CREOSOTE BUSH

US/IBP SYNTHESIS SERIES

This volume is a contribution to the International Biological Program. The United States' effort was sponsored by the National Academy of Sciences through the National Committee for the IBP. The lead federal agency in providing support for IBP has been the National Science Foundation.

Views expressed in this volume do not necessarily represent those of the National Academy of Sciences or of the National Science Foundation.

US/IBP SYNTHESIS SERIES | 6

CREOSOTE BUSH

Biology and Chemistry of *Larrea* in New World Deserts

Edited by

T. J. Mabry
University of Texas at Austin

J. H. Hunziker
Universidad de Buenos Aires

D. R. DiFeo, Jr.
University of Texas at Austin

Dowden, Hutchinson & Ross, Inc.
Stroudsburg Pennsylvania

Library of Congress Catalog Card Number: 76-5838
ISBN: 0-87933-282-4

79 78 77 1 2 3 4 5
Manufactured in the United States of America.

LIBRARY OF CONGRESS CATALOGING IN PUBLICATION DATA
Main entry under title:
Creosote bush.
(U.S./ IBP synthesis series; 6)
Bibliography: p. 257
Includes index.
1. Larrea. 2. Desert ecology–America. I. Mabry, Tom J. II. Hunziker, J. H. III. DiFeo, D. R. IV. Series.
QK495.Z9C73 583'.214 76-58381
ISBN 0-87933-282-4

Exclusive distributor: **Halsted Press**
A Division of John Wiley & Sons, Inc.
ISBN: 0-470-99233-6

FOREWORD

This book is one of a series of volumes reporting results of research by U.S. scientists participating in the International Biological Program (IBP). As one of the 58 nations taking part in the IBP during the period July 1967 to June 1974, the United States organized a number of large, multidisciplinary studies pertinent to the central IBP theme of "the biological basis of productivity and human welfare."

These multidisciplinary studies (Integrated Research Programs), directed toward an understanding of the structure and function of major ecological or human systems, have been a distinctive feature of the U.S. participation in the IBP. Many of the detailed investigations that represent individual contributions to the overall objectives of each Integrated Research Program have been published in the journal literature. The main purpose of this series of books is to accomplish a synthesis of the many contributions for each principal program and thus answer the larger questions pertinent to the structure and function of the major systems that have been studied.

Publications Committee: US/IBP
Gabriel Lasker
Robert B. Platt
Frederick E. Smith
W. Frank Blair, Chairman

PREFACE

The origin, structure, and functioning of desert scrub ecosystems was investigated under the auspices of the Structure of Ecosystems Integrated Research Program of the U.S. International Biological Program. The sites selected for intensive comparative investigation were similar desert areas in Arizona and Catamarca (Argentina). Since *Larrea* is a dominant element in both areas it became apparent early in the investigations that basic knowledge with regard to this genus was essential to understanding the functioning of the two ecosystems. Thus, the present volume is the result of more than six years of research, which began in 1969, on different aspects of the biology of *Larrea.* We now recognize a variety of characteristics (many of which are unique) of *Larrea* that evolved in the course of its survival in desert ecosystems.

Although *Larrea* consists of only five species–four in South America and one in North America–it nevertheless shows a remarkable diversity concerning vegetative habit, ecological, morphological, genetical and chemical variation, polyploid levels, natural interspecific hybridization, and breeding systems.

Some of its species have developed into the most successful plant species for colonization of the driest and hottest semidesert regions of North and South America, where they presently cover hundreds of thousands of square miles and thus dominate the semidesert landscapes throughout enormous expanses of territory. This numerical and biomass dominance of *Larrea divaricata, L. tridentata,* and *L. cuneifolia,* all of which form almost pure stands in many regions, makes them an especially important habitat component for animal life in the deserts where they occur. These three species are among the more extreme shrubby xerophytes in both North and South America.

Larrea divaricata ("jarilla") and its closely related North American vicariad *L. tridentata* ("creosote bush," "gobernadora") constitute one of the most interesting and still puzzling cases of amphitropical disjunction. The origin of the vicarious species-pair, though very likely South American, is still a matter of dispute.

Other notable features of *Larrea* include the various physiological, morphological, and anatomical adaptations with which several of its species can cope with extreme arid conditions and which are directly related to their success as desert shrubs. As a consequence of their success in semi-arid environments *L. divaricata* and *L. tridentata* are at present expanding their ranges and behaving as woody weedy colonizers in areas that are either overgrazed or otherwise disturbed by man.

Last, but not least, among the remarkable features of *Larrea,* are the chemical defenses of the plant against herbivores, including nordihydroguaiaretic acid (NDGA) and a complex array of flavonoid methyl ethers that are deposited on the leaf surfaces of all members of this genus.

Hopefully, the information concerning the biology and chemistry of *Larrea* presented in this volume will be of value in understanding the functioning of semidesert ecosystems and in their management and rational use by man.

The authors of Chapter 2 wish to express their gratitude to several institutions or persons that in one way or another assisted in their research. Financial support from the National Science Foundation (U.S.A.) through a grant to Professor Otto T. Solbrig is gratefully acknowledged (Origin and Structure of Ecosystems Program of the U.S. International Biological Program).

Several grants by the "Consejo Nacional de Investigaciones Científicas y Técnicas" and the "Comite Nacional del Programa Biológico Internacional," both of Argentina, are gratefully acknowledged.

J. H. Hunziker, C. A. Naranjo, and R. A. Palacios belong to the "Carrera del Investigador Científico," Consejo Nacional de Investigaciones Científicas y Técnicas, Argentina, whose continuous support is acknowledged.

T. W. Yang wishes to express his deep appreciation especially to the following individuals and institutions that have supported his extended research in *Larrea* over the years: R. R. Humphrey, J. W. Hallowell, W. V. Brown, J. E. Endrizzi, Western Reserve Academy, University of Texas, University of Arizona, and National Science Foundation.

The senior author of Chapter 5 (T. J. Mabry) would like to thank the Potts-Sibley Foundation for financial support and Dr. D. J. Sibley, Jr., for his personal interest in the research and for the use of his ranch in the Glass Mountains of west Texas for field studies.

The author of Chapter 6 wishes to thank G. H. Orians, J. C. Shultz, R. G. Cates, and M. L. Paulson for discussion, advice, and aid in the collection of plant material and insects. This research has been supported by grants GB 11193 and BMS 75-03136 from the National Science Foundation.

The ideas presented in Chapter 7 have developed at least in part through discussions with Rex G. Cates, David Rhoades, and Gordon H. Orians. J. Schultz wishes to thank P. Bierzychudek, A. Joern, W. K. Milsom, Mrs. D. R. Paulson, and T. D. Schultz for aiding and abetting in field work. We thank the Instituto Miguel Lillo, The Department of Entomology at the University of Arizona (especially Floyd Werner), and the U.S. National Museum (especially W. D. Duckworth) for permitting access to their collections and for aiding in determinations.

The editors wish to thank all the contributors for their dedicated and conscientious efforts to integrate their individual data with results from other investigators and other disciplines. Also, the assistance of Cathy Osborn in preparing the manuscript is gratefully acknowledged.

Finally, we wish to acknowledge the invaluable assistance of Marilyn Whitehouse who for more than three years organized and participated in all aspects of the preparation of the volume.

Tom J. Mabry
Juan Hunziker
Dan R. DiFeo, Jr.

CONTENTS

LIST OF CONTRIBUTORS

Samuel A. Bamberg
Laboratory of Nuclear Medicine and Radiation Biology, Mercury, Nevada

Michael G. Barbour
University of California, Davis

Charles F. Bohnstedt, Jr.
The University of Texas at Austin

Gary Cunningham
New Mexico State University, Las Cruces

Dan R. DiFeo, Jr.
The University of Texas at Austin

Frank Enders
The University of Texas at Austin

Arthur C. Hulse
Indiana University of Pennsylvania

Juan H. Hunziker
Universidad de Buenos Aires, Argentina

John A. Ludwig
New Mexico State University, Las Cruces

Tom J. Mabry
The University of Texas at Austin

James A. MacMahon
Utah State University, Logan

Michael A. Mares
University of Pittsburgh, Pennsylvania

Andrew R. Moldenke
University of California, Santa Cruz

Carlos A. Naranjo
Universidad de Buenos Aires, Argentina

John L. Neff
University of California, Santa Cruz

Walter C. Oechel
McGill University, Montreal

Daniel Otte
Philadelphia Academy of Natural Sciences, Pennsylvania

Ramon A. Palacios
Universidad de Buenos Aires, Argentina

Lidia Poggio
Universidad de Buenos Aires, Argentina

David F. Rhoades
University of Washington, Seattle

Masayuki Sakakibara
University of Tokyo, Japan

John C. Schultz
Dartmouth College, Hanover, New Hampshire

David Seigler
The University of Illinois at Urbana

Beryl B. Simpson
Smithsonian Institution, Washington, D.C.

Otto T. Solbrig
Harvard University, Cambridge, Massachusetts

Barbara N. Timmermann
The University of Texas at Austin

Tien Wei Yang
University of Arizona, Tucson

CREOSOTE BUSH

1

The Adaptive Strategies of *Larrea*

O. T. Solbrig

From Palm Springs, California, to the Pecos River in Texas and from central Arizona and New Mexico to the state of San Luis Potosí in Mexico, the traveler meets with vast expanses of semi-arid vegetation interrupted by chains of mountains. Over the greater part of this region, the vegetation is formed primarily by globose shrubs of up to two meters high and by cacti and other succulents of different sizes and shapes. These succulents range from small, almost insignificant plants barely protruding above the soil to sahuaro (*Cereus giganteus* Engelm.) and organpipe cacti (*Lemaireocereus thurberi* [Engelm.] Britt. and Rose). Along streams and washes trees are found: cottonwoods (*Populus* L.), hackberries (*Celtis* L.). and mesquites (*Prosopis* L.). In the flats the vegetation is sparse and abundant bare ground can be seen.

However, in the spring, particularly after a wet winter, much of that bare ground will be covered by a carpet of colorful ephemeral herbs. The species composition of the flora varies somewhat from place to place according to the variations in rainfall. To the southeast of this vast region, summer precipitation is the norm; in the northwest, only winter rains fall; in between (southeastern Arizona and northern Sonora, Mexico), both summer and winter rains are to be found. The differences in the rainfall pattern and the fluctuations in yearly amounts of precipitation are among the principal factors controlling species distribution.

Three major floristic regions that correspond to the three main rainfall patterns can be recognized within this large area:

1. The Mojave Desert in California, which has only winter rains. This region also has the lowest total precipitation.
2. The Sonoran Desert, which includes roughly central and southern Arizona and the states of Sonora and Baja California in Mexico. Summer and winter rains are the norm in the northern part of the Sonoran Desert, with winter precipitation prevailing in Baja California and summer precipitation in southern Sonora.

3. The Chihuahuan Desert, which comprises central and southern New Mexico, southwest Texas, and the states of Chihuahua, Sinaloa (in part), and San Luis Potosí (in part), Mexico. This region has almost exclusively summer rains, and the amounts vary between the areas considerably.

Although species composition differs from region to region, one species dominates the vegetation throughout all of this area: the creosote bush, *Larrea tridentata* (DC.) Coville. The creosote bush belongs to a small genus of only five species in the family Zygophyllaceae. *Larrea tridentata* is the only species of this genus that grows in North America; the other four species are found in temperate South America, from southern Peru and Bolivia to central Patagonia in Argentina (see Figures 2-1 through 2-5).

Two of the South American species, *L. divaricata* Cav. and *L. cuneifolia* Cav., resemble the North American creosote bush in habit and in form of leaves and flowers. *Larrea divaricata* is so similar to *L. tridentata* that it can only be distinguished by minute technical differences in the shape of the stipules (see Chapter 2). These two South American species are found growing in areas that are very similar in rainfall pattern, climate, and topography to the areas in North America where creosote bush grows. The region where these species are most abundant in South America is the so-called Monte region of Argentina.

The vegetation of the Monte region is formed by a mixture of globose shrubs, succulents, and annuals in the flats and by small trees along washes. Physiognomically, this vegetation is very similar to that of the North American warm deserts. However, the species found in South America are for the most part different from those that grow in North America. This phenomenon, namely, similarity in structure but dissimilarity in species composition, is also observed in the Old World deserts that have physical environments similar to those of the Sonoran Desert and the Monte.

This book brings together the results of studies on the biology, ecology, and chemistry of the species of *Larrea* that grow in two widely separated, but climatically similar, regions. Most of these studies were part of an International Biological Program known as the Origin and Structure of Ecosystems Project. The primary objective of this project was to understand the process of convergent evolution in warm desert regions (Orians and Solbrig 1977).

Because of the nature of this study, as outlined below, we did not attempt to investigate all of the species of *Larrea* with the same intensity, but rather tried to obtain a thorough knowledge of the species of *Larrea* that occur in the two localities chosen for intensive study by the Structure of Ecosystems Project. Consequently, in this introductory chapter we will first look at the objectives of the overall research project and then place *Larrea* in the gradient of microhabitats found in the desert study areas. Finally, we will examine the general adaptive strategies of desert shrubs.

THE ORIGIN AND STRUCTURE OF ECOSYSTEMS PROGRAM

For a long time we have known that throughout the world in areas of climatic similarity, the physiognomy of the vegetation is also similar. These similarities have allowed the classification of vegetation into broad general types that more or less coincide with certain climatic features (Schimfper 1903; DuRietz 1931; Raunkier 1934; Cain 1950; Good 1964). This knowledge has also led to attempts to predict vegetation by using solely climatic features, but results have been inconclusive (Köppen and Geiger 1936; Holdridge 1947; Tossi 1960). Although the details of the different predictions are subject to question, the premise that climate is a determinant of vegetational physiognomy is generally accepted. From this premise follows the corollary that environmental similarity will produce similarity in the vegetational structure independent of the floristic composition.

If similar climates produce physiognomically similar vegetation, this occurrence is because each combination of climatic factors (temperature, humidity, insolation) produces a unique set of physical stresses to which there exist limited, successful adaptive strategies. From a theoretical point of view, what is called for is the identification of the physical stresses created by the so-called desert climate and the prediction of the adaptive strategies that will solve the various stresses that exist in this environment.

To study more fully these problems, two parallel studies were undertaken as part of the Origin and Structure of Ecosystems Program: the Mediterranean shrub and the desert scrub projects. The selection of Mediterranean and hot desert systems as the focus of these two parallel studies was determined by the interests of the investigators who were influential in starting the projects. General results of these studies are being published separately (Mooney 1977; Orians and Solbrig 1977).

The immediate objective of the desert scrub project was to determine the structural similarities of the desert ecosystems of central and northern Argentina (the Monte) and those of the southwestern United States (Sonoran Desert). The study consisted of (1) a comparison of the structural attributes of the vegetation of two sites with similar physical environments in Argentina and the United States; (2) a study of the structural and behavioral features of some representative species of plants, invertebrates, and vertebrates in the community; and (3) an investigation of the interactions between certain functional types in the community—that is, plant-leaf herbivore, flower-pollinator, and seed-seed eater (disperser) interactions.

The areas selected for the intensive study were chosen exclusively on the basis of the similarity of their physical environment, primarily climate. The sites that were selected were the Bolsón de Pipanaco, near the city of Andalgalá, province of Catamarca in Argentina, and the Avra Valley, near Silver Bell and Tucson, Arizona. Although a great effort was made to select two sites with identical physical environments, this goal was not possible simply because no two points in the world have this dimension. In our system the greatest difference is in rainfall pattern (Bailey 1977). The precipitation in Andalgalá is mostly in the form of summer rains, while in Arizona rainfall is equally divided between summer and winter rains.

Given that the physical environment is not identical, but still quite similar, at the two sites, the possibility exists of attributing the differences found in the organisms to differences in the physical environment, while explaining the convergences in the biota as a result of the similarities in the physical environment at the two sites. To avoid such rationalizations, hypotheses have been formulated that predict the similarities and differences that should exist in the two ecosystems under the physical environments that prevail at the two sites. These hypotheses are based on the theory of natural selection and an understanding of the basic biology of the organisms under study. They are reported extensively elsewhere, together with their underlying rationale (Orians and Solbrig 1977).

ADAPTIVE STRATEGIES OF DESERT PLANTS

One generally recognized basis for the high degree of convergence in plant form found in desert areas is that these environments pose serious limitations to plant growth. Although we usually accept that water availability is the most obvious selective force, a number of other factors also exist—for example, severe temperature stresses (Gates 1968). Furthermore the water available to the plant is dependent not only on rainfall distribution, but also on exposure, topography, and soil particle size and type, so that the formulation of a predictive theory requires a finer input than only average temperature and rainfall data.

Desert and semideserts are regions where during extensive parts of the year precipitation is insufficient to maintain active plant growth. The figure of 200 mm of rainfall a year is cited as the upper limit for desert regions (Morello 1958; Barbour and Diaz 1973), but this amount depends as much on distribution and potential evapotranspiration as on total rainfall itself (Sarmiento 1976). The Brazilian Caatinga, for example, with rainfall in excess of 600 mm is a typical semidesert in spite of the high rainfall, since all plants are subjected to intense water stresses during much of the year. Another characteristic of deserts is intense solar radiation (Barbour and Diaz 1973). Although high air temperatures are often associated with deserts, such heat is not necessarily the case, particularly at night.

Normally, plants will derive a competitive advantage from maximizing photosynthetic production within the constraints set by their environment. This characteristic allows the plant to produce more seeds, and/or more vegetative biomass, and/or more chemical defenses, and thereby increase its overall fitness. For desert plants the evolutionary dilemma is how to capture abundant light and carbon dioxide, while trying to economize on water, which is the limiting factor. The dilemma exists because of the inevitable association between carbon dioxide gain and water vapor loss through stomata. To maximize carbon dioxide flux, the plant has to possess low stomatal resistance, which, however, results in high water loss.

There are partial solutions that increase carbon dioxide flux without changing water vapor flux. One such solution is to open only the stomata when ambient humidity is high. This method decreases somewhat the rate of water loss without affecting carbon dioxide flux. Another solution is to possess biochemical machinery (the so-called C_4 photosynthesis) that concentrates carbon dioxide (in the form of C_4 acids) in the cell and thereby increases carbon dioxide flux without affecting water loss. However, both of these methods have associated costs and do not appear to be clearly superior strategies. Consequently, there appear to be several equally successful ways to increase photosynthetic production under desert conditions.

One extreme adaptive strategy is to acquire a leaf and canopy structure that maximizes light interception and produces the maximum amount of photosynthate. This solution calls for a high carbon dioxide flux to be functional and results in high transpiration. Plants with this strategy will have relatively large leaves and low stomatal resistances and will be kept from overheating by evaporative cooling. However, as soon as the dry season sets in, such leaves must be dropped. Otherwise, respiration in the overheated leaves will be very high, and the leaves will constitute a great energy drain to the plant. Permanent wilting will probably also set in. We call such leaves *mesophylls.*

The opposite extreme adaptive strategy is to possess small leaves with thick cuticles and high stomatal resistances that will not overheat excessively even when the stomata are closed, and no transpiration and concomitant evaporative cooling is possible. Such microphylls will be photosynthetically inefficient under condition of adequate moisture compared to the larger leaves of the first strategy, but since they do not overheat as much and lose little or no water when the stomata close, they need not be dropped during the dry season. In effect, since respiration is a function of temperature, the respiration rates will be lower and the energy drain less than in the case of the corresponding mesophyll. Furthermore, since some water is available during the dry season, photosynthesis can proceed throughout the year. Consequently, this type of leaf will be energetically profitable even during the dry season. We call such leaves *xerophylls* (Orians and Solbrig 1976).

All desert species are subjected to periods of drought of varying lengths, even during the rainy season. Plants with extreme mesophylls are therefore not viable in the desert. Furthermore, as a result of local spatial and temporal variations in humidity, a certain degree of variation among species is expected in the exact characteristics of their photosynthetic machinery. These two strategies are therefore to be viewed as general syndromes with continuous intergradations of strategies.

The mesophytic leaf is typical of the ephemeral desert plants. Studies by Mooney et al. (1977) on *Camissonia oblongifolia,* a typical desert ephemeral, show this plant to have the highest photosynthetic rate recorded so far and also extremely high transpiration rates. An example of an extreme xerophyll is given by cacti and other succulents. These plants can exist under conditions of extreme water stress. Their photosynthetic rates are, however, among the lowest known. The soil water potential in time and space will determine the competitive advantage of each of the two strategies and the exact details of structure and function of species possessing these opposite types of photosynthetic surfaces.

If there are extensive periods during which soil water is readily available to plants, then plants possessing mesophylls will be able to produce more photosynthate during the wet season than plants with xerophylls throughout the year. Such is the situation encountered in a tropical savanna. As the amount of time favorable to the mesophyll decreases, the relative advantage of the xerophyll increases until a point is reached when both are equally competitive in their ability to produce photosynthate. As the wet season diminishes even further, the vegetation should be dominated increasingly by plants with xerophytic photosynthate surfaces. However, the mesophyte will not disappear entirely. In effect, the carrying capacity of xerophytes will be determined by how many plants can be sustained during the dry season. Consequently, during the wet season there is always an excess of soil moisture that can be utilized by ephemeral plants and by perennials with an opportunistic, mesophytic, canopy structure.

Soil moisture varies not only in time but also in space due to topography and soil texture. Water will flow towards depressions, and coarse desert soils will accumulate more water at a depth where it is better protected from evaporation. If the moisture accumulation is sufficiently great, the competitive advantage can tip back in favor of plants with mesophylls in certain areas. Such is often the case along washes, where sufficient moisture accumulates at lower depths to permit plants with mesophylls and deep roots to function during the climatically dry season. Desert oases are basically similar habitats. On the other hand, if soils are fine textured and runoff and surface evaporation are high, xerophytes may predominate in spite of a high precipitation. The already mentioned case of the Brazilian Caatinga is an example.

THE ADAPTIVE STRATEGY OF DESERT SHRUBS

A familiar life form in the desert is the globose shrub. Although absent in the extreme dry desert, such as the Atacama Desert in Chile, xerophytic shrubs are usually the most abundant life form in deserts. They possess small, xerophytic leaves, or they lack leaves altogether and instead possess green photosynthetic branches with or without ephemeral leaves–for example, species of *Cercidium* and *Bulnesia.* Sometimes they possess two types of leaves: small xerophytic leaves in the dry season and larger, more mesophytic leaves during the wet season–for example, *Zygophyllum dumosum* in Israel. The leaves are typically covered with either hairs or resins, and in many cases, both are employed. They tend to possess thick cuticles, sunken stomata in the leaves, palisade parenchyma on both leaf surfaces, and a number of other structures that have been interpreted as being adaptive to water loss (Schimper 1903).

At one time the belief was that these plants were efficient users of water and that their transpiration rates were low. However, the contrary is true when soil moisture is available; transpiration rates in these plants are very high (Maximov 1929; Walter 1931). However, when soil moisture is low and stomata are closed, water loss in these leaves is almost nonexistent. They are therefore capable of withstanding extensive periods of drought. Because of their size and position, leaves of desert shrubs do not overheat extensively (Loomen et al. 1970).

Another very important characteristic of many desert shrubs is their ability to withstand high internal water stresses (see Chapter 3). This characteristic allows the plants to extract water from the soil solution at -20 to -50 bars and to remain photosynthetically active under conditions when other plants are unable to function. Another conspicuous difference is in the size of the shrubs. There is a tendency for all shrub species to belong to limited size classes. By and large, in warm deserts with summer rain, the shrub of 1.5-2.5 meters in height predominates, while in cooler deserts, or in areas with only winter rain, the smaller shrub of about 0.5 meters is found. Since competition for light is not a factor, the size of shrubs is most likely an adaptation to temperature. In predominantly winter-active shrubs or in areas of cold air temperatures, the short shrub will have a competitive advantage since air temperatures near the ground will be closer to the photosynthetic optimum. In warm deserts, and particularly when shrubs are predominantly summer active, air temperatures near the ground will be excessive, and there will be an advantage in placing the leaves away from the ground in order to minimize the effect of ground radiation and to expose the leaves to the wind.

IBP STUDIES OF *LARREA*

Since species of *Larrea* are a dominant element of the vegetation at both of the primary study sites, they were singled out for intensive study. The species found at the northern site is the tetraploid race of *L. tridentata,* while at the South American site the dominant species is *L. cuneifolia,* also a tetraploid. In the region of Andalgalá, a second species of creosote bush is present, *L. divaricata,* which is morphologically very similar to the North American *L. tridentata* (see Chapter 2). In the following pages we present the results of these in-depth studies, as well as data from species of *Larrea* not in these deserts per se.

A well-known phenomenon is that shrub communities in deserts are usually dominated by one or two species. We were therefore interested in knowing why *Larrea* species are so dominant in these deserts. Finally, we also wanted to study the evolutionary history and the phylogenetic relationships of the genus. Therefore, detailed studies of the biology and chemistry of *Larrea* were undertaken.

SUMMARY

Desert plant life forms vary from small almost undetectable succulents to large shrubs and trees. In the desert shrub program of the IPB Origin and Structure of Ecosystems Project, one major life form prevails: the globose shrub or more specifically the creosote bush, *Larrea* Cav. (Zygophyllaceae).

Two main strategies may be employed by desert plants. In the first of these, the plants produce large canopies with low stomatal resistance and are cooled by evaporation. These plants, as soon as the dry season sets in, must drop their leaves and senesce until the next rainy season begins.

The second type of strategy employed is for a plant to produce small leaves with thick cuticles and high stomatal resistances that have little overheating even when stomata are closed. This type of strategy is the one we might expect for *Larrea.*

The intent of this detailed study of *Larrea* is to see whether *Larrea* does utilize either of these extreme strategies and also to study *Larrea* in a more detailed fashion to delimit specifically what strategies are used.

RESUMEN

Las formas de vida vegetales en el desierto van desde diminutas suculentas, casi indistinguibles, hasta arbustos grandes y árboles. En el programa de arbustos de zonas desérticas, en el proyecto Origen y Estructura de Ecosistemas, del IBP, prevalece una forma de vida principal, el arbusto globoso, o más específicamente, la "jarilla" (o "gobernadora", en México), *Larrea* Cav. (Zygophyllaceae).

Las plantas del desierto emplean dos estrategias principales. Una de éstas es la producción de abundante follaje con baja resistencia estomática y enfriamiento por evaporación. Las plantas que emplean esta estrategia pierden sus hojas tan pronto como comienza la estación de secas y entran en un período de vida latente hasta que comienza la siguiente estación de lluvias.

El segundo tipo de estrategia empleado, es la producción de hojas pequenas con cutícula gruesa y alta resistencia estomática, que tienen poco sobrecalentamiento, aun cuando los estomas se encuentren cerrados. Este es el tipo de estrategia que puede esperarse en *Larrea.*

El propósito de este estudio detallado de *Larrea* es averiguar si ésta utiliza alguna de estas dos estrategias extremas y a la vez estudiarla du una manera más detallada, con el fin de delimitar específicamente las estrategias empleadas.

2

Geographic Distribution, Morphology, Hybridization, Cytogenetics, and Evolution

J. H. Hunziker, R. A. Palacios, L. Poggio, C. A. Naranjo and T. W. Yang

GEOGRAPHIC DISTRIBUTION

The genus *Larrea* constitutes an interesting case of disjunct amphitropical distribution covering arid and semi-arid regions of Argentina, Chile, Bolivia, Peru, Mexico, and southwestern United States. It is composed of five species: four in South America and one in North America.

Two diploid species, *L. nitida* Cav. and *L. ameghinoi* Speg., constitute section *Larrea* and have multifoliolate leaves and rather small flowers (Palacios and Hunziker 1972). *Larrea nitida* is a shrub occurring in western Argentina and in Chile (Coquimbo, Aconcagua, Santiago) (Figure 2-1). *Larrea ameghinoi* is a woody chamaephyte occurring from Santa Cruz Province to Neuquén, Argentina (Figure 2-2).

The remaining species have bifoliolate leaves and larger flowers and belong to section *Bifolium;* these are *L. divaricata* Cav., *L. tridentata* (DC.) Coville, and *L. cuneifolia* Cav.

Diploid *L. divaricata* is the dominant shrub in the Monte, or central semidesert of Argentina, where its area is largely continuous. It occurs also on the other side of the high Andean Cordillera in Chile (Atacama, Aconcagua) and in isolated regions of Bolivia (Tarija) and Peru (Chuquibamba, Aplao) (Figure 2-3).

A vicarious taxon, *L. tridentata,* which is considered conspecific with *L. divaricata* by most recent authors, is the dominant shrub in comparable deserts of North America. It has been shown to consist of diploid (Chihuahuan Desert), tetraploid (Sonoran Desert), and hexaploid taxa (Mojave Desert) (Yang 1967a, 1968, 1970; Yang and Lowe 1968; Barbour 1969a) (Figure 2-4).

Tetraploid *L. cuneifolia* is another bushy species of the Monte of Argen-

FIGURE 2-1. *Geographic distribution of* L. nitida.

tina that has a wide distribution, mainly in the western part of Argentina (Figure 2-5).

Larrea divaricata has a disjunct area in South America that can be placed into a general distributional pattern. Weberbauer (1945) has noted that in South America xerophytes grow in different geographic areas: in Peru and in Argentina. He cites the examples of *Bougainvillea spinosa* and *Bulnesia retama,* which have restricted ranges in Peru and much wider ranges in Argentina. The first example occurs in Peru in the Department of Moquequa, at altitudes of up to 2,300 m above sea level, while the second extends in the south from Tarija (southern Bolivia) to 43° south latitude at Chubut, Argentina. Almost the same pattern occurs with *L. divaricata* in South America (see Figure 2-3) although Weberbauer does not cite this example.

The explanation offered by Weberbauer is as follows: At the beginning of

FIGURE 2-2. *Geographic distribution of* L. ameghinoi.

the Quaternary, the Bolivian Andes were lower than they are today. Fossil remains of a macrothermic Tertiary flora exists in the Cerro del Potosí at a level of 4,000 m or more, and stretches of Quaternary beach can be seen several hundreds of meters above the Pacific Ocean. These data suggest that the area of these xerophytes might have been continuous at the beginning of the Quaternary and that later the present disjunction arose because these shrubs could not resist the cold climate of high altitudes caused by the elevation of the Andes

Since *L. divaricata* and diploid *L. tridentata* have genomes that are homologous and both taxa are so closely related that they can be considered semispecies, knowing how the present amphitropical disjunct distribution originated is of great interest.

In the last section of this chapter the three basic theories concerning the origin of this disjunction are outlined. Contrary to the opinion of some recent authors, we believe that *L. divaricata* and its allies (including *L. tridentata*)

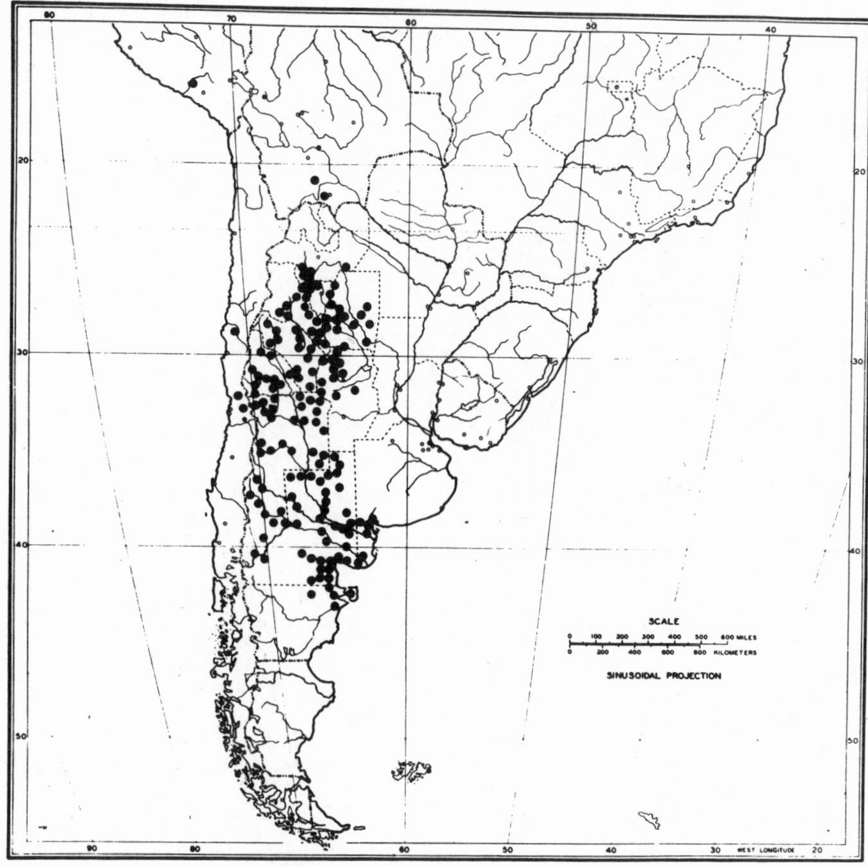

FIGURE 2-3. *Geographic distribution of* L. divaricata.

originated in South America. If this theory is so, we still have the interesting problem of how *Larrea* reached North America from South America.

MORPHOLOGY

In this section we shall deal with the morphology of the leaf, the stipules, the fruit, and the seed. Flower morphology is described later (see Chapter 4) and, therefore, will not be treated here. Other general morphological characteristics of the sections (Palacios and Hunziker 1972) or species (Descole et al. 1940, 1943) have been described elsewhere.

Leaf

Larrea has opposite, subsessile, unpaired pinnately compound leaves, with stipules and with 2 to 17 sessile folioles, the terminal one of which is well

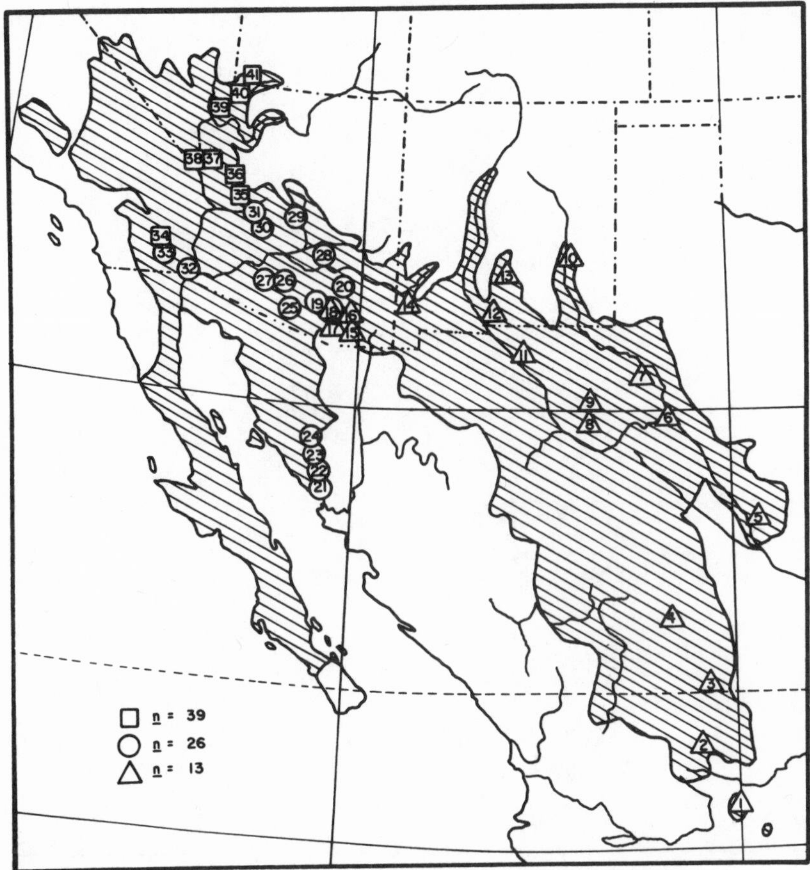

FIGURE 2-4. *Geographic distribution and chromosome numbers of creosote bush populations in North America* (L. tridentata).

developed or much reduced. The species of *Larrea* are quite distinct in the form of their leaves (Figure 2-6). As mentioned earlier, there are two sections within the genus: the multifoliolate section, *Larrea* (*L. nitida, L. ameghinoi*), and the bifoliolate section, *Bifolium* (*L. divaricata, L. tridentata, L. cuneifolia*). The multifoliolate group seems to be more primitive, since the majority of the genera in the Zygophyllaceae have multifoliolate species and the rarer bifoliolate species seem to represent a reductional trend in response to aridity.

In the multifoliolate species the number of leaflets is quite variable, and there is always a terminal foliole. In *L. nitida* it varies from 9 to 17, and the leaflets usually show some overlapping. In *L. ameghinoi,* on the other hand, there are 3 to 7 leaflets. These are well separated from each other, with little overlapping, and are rather asymmetrical and uneven in size (see Figure 2-6).

FIGURE 2-5. *Geographic distribution of* L. cuneifolia.

In section *Bifolium* the number of leaflets is always 2. Each has a very much reduced foliole at the tip in the form of a filiform mucron (see Figure 2-6). Considerable variation in leaf morphology is found in *L. divaricata* among regions (G and H in Figure 2-6). Some of the populations have leaflets that are large and are fused along a small portion of their length; others have smaller leaflets that have round tips and are fused along a greater proportion of their length (G in Figure 2-6). In *L. divaricata* the folioles are usually divergent and convex; in diploid *L. tridentata* they are bifalcate and concave (G, H, and I in Figure 2-6). In tetraploid and hexaploid *L. tridentata* the folioles are not falcate, but are either straight or convex (Hunziker et al. 1972b, Figure 6).

There is intrapopulational variation in the amount of fusion between the leaflets of *L. cuneifolia* as well as in the length-width ratio of the folioles. Leaflet fusion in *L. cuneifolia* produces what is basically an entire leaf derived from a multifoliolate pattern.

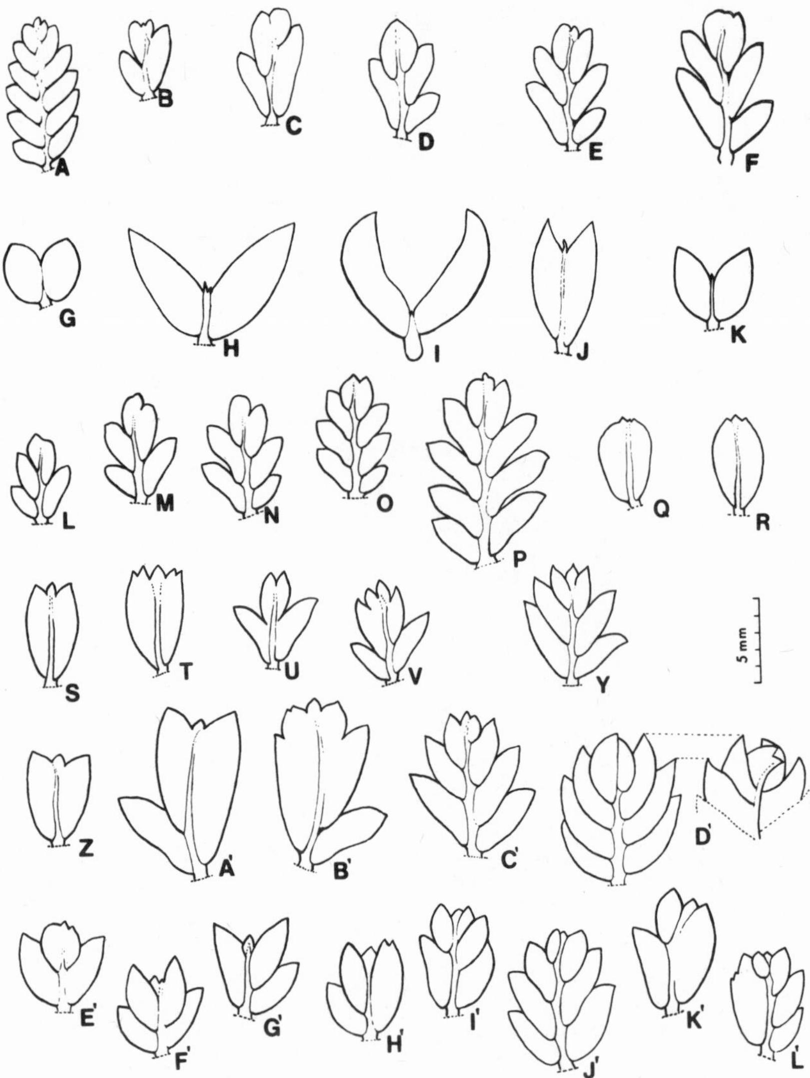

FIGURE 2–6. *Leaves of the species of* Larrea *and their natural hybrids.*

Stipules

The apex of the stipule is acute in all *Larrea* species, except in the Bolivian, Chilean, and Argentine *L. divaricata* populations where it is obtuse (Hunziker et al. 1972b, Figure 3). In the diploid Chihuahuan *L. tridentata* the apex is acute, and in the hybrids between *L. divaricata* and *L. tridentata* (Yang et al. 1976) it is intermediate. In *L. divaricata* from Peru the stipule apex is also intermediate, as it is in the hybrids (Hunziker et al. 1972a). The

Peruvian populations are diploid, as are all South American taxa so far studied (Yang et al. 1976).

Fruit

The fruit is a schizocarp that eventually splits into 5 mericarps, each of which contains a single seed. The walls are relatively soft in section *Bifolium* and harder in section *Larrea.*

In section *Bifolium* the mericarps are hairy and easily separate at maturity. They are preadapted for epizoic dispersal. Presumably mammals or birds may transport the seed, at least for short distances.

The mericarpal walls in diploid *L. tridentata* (Chihuahuan race) are considerably harder than in its South American counterpart, *L. divaricata* (Yang et al. 1976).

The mericarps in section *Larrea* are puberulous and remain associated at maturity. In *L. ameghinoi* the mericarps are verrucose and brown-red in color, and the walls are not extremely hard. On the other hand, in *L. nitida* the mericarps are smooth, are of burnt stone color, and have hard walls.

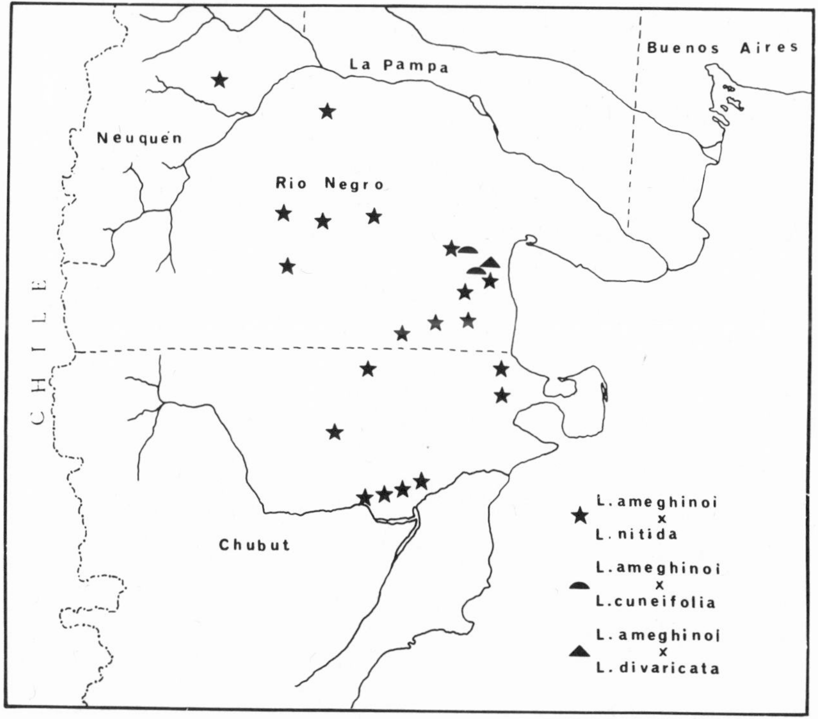

FIGURE 2-7. *Geographic distribution of some interspecific* Larrea *hybrids in northern Patagonia.*

An interesting correlation exists between the seed coat structure and the strength of the mericarp wall. In section *Larrea* the internal layers of the mericarp are sclerified and the external seed coat (testa) is membranaceous. But in the species of section *Bifolium* the mericarp has nonsclerified internal layers and the external seed coat is thick. This correlation is probably related to the protection of the seed before it germinates.

Seed

Most of the species can be distinguished by the shape or color of their seeds. In section *Larrea, L. ameghinoi* has chestnut-colored to occasionally black seeds; *Larrea nitida* seeds are olive brown. The seeds of *L. divaricata* and diploid *L. tridentata* can be easily separated because those of the latter species have a much more triangular contour, or a "boomerang" shape (Yang et al. 1976, Figure 1).

A transverse section of the seeds of *L. divaricata* and *L. tridentata* is always elliptical or obovate, while in *L. cuneifolia* it is ovate.

The embryo in *L. divaricata* and *L. tridentata* has the cotyledons parallel to the longitudinal plane of symmetry, whereas *L. cuneifolia* has the cotyledons perpendicular to the plane.

HYBRIDIZATION

Distributional and Ecological Observations on Natural Hybrid Swarms in Patagonia

Hunziker et al. (1969) have reported the occurrence of natural hybridization between the four South American species and described the hybrids *L. ameghinoi* × *L. nitida* and *L. ameghinoi* × *L. cuneifolia* with regard to leaf morphology, growth habit, phenotypic plasticity, and morphological segregation in later hybrid generations. They pointed out the fact that hybrid populations occur in ecologically intermediate habitats. More recently, Hunziker et al. (1972a, b) have dealt briefly with the chromosome behavior of some of these interspecific hybrids and have also presented results concerning phenolic compounds and seed albumins.

The area that was intensely studied for hybridizing populations includes eastern Neuquén, Río Negro, and northern Chubut provinces in Argentina. Five out of six possible di-hybrid combinations have been found. These are, in order of abundance: *L. ameghinoi* × *L. nitida, L. ameghinoi* × *L. cuneifolia, L. cuneifolia* × *L. divaricata, L. ameghinoi* × *L. divaricata,* and *L. cuneifolia* × *L. nitida.* Hybrid swarms between *L. ameghinoi* and *L. nitida* are very common where these two species are parapatric (Figure 2-7). One extensive hybrid population was studied in detail through metroglyphic analysis, in an area 71 km west of Sierra Grande, Dep. Valcheta, Río Negro (Hunziker et al. 1976).

Numerous hybrids and segregants originating from crosses between *L. ameghinoi* and *L. cuneifolia* were observed in several localities of the Río Negro Province (see Figure 2-7).

Only one hybrid plant of *L. ameghinoi* × *L. divaricata* was found. The location was near Highway No. 3, 59 km south of San Antonio Oeste, Río Negro Province; its phenolic pattern indicated its origin. Previously, this hybrid had been erroneously thought to be a derivative of an F_1 hybrid between *L. ameghinoi* and *L. cuneifolia,* on the basis of morphological similarity of its leaf shape with the leaf shape of some of the leaves of a putative hybrid derivative between *L. ameghinoi* and *L. cuneifolia* (Hunziker et al. 1969).

In the same locality a single hybrid individual of *L. cuneifolia* × *L. nitida* has been discovered. Actually, in this locality all five hybrids exist in or near a depression of about 400 × 300 m. A sketch of this place has been published in a previous paper (Hunziker et al. 1969, Figure 1). The hybrid swarms of *L. ameghinoi* × *L. cuneifolia* and a single unusually large hybrid *L. ameghinoi* × *L. divaricata* occupy intermediate zones forming a hybrid belt circling the botton of the depression (Figures 2-8, 2-9, and 2-10; see also Hunziker et al. 1969, Figures 1 and 2).

The slope has an approximate grade of 1/100, and the bottom of the depression is approximately 2 m below the higher level where the bushy *L. divaricata* and *L. cuneifolia* prevail (Hunziker et al. 1976). As has been noted earlier, in this depression *L. ameghinoi* dominates the bottom and the other two species occur on higher sandy soils (Hunziker et al. 1969). Soil in the bottom of the depression (A in Figure 2-8) has higher percentages of clay, silt, N, C, P, Ca, Na, and K than the soil in the higher peripheral areas where the shrubby species dominate (C in Figure 2-8). The intermediate and narrow sites (B in Figure 2-8), where the hybrids grow and form a belt, show intermediate edaphic characteristics (Table 2-1). That these edaphic factors are limiting and very important is shown by the almost complete ecological separation of the species in their respective zones and also by the narrow belt of hybrid swarms in the intermediate zones that have intermediate edaphic conditions (Hunziker et al. 1976).

Hybridization in the Experimental Garden

Larrea divaricata and *L. tridentata* were transplanted as two-year-old plants in 1967 to the La Creciente Experimental Plot in Tucson, Arizona. Plants of each taxon were planted next to each other with their branches growing side by side. Bees were observed visiting the flowers without discrimination. Mature seeds were collected from these branches. Hybrid seed-

FIGURE 2-8. Larrea *vegetation at the depression of km 1193, Ruta 3, 59 km south of San Antonio Oeste, Río Negro Prov., Argentina.*

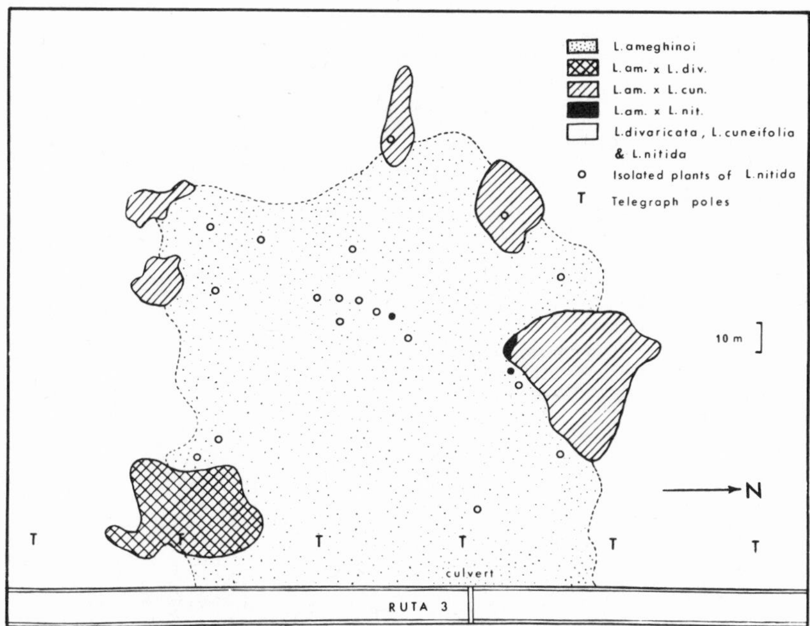

FIGURE 2-9. *Distribution of species of* Larrea *and hybrid plants or swarms in the depression of Figure 2-8.*

lings could be readily identified by their leaves and stipules prior to being transplanted to the outdoor plot. Most of the hybrids produced flowers and set seeds in two years and provided the materials for morphological and cytological studies (Yang et al. 1976).

Morphological Comparisons of Hybrids and Progenitors

Hybrid individuals were, in general, intermediate in leaf morphology and habit (Figure 2-11; also see Figure 2-6). This characteristic is especially true of all hybrids that are sterile, or almost completely so, and putative or are known F_1 hybrids, such as *L. ameghinoi* X *L. divaricata, L. divaricata* X *L. cuneifolia, L. cuneifolia* X *L. nitida,* and *L. divaricata* X *L. tridentata* (Hunziker et al. 1976; Yang et al. 1976). In the case of the last hybrid, several indices were devised for an exact comparison of the hybrids with the parental species (Yang et al. 1976).

The intersectional hybrids showed considerably more phenotypic plasticity than their parental species. This trait is very notable in *L. ameghinoi* X *L. divaricata, L. cuneifolia* X *L. nitida,* and *L. ameghinoi* X *L. cuneifolia* (see Figure 2-6).

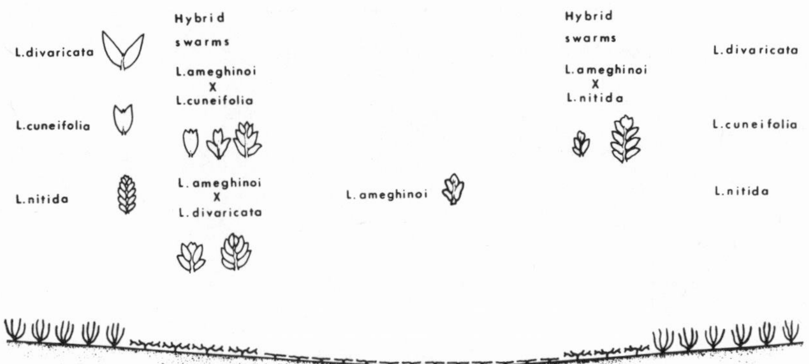

FIGURE 2-10. *Vegetation profile of the depression represented in Figure 2-8.*

Metroglyphic Analysis and Introgression

Hunziker et al. (1976) used metroglyphic analyses of hybrid swarms that are abundant in Río Negro Province, Argentina, to show the correlation of characters. Some of the hybrid individuals were intermediate, while others approached the morphological variation of the parental populations, with a continuous array of hybrid individuals going from one species to the other. Total resin content of the leaves was used as a discriminating character; the high (12.3-26 percent) was found in *L. nitida;* the low (5.3-10.9 percent) in *L. ameghinoi,* and the intermediate (8-17.4 percent) in the hybrids. The conclusion is that a few individuals apparently belong either to *L. ameghinoi* or to *L. nitida,* which were at the extreme of their variation spindle, and they possibly represent individuals resulting from introgression. The same authors (Hunziker et al. 1976) have analyzed the data of Mizrahi (1967) and found evidence of hybrid origin (*L. nitida* X *L. ameghinoi*) in some of the supposed *L. nitida* samples from Chubut, Argentina. These authors have also mentioned a few populations that could be classified as either *L. nitida* or *L. ameghinoi,* but since these slightly approached one or the other species in one or more characteristics, the authors speculated that the latter could have been derived through introgression long ago (Hunziker et al. 1976).

Chromatography of Phenolics in the Study of Hybridization

Hunziker et al. (1972a, b, 1976) have studied the phenolic patterns of all species and natural hybrids of *Larrea.*

Phenolic constituents of *Larrea* have been characterized and are discussed in Chapter 5. The discussion here will only report the chromatographic results obtained from the hybrid populations.

TABLE 2-1 *Edaphic Characteristics of Top Soils at Different Parts of the Depression in Rio Negro Province, 59 km South of San Antonio Oeste, Argentina (from Hunziker et al. 1976).*

	Texture in %							Mg per 100 g of soil				
Zone	Clay	Silt	Fine sand	Coarse sand	pH of soil paste	Total N %	Total C %	P	Ca	Mg	Na	K
A	21.5	42	33	3.5	8	0.14	0.93	1.66	660	48	24.6	145
B	18.3	38.5	32	11.17	7.5	0.10	0.67	1.05	350	54	12.3	128.7
C	6.75	14	53.7	25.5	8.1	0.06	0.34	0.9	340	Vest.	8.9	88.9

Note: *A* = Bottom of the depression where *L. ameghinoi* dominates; *B* = Intermediate narrow zone where *L. ameghinoi* × *L. divaricata*, *L. ameghinoi* × *L. cuneifolia*, and *L. ameghinoi* × *L. nitida* thrive; *C* = High border of the depression where *L. cuneifolia*, *L. divaricata*, and *L. nitida* dominate.

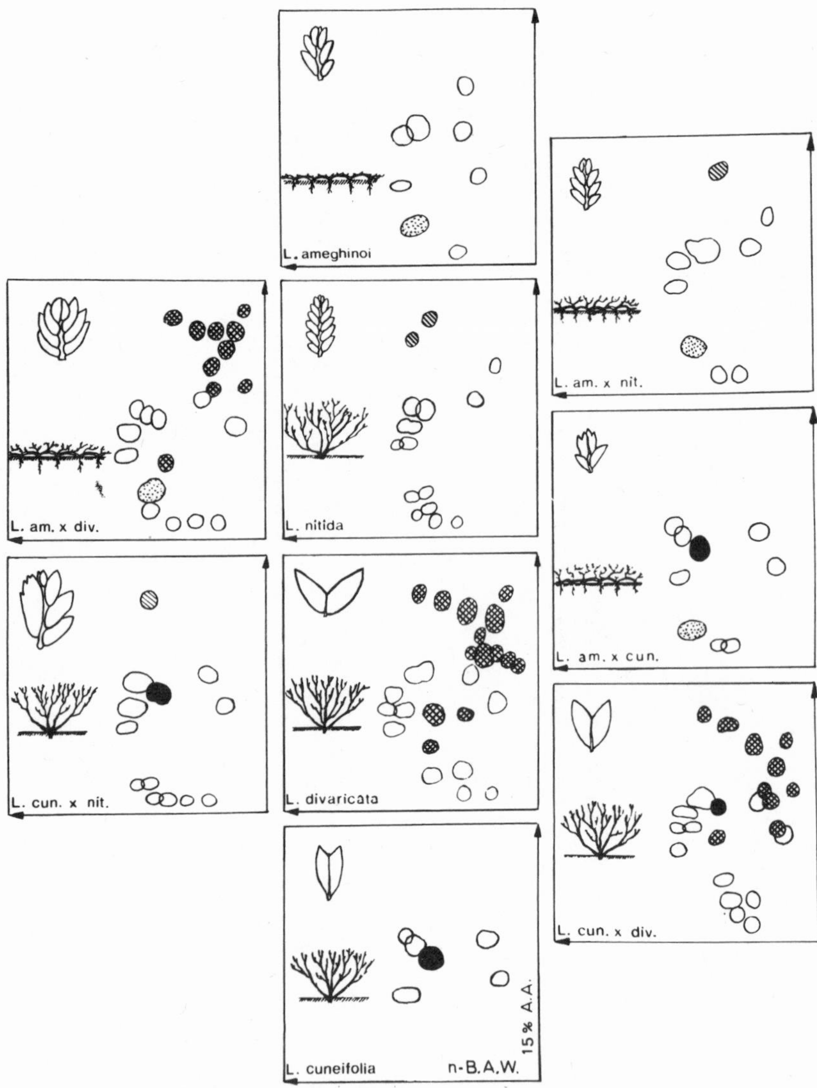

FIGURE 2-11. *Leaves, growth habit, and phenolic compounds of north Patagonian species and hybrids of* Larrea.

In general the chromatograms of the five hybrids show intermediacy and total or almost total addition of the phenolic compounds found in the parental species. In the hybrids in which either *L. ameghinoi* or *L. cuneifolia* was a parental species, the distinctive spot characterizing each species is shown (see Figure 2-11).

In hybrids involving *L. divaricata,* a constellation of 8 to 10 spots characteristic of this species was observed, and in the hybrids originated by *L. nitida,* only one of the two *L. nitida* marker spots could usually be observed (see Figure 2-11).

Due to the addition of marker compounds in the hybrids, chromatography has been highly valuable in this study for the correct identification of the parental species, especially in the case of *L. ameghinoi* × *L. divaricata.* The latter hybrid had not flowered for several years, and consequently the morphological information was incomplete (only vegetative and fruit characters) for some time. Originally it was believed to have arisen as a segregant from the *L. ameghinoi* × *L. cuneifolia* hybrids (Hunziker et al. 1969). Its chromatogram clearly indicates that this hybrid results from *L. ameghinoi* and *L. divaricata* (see Figure 2-11).

Protein Electrophoresis and Hybridization

Water soluble seed proteins have been studied by Hunziker et al. (1972a, b, 1976). In polyacrylamide gel each of the South American species has a characteristic pattern. Section *Larrea* has been shown to possess two fast moving bands that are absent in section *Bifolium. Larrea nitida* is characterized by a fast, extremely dense band.

Hunziker et al. (1976) have studied the electrophoretic patterns of *L. ameghinoi, L. nitida,* and four natural hybrids. The *L. ameghinoi* and *L. nitida* genomes could always be distinguished by using the fast moving albumins as markers (Figure 2-12). Hybrid 8818 clearly showed the two protein bands, and morphologically it looked like an F_1 hybrid in that it was 0.5 m high and had 6 to 9 leaflets. This plant was intermediate for 10 of the 12 traits used in the metroglyphic analysis and approached *L. ameghinoi* in the length of the mericarp hairs and *L. nitida* in the endocarp brightness. We should also point out that the fast bands of each species segregate independently of quantitative morphological traits and phenolic compounds.

Hybrid derivative 8873 showed the "*ameghinoi*" marker band and was intermediate for 8 morphological characteristics, while 3 approached *L. ameghinoi* and 1 approached *L. nitida.* Hybrid derivative 8678 showed the "*ameghinoi*" protein band and was intermediate for 7 morphological traits, while 3 approached *L. nitida* and 2 approached *L. ameghinoi.* Chromatography showed one phenolic marker spot from *L. ameghinoi* and one from *L. nitida.*

Hybrid derivative 8702 had the *L. nitida* protein band and had 3 morphological traits of *L. nitida,* 6 intermediate, and 3 of *L. ameghinoi.* Chromatography showed that it had the phenolic marker spot of both *L. nitida* and *L. ameghinoi.*

Luxuriance of Some of the Hybrids

All natural interspecific hybrids appeared vigorous when compared to their parents. Most notable were those involving *L. cuneifolia* × *L. divaricata, L. ameghinoi* × *L. cuneifolia,* and *L. ameghinoi* × *L. divaricata.* The latter

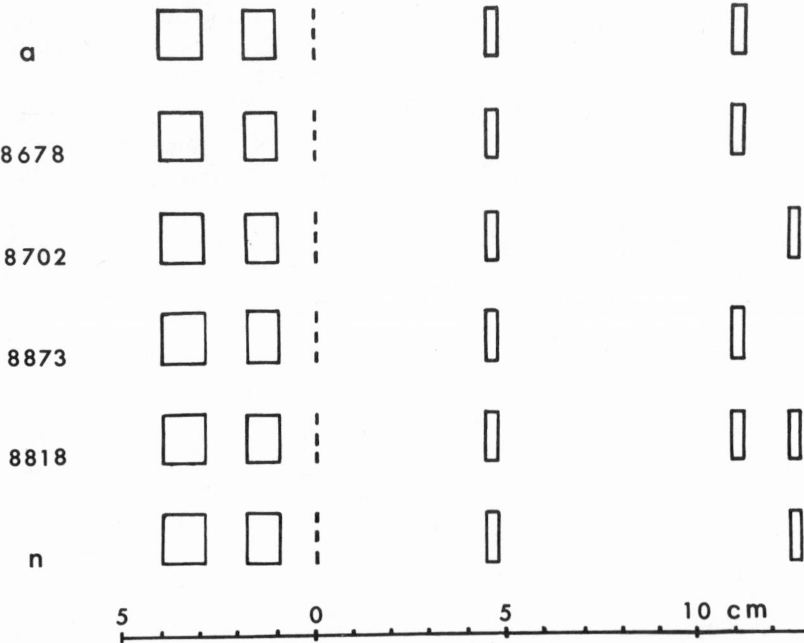

FIGURE 2-12. *Polyacrilamide gel electrophoresis of seed albumins of* L. ameghinoi, L. nitida, *and their hybrid derivatives.*

two showed a remarkably vigorous prostrate growth that allowed single individuals of these hybrid combinations to occupy a surface area of approximately 250 to 400 square meters. Due to breakage and death of some of the branches, the individual appeared to be subdivided into many smaller bushes, but these were identical in all characteristics. Evidently, they originated by vegetative reproduction of a single hybrid genotype. The prostrate rooting stem trait of *L. ameghinoi* produces in the hybrid an enormously extensive semiprostrate bush. Vegetative reproduction in these hybrids is indeed developed to a maximum.

CYTOGENETICS

Chromosome Behavior and Fertility

Hunziker et al. (1976) have studied the meiotic behavior in several individuals of all South American species and five interspecific hybrids (Table 2-2). *Larrea ameghinoi* has regular meiosis, usually with 13 bivalents at first metaphase. Similar regular meiotic behavior has been observed in the other diploid species, *L. nitida* and *L. divaricata.* One individual of *L. divaricata*

TABLE 2-2 *Chromosome Behavior at First Metaphase and Prometaphase in Species and Hybrids of* Larrea *(from Hunziker et al. 1976).*

Species or hybrid	Herbarium number (field tag number)	Chromosome number ($2n$)	Chromosome associations: Mean and range per cell in MI and prometaphase — III	II	I	Number cells studied	Closed II per cell Mean ± SE and range Metaphase I	Number cells studied	Pollen fertility %	Mericarps with seed %
L. ameghinoi	9001	26	–	13	0	70	12.61 ± 0.12 (11–13)	26	92–97[a]	77[a]
L. nitida	8999	26	–	13	0	100	12.21 ± 0.08 (10–13)	100		
L. nitida	8581 (8)	26	–	12.95 (12–13)	0.1 (0–2)	80	10.40 ± 0.30 (6–13)	22	98–100[a]	71–90[a]
L. divaricata	8587	26	–	12.83 (11–13)	0.34 (0–4)	47	10.36 ± 0.33 (6–13)	30	0 99–100[a]	62–72[a]
L. cuneifolia	8955 (19)	52	–	25.99 (25–26)	0.02 (0–2)	100	23.07 ± 0.16 (19–26)	100	95–100[a]	54–66[a]
L. ameghinoi × *L. nitida*	8602 (22)	26	–	12.93 (12–13)	0.13 (0–2)	15	– –	– –	98–99.5	21–71[a]
L. cuneifolia × *L. divaricata*	8619 (29)	39	0.09 (0.1)	12.35 (10–14)	14.03 (11–19)	66	11.79 ± 0.14 (9–13)	63	7.8–9.3	0

Note: All individuals from km 1193, Ruta 3, Dep. San Antonio, Río Negro, Argentina.
[a]Plants of the same locality but different individuals than those studied cytologically.

(8587) did not show a completely regular meiosis. Other individuals of *L. divaricata* from the same region or from other parts of Argentina–such as Salta, Tucuman, La Rioja, and Mendoza–proved to be diploids forming 13 bivalents at first metaphase.

Tetraploid *L. cuneifolia* showed 26 bivalents; other individuals from northwestern Argentina were also determined to be tetraploids with $n = 26$. The fact that no multivalents were detected in this species suggests that it is an allopolyploid.

Meiosis in the hybrids presented some peculiar features: the intrasectional hybrids either did not show cytomixis (*L. ameghinoi* × *L. nitida*) or showed it only to a moderate extent (22.3 percent of the cells in *L. cuneifolia* × *L. divaricata*). On the other hand, in intersectional hybrids most of the cells showed cytomixis, which made a detailed study of meiotic associations impossible (and meaningless from a phylogenetic point of view).

The hybrid between the multifoliolate species, *L. ameghinoi* and *L. nitida,* showed regular meiosis and had an average of 13 bivalents at first metaphase. At second metaphase more than one hundred cells had 13 chromosomes. The percent of mericarps with seed in this hybrid reached 71 percent and is comparable to that of the parental species.

The sterile hybrid between the two bifoliolate species, *L. cuneifolia* and *L. divaricata,* were found to be triploid as expected and showed 13 bivalents and 13 univalents in nearly 50 percent of the cells. In addition to the 66 cells listed in Table 2-2, 19 cells were observed that had numbers deviating from $2n = 39$. One had 37, 6 had 38, 7 had 40, 4 had 41, and 1 had 42. These probably originated from cytomixis. The significance and possible origin of this cytomixis in *Larrea* had been discussed elsewhere (Hunziker et al. 1976). The same authors have shown that the sterile triploid hybrid, *L. cuneifolia* × *L. nitida,* also underwent cytomixis. Cells were observed that were joined through cytoplasm. At first metaphase different configurations and chromosome numbers were found:

1 III + 4 II + 38 I = 49
9 II + 26 I = 44
8 II + 27 I = 43
9 II + 20 I = 38
10 II + 16 I = 36

Other cells from a single anther showed variable numbers of chromosomes (17 to about 51) at first anaphase.

In the triploid hybrid, *L. ameghinoi* × *L. cuneifolia,* irregular meiosis as well as several different chromosome numbers and associations were observed, again due to cytomixis. Several individuals were studied, and the number of univalents out of the metaphase plate was counted and observed to vary from 1 to 19. In spite of the irregular meiosis these hybrids were partially fertile. The percentage of pollen fertility ranged from 0 to 86 and that of seed-bearing mericarps varied from 15 to 19.4. Quite surprisingly, this intersectional triploid hybrid, with its highly irregular meiosis and nearly all of its cells showing cytomixis, still shows nearly 20 percent of mericarps bearing seed.

In the natural diploid hybrid, *L. ameghinoi* × *L. divaricata,* only estimating the mean number of univalents lying outside the metaphase plate in 52 cells (mean = 7.5) was possible. In spite of these meiotic abnormalities, the hybrid showed 8.5-11 percent pollen fertility and about 4 percent of the mericarps with seed (1 seed in 25 mericarps).

Yang et al. (1976) have recently made meiotic studies of the two vicarious taxa, *L. divaricata* and *L. tridentata.* Both have regular meiosis with 13 bivalents at first metaphase (Table 2-3). *Larrea divaricata* has a lower mean of closed or ring bivalents per cell (9.47 ± 0.14) than *L. tridentata* (12.40 ± 0.07). This difference was found to be highly significant.

Another strain of *L. divaricata* from Río Negro, Argentina, has been studied elsewhere (Hunziker et al. 1976). It also has a lower frequency of closed bivalents (10.36 ± 0.34) than *L. tridentata.* Yang et al. (1976) found that meiosis in the hybrids was relatively regular (see Table 2-3); their frequency of bivalents was slightly lower than in the parental strains. The frequency of closed bivalents was intermediate between those of the parental strains. Univalents were present in the hybrids at low frequencies; these were not observed in the parental strains (Figure 2-13; also see Table 2-3).

The difference in the frequency of closed bivalents between the hybrids and the parental species was highly significant, while the differences between the hybrids were lower. The frequency of closed bivalents depends on chiasma frequency. If chiasma frequency is under genetic control and subject to selection, in all possibility their frequency is controlled by multiple factors with additive effects. If this is the case, an F_1 with intermediate values is what would be expected (Yang et al. 1976).

The cause of sterility in the three hybrids, *L. ameghinoi* × *L. cuneifolia, L. cuneifolia* × *L. divaricata,* and *L. cuneifolia* × *L. nitida,* is believed to be a chromosomal barrier. In *L. cuneifolia* (4*n*) × *L. divaricata* (2*n*) there is good pairing of two genomes and only one genome is unpaired. In a triploid with such a pairing we would expect some fertility; however, it is completely sterile, which suggests that genic sterility is also involved.

Chromosomal behavior and seed fertility in the six interspecific hybrids can be easily appreciated in a crossing polygon (Figure 2-14).

Simpson et al. (see Chapter 4) have found differences in the breeding systems of the different species of *Larrea.* They have demonstrated that all of the species are self-compatible, but that *L. tridentata* (4*n*), *L. cuneifolia,* and *L. divaricata* exhibit an increasing series in their levels of natural self-pollination. Possibly, in *Larrea* the differences in closed bivalents and chiasma frequency are correlated with different degrees of natural self-pollination. Research has shown that in several genera (*Agropyron, Gilia,* and so forth) self-pollinating species possess a higher number of chiasmata than cross-pollinating ones (Grant 1958).

The A-T 219-110 hybrid was slightly more irregular than A-T 202-102

TABLE 2-3 *Chromosome Behavior at First Metaphase and Prometaphase of* L. divaricata, L. tridentata, *and Their Hybrids (from Yang et al. 1976)*

		Chromosome associations. Means ± S.E. and range per cell in MI and Prometaphase.			Metaphase I: Number of closed bivalents per cell	Metaphase I: Number of chiasmata per cell			
Species or hybrids	Herbarium number of culture number	II	I	Number cells studied	Mean ± S.E. and range	Mean ± S.E. and range	Number of cells studied	Pollen fertility (%)	Mericarps with seed (%)
L. divaricata	A-T 219	13	–	92	9.47 ± 0.14 (5–12)	22.47 ± 0.14 (18–25)	91	99[a]	62–72[a]
L. divaricata (A-T 202) × *L. tridentata* (T-Z 241)	A-T 202–102	12.97 ± 0.03 (12–13)	0.06 ± 0.06 (0–2)	34	11.44 ± 0.31 (7–13)	24.44 ± 0.31 (20–26)	25	37–67	4–40
L. divaricata (A-T 219) × *L. tridentata* (T-P (W))	A-T 219–110	12.59 ± 0.12 (8–13)	0.80 ± 0.23 (0–10)	69	10.47 ± 0.24 (5–13)	23.02 ± 0.35 (13–26)	55	55–78.8	5–17.7
L. tridentata	T-Z 151	13	–	100	12.40 ± 0.07 (10–13)	25.40 ± 0.07 (23–26)	100	97–99	82[a]

[a]Plants other than those studied cytologically.

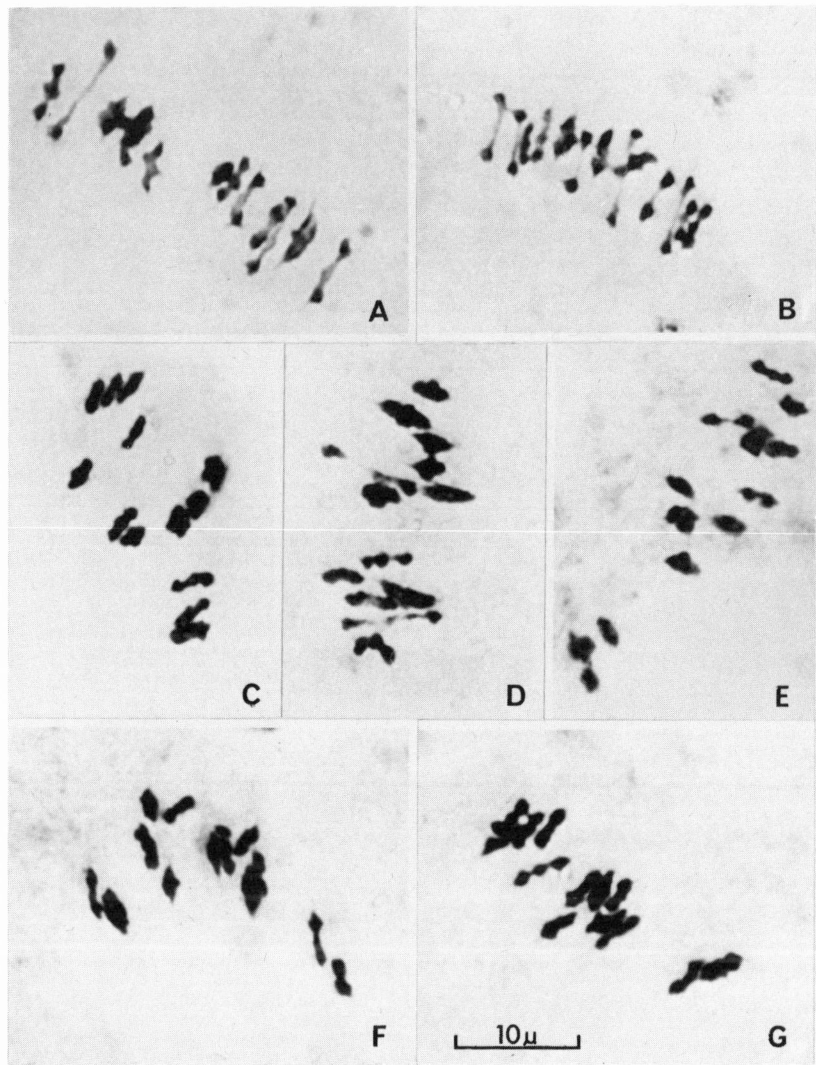

FIGURE 2-13. *First meiotic metaphase of* L. divaricata, L. tridentata *and their hybrid.*

(both *L. divaricata* × *L. tridentata*). It had fewer bivalents and closed bivalents as well as more univalents, and these differences were significant (Yang et al. 1976).

Pollen fertility in the hybrids was not complete, and great variation existed in the size and stainability of the pollen grains depending on the time of the year. This condition probably was due to low buffering of the hybrids to cope with environmental stresses. The hybrids had a lower percentage of

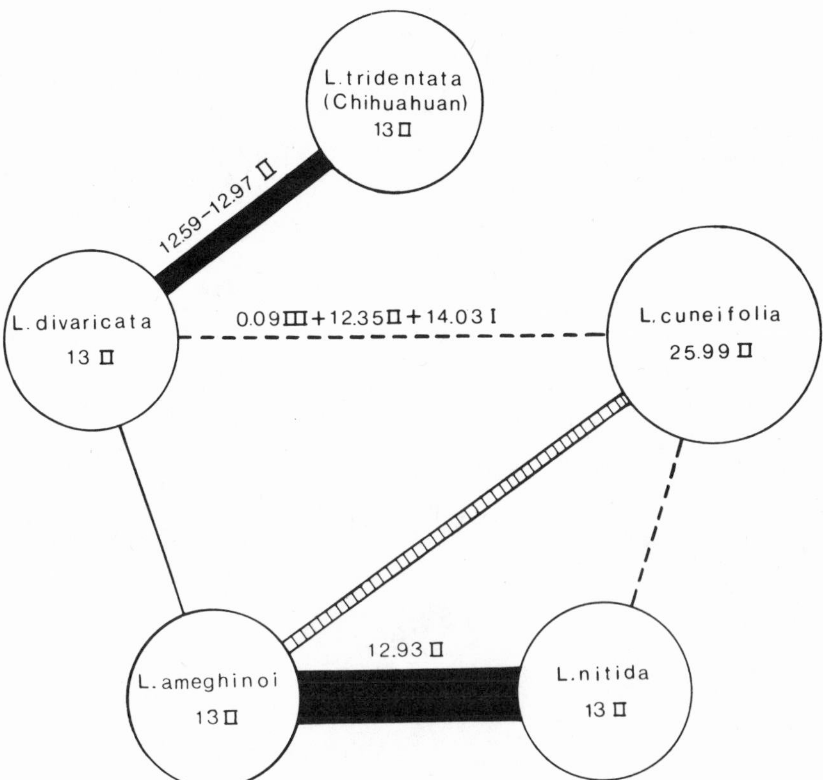

FIGURE 2-14. *Putative crossing relationships of the species of* Larrea *and their hybrids.*

pollen and seed fertility than pure *L. divaricata* and *L. tridentata* (Yang et al. 1976).

Progeny Tests

Hunziker et al. (1976) have performed progeny trials with seed from open pollination (collected in northern Patagonia) on hybrid individuals. The progeny under cultivation were analyzed with regard to growth habit, vigor, and leaf morphology. This analysis could only be done with two of the five natural hybrids since three of them are either completely or largely sterile.

Progeny consisting of 38 plants were derived from 111 seeds collected from *L. ameghinoi* × *L. cuneifolia* hybrids. They were generally weak and showed segregation for vigor, growth habit, and other morphological characteristics. Of the 23 plants that remained alive one year after germination, 10 showed cuneiform leaves (A, B, and C in Figure 2-15); 4 had multifolio-

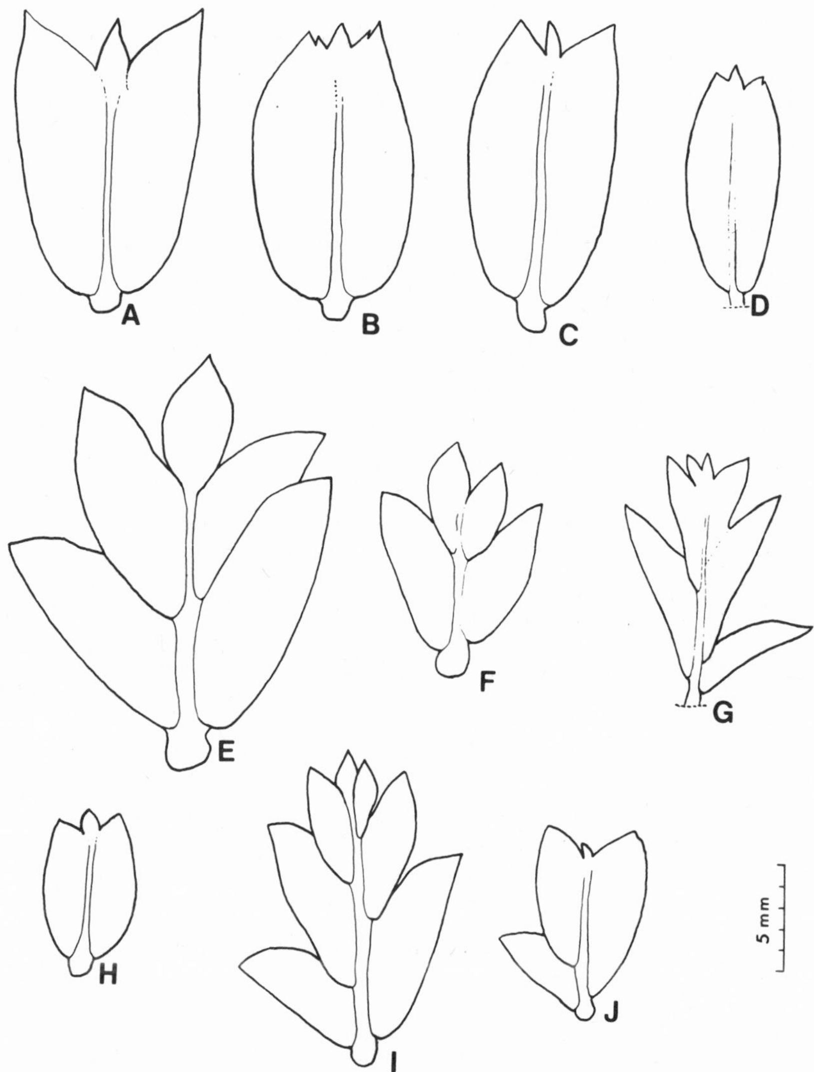

FIGURE 2-15. *Leaves from segregants from progeny trials originating from seed collected on natural* L. ameghinoi × L. cuneifolia *hybrids.*

late leaves with an acute apex (E, F, and G in Figure 2-15); and 9 had both types of leaves on the same individual (H, I, and J in Figure 2-15). The latter plants displayed considerable phenotypic plasticity, but did not reach the typical extreme foliar type of both parents. In most cases the cuneiform leaves had a minute apical leaflet or mucron. Some of the plants showed transgressive segregation, with leaflets more fused than in *L. cuneifolia,* and they had a three-dimensional navicular conformation resembling a spoon

(D in Figure 2-15). Many of the plants were weak and died. Two and a half years after germination only 4 plants remained alive. In all likelihood, a large part of the observed segregation for habit, vigor, and leaf morphology was due to aneuploidy or dysploidy in the progeny of triploid *L. ameghinoi* × *L. cuneifolia.*

The 409 seeds collected from various *L. ameghinoi* × *L. nitida* hybrids yielded 137 seedlings. These showed segregation for vigor, growth habit, and foliar characteristics. Of 111 plants that remained alive fourteen months after germination, 44 showed 9 to 13 leaflets as in *L. nitida,* 22 had 3 to 7 leaflets as in *L. ameghinoi,* and 45 showed intermediate numbers (6 to 9). Most of the plants were semi-erect or erect; only 3 were prostrate as *L. ameghinoi.*

In general, the plants tended to resemble *L. nitida* regarding growth habit and number of leaflets. Some of them actually could be taken as true *L. nitida.* Only one individual resembled *L. ameghinoi;* it had a prostrate growth and 5 to 6 leaflets. This resemblance could mean that most of the flowers had been pollinated with *L. nitida* pollen.

Larrea species and hybrids do not grow well under cultivation in Buenos Aires. After seven years of cultivation in the field, only 25 of 137 remained alive. A smaller sample of pure *L. nitida* plants showed a much lower survival rate in the same locality under the same conditions. Several hybrid derivatives reached flower after three years. Only one plant flowered after two and a half years, and it produced 4 fruits yielding 6 seeds, which were the result of selfing, since there were no other plants in flower (Hunziker et al. 1976).

Yang et al. (1976) also raised an F_2 from 152 seeds collected in the experimental garden on a hybrid *L. divaricata* × *L. tridentata.* After germination (facilitated by scarification) of these, 22 seedlings were obtained, which by the third month showed a strong segregation for vigor: 3 plants were very vigorous, 5 vigorous, 5 average, 7 weak, and 2 extremely weak. In all probability a large proportion of the 130 seeds that did not germinate represent lethal genotypes.

EVOLUTION

Isolating Mechanisms

Hunziker et al. (1976) have discussed the isolating mechanisms that prevent or reduce gene interchange among the four South American species. There is seasonal isolation in respect to flowering. *Larrea ameghinoi* and *L. nitida* flower first, *L. cuneifolia* follows, and *L. divaricata* is last.

There are ecological differences among the species that are effective in isolating each from the others (see the section on distributional and ecological observations on natural hybrid swarms).

There are also postzygotic mechanisms that operate in the following cases:

1. The hybrid *L. ameghinoi* × *L. divaricata* apparently flowers sporadically and is almost sterile.
2. The *L. cuneifolia* × *L. divaricata* and *L. cuneifolia* × *L. nitida* hybrids are completely sterile.
3. The partly fertile hybrids of *L. ameghinoi* × *L. cuneifolia* and *L. divaricata* × *L. tridentata* show degeneration of the hybrid progeny in the F_2.

Species Relationships

As mentioned earlier, there are two sections within the genus. The affinities of the species within each section is supported by cytogenetics and protein data. The multifoliolate pair, *L. nitida* and *L. ameghinoi* (section *Larrea*), is so closely related that its hybrid shows regular formation of bivalents and is fully fertile. Hybridization between the two taxa is a common phenomenon in Patagonia. Both taxa could be regarded as partly sympatric semispecies and as constituents of a syngameon (Grant 1971).

The South American members of the bifoliolate pair, *L. divaricata* and *L. cuneifolia,* also are closely related to the extent that cytogenetic evidence from their interspecific hybrid indicates that *L. divaricata* (or a species very closely related to it) has been one of the progenitors of tetraploid *L. cuneifolia.* The close relationship of these two bifoliolate species has been pointed out by Cozzo (1948) on the basis of the similarity of the wood anatomy, which makes them appear as "forms of a common species and not as two different ones."

The relationships between taxa of the two sections cannot, unfortunately, be assessed with precision on cytogenetic grounds; due to cytomixis, gaining sufficient data on the intersectional hybrids–namely, *L. ameghinoi* × *L. cuneifolia, L. ameghinoi* × *L. divaricata,* and *L. cuneifolia* × *L. nitida*–has not been possible. The relationships of the species of *Larrea* based on chromosome behavior and the percentage of mericarps with seed for the six interspecific hybrids can be visualized as shown in Figure 2-14. A tentative phylogenetic tree has been published elsewhere (Hunziker et al. 1972a).

Except in the cases of *L. divaricata* and *L. tridentata,* the chromatographic patterns of phenolics do not reveal obvious affinities. Our preliminary studies of the phenolics have shown that the chromatographic profiles of *L. divaricata* and *L. tridentata* are very similar (see Figure 2-11). The same is shown by the recent and more detailed studies of Mabry et al. (see Chapter 5). On the other hand, the two closely related diploids, *L. nitida* and *L. ameghinoi,* share an homologous genome but have different chromatographic profiles (see Figure 2-11). This pattern is also shown in the recent studies by Mabry et al. (see Chapter 5) who found differences between these two species in 6 flavonoid aglycones and 3 flavonoid glycosides. In all probability, rather few gene differences could produce different phenolic patterns in species that have largely homologous genomes.

The close pairing in the *L. cuneifolia* × *L. divaricata* hybrid showed that either *L. divaricata* or a closely related species has been one of the progenitors of tetraploid *L. cuneifolia.* However, if one of the diploid progenitors was contemporary *L. divaricata, L. cuneifolia* should have all or most of the phenolic compounds of *L. divaricata* due to the addition of compounds in the hybrids. This characteristic is not observed in our preliminary chromatographic studies nor in the more recent studies by Mabry et al. (see Chapter 5). These authors have shown that *L. cuneifolia* lacks 8 flavonoid aglycones that are present in *L. divaricata.* Apparently there is genome homology, but possibly the ancestor of *L. cuneifolia* was somewhat different from the present-day Argentine *L. divaricata.* This ancestral difference is not surprising because the Peruvian race of *L. divaricata* is even poorer than *L. cuneifolia* in that it has only 9 flavonoid aglycones while *L. cuneifolia* shows 11 and *L. divaricata* from Argentina has 20.

The hybrids of *L. divaricata* × *L. tridentata* have regular meiosis, which indicates that the genomes are homologous. As shown in Table 2-2, both hybrids show differences in the average number of bivalents, univalents, and closed bivalents that are statistically significant. These differences could be due to different environmental conditions prior to fixation or to genotypic differences (Yang et al. 1976). Both hybrids were semisterile with respect to pollen and seed fertility; they had considerably lower values than the parental strains. The sterility could be genic or chromosomal or both. It could be developmental, but probably is predominantly segregational (Stebbins 1966). In addition to genic differences, both amphitropical taxa could possibly have diverged in a few minute chromosomal differences through reciprocal translocations, transpositions, or inversions that would not affect chromosomal pairing as observed at first metaphase, but could produce deficiencies and duplications in the gametes. This condition has been termed *cryptic structural hybridity* by Stebbins who has shown that heterozygosity for small structural differences may cause partial sterility (Stebbins 1950, Figures 23, 24).

As pointed out by Yang et al. (1976), the relationship between South American *L. divaricata* and North American *L. tridentata* has been a matter of controversy for some time. Some authors have been inclined to consider them as different species; others have considered them as different races or subspecies of a single amphitropical species.

The phenolic chromatographic patterns of diploid, tetraploid, and hexaploid North American *L. tridentata* and South American *L. divaricata* were studied. Even when they presented some differences, they were found on the whole to be strikingly similar (see Chapter 5). On the other hand, each one of the four South American species of *Larrea* could be characterized by different phenolic markers (Hunziker et al. 1972a, b, 1976).

The protein electrophoretograms obtained by these authors also showed that there were few differences among diploids of *L. divaricata* from Northern Patagonia and diploid *L. tridentata* from New Mexico. They found small differences depending upon the particular geographic locality of the *L. tridentata* strains. The results obtained by Yang et al. (*submitted*) were similar. The similarity of the Chihuahuan, Peruvian and Argentine patterns may be observed in Figure 2-16.

The overall similarities between strains of *L. divaricata* and *L. tridentata* were only slightly fewer than those within *L. tridentata* and *L. divaricata.* This comparison demonstrates the high degree of protein fraction homology between *L. divaricata* and *L. tridentata.* In this respect we should note that protein patterns are different in the four South American species of *Larrea* and thus support the affinities of the species as indicated by morphological and cytogenetic data (Hunziker 1971).

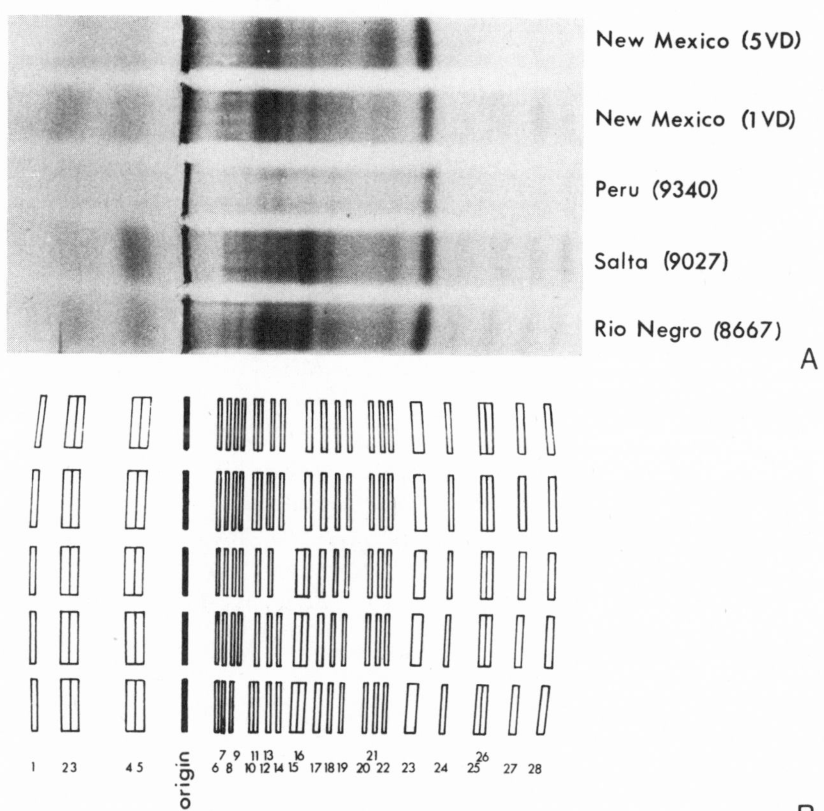

FIGURE 2-16. *Seed protein electrophoresis of* L. divaricata *and* L. tridentata.

The protein electrophoretic data not only separate the four South American species but also show the affinities between the two species of the multifoliolate group and between the two of the bifoliolate group. The multifoliolate group of species has two fast bands that are absent in the bifoliolate one (Hunziker et al. 1976).

Hunziker et al. (1972b) also found high protein homologies between different ploidy levels of *L. tridentata* and concluded, by also taking into account morphological and chromatographic data, that interracial polyploidy was involved in the origin of the tetraploid and hexaploid populations.

On the basis of morphological, phenolic, and protein data, these authors concluded that in all likelihood *L. divaricata* and diploid *L. tridentata* were conspecific and, accordingly, treated them as subspecies. They emphasize, however, that the final answer to this question comes from the analysis of the hybrid (Hunziker et al. 1972b). Recent results by Yang et al. (1976), as already mentioned, have revealed the presence of a partial reproductive barrier in the hybrids that makes them semisterile. If these taxa were sympatric, gene interchange between them would be greatly reduced. Since the development of the reproductive barrier is not complete biologically, these taxa fall within a category intermediate between a species and a subspecies. They could be considered "allopatric-semispecies." This category applies to allopatric taxa that have not yet attained complete reproductive isolation and are at intermediate stages of divergence (Grant 1963, 1971).

Both entities are still very closely related as indicated by their morphology, the homology of their proteins, the phenolic patterns, the regular chromosome behavior in the hybrids, and the partial gene exchange still possible between them through a semisterile hybrid. According to general use in similar plant cases, a more practical approach may be to give them specific taxonomic rank. Both taxa may be considered as integrating a superspecies (Mayr 1942, 1963, 1970; Grant 1963). We may refer to it as the *L. divaricata–tridentata* superspecies.

Finally, as has been pointed out by Hunziker et al. (1976), clarifying the relationship of the three North American cytotypes (or taxa) among themselves is important. The similarity of the electrophoretic and chromatographic patterns as well as the morphological, physiological, and anatomical similarities suggest that interracial autoploidy has occurred since there is no increase of protein fractions and phenolics, nor abrupt morphological differentiation with increased ploidy (see Chapter 5).

Primitive and More Recent or Specialized Adaptations

The multifoliolate species of section *Larrea* (*L. nitida, L. ameghinoi*) are more mesophytic and microthermic than the extreme xerophytes of section *Bifolium.* In northwestern Argentina (Cordillera de La Rioja), *L. nitida* is only found from 2,500 m above sea level to 3,150 m whereas *L. divaricata* and *L. cuneifolia* are found from 1,800 m or less to 3,000 m (Hunziker 1952). Because of the morphology and smaller size of the flowers and their early flowering (at a time when there are few insects), they seem to make more use of self-fertilization than the species of *Bifolium* (see Chapter 4).

Multifoliolate *L. nitida* is regarded as a taxon representing primitive *Larrea* types. This species is, according to Morello (1955), a phreatophyte.

Larrea ameghinoi, with its lower number of leaflets and prostrate growth habit, is obviously adaptated to the cold, windy Patagonian climate.

Larrea divaricata, L. tridentata, and *L. cuneifolia* probably represent an adaptation to aridity by reduction in the number of leaflets along with other morphological and physiological adaptations. In *L. cuneifolia* the leaf is reduced basically to an emarginate single blade, due to extreme fusion of the folioles. Moreover, this species has acquired (possibly through crossing to a now extinct diploid) the extraordinary ability to orient the leaves so that most epiphylls face the east. At midday its leaves receive the strong sun rays in a tangential manner (Hunziker et al. 1972a). This ability is another adaptation that allows *L. cuneifolia* to be a more extreme xerophyte than *L. divaricata.* In fact, *L. cuneifolia* may be present at drier sites than *L. divaricata* (Morello 1955; Ragonese 1951). Tetraploid *L. cuneifolia* probably represents the most advanced and xerophytically specialized taxon of the genus.

The Geographical Origin of *Larrea*

The possible geographical origin of *Larrea* has been considered recently (Barbour 1969a; Hunziker et al. 1972a, b; Turner 1972; Porter 1974; Hunziker1975). Contrary to the opinion of some of these authors, and based on several lines of evidence, we believe that the *L. divaricata* complex has originated in South America.

Theories About the Center of Origin of Larrea

Basically there are three hypotheses concerning the center of origin of *Larrea* (see Chapter 5).

Johnston (1940) proposed a South American origin for the genus *Larrea.* This theory is sustained by us on the basis of new investigations (Hunziker et al. 1972a, b; see also Hunziker 1975). Axelrod (1950) has noted that the present occurrence of relic austral types, such as *Larrea* in North America, can be explained by transtropic migration in the late Cenozoic. Long-distance dispersal of *Larrea* across the tropics may have occurred through an intermediate series of appropriate semi-arid habitats that served as "way-stations" (Raven 1963), a situation which might have arisen as a result of the expansion of the world's arid climates in the late tertiary and early Quaternary (Axelrod 1970; Porter 1974).

On the basis of the similarities between *Larrea* of the Chihuahuan and the Argentine areas, Barbour (1969a) has postulated a transtropic prototype that later became extinct. Its disappearance would have produced the present North-South American disjunction.

Turner (1972) proposed that *L. tridentata* developed as a diploid population in North America millions of years ago and subsequently became established in South America through long-range dispersal. Porter (1974) also supports this view.

Evidence for a South American Origin

Several lines of evidence that indicate a South American origin for the genus *Larrea* are outlined below.

Besides bifoliolate *L. divaricata, L. tridentata,* and *L. cuneifolia* (section *Bifolium*), there are two other more mesic species of *Larrea* in South America, the multifoliolate *L. ameghinoi* and *L. nitida* (section *Larrea*) (Palacios and Hunziker 1972; Hunziker 1975). As has already been mentioned, reduction of leaflet number would represent an adaptation to aridity and thus a derived condition. Since both multifoliolate, more mesic species are presently in Argentina and Chile, a South American origin is favored. This argument does not necessarily mean that the center of origin of *Larrea* coincides with the present-day range of the multifoliolate species.

Larrea divaricata and *L. cuneifolia,* with only two leaflets, would represent more recent types within the genus resulting from adaptations to the semidesert and desert environments in which they occur. In contrast, both of the multifoliolate species, *L. nitida* and *L. ameghinoi,* frequently occur in less xeric, cooler habitats.

The South American genus *Bulnesia,* which is one of the genera most closely related to *Larrea,* is composed of six multifoliolate species and only one bifoliolate species. As suggested by Porter (1974), the *Bulnesia* of southern South America are derived from tropical progenitors represented today by the multifoliolate arboreal *B. arborea* and *B. carrapo* (Venezuela and Colombia).

Larrea cuneifolia (n = 26), which has a wide range in Argentina, contains the genome of *L. divaricata* (n = 13). The cytogenetic analysis of the hybrid between tetraploid *L. cuneifolia* and diploid *L. divaricata* indicates that the two species have a genome in common and suggests that *L. divaricata* is probably one of the two diploid progenitors of *L. cuneifolia* (Hunziker et al. 1972a, b, 1973). Since *L. cuneifolia* has a wide distribution in Argentina and possesses at least two specialized adaptations (leaflet fusion, orientation of epiphylls to the east, both of which would require considerable time to develop), it is most likely a relatively old species. The presence of the *L. divaricata* genome in *L. cuneifolia* would indicate that the *L. divaricata* genome is an ancient one in South America. On the other hand, we know that this ancient South American genome is largely homologous to the diploid *L. tridentata* genome (Yang et al. 1976). The other genome of *L. cuneifolia* could have come from a species that is now extinct (Hunziker et al. 1972a).

The genera in the Zygophyllaceae that are most likely to be closely related to *Larrea* have contemporary distributions that suggest a northern South American origin for most of them. Axelrod (1950) has noted that *Larrea* belongs to a family "of tropical and border-tropical affinity. . . . This suggests a long history on the margins of the tropics in austral areas, particularly at low to middle latitudes where tropical savanna and similar environments have long been in existence."

In this connection, we should note that *Bulnesia* is restricted to South America and has also evolved on this continent. Two species can be found in Colombia and Venezuela (north of the equator), and five have a southern distribution (Argentina, Chile, Peru, and Paraguay). Six of its seven species that have been studied so far have proven to be diploids (Poggio, *unpublished*). Apparently, in this genus as in *Larrea,* primary speciation occurred in South America, but polyploidy and long-distance migration to North America did not occur in *Bulnesia* (possibly because the seeds were less suited for long-distance dispersal since their integuments offer little protection). So far *Larrea, Bulnesia, Plectrocarpa,* and *Porlieria* (Poggio, *unpublished*) are the only genera in the subfamily Zygophylloideae known to have a chromosome number of $x = 13$. Knowing the basic number of *Metharme* (Porter 1974), which is also restricted to South America, would be interesting. *Plectrocarpa* and *Metharme* are, according to Engler (1896), so close to *Larrea* that they can be considered as early derivations of a *Larrea* ancestral type. Porter (1974) has pointed out that "phylogenetic relationships with the Zygophyllaceae are still somewhat hazy" and that *Larrea* appears to belong to a series of poorly known, mainly monotypic, shrubby desert genera. According to Porter, these genera are *Metharme* (monotypic, Chile), *Neoluederitzia* (monotypic, S.W. Africa), *Plectrocarpa* (two species, Argentina), *Sericodes* (monotypic, Mexico), and *Sisyndite* (monotypic, S.W. Africa). Of about eight genera within the subfamily Zygophylloideae related to a greater or lesser extent to *Larrea,* only one has a strictly North American distribution, namely, the monotypic genus, *Sericodes. Guaiacum* ranges from North to South American through the tropics. Of the others, four have a South American distribution (*Plectrocarpa, Metharme, Bulnesia, Porlieria*) and two are South African (*Neoluederitzia, Sisyndite*). This distribution supports Axelrod's idea of a long history of the family on the margin of the tropics in austral areas (Hunziker 1975).

Porter (1974) has suggested that *Larrea* may be most similar morphologically (in terms of flowers and fruits) to *Sericodes,* a monotypic genus that is exclusively North American. The latter, however, has simple leaves and hairy mericarps, while the primitive species of *Larrea* (represented today by taxa such as *L. nitida*) probably had multifoliolate leaves and puberulous and indehiscent fruits.

In connection with the origin of *Larrea* and *Sericodes,* we should note that the light, hairy mericarps of *Larrea tridentata* and *Sericodes greggii* may be adapted for epizoic as well as endozoic dispersal. *Sericodes* compared to *Larrea* may represent a much earlier arrival from South America that originated from other members of the Zygophyllaceae of the tropics. On the other hand, multifoliolate *Larrea* species (section *Larrea*) are not suitable for epizoic dispersal because they have heavy puberulous mericarps.

Recent cytological data obtained by Poggio (*unpublished*) indicate that *Plectrocarpa tetracantha* has $n = 13$; *Porlieria microphylla,* $2n = 52$; six species of *Bulnesia,* $n = 13$; *Pintoa chilensis,* $2n = 20$; *Sisyndite* sp., $2n = 20$; and *Sericodes greggii,* $n = 15$. These data obviously suggest a closer relationship of *Larrea* ($n = 13$) with South American *Plectrocarpa, Bulnesia,* and *Porlieria,* all of which have $x = 13$, and a more distant one with North American *Sericodes,* South African *Sisyndite,* and South American *Pintoa.*

As shown by Hunziker et al. (1972b), within *L. tridentata* there are no marked differences in the protein patterns of the different chromosomal races. The diploid protein spectra present some slight differences among themselves. There are no obvious differences in the presence or absence of bands among the tetraploids except concentrations of certain fractions. The hexaploids also show slight variation. The absence of major differences among di-, tetra-, and hexaploid patterns strongly suggests that interracial autoploidy is involved in the origin of tetra- and hexaploid populations of *L. tridentata.* If alloploidy were involved, the tetra- and hexaploid protein spectra would be more complex than the diploids because in amphiploids generally, there is some addition of protein fractions from the original diploids (Hunziker et al. 1972b).

The protein electrophoretograms obtained by these authors also showed that there are few differences between diploids of *L. divaricata* from northern Patagonia and *L. tridentata* from New Mexico. Similar results were also obtained in a subsequent investigation. The high coefficients of similarity obtained when *L. divaricata* and *L. tridentata* patterns are compared show the high homology of protein fractions between the two taxa (Yang et al. *submitted*). It should be noted in this respect that protein spectra are quite different in the four South American species of *Larrea* and support the affinities of the species as indicated by morphological and cytogenetic data (Hunziker 1971).

Hunziker et al. (1972a, b) found no major differences in the phenolic patterns by two-dimensional chromatography in their preliminary studies of South American *L. divaricata* and the three chromosomal races of *L. tridentata.*

The discovery that all three ploidy levels of *L. tridentata* have the same

20 flavonoid aglycones on the surface of the leaves and largely the same internal flavonoid glycosides suggests a recent autoploid origin for these taxa. Altogether, small variation in the extensive North American populations, which is contrasted with the highly variable and complex chemical patterns found in the South American *Larrea* taxa, is in accord with a South American origin for the genus and a relatively recent introduction into North America (see Chapter 5).

On the basis of radiocarbon dating, there are no wood rat midden deposits (*Neotoma*) containing authenticated *Larrea* older than 10580 ± 550 Y.B.P. in the Sonoran Desert (Van Devender 1973; Wells 1976).

Wells maintains the opinion that the present geographical range of *Larrea* in North America may be of very recent origin. According to him a large portion of the present area of the warm desert areas of North America were occupied by pluvial woodlands until the end of the Wisconsin glacial (about 11000-12000 Y.B.P. at the low subtropical latitudes of the Sonoran and Chihuahuan deserts or until around 9000 Y.B.P. at higher elevations of the Mojave Desert) (Wells and Berger 1967; Wells 1969; 1976; Wells and Hunziker, *in press*). The available fossil evidence, therefore, does not indicate an ancient distribution of *Larrea* in North America.

Possible Dispersal Agents

If one accepts that long-distance dispersal of *Larrea* from South America to North America did happen, then possible dispersal agents must be considered. One possibility is long-distance transport by birds. Cruden (1966) has not favored long-distance transport of seed by birds as a way of explaining the North–South American disjunctions. He has pointed out some of the difficulties for these explanations, particularly the fact that the passage of seeds through a bird would take but a few hours. Proctor (1968), however, has shown by experimental feeding of caged birds that the killdeer plover (*Charadrius vociferus*) retains some viable seeds in its gizzard for periods as long as 77 to 160 hours and sometimes up to 340 hours. Wells (1977) has suggested that the related golden plover (*Pluvialis dominica*) or the upland plover (*Bartramia longicauda*), which migrate between Argentina and the Northern hemisphere could have been the carriers of *Larrea* seed (Wells and Hunziker, *in press*). On the other hand, Dr. K. Ollrog (*personal communication*) suggested to us that the *Larrea* seed could have been carried from South America to North America by the migratory peregrine falcon (*Falco peregrinus*) or the Swainson's hawk (*Buteo swainsoni*) that eat birds and rodents, respectively.

Conclusions

As pointed out by Hunziker (1975), data from comparative anatomy, morphology, cytology, and palynology for all the genera related to *Larrea* are badly needed in order to have further evidence on its origin. In the genus *Larrea* there has been primary speciation at the diploid level (*L. nitida, L. ameghinoi, L. divaricata,* and *L. tridentata*) with occasional hybrid speciation involving allotetraploidy (*L. cuneifolia*). Both processes have occurred in South America. This situation parallels that of the related genus *Bulnesia,* except for the occurrence of polyploidy (Hunziker 1975).

Yang (1968, 1970) and Barbour (1969a) have established the existence of diploid, tetraploid, and hexaploid chromosomal races within *L. tridentata* that replace each other from southeast to northwest in the Chihuahuan, Sonoran, and Mojave deserts, respectively. There is an increase in the ploidy level with increased aridity of the deserts, and the present distribution suggests a northwestward pattern of migration from Mexico to California, Nevada, and Utah.

After assessing all the available evidence, we suggest that *Larrea tridentata* is derived from ancestral South American populations of *L. divaricata* and has reached North America from South America as a diploid. We suggest that after adaptation, differentiation, and colonization of the Chihuahuan Desert, *L. tridentata* underwent interracial autopolyploidy in North America, with Chihuahuan desert diploids giving rise to the Sonoran Desert tetraploid race. By combination of unreduced and reduced gametes, this race could in turn have given rise to the hexaploid race that now occupies much of the Mojave Desert. Wells (1977) thinks that the most important features of the present geographic pattern of *L. tridentata* probably originated during the climatic transition from the late Wisconsin glacial to the Holocene, when a dry climate eliminated the pluvial woodlands that existed in the lowlands of southwestern North America. In the vacant niches of this new, vast, and varied desert environment a burgeoning *Larrea* population could have expanded and differentiated explosively (Wells 1977).

The migration of *L. divaricata* to North America and its subsequent differentiation into *L. tridentata* and further into tetraploid and hexaploid races has been a less radical and probably more recent and rapid development than the primary speciation that occurred in South America. In North America there has been merely semispecific differentiation and interracial polyploidy as suggested by meiotic chromosome studies, protein electrophoretic data, chromatography of the phenolic compounds, and exomorphology (see Chapter 5; see also Hunziker et al. 1972a, b; Hunziker 1975; Yang et al. 1976).

That *Larrea* is probably a recent element in the North American desert vegetation is further supported by the absence of older macrofossil evidence of *Larrea* in Pleistocene *Neotoma* deposits as discussed earlier.

SUMMARY

Distributional, morphological, cytogenetical, and evolutionary aspects of the five species of *Larrea* and six interspecific hybrids are discussed. Other problems under consideration are the significance of hybridization and introgression in the variation of *L. nitida* and *L. ameghinoi,* results of progeny trials of some of the hybrids, the importance of chromatography of phenolics, and electrophoresis of seed proteins in the identification of hybrids and hybrid derivatives, isolating mechanisms, and relationships between species.

Evidence from the meiotic behavior in the sterile hybrid *L. cuneifolia* × *L. divaricata* suggests that *L. divaricata,* or a species very closely related to it, has been one of the progenitors of tetraploid *L. cuneifolia.* The regular chromosome behavior and high fertility of the hybrids between *L. ameghinoi* and *L. nitida* indicate that the two taxa are closely related and that they should be regarded as partially sympatric semispecies integrating a syngameon.

The behavior of the chromosomes in the hybrid between *L. divaricata* and *L. tridentata* was normal, thereby indicating that the *L. divaricata* and *L. tridentata* genomes are homologous. *L. tridentata* showed a higher mean of closed bivalents than *L. divaricata.* The interspecific hybrids had an average number of closed bivalents that was intermediate between the values for the parental strains, and they were semisterile with respect to pollen and seed fertility. The analysis of the hybrids indicates that *L. divaricata* and *L. tridentata* constitute a borderline case between species and subspecies and, therefore, may be considered as allopatric semispecies.

Other hybrids were either partially, almost complëtely, or absolutely sterile (*L. ameghinoi* × *L. cuneifolia, L. ameghinoi* × *L. divaricata,* and *L. cuneifolia* × *L. nitida,* respectively).

The available evidence concerning the center of origin of *Larrea* is also reviewed. It suggests that *Larrea* reached North America from South America through long-distance dispersal.

RESUMEN

En el presente trabajo se discuten diversos aspectos de la distribución geográfica, la morfología, citogenética y evolución de las cinco especies de *Larrea* y seis de sus híbridos interespecíficos. Otros problemas que se tratan son los siguientes: la trascendencia de la hibridación e introgresión en la variación de *L. nitida* y *L. ameghinoi,* los resultados de pruebas de progenie de algunos de los híbridos, la importancia de la cromatografía de compuestos fenólicos y de la electroforesis de proteínas seminales en la identificación de híbridos y derivados híbridos, los mecanismos de aislamiento y las relaciones entre las especies.

La evidencia obtenida a través del estudio del híbrido estéril entre *L. cuneifolia* y *L. divaricata* indica que *L. divaricata* o una especie muy relacionada con ésta, ha sido uno de los progenitores del tetraploide *L. cuneifolia.*

El apareamiento cromosómico regular y elevada fertilidad de los híbridos entre *L. ameghinoi* y *L. nitida* sugiere que ambos taxa están estrechamente relacionados y que pueden ser considerados como semiespecies parcialmente simpátricas, integrando un singameon.

El comportamiento de los cromosomas en el híbrido entre *L. divaricata* y *L. tridentata* es normal indicando que los genomios de *L. divaricata* y *L. tridentata* son homólogos. *L. tridentata* muestra un promedio de bivalentes cerrados mayor que *L. divaricata.* Los híbridos interespecíficos tienen un promedio de bivalentes cerrados intermedios respecto al valor de ambos padres y son semiestériles con respecto a fertilidad de polen y porciento de mericarpios con semilla. El análisis de estos híbridos indica que *L. divaricata* y *L. tridentata* constituyen un caso límite entre especie y subespecie y que, por lo tanto pueden ser considerados como semiespecies alopátricas.

Se hace una revisión de la evidencia disponible acerca del centro de origen de *Larrea.* Se sugiere que *Larrea* llegó a Norteamérica desde Sudamérica mediante transporte a larga distancia.

APPENDIX 2A
A TAXONOMIC KEY TO THE SPECIES OF *LARREA*

1. Leaves with 3 to 17 leaflets, imparipinnate, with terminal leaflet developed. Mericarps puberulous, remaining associated at maturity. Flowers small, with petals 4 to 6.9 mm long.
    2. Leaves with 3 to 7 leaflets. Mericarps verrucose, brown-red, and with not too-hardened walls. Seeds chestnut to occasionally black in color. Ligneous prostrate chamaephyte. *L. ameghinoi* Speg.
    2′. Leaves with 9 to 17 leaflets. Mericarps smooth, of burnt yellow stone color, with hard walls. Seeds olive brown in color. Erect shrub. *L. nitida* Cav.

1′. Leaves with two leaflets. Mericarps hairy, easily separating at maturity. Flowers big, with petals 7.5 to 10 mm long.
    2. Leaflets fused up to 1/4 to 1/3, rarely almost 1/2 of their length, divergent to falcate.
        3. Obtuse stipules. *L. divaricata* Cav.
        3′. Acuminate stipules. *L. tridentata* (DC.) Coville
    2′. Leaflets fused up to 2/3-3/4 of their length, more or less parallel. Leaves cuneiform. Acuminate stipules. *L. cuneifolia* Cav.

3

Growth and Development, Form and Function

M. G. Barbour, G. Cunningham, W. C. Oechel, and S. A. Bamberg

This chapter summarizes what is know about *Larrea* germination, seedling survival, anatomy, shrub architecture, photosynthesis, water relations, carbon allocation (productivity), phenology, and life span. Some of these topics have been examined in some detail by other workers, and consequently there is a considerable literature to review. The topics include anatomy, morphology, water relations, and photosynthesis, but even in these areas, conclusions are tenuous.

The taxa reviewed here are those of most interest to the IBP projects that we have contributed to: *L. tridentata* of North America, *L. divaricata* of South America, and *L. cuneifolia* of South America.

GERMINATION AND SEEDLING SURVIVAL

We have very little historical literature on *Larrea* germination and survival, and little has been added from IBP studies, because the IBP was not aimed in this direction.

Seed Reserves in the Soil

Seed reserves in the soil have recently been investigated in IBP Desert Biome Studies at Rock Valley, Nevada (Childs and Goodall 1973; Chew et al. 1973). As expected, *Larrea* seeds were most abundant beneath *Larrea* bushes, and their number rapidly decreased with depth and distance from the shrubs. About two-thirds of all seeds encountered were found on the soil surface, and only 10 percent were found between 1 and 10 cm (none were found below 10 cm). The seed density varied markedly from year to year, with 6.5 seeds per dm^2 found beneath *Larrea* shrubs in 1971 and only 0.07 per dm^2 in 1972. Seed densities in the open were about one-tenth of those beneath *Larrea* shrubs. At two other Desert Biome sites, Silver Bell and Jornada, *Larrea* seeds were practically nonexistent at the time of sampling.

Most *Larrea* seeds are shed in spring and early fall in the Mojave and

Sonoran deserts and in early fall in the Chihuahuan Desert. In addition, *Larrea* can continue flowering and fruiting as long as abundant moisture is available and temperatures are warm, but seed crops that result from this extended flowering are not the major ones.

Germination and Survival in the Field

Quantitative studies on the germination requirements of *Larrea* are not extensive. Indeed, only two reports of *Larrea* germination in nature appear in the literature for the Mojave Desert. Went and Westergaard (1949) observed seedlings in abundance in Death Valley following exceptionally heavy late summer rains (of 16 mm). The following year almost the same rainfall pattern was duplicated, but no *Larrea* seedlings were observed. These workers therefore concluded hat temperature, as well as moisture, was critical: If daily maximum/minimum temperatures are high for two weeks following the rain (32/15° C the first year), then *Larrea* germinations are numerous. If daily maximum/minimum temperatures are low (20/9° C the second year), then *Larrea* doesn't germinate. Of the thousands of seedlings seen one year, few survived to the following October. Sheps (1973) also noted natural germination in Death Valley following September rains of 30 mm, with mean maximum/minimum temperatures of 34/23° C. After twenty-one months, mortality for these seedlings averaged 94 percent for five sites. Mortality seemed to be most severe, at earlier times, for seedlings close to mature *Larrea* shrubs. In addition, Sheps artificially sowed seeds and planted seedlings in the field in all seasons. Germination only occurred when night temperatures were above 20° C. The highest rate of germination appeared to be 40 percent, but in all cases survival was low. Survival was lowest close to *Larrea* shrubs and was highest at some distance from *Larrea* shrubs, especially if fungally infected *Larrea* litter was added to the soil around seedlings.

Valentine and Gerard (1968) artificially sowed *Larrea* seed in several Chihuahuan Desert sites from 1956 to 1959. Germination averaged about 6 percent, but mortality was 100 percent by 1963. The cause of death was mainly attributed to drought and damping-off disease. Germination was enhanced as precipitation during the growing season increased from 50 to 250 mm, but the authors did not state the time of maximum germination.

Germination and Survival in Laboratory Studies

Barbour (1967, 1968) conducted extensive germination trials with seed from all three warm deserts of North America. He found no evidence for ecotypic differentiation and in fact reported that germination requirements for temperature, moisture, pH, salinity, and light were remarkably mesic and not adapted to desert conditions. He concluded that germination in nature might be a rare event. Optimum germination conditions included: 23° C (constant), darkness, leaching of the mericarps prior to sowing, water potential around seeds near zero, pH 6, and NaCl concentration 500 ppm or less. Exposure of dry seeds to 71° C for a week, or of wet seeds to 40° C for three days, resulted in a significant decline in viability, compared to seeds kept at room temperature. (When seeds are stored in their mericarps in paper sacks in the dark at room temperature, Barbour has found most of his collections retain some low germinability even after eight years.)

Other germination and seedling growth studies have been conducted by Dalton (1962), Knipe and Herbel (1966), Beatley (*personal communication*), Gerard (*personal communication*), Kurtz (1958), Yang (1967b and *personal communication*), Wallace and Romney (1972), and Sheps (1973). The results of these studies do not always agree with each other or with the results of Barbour. None of the investigators, however, has shown allelopathy between *Larrea* shrubs and *Larrea* seedlings to be a significant factor in the laboratory situation, despite indications from the field that it may be a factor in seedling survival and shrub distribution. To date, we do not know whether seeds produced in the spring have different germination requirements from those produced in the fall in areas where two crops of seeds are produced (see also Koller 1955). The role of "new" factors in seedling establishment continue to appear in the literature. Most recently, Adams et al. (1970) have shown that a hydrophobic layer may form beneath *Larrea* shrubs and that this condition may prevent seedling establishment; also Lunt et al. (1973) have shown that *Larrea* is relatively demanding of soil oxygen and may be restricted from fine-textured, bottom-land sites because of low soil oxygen concentrations.

Virtually no germination work has been published on South American taxa of *Larrea.*

ANATOMY, MORPHOLOGY, AND SHRUB ARCHITECTURE

Subtle differences in leaf anatomy, the morphology of various organs, and shrub organization exist between various *Larrea* taxa. The ecological significance of these differences has not been demonstrated, but we can hypothesize for some that drought resistance is affected.

Stem Anatomy

Cozzo (1948) has examined the secondary wood of all South American *Larrea* taxa in some detail; later papers by Ragonese (1960) and Cabrera (1961) added very little new information. Cannon (1908), and to some extent Webber (1936) and Barbour (1969a), have much less thoroughly examined *L. tridentata.*

The Zygophyllaceae as a whole is characterized by "highly specialized" wood (Metcalfe and Chalk 1950) that is very advanced in a phylogenetic sense with numerous diffuse-porous vessels and many horizontal and vertical rays. Growth rings are absent or rare in South American *Larrea* according to Cozzo (1948), but Chew and Chew (1965), Dye (1968), and Barbour (1969b) have been able to count rings in North American *Larrea.*

The major difference in wood anatomy between *L. divaricata* and *L. cuneifolia* is that the density of vessels and crystals is much greater in the latter species (Cozzo 1948). Apparently, all taxa exhibit chlorenchyma. Young twigs of *L. tridentata,* within 20 cm of the stem apex or of diameter less than 3 mm, possess a 50 μ thick band of chlorenchyma tissue just below the epidermis (Cannon 1908). Morello (1955) drew a 100 μ thick chlorenchyma band for *L. divaricata* and *L. cuneifolia,* but Ragonese (1960) and Cabrera (1961) did not mention such a tissue for their South American material.

The fact that chlorenchyma is present should be borne in mind when we review photosynthesis measurements that have been expressed on a leaf area or leaf weight basis. These values may be too high, for the photosynthetic twig area of a leafy branch may be 10 to 15 percent of adjacent leaf area (Barbour et al. 1974).

Cozzo (1948) tabulated differences in size of vessels, fibers, and fiber-tracheids between *L. divaricata* and *L. cuneifolia* (Table 3-1), but he apparently did not consider them to be significant. Barbour (1969a and Table 3-1) found differences in fiber length between *L. divaricata* and *L. tridentata* and also between the three races of *L. tridentata*, and he showed them to be statistically significant. Fiber length increased in the progression: *L. divaricata,* Chihuahuan *L. tridentata,* Sonoran *L. tridentata,* and Mojave *L. tridentata.* His mean for *L. divaricata,* 533 μ, was very similar to the 557 μ mean length determined by Cozzo. Morello (1955) recognized races or ecotypes within both *L. cuneifolia* and *L. divaricata* based on a number of traits (see Table 3-1), but apparently they do not differ in stem anatomy.

Webber (1936) examined the wood of seventy California species and found *Larrea* to have to lowest density of vessels. Cannon (1905) found that vessel density could be reduced even further by watering *Larrea* in situ near Tucson; seven other desert species did not respond as dramatically.

Leaf Anatomy

There are several references to *Larrea* leaf anatomy in the literature (Ashby 1932; Runyon 1934; Morello 1955; Cabrera 1961; Duisberg 1952a; Dalton 1962; Wellendorf 1963; Hull et al. 1971), but none examines anatomy extensively both within and between taxa. Generally, the conclusions of these

TABLE 3–1 *Anatomical, Morphological, and Growth Traits of Some of the* Larrea *taxa.*

Traits	*L. tridentata* races or ecotypes			*L. divaricata* ecotypes		*L. cuneifolia* ecotypes	
	Mojave	Sonoran	Chihuahuan	Monte	Chaqueña	Monte	Chaqueña
Leaf anatomy		partly isolateral[a]		isolateral[b]		isolateral[b]	partly isolateral[b]
total thickness (mm)				0.17[b]		0.23[b]	0.40[b]
upper/lower epidermis thickness (μ)				15/20[b]		28/18[b]	
outer resin coat thickness (μ)				10[b]		33[b]	40[b]
major lateral veins per leaf				11[b]	8–9[b]	14[b]	16[b]
area (one face, mm^2)				53[b]	150[b]	60[b]	110[b]
upper or upper/lower stomate density per mm^2, field plants		208[a]		104/130[b] 305[a]		145/165[b] 162[a]	90/120[b]
stomate density, greenhouse plants	120[c]	138[c] 158[a]	176[c]	222[c] 195[a]		135[a]	
longevity (yr)		2[m]	1–2[d]	1[b,e]		2[b,e]	
Leaflet shape and % fusion	divaricate[c]	neutral[c]	falcate[c]	divaricate,[c] < 40%[a] divaricate-falcate[b]		divaricate[b] > 60%[a]	
pubescence	abundant[c]	moderate[c]	scanty[c]	moderate,[c] present[b]		present[b]	
area/weight (cm^2/gdw)		62[a]		72[a]		63[a]	

cotyledon area (mm^2)	31[c]	32[c]	42[c]	36[c]		
leaf orientation		random[a]		random[a]	sprays facing east-west[a]	
Stem anatomy						
fiber length (μ)	873[c]	799[c]	628[c]	533[c] 557[f]	441[f]	
vessel density per mm^2				83[f]	162[f]	
vessel diameter (μ)				40[f]	33[f]	
vessel length (μ)				90[f]	98[f]	
Fruit						
mericarp length (mm)	4.3[c]	4.9[c]	5.2[c]	4.5[c]		
hair length (mm)	1.7[c]	1.3[c]	0.9[c]	1.2[c]		
texture	soft[c]	medium[c]	hard[c]	medium[c]		
color	tan[c]	brown[c]	red[c]	brown[c]		
Stipules		large, acute, light color[c,g]		small, obtuse, dark[c,g]		
Flowering time	spring and sometimes late summer[h]	early summer and fall[h]	spring and late summer[h]	fall thru winter[h]	after spring rains[b]	before spring rains[b]
Internodes					Y	2.5(Y)
Growth pattern						
leaf emergence rate, seedling	0[c]	3[c]	13[c]	59[c]		
height growth rate, seedling	49[c]	73[c]	57[c]	97[c]		

TABLE 3–1 (Continued)

Traits	*L. tridentata* races or ecotypes			*L. divaricata* ecotypes		*L. cuneifolia* ecotypes	
	Mojave	Sonoran	Chihuahuan	Monte	Chaqueña	Monte	Chaqueña
rate of branching, seedling	59[c]	80[c]	97[c]	61[c]			
seedling weight (3 mo., seedling)		1.31[a]		2.50[a]		1.52[a]	
root/shoot ratio (3 mo., seedling)		0.19[a]		0.33[a]		0.32[a]	
average shrub height (cm, field plants)	112[i,j]	138[i,j,k]	86[i,j]	150[b]	250[b]	112[k] 120[b]	205[b]
ground area covered by canopy (m^2)				10[b]	15.5[b]	10[b]	13.5[b]
surface area of canopy (m^2)							
spring				2.40[b]		1.65[b]	
winter				0.75[b]		0.60[b]	
root system	general[n]	general[m,o]	general[l]	lateral[b]	vertical[b]	general[b]	
ground surface occupied by roots (m^2)						85[b]	

Souces: [a]Barbour et al. 1974; [b]Morello 1955, [c]Barbour 1969a; [d]Burk and Dick-Peddie 1973; [e]Morello 1958; [f]Cozzo 1948; [g]Porter 1963; [h]data developed in this chapter; [i]Barbour 1969b; [j]Barbour 1968; [k]Barbour and Diaz 1973; [l]Ludwig 1974; [m]Chew and Chew 1965, [n]Wallace and Romney 1972; [o]Cannon 1911.

workers have been that leaf anatomy is rather consistent within the genus. The leaf is isolateral, with two or more layers of palisade parenchyma beneath each epidermis and a thin layer of spongy mesophyll in the center. The epidermal cells are rather large and their walls are strikingly thick; these cells are sometimes filled with tannins and resins. Calcium oxalate crystals are often apparent throughout the leaf. A resin coats the epidermis but does not plug the stomata.

Barbour et al. (1974), however, have reported differences in leaf anatomy between *L. divaricata, L. tridentata,* and *L. cuneifolia.* They examined both greenhouse seedlings and herbarium material and found that only the *L. cuneifolia* leaves showed well-developed palisade parenchyma on both leaf surfaces (Figure 3-1). The *L. tridentata* and *L. divaricata* sections showed palisade only on the upper face and either spongy parenchyma alone or some mixture of spongy and palisade on the lower face (Figures 3-2 and 3-3). Epidermal cells are much larger in *L. cuneifolia.* They did not speculate on the ecological significance of this difference. Perhaps it is related to the orientation of the leaves: On *L. divaricata* shrubs, the leaves are oriented randomly, but generally seem to be roughly horizontal to the ground; on *L. cuneifolia* shrubs, the leaves are oriented more vertically in two-dimensional sprays and generally face east-west so that both faces may be exposed to direct insolation during the course of one day. The thickness of the palisade layer(s) and of the entire leaf were greater for field material than for greenhouse seedlings. *Larrea divaricata* leaves often seemed to be thinner (with a higher area-weight ratio; see Table 3-1) than *L. cuneifolia* or *L. tridentata* leaves, but the differences were not statistically significant.

Morello (1955) reported differences in leaf anatomy for the races, or ecotypes, of *L. cuneifolia* and *L. divaricata* (see Table 3-1).

For any given taxon, race, or leaf, stomatal density is roughly equal on both leaf faces. Beyond this generalization, finding good agreement on stomate density from one author to another is difficult. This variability probably reflects genetic heterogeneity and growing conditions of the plants selected. Greenhouse seedlings of *Larrea,* for example, exhibit a lower stomatal density than field plants, a phenomenon duplicated by some cultivated plants when grown in lower light intensity or under more mesic conditions (Knecht and O'Leary 1972; Penfound 1931). Average stomate density, considering all variation, is around $160 \cdot mm^{-2} \cdot face^{-1}$.

Barbour (1969a and Table 3-1) has shown a cline of decreasing stomate density from the relatively mesic Chihuahuan Desert westward into the Sonoran and finally into the very arid Mojave. This pattern differs from the one Evenari (1960) proposed as typical for most plants: Stomatal density increases with increasing aridity. *Larrea cuneifolia* ecotypes do behave as Evenari predicts: The mesic chaco ecotype has a lower density than the xeric Monte ecotype, and the mesic, weedy, almost phreatophytic *L. divaricata* has a

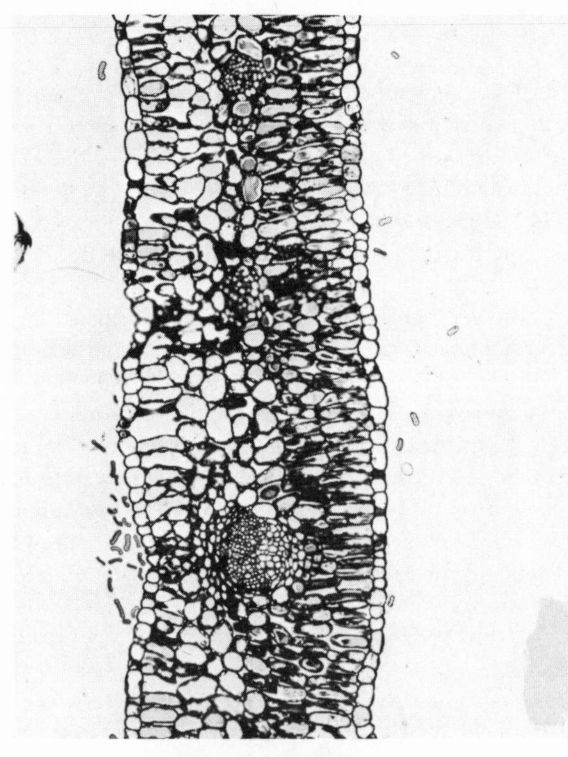

FIGURE 3-1. *Cross section through representative leaves of greenhouse-grown* L. cuneifolia *seedlings. Courtesy of David Diaz.*

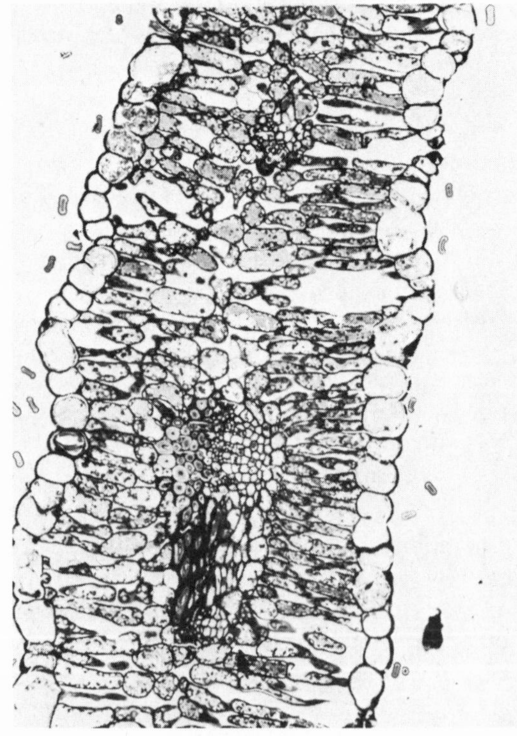

FIGURE 3-2. *Cross sections through representative leaves of greenhouse-grown* L. divaricata *seedlings. Courtesy of David Diaz.*

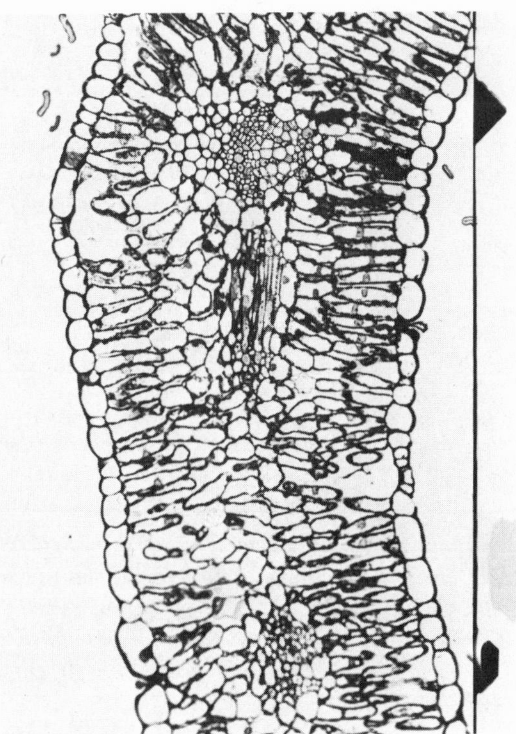

FIGURE 3-3. *Cross section through representative leaves of greenhouse-grown* L. tridentata *seedlings. Courtesy of David Diaz.*

lower stomate density than the xeric Monte *L. cuneifolia* (Morello 1955 and Table 3-1).

Within an ecotype, however, whether *L. cuneifolia* or *L. divaricata,* Barbour et al. (1974) found no correlation between stomatal density and degree of site aridity (Figure 3-4). Evidently, fine adjustment to site aridity does not include modification of stomate density.

Morphology

From an examination of herbarium specimens, Porter (1963) concluded that three morphological differences consistently separated *L. divaricata* from *L. tridentata.* Leaflets are falcate (the tips point toward each other) in

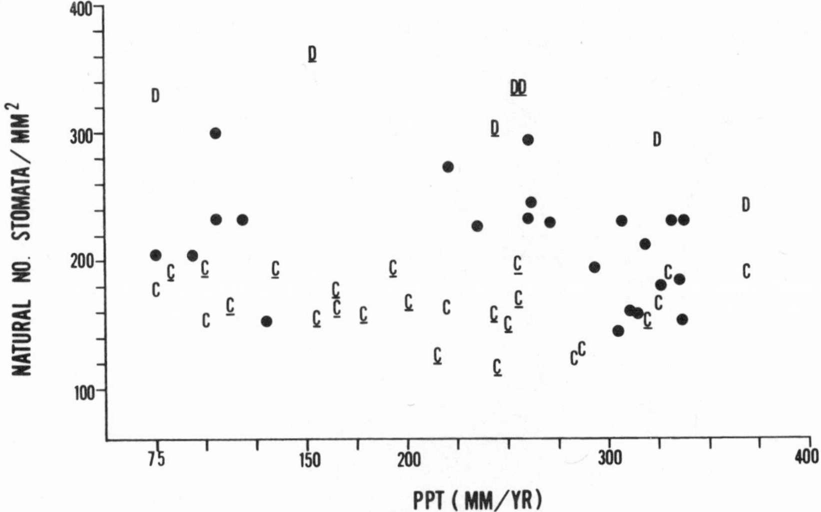

FIGURE 3-4. *Relationship between leaf stomatal density of field plants ("natural number of stomata" per mm², average of both faces) and the yearly precipitation at the field site. Closed circles are Sonoran* L. tridentata; *D indicates* L. divaricata; *and C indicates* L. cuneifolia. *Underlined D and C sites, and all* L. tridentata *sites, have the most reliable precipitation estimates. From Barbour et al. (1974).*

L. tridentata and are divergent (point away from each other) in *L. divaricata*; pubescence on leaf face and margin is heavier for *L. divaricata*; and *L. tridentata* stipules are larger, more acute, and of lighter color than *L. divaricata* stipules. Shreve and Wiggins (1964) cite the same three characteristics. Work by others, especially Monticelli (1939), Barbour (1967, 1969a), Yang (1967), and Hunziker et al. (1972a) have both minimized Porter's conclusion and added to them. Stipule size and shape remain definite distinguishing characters, but leaflet shape and pubescence vary to such a degree within the *L. tridentata* races that *L. divaricata* is not unique (see Table 3-1).

Fruit texture, color, pubescence, and cotyledon area also vary considerably in *L. tridentata* material, with *L. divaricata* material falling within the clines or at one extreme (see Table 3-1).

Leaf morphology is the major character distinguishing *L. cuneifolia* from *L. divaricata* taxa. *Larrea cuneifolia* leaflets are fused together for 60 percent or more of their length, while *L. divaricata* leaflets are fused together for 40 percent or less of their length. The leaflets of *L. divaricata* and *L. tridentata* fold together, and only the underside faces are exposed in a vertical orientation at night (Runyon 1934) or in daylight under various stresses (Barbour 1967). *Larrea cuneifolia* leaflets do not close. Leaflet closure may reduce heat load and transpiration in *L. divaricata* and *L. tridentata,* but since there is no direct evidence at present to support this theory, the ecological value of *L. divaricata* leaflet closure may or may not be significant. Leaf morphology of *L. tridentata* may change with season or plant water status (Cunningham 1968).

Morello (1955) discussed some of the same differences as described above and added others that distinguish *L. cuneifolia* from *L. divaricata* and ecotypes within each (see Table 3-1). These differences included leaf longevity, leaf area, leaf anatomy, number of prominent lateral leaf veins, time of flowering, and internode length.

Shrub Architecture

Major differences exist in shrub architecture between the taxa and races; these differences relate to shrub height, compactness of foliage, degree of branching, and orientation of leaves.

Larrea cuneifolia leaves (Figure 3-5) are borne in two-dimensional sprays along much of the length of short branches. The sprays are usually oriented to face east-west, but sometimes they face other directions (D. Diaz, *personal communication;* Morello 1955). The shrubs are dense and short; average height was 107 cm for plants in twenty-one sites sampled by Barbour and Diaz (1973). Morello (1955) reported Monte *L. cuneifolia* to average 120 cm tall and cover 10 m^2 of ground; chaco plants averaged 210 cm and 13.5 m^2 (see Table 3-1).

Larrea divaricata (Figure 3-6) strongly contrasts with *L. cuneifolia.* These plants are considerably taller, more spindly, retain fewer leaves along the stems, and the leaves are oriented in random directions. Monte *L. divaricata* average 145 cm tall and 10 m^2 cover; chaco *L. divaricata* average 250 cm and 15.5 m^2 (Morello 1955 and Table 3-1).

Larrea tridentata plants (Figure 3-7) look quite different from *L. divaricata* plants, both in the field and in greenhouse growth trials. Barbour (1969a) measured plant height and rate of branching (number of branches per centimeter of branch length) during the first six months of life for several hundred seedlings of *L. tridentata* races and *L. divaricata.* The seedlings were grown under moderately controlled parameters in the same greenhouse at the same time. Table 3-1 shows that *L. divaricata* plants exhibited rapid growth in height, but a low branching rate, a combination not shared by any of the three *L. tridentata* races. Barbour concluded that the genetic growth patterns are distinct: Chihuahuan plants are relatively short, with considerable branching; Sonoran plants are much taller (but not as tall as *L. divaricata*) and exhibit a moderate amount of branching; and Mojave plants are simply slow growing, with little branching. Field plants show similar differences. According to data from Barbour (1967, 1969a,b) and Barbour and Diaz (1973), some twelve Mojave sites exhibited an overall mean *Larrea* height of 112 cm;

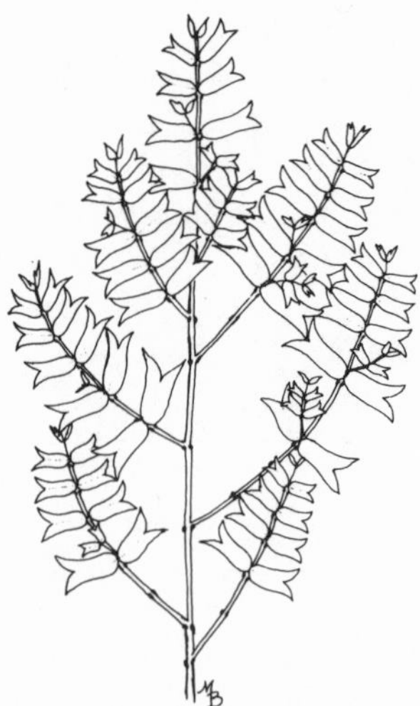

FIGURE 3-5. *Leaf orientation on twigs of greenhouse-grown* L. cuneifolia. *Drawing by Mary Breckon.*

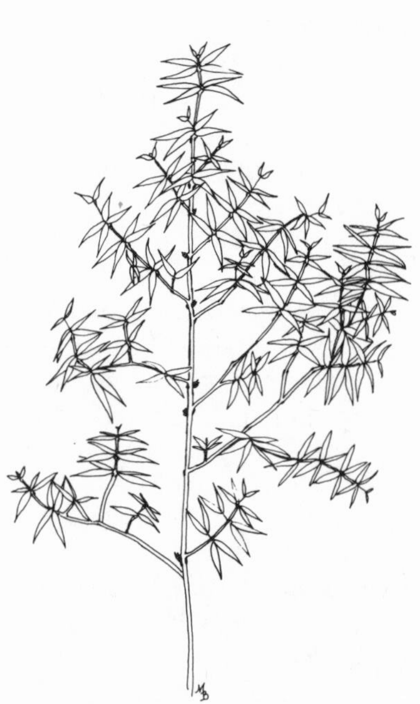

FIGURE 3-6. *Leaf orientation on twigs of greenhouse-grown* L. divaricata. *Drawing by Mary Breckon.*

FIGURE 3-7. *Leaf orientation on twigs of greenhouse-grown Sonoran* L. tridentata. *Drawing by Mary Breckon.*

34 Sonoran sites had a mean of 138 cm; and 19 Chihuahuan sites had a mean of 86 cm (see Table 3-1).

Even at the very earliest seedling stage, the various *L. tridentata* taxa are unique. Total cotyledon area (2 × length × width; thus upper surface of both cotyledons) shows an increasing cline from west to east in North America, with *L. divaricata* being intermediate, and yet leaf emergence rate (percent of seedlings showing true leaves visible to the naked eye at an age of fifteen days) shows an opposite cline (Barbour 1969a and Table 3-1). Both clines are statistically significant.

In a more recent growth trial, Barbour et al. (1974) compared the root and shoot growth of three-month-old *L. cuneifolia, L. divaricata,* and Sonoran *L. tridentata.* Again, *L. divaricata* exhibited the fastest shoot growth rate and total biomass accumulation (Table 3-1), but it also exhibited rapid root growth. Thus its root-shoot ratio was virtually identical to that of *L. cuneifolia,* and it was considerably greater than that of *L. tridentata.* Since *L. divaricata,* when compared to the habitats of *L. cuneifolia* and *L. tridentata,* is a mesophyte (Morello 1955), we might expect it to have a low root-shoot ratio, but this was not consistently the case (see Table 3-1).

Barbour (1973, 1976) has recently reviewed the literature on *L. tridentata* root-shoot ratios for seedlings and mature field plants. He found the ratio to vary between 0.22 and 1.08. Depth of soil is one factor that is very effective in modifying the root-shoot ratio: In a sandy wash, Wallace and Romney (1972) found *L. tridentata* ratios ranged from 0.96 to 1.51; this soil lacked the typical caliche hardpan at 10 to 70 cm depth present beneath surrounding Mojave Desert terrain. Root-shoot ratios are discussed in more detail later in this chapter.

The root system of *L. tridentata* is typically general—that is, it consists of both lateral and vertical potential, depending on soil conditions (Cannon 1911; Chew and Chew 1965; Wallace and Romney 1972; Ludwig 1975). It is generally fibrous and shallow and even in the absence of a carbonate deposition layer, it may penetrate only 170 cm but extend outward 4 m. In deep sands, the system may contain both deep tap and massive lateral roots. If a caliche layer is present, a tap root is often unable to penetrate. Entire individual root systems can be limited to 10 to 25 cm of soil above the caliche layer. The root tip, which is not particularly fast growing, averages about 10 mm day^{-1} in young plants under optimum laboratory conditions (Barbour 1967, 1968). The optimum temperature for root growth was determined to be 29° C. Wallace et al. (1970) reported that root-shoot ratios of Mojave *L. tridentata* seedlings could be modified by temperature manipulation.

Apparently, the root system of *L. divaricata* is ecotypically differentiated (Morello 1955 and Table 3-1): The mesic chaco ecotype is characterized by a root system dominated by vertical roots, while the xeric Monte ecotype is characterized by horizontal, lateral roots. The *L. cuneifolia* ecotypes uniformly possess a general root system.

The shallow root system of *Larrea* lacks water storage tissue and, therefore, provides an often small and intermittent supply of water to the shoots. Although this type of system can be responsive to rain input and possibly to distillation from below (Stark and Love 1969; Syvertsen et al. 1975), it is unable to supply large quantities during droughts. Usually large water quantities are provided only by species that tap subterranean reserves—such as *L. nitida*—but *L. divaricata* can be phreatophytic on some sites (Morello 1955).

Barbour et al. (1974) suggest that critical ecological differences between *L. cuneifolia, L. divaricata,* and *L. tridentata* may be due to shrub architecture rather than shrub physiology or leaf anatomy—that is, the degree of xerophytism may be due to a complex of factors such as stomate density, transpiration rate, degree of leaf retention during stress, total leaf area, orientation of the leaves, root-shoot ratio, and type of root system. With the help of some detailed field measurements, a model of a *Larrea* shrub could be manipulated in a mathematical sense to test the effect of various environmental factors on heat budget, water status, and productivity. This approach could well be a profitable direction for future research. Morello (1955) has already collected some of the data that could be used in such calculations—for example, total canopy surface area and root volume (see Table 3-1).

PHENOLOGY AND LIFE SPAN

Since virtually all the data on the phenology of *Larrea* has been gained by passive observation, we cannot definitely state which factor (moisture, temperature, day length, and so forth) is most critical in triggering phenological events. Even less is known of the potential life span of *Larrea.*

Phenology: North America

Most floras and investigators list the flowering period of *L. tridentata* as April through May regardless of desert location, but they commonly recognize that local pockets of shrubs, or scattered individuals that may receive additional moisture in the form of runoff, can be found flowering virtually any time of year. Because of such variability, flowering (and other phenological events) are thought to be mainly moisture and temperature dependent (for example, Dalton 1962; Chew and Chew 1965; Barbour 1967; Ackerman and Bamberg 1974).

The longest phenological record has been compiled recently for *L. tridentata* from the Mojave Desert in Rocky Valley, Nevada, by Ackerman and Bamberg (1974). As shown in Figure 3-8, leaf and twig production were pronounced within the limits of March through October despite major fluctuations in winter or summer rainfall during the years 1968 to 1974. Some years, leaf

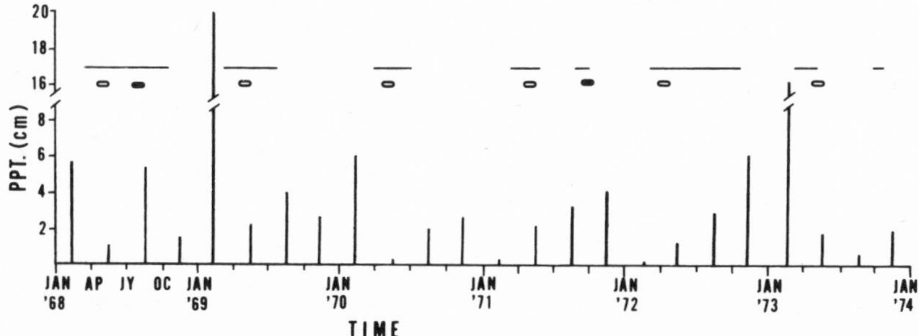

FIGURE 3-8. *Phenology of Mojave* L. tridentata *from Rock Valley, Nevada. Height of the vertical lines indicates total precipitation within the three-month periods described along the time axis. Horizontal lines indicate time of maximum shoot growth. Open circles indicate spring flowering peak; dark circles indicate late summer flowering peak, if present. Summarized from data by Ackerman and Bamberg (1974).*

and stem production stopped well before October; in other years it stopped during midsummer and then resumed. These variations do not correlate with rainfall. For example, although 1969 was an exceptionally wet year in which rainfall was well distributed through every season, the period of leaf production was much shorter (March through July) than in the drier years of 1968 and 1972. Also the period was the same length in 1969 as in the exceptionally dry year of 1970. Perhaps fluctuations in temperature were more critical to leaf development than fluctuations in moisture.

Onset of spring flowering in Rock Valley was consistently late April through early May despite major fluctuations in rainfall the preceding winters. Flowering even occurred after the minimal winter rains (October to April) of 2.5 cm in 1970-71. Burk and Dick-Peddie (1973) concluded from observations in the Chihuahuan Desert that once sufficient rain had fallen to trigger an event, additional rain did not increase the intensity of that event, which to a large extent has been substantiated by watering experiments of Cunningham et al. (1974). If this conclusion is the case, then the minimum winter rainfall sufficient to trigger Mojave *L. tridentata* flowering and the onset of leaf production is 2.5 cm or less. This amount is very close to the 2 cm of rain that Bamberg et al. (1973) conclude is sufficient to trigger increased leaf production and net photosynthesis for most Mojave perennials that they examined.

What is only now becoming clear is that flower bud enlargement is triggered by increased soil moisture, and the ultimate process of flowering takes place as the plants and soil dry down. Microenvironmental data for Rock Valley in 1972 showed that flower buds developed in March and early April, when soil moisture at 15 to 30 cm depth was at a maximum (about -10 bars) and that flowers appeared as soil moisture rapidly fell in April. Fruit was maturing in May and June when soil moisture was -50 bars. A series of watering experiments on the Jornada bajada of New Mexico by Cunningham et al.

(1974) led those authors to conclude "... that plants with less than maximal soil moisture divert a significantly greater amount of carbon and energy to reproduction." If moisture levels remain high, flowering and fruiting still occur, but assimilates are channeled preferentially towards vegetative growth. A six-year study by Valentine and Gerard (1968) in New Mexico also showed a significant negative correlation between rainfall and fruit production. More information on this topic is presented later in this chapter.

Late summer flowering occurred at Rock Valley in two of the six years, but as seen from Figure 3-8, there was no correlation with either summer rainfall (July to October) or annual rainfall. Possibly the intensity of the rains (not shown in this summary) or temperatures had a more critical role. Fruit development was very minimal following late summer flowering in both years, and yet its ripening was hastened compared to fruit initiated in spring: Fruit from both spring and late summer flowers reached a peak of maturity in August through October. Whether the same shrubs flower both times, or different shrubs flower each time, is still not clear.

More arid sites may show a shorter growing season than Rock Valley's, and a second flowering peak may be absent, according to the little data we have. Stark and Love (1969) reported that *Larrea* begins growth in Death Valley in March, flowers in April, and terminates growth in June. Oechel et al. (1972a) reported that *Larrea* in Deep Canyon (in the northwestern, Colorado portion of the Sonoran Desert of California, annual precipitation 5 to 8 cm) began active growth in January, flowered in April, matured fruit in June, and fell back to a low growth rate thereafter.

Phenology of Sonoran and Chihuahuan *L. tridentata* generally parallels the Rock Valley population. A one-year study of a site at Saguaro National Monument near Tucson, Arizona, by Yang and Abe (1973a, b) is summarized in part in Figures 3-9 and 3-10. A major peak of flowering occurred in July and August of 1972, a bit later than usual, due to a dry year; flowering was in May and June in 1973. A minor peak of flowering occurred in November and early December. The number of plants with maturing fruit showed a long decline from September through the following January, with the second flowering peak adding a slight increase in January. Unpublished summaries of IBP work in Arizona reveal that there are two modes of vegetative activity among the perennials. *Larrea, Simmondsia chinensis, Krameria grayi,* and *Ambrosia deltoidea* are active throughout the year; most other species are winter dormant for three to five months. *Larrea, Simmondsia,* and *Krameria*—all xerophytic, evergreen shrubs—bloom heavily with the onset of winter or summer rains. In addition, they show a tendency toward production of a few flowers throughout the dry fall and spring, which can be interpreted either as an opportunistic strategy or a mixed blooming pattern. Many of these sporadic flowers do not produce fruits and seeds, but some do. These shrubs are presumably photoperiodically neutral.

A three-year study in southern New Mexico by Burk and Dick-Peddie

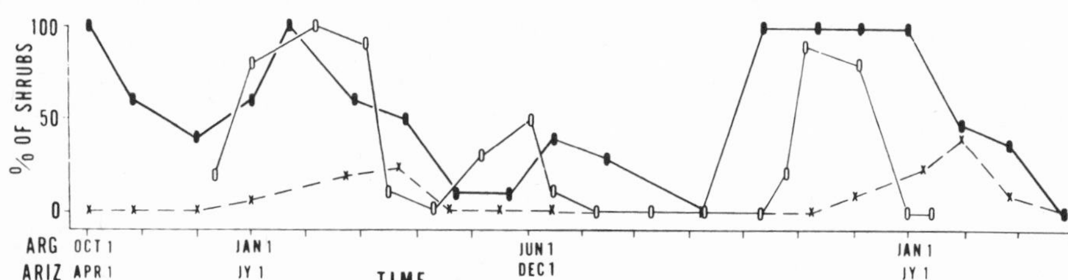

FIGURE 3-9. *Flowering of Sonoran* L. tridentata *(open circles),* L. divaricata *(dark circles), and* L. cuneifolia *(dotted line). Arizona data from Saguaro National Monument are for the period June 1972 to July 1973 and are taken from Yang and Abe (1973a, b). Argentina data from the Andalgalá area are for the period October 1972 to April 1974 and are taken from leClaire et al. (1973a, b) and leClaire and Brown (1974a, b);* L. divaricata *is from their site 1 (annual ppt 100 mm);* L cuneifolia, *from sites 1–4, K6, K34, K66, and K96 (mean ppt 200 mm). The Sonoran site averages 250 mm.*

(1973) showed onset of growth in March or April, a major flowering peak in May and early June, and a consistent second flowering period in late July and August. Abscission of immature fruits was much greater after the second flowering peak. Surprisingly, mature fruit from both flowering periods peaked in August through October.

The relative importance of moisture, temperature, and day length is not agreed on by all investigators, even though we conclude in our review that most investigators view moisture as the most important factor in driving phenological events. Dr. Janice Beatley (*personal communication*) has unpublished data that lead her to believe that photoperiod is most important, at least for *Larrea* in the Mojave Desert. Certainly, some desert perennials do appear responsible to photoperiod. Turner (1963) found that in *Prosopis juliflora* and *Cercidium floridum* stem growth began several weeks before the onset of summer rains in Arizona, and that flowering was initiated by photoperiod ". . . although subsequent weather may not permit flowering or the

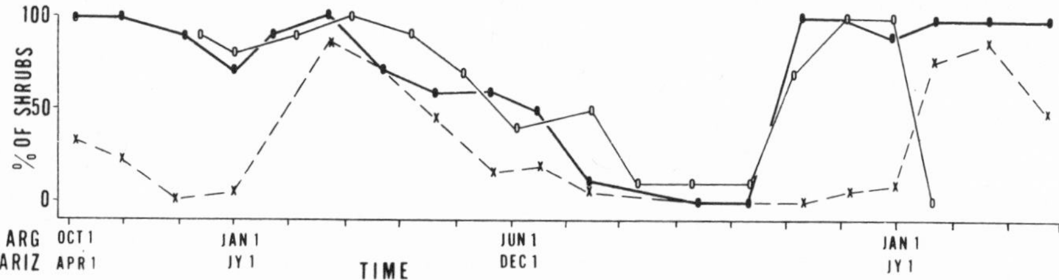

FIGURE 3-10. *Plants showing maturing fruit for Sonoran* L. tridentata *sites (open circles),* L. divaricata *(dark circles), and* L. cuneifolia *(dotted line). For sources of data, see caption for Figure 3-9.*

setting of seed." Morello (1955 and Table 3-1) claims that one of the *L. cuneifolia* ecotypes flowers prior to spring rains.

Chew and Chew (1965) examined a stand of *Larrea* in a very mesic site in southeastern Arizona and concluded: "Growth was largely independent of rainfall and soil moisture." They believed that onset and termination of vegetative growth most closely correlated with soil temperature at 15 cm depth rising above and falling below 17° C. While not recognizing the primacy of temperature, Burk and Dick-Peddie (1973) nevertheless did find a similar correlation between soil temperature and *Larrea* growth in New Mexico. Their "critical" 15 cm depth temperature, however, turned out to be 12° C, and they speculated about ecotypic variation within the species. In his unpublished Ph.D. dissertation, Dalton (1962) reported that growth of *Larrea* near Tucson would only respond to a heavy rain ending a dry spell if the daily maximum/minimum air temperatures were above 27/4° C.

Recent data by Oechel et al. (1972 a,b), who established correlations between net photosynthesis, temperature, and water stress, clearly show that change in water stress are much more effective in influencing plant metabolism than changes in temperature, at their particular Sonoran research site.

Increasing elevation sets back phenology, but from the few observations reported, determining whether moisture or temperature is ultimately responsible is impossible. Barbour (1967) summarized differences in phenology that he witnessed on the same day for six pairs of sites (Table 3-2). The effect of elevation was pronounced for differences of 968 m or more, and the effect was minimal or nil for differences of 225 m or less.

Phenology: South America

Flowering and fruiting of *L. divaricata* and *L. cuneifolia* are summarized in part in Figures 3-9 and 3-10. As explained more carefully in the legend for Figure 3-9, these data are from sites near Andalgalá, Argentina (leClaire et al. 1973a,b; leClaire and Brown 1974a,b); the data are superimposed on Sonoran *L. tridentata* graphs so that phenological relationships between all three taxa can be examined. We can see that patterns of flowering and fruit maturation for *L. divaricata* and *L. tridentata* are quite similar, despite the fact that the *L. divaricata* site is relatively arid (receiving about 100 mm annual precipitation), while the *L. tridentata* site is relatively mesic (receiving about 250 mm).

Two poorly defined groups of perennials in the Andalgalá region can be recognized in relation to the pattern of leaf and shoot initiation. Members of one group resume vegetative growth as soon as temperatures increase in the spring (approximately September). Both *Larrea* species (*L. cuneifolia* and *L. divaricata*) and indeed the majority of the common perennials belong to this group. Another group delays such growth until the onset of the rainy season during November to January. Of the perennials, *L. cuneifolia*, *Cassia aphylla*, and *Trichomeria usillo* tend to have the longest growing season. All have

TABLE 3-2 *Effect of Elevation on Timing of Flower and Fruit Development in Pairs of Nearby* L. tridentata *Sites Visited on the Same Day (from Barbour 1967).*

Pair no., desert, and state	Location of sites	Elev. (m)	Difference in elev. (m)	Notes
1. Mojave (California)	Daylight Pass, Death Valley National Monument	1,387	1,452	fruit green
	Floor of Death Valley	-65		fruit ripe
2. Sonoran (California)	Jumbo Rocks, Joshua Tree National Monument	1,420	1,087	flowers present, fruit green
	Near Twentynine Palms	333		flowers absent, fruit ripe
3. Chihuahuan (Texas)	Big Bend National Park	1,742		some flowers, fruit ripe
	Big Bend National Park	774		no flowers, fruit dropped
4. Chihuahuan (New Mexico)	Near Cloudcroft, New Mexico	1,870	451	fruit ripe, some dropped
	Near Alamogordo, New Mexico	1,490		fruit ripe, most dropped
5. Mojave (California)	Near Barstow, California	580	225	fruit ripe
	Near Baker, California	355		fruit ripe
6. Sonoran (Arizona)	Organ Pipe Cactus National Monument	807	194	most fruit dropped
	Organ Pipe Cactus National Monument	613		most fruit dropped

photosynthetic twigs to some extent, and *Larrea* keeps some leaves throughout the winter. Both *Larrea* species exhibit the same mixed or opportunistic blooming pattern that *L. divaricata* shows in the Sonoran Desert–that is, they bloom heavily with the onset of summer rains, but bloom sporadically during the dry season as a result of off-season rains. This pattern is unexpected for the phreatophytic *L. divaricata*, because three other phreatophytes bloom during the dry spring and drop their seeds in January at the beginning of the rainy season (*Cercidium praecox, Prosopis chilensis,* and *Acacia aroma*).

According to the IBP data in Figure 3-9, considerably fewer *L. cuneifolia* shrubs produced flowers and fruits compared to *L. divaricata*. The raw data (not included in Figure 3-9) show that this pattern held true in sites throughout a 100 to 300 mm range of annual precipitation. This relationship between *L. divaricata* and *L. cuneifolia* may have been true in the Andalgalá region, but it did not hold true throughout the Monte. Barbour and Diaz (*unpublished data*) found *L. cuneifolia* blooming vigorously between Catamarca and Mendoza in January 1973; in the Andalgalá area at the same time only about 10 percent of *L. cuneifolia* shrubs were in flower, according to Figure 3-9.

Morello (1955) distinguished the chaco and Monte ecotypes of *L. cuneifolia* by their flowering time: Although both commence flowering in general at the same time of year (November), the time for the Monte ecotype is after the start of spring rains, but prior to spring rains for the chaco ecotype (see Table 3-1). His observations have not been investigated further by any other workers to our knowledge. Simpson et al. (see Chapter 4) has shown quantitative differences between reproductive effort of *L. divaricata, L. cuneifolia,* and *L. tridentata:* Nectar expended per shrub is very high for *L. cuneifolia,* moderate for *L. divaricata,* and low for *L. tridentata.*

Not only is the quantitative phenology of *L. cuneifolia* unique, according to IBP data, but so is timing. Onset of flowering is later than for other *Larrea* species. The peak in fruit maturation in February 1973, prior to a peak in flowering (see Figures 3-9 and 3-10) is anomalous.

According to Morello (1958), both *L. divaricata* and *L. cuneifolia* exhibit maximum shoot growth during the September to May period. This period is equivalent to the March through November period in North America; hence the pattern is remarkably similar to the vegetative growth cycle of *L. tridentata.* Leaves are retained for two years for *L. cuneifolia* shrubs and one year for *L. divaricata* (Morello 1955, 1958). Chihuahuan *L. tridentata* leaves are retained one year if the shoot is growing rapidly and two years if it is growing slowly (Burk and Dick-Peddie 1973). In the mesic Sonoran *L. tridentata* site examined by Chew and Chew (1965), leaves were retained two years.

Life Span

Morello (1955, 1958) thought that *L. cuneifolia* and *L. divaricata* live for about twenty-five to thirty years, but he presented no evidence. This life span would be exceptionally short compared to what little we know about *L. tridentata.*

Shreve (1951) and Shreve and Hinkley (1937) also offer merely an educated guess when they state that *L. tridentata* may reach an age well in excess of one hundred years. Cetainly, *Larrea* communities seem to change very little in a human generation. Simmons (1966) compared an 1894 photograph of a boundary marker in Arizona with one taken seventy-two years later and concluded that some of the same creosote bushes could have been in both photographs, with little evident change of size.

Larrea wood does exhibit rings (despite the claim of Cozzo [1948]), and some investigators have made ring counts of several populations, but we have no firm evidence that rings always correspond to age in years on a 1:1 basis. In southern New Mexico, Dye (1968) sampled 35 shrubs of various canopy volume and counted rings at the root crown level. As shown in Figure 3-11, the counts ranged from 16 to 54, and they were positively correlated logarithmically, to canopy volume. *Larrea* is known to be an invader in much of New Mexico during the past 75 to 100 years (Gardner 1951), and possibly the oldest *Larrea* on the site is indeed not older than 54 years—that is, ring count could be equal to age in years.

A similar study was conducted by Chew and Chew (1965) in southeastern Arizona. Their counts, for 61 plants, showed a maximum count of 65 rings (see Figure 3-11) and were also logarithmically related to canopy volume. Unfortunately, this area also has been subject to *Larrea* invasion in the recent past, so that very old shrubs would not be expected.

Barbour (1967, 1969a) made ring counts throughout the southwestern United States, but unfortunately only counted rings at the base of the tallest stem of each plant—not at the root crown. He found that ring count correlated well with branch height on most sites and that these counts were rather low for some large stems at arid sites. One Sonoran Desert site, for example, with a yearly rainfall of 125 mm, had a 270 cm tall branch with a ring count of only 13. Barbour doubted that such growth could occur on that site in only 13 years, and he proposed that rings were laid down in only exceptionally wet years. However, he had no direct evidence that this amount of wood could not have been produced in 13 years.

Whether age correlates best with shrub volume or height is still not clear. Shreve and Wiggins (1964) and Chew and Chew (1965) thought volume to be best. Valentine and Gerard (1968), however, reported a linear relationship between *Larrea* height and age for young plants up to the age of ten years. They added that trampling by cattle kept some older plants relatively short. Gardner (1951) also found height to correlate with age in another small, homogeneous Chihuahuan site.

The period of juvenility may be prolonged. Chew and Chew (1965) estimated that flowering and fruiting did not begin until shrubs were over thirteen years old on one relatively mesic site. There have been few comparable studies on arid sites. Valentine and Gerard (1968) reported onset of fruit

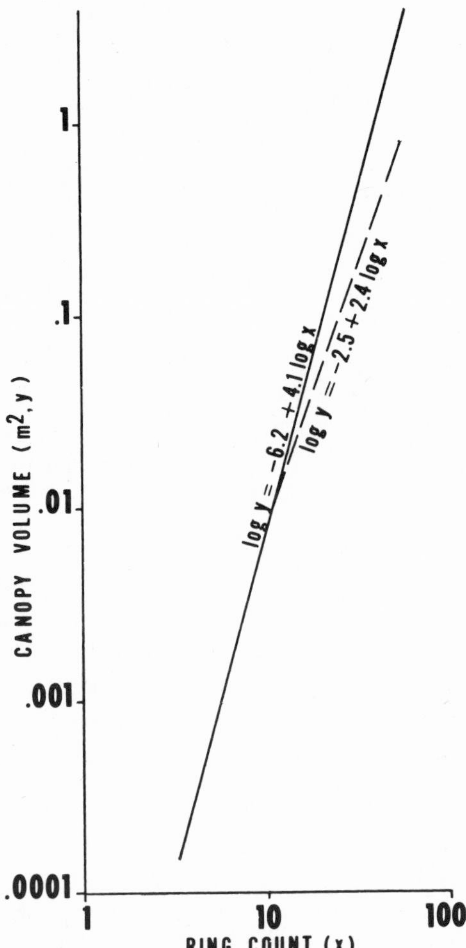

FIGURE 3-11. *Regression between ring count and canopy volume obtained by Dye (1968, dotted line) for Chihuahuan* L. tridentata *and by Chew and Chew (1965, solid line) for Sonoran* L. tridentata. *Both sites may have been recently invaded by* Larrea *in the past 75 years.*

production in the fourth and fifth year for New Mexico plants on a site with 225 mm annual precipitation. In greenhouse situations and in irrigated plots, Dr. Tien Wei Yang at the University of Arizona (*personal communication*) has found that all *Larrea* taxa can be brought to flowering by the age of two years.

Several authors have pointed out that *L. tridentata* reproduces asexually and produces clumps or circles of eventually distinct plants (Muller 1953; Barbour 1969b; Wright 1970; Vasek et al. 1974). The age of these asexually derived clumps may have more intrinsic impact on community structure or stability than the age of individual shrubs. *Larrea* shrubs may have their lower branches covered by wind- or water-borne sediment, and these branches may take root and eventually produce new, independent individuals. Alternatively, the root crown may split due to aging or mechanical damage from material washing down a bajada. In the Tucson area, Wright (1970) believes that most clumps of *L. tridentata* arose from both a nurse plant effect and vegetative reproduction. Vasek et al. (1974 and *personal communication*) have some data to indicate the outward spread of a ring of creosote bushes may be as slow as thirty-nine years per cm radius. In view of the fact that some of the rings they have photographed measure many meters in diameter, such larger groups may have ages of several hundred to several thousand years (see Chapter 9).

PHOTOSYNTHESIS AND WATER RELATIONS

A plant's growth and distribution are determined by many independent physiological attributes that enhance not only its capacity to set viable seed, to germinate, and to establish, but also its ability to correctly portion photosynthate into various metabolic and growth product pools. Many of these attributes relate to water relations and photosynthesis. Extremes of high temperature and moisture seem to be the main environmental parameters limiting the distribution of *Larrea*. Sonoran *L. tridentata* is known to maintain positive photosynthesis throughout the entire year—that is, spanning hot, cold, wet and dry periods. This trait may be true for other species and races of *Larrea*.

Water Relations

Rates of water uptake in *Larrea* are regulated by root resistance (r_{root}) and by the water potential gradient between soil and root (Ψ_{soil}-Ψ_{root}). Since distribution of soil moisture is not homogeneous, the root distribution of *Larrea* is obviously important. The questions of how extensive *Larrea* root systems are and whether competition for moisture between adjacent *Larrea* shrubs goes on have been reviewed most recently by Barbour (1973, 1974). We believe that these questions have not yet been satisfactorily resolved.

Larrea appears to be able to utilize water distilled from lower soil horizons. Such water often condenses on the underside of rocks that cool at night more rapidly than does the surrounding soil (Stark and Love 1969; Syvertsen et al. 1975). In addition *Larrea* leaves may be able to take up water from both vapor and liquid present on the leaf surfaces (Spalding 1904; Stark and Love 1969; Wallace and Romney 1972). However, whether foliar exposure to liquid water or to high relative humidities allows significant water uptake is doubtful. The difficulty is in separating the effect of direct foliar water absorption from nighttime recovery.

Among water-conserving shoot adaptations of *Larrea* is its ability to shed tissue (Stark and Love 1969; Strain and Chase 1966; Morello 1955). This reduction helps bring the rates of water loss and water uptake into equilibrium, thus protecting the remaining tissue from desiccation. *Larrea* can continue to lose tissue until only a few small, young leaves and the apical buds are left alive (Dalton 1962; Runyon 1934). Further desiccation may result in the death of a portion of the branches, and *L. tridentata* cannot survive complete drought induced defoliation (Runyon 1934).

Moisture stress levels induce morphological variations. Increased moisture causes more and larger leaves, larger plants, and augmented twig growth in *L. tridentata* (Dalton 1962). Similar phenomena occur in *L. cuneifolia* and *L. divaricata* (Morello 1955 and Table 3-1). Morello found that during their annual period of "rest," both South American species reduced their transpiration surfaces by 60 to 80 percent. Older, more expanded leaves were lost preferentially, thereby leaving the overall leaf size on a stressed shrub smaller than on a nonstressed shrub.

Higher leaf numbers under low moisture stress probably occur because of both increased rates of leaf and node formation and increased periods of leaf retention (Oechel et al. 1972a). Differences in leaf length and width among stressed and unstressed Mojave *L. tridentata* seasonal phenotypes may vary by at least 50 percent (Wallace and Romney 1972). No researcher has yet developed a quantitative understanding of the effect of variations in leaf size, morphology, and numbers on *Larrea* water use economy.

Early investigators felt that *L. tridentata* leaves manifest few xeromorphic adaptations to an arid environment (Ashby 1932; Runyon 1934); however, Oppenheimer (1960) subsequently reviewed the literature and concluded that *L. tridentata* exhibits very low cuticular transpiration rates and that it efficiently restricts stomatal water loss under stress conditions. Four anatomical modifications may be relevant: (1) the resin coating of the leaf may increase cuticular resistance (r_c); (2) lips of the guard cells may increase stomatal resistance (r_s); (3) epidermal hairs may be important in increasing boundary layer reistance (r_a); and (4) further increase may be brought about by the leaf anatomy with its scarcity of spongy mesophyll and intercellular space and with its thick compact layer of palisade tissue.

Larrea tridentata growth and distribution are limited by both high and low moisture levels. Wallace and Romney (1972) reported that the shoots of two-year-old seedlings died during a ninety-day period of a combination of salinity, poor aeration, and continuous water exposure in moist areas near Nevada playas. Beatley (1974) has recently developed an hypothesis that the northern and upper elevation limits to *L. tridentata* in Nevada ". . . are determined primarily by rainfall in excess of a critical amount. . . ." That amount was estimated to be 183 mm "[which] . . . is not the average annual total but that of the late autumn-winter season. . . ."

Transpiration Measurements

Transpiration data taken from different locations are extremely difficult to compare because of environmental and genotypic variables. In addition, transpiration is sometimes expressed on a leaf area basis and sometimes on a weight basis, but without knowing the area-weight factor, converting values so that comparisons can be made is impossible. Nevertheless, we propose to abstract a few absolute values from the literature.

Transpiration rates of several species growing in situ in Rock Valley, Nevada, were measured at various temperatures several times during the year (Bamberg et al. 1973). For *L. tridentata,* maximum rate was 1.3 in March, and minimum was 0.1 in June (g $H_2O \cdot$ g dry $wt^{-1} \cdot hr^{-1}$). Of the several species measured, *Larrea* was clearly the most efficient in restricting transpirational loss of water. Schratz (1931) showed that maximum transpiration for Sonoran *L. tridentata* in situ near Tucson was also 1.3 $g \cdot g^{-1} \cdot hr^{-1}$, which occurred during early October, between 1300 and 1600 hours, when the temperature was about 31° C.

These in situ transpiration rates are intermediate in terms of stressed and unstressed six-month-old greenhouse plants recently measured by Barbour et al. (1974). Unstressed plants, with an average tissue water potential of -15 bars, as determined by Scholander bomb, showed the following values: Sonoran *L. tridentata,* 2.9; *L. divaricata,* 5.4; and *L. cuneifolia,* 3.2 $g \cdot g^{-1} \cdot hr^{-1}$. Stressed plants, with an average tissue water potential of -45 bars, showed the following: Sonoran *L. tridentata,* 0.1; *L. divaricata,* 0.5; and *L. cuneifolia,* 0.9. The high, unstressed transpiration rate of *L. divaricata* was significantly greater than the rate for the other two taxa, but stressed rates were not statistically significantly different (90 percent level). Stress brought a 73 to 96 percent decline in transpiration for *L. tridentata,* the taxon most severely reduced. When Barbour et al. calculated unstressed transpiration rate on a per stomate basis, their value of 9.6×10^{-4} mg $H_2O \cdot hr^{-1}$ was remarkably similar to a value obtained by Ashby (1932) for a well-watered *L. tridentata* bush near Tucson.

Water loss rates of detached leaves have been measured for Sonoran *L. tridentata* and expressed as a percentage of turgid water content (Odening et al. 1974). Both the transpiration rate and tissue water content are combined in their measure. *Larrea tridentata* lost the greatest percentage of its weight during the first 10 minutes, compared to *Chilopsis linearis,* which lost only 5 percent, and *Encelia farinosa,* which lost 22 percent. These results indicate that *Larrea's* nonsucculent leaf is very dependent on a continuous water supply, for it is not able to recoup losses from foliar moisture reserves.

Small leaf size and relative lack of pubescence are probably also water conserving adaptations (Oechel et al. 1972b) in that the bulk of heat loss can be handled via convection rather than transpiration. Other species may expend significant quantities of water in order to cool the leaf below lethal limits, whereas *L. tridentata's* low r_a and small leaf mass result in near-ambient leaf temperatures, despite stomatal closure. Recent measurements of tissue temperatures show *L. tridentata* leaves to be within 1° C of air temperature at 32° C with no wind, or at 44° C with wind and irrigated. Under similar conditions, *Yucca* and *Opuntia* species were 7-13° C above air temperature. When sufficient moisture is available, of course, *Larrea* is able to "take advantage" of transpirational cooling, and it transpires at rates comparable to those of mesophytes (Wallace and Romney 1972; Ashby 1932).

Water Potential Measurements

Despite its control of transpiration, *L. tridentata* can exhibit one of the lowest seasonal levels of tissue water potential, among coexisting desert species. At Deep Canyon, California, *Larrea* showed a range of maximum (dawn) xylem water potentials from -24.5 bars in February 1969 to -56 bars in September 1969. Minimum xylem pressure potentials ranged from less than -40 bars in February 1969 to less than -65 bars in September 1969 (Oechel et al. 1972a). A subsequent study (Odening, Strain, and Oechel, *unpublished data*) demonstrated that during much of the year tissue moisture levels are sufficiently low to place *L. tridentata* at Deep Canyon under conditions of negative turgor pressure. This demonstration may explain why node formation of *L. tridentata* can continue all year, but cell elongation is restricted to brief periods when tissue water potential and thus cell turgor pressure are above critical levels (Oechel et al. 1972a).

Turning to the Mojave Desert, Bamberg et al. (1973) reported *L. tridentata* water potential to range between -51 and -65 bars from May 1, 1972, to June 19, 1972. These stresses are similar to those reported for *Krameria parvifolia* (-48 to -72 bars), *Lycium andersonii* (-41 to -52 bars), and *L. pallidum* (-44 to -51 bars). These three species were dormant by June. Watering *Larrea* plants during the summer of 1972 at Mercury, Nevada, increased tissue water potential to between -1 and -22 bars.

A caliche layer affects the moisture status of *L. tridentata.* Cunningham and Burk (1973), working in southern New Mexico, found that during periods of heavy precipitation, the absence of such a layer improves the water status of *Larrea.* From August to October 1969, xylem water potential fluctuated between about -52 and -22 bars in areas lacking caliche and between -70 and -23 bars where caliche is present. From May to September 1970, a much drier year, water potentials ranged between about -105 and -30 bars without caliche and between -115 and -38 bars with caliche.

However, it should be pointed out that in low rainfall areas or during drought periods, the most xeric conditions and the highest desiccation levels would be expected where there is not a caliche layer.

Recently, some evidence for anomolous diurnal patterns of water potential have been reported for *L. tridentata.* Working at the northern edge of the Sonoran Desert in Arizona, Halvorson and Patten (1974) showed that dawn water potentials (as determined by Scholander bomb) were sometimes more negative at dawn than in the early afternoon. On March 3, for example, dawn water potential of *L. tridentata* shrubs averaged -25 bars; it dropped to -27 bars around 1100 hours then rose to -20 bars at 1300 hours. On July 10, both dawn and 1300 hours water potentials were -50 bars. *Ambrosia deltoidea* and *Cercidium microphyllum,* examined at the same times, exhibited "normal" cycles, with water potential declining from dawn to midafternoon.

Syvertsen et al. (1975) showed similar patterns for Chihuahuan *L. tridentata.* When shrubs in situ were watered, so that dawn water potential was about -20 bars, water potential curves during the day were "normal." But when shrubs were left unwatered in dry soil, so that dawn water potential was -40 bars or less, an anomolous rise occurred in midafternoon to bring water potential back to or considerably above dawn water potential. They ascribed this rise to vertical water vapor movements in the soil profile in response to temperature gradients—that is, water moves up out of the rooting zone at night and back down during the day. "The occurrence of this phenomenon probably enhances the ability of *Larrea* shrubs to maintain photosynthetic activity when soil water potentials are low and makes questionable the use of predawn stem xylem water potential measurements to assess seasonal trends in plant water status."

Photosynthetic Response to Tissue Water Content

Photosynthesis rates even more than transpiration rates show a great deal of variation due to time of day, season, location, light intensity, soil moisture, temperature, genetic stock, and method of measurement used by the experimenter.

Several workers have suggested that *Larrea's* principal adaptation to desert environments lies not in xeromorphic properties to obtain moisture or to conserve water loss but rather in resistance to the damaging effects of low tissue water potential levels (Ashby 1932; Odening et al. 1974; Oechel et al. 1972a). *Larrea* can definitely maintain high photosynthesis and cell division levels at water potentials far lower than most other species.

Diurnal measurements of photosynthesis in *L. tridentata* under ambient conditions of temperature, light, and water potential have been taken by

Oechel et al. (1972a). Subsequent stepwise multiple correlation of the resulting data showed that tissue water potential was the most important factor most highly correlated with daily photosynthesis totals. Correlation between dawn water potential (Scholander bomb readings) and total daily photosynthesis was $r^2 \approx 0.86$. The maximum water potential experienced was -25 bars; at that level, maximum daily productivity of 75 mg $CO_2 \cdot$ g dry wt^{-1} was noted. Decreases in dawn water potential to -55 bars correlated with reduction in daily productivity to 9 mg • g dry wt^{-1}.

In field studies the range of measurable environmental and physiological conditions is necessarily limited. Odening et al. (1974) have investigated the influence of water potential (as measured with Scholander bomb) on instantaneous photosynthesis of Sonoran *L. tridentata, Encelia farinosa,* and *Chilopsis linearis.* Data from field experimental gardens and phytotron studies are included in Figure 3-12 to present photosynthetic responses over a wide range of conditions. *L. tridentata* maintains the highest photosynthetic levels of the three species over most of the water potential range measured except above -10 bars. *L. tridentata* also shows compensation at the lowest water potentials, for positive photosynthesis is continued to at least -78 bars, while *Chilopsis* reaches compensation at -35 bars and *Encelia* at -47 bars. Mojave *L. tridentata* has also shown positive net photosynthesis at tissue water poten-

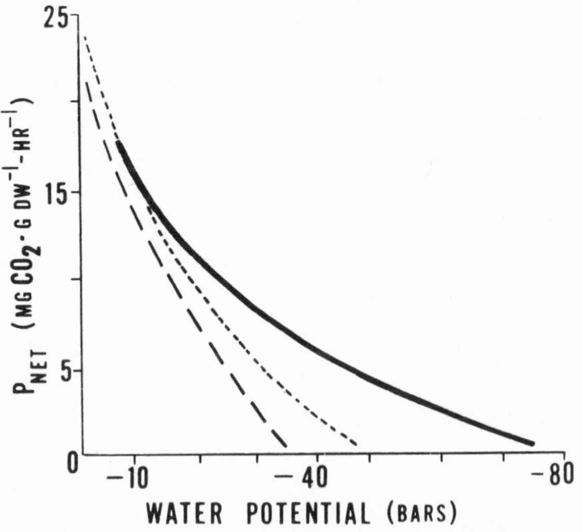

FIGURE 3-12. *Relationship between water potential and net photosynthesis in Sonoran* L. tridentata *(solid line),* Chilopsis linearis *(dashed line), and* Encelia farinosa *(dotted line). Tissue water potential was measured with Scholander bomb. Data were collected from in situ field, experimental garden, and phytotron plants. Adapted from Odening et al. (1974).*

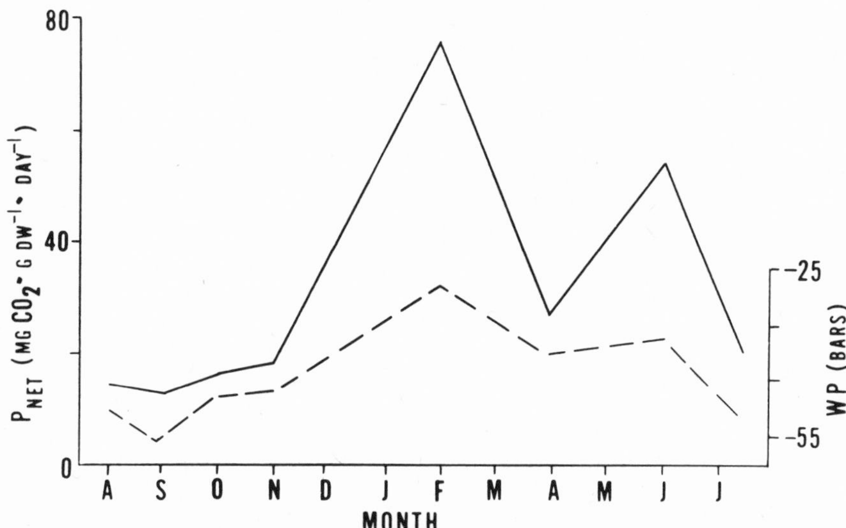

FIGURE 3-13. *Seasonal pattern of dawn water potential (dotted line) and daily total net photosynthesis (solid line) for in situ Sonoran* L. tridentata. *Tissue water potential was measured with Scholander bomb; minimum values were also measured but are not shown; they averaged 15 bars lower than dawn readings. Adapted from Oechel et al. (1972a).*

tial as low as -50 to -60 bars (Bamberg et al. 1973). Strain's observation (1969) that *L. tridentata* was unique among several shrub species in being able to exhibit the same rate of photosynthesis during the hottest, driest month of the year as it did during the most mesic has not been substantiated by later work (Figure 3-13; see also, for example, Oechel et al. 1972a).

Generally, net photosynthesis values for *Larrea* fit well into the range of values summarized by Mooney (1972a, b) for semi-arid, evergreen, sclerophyllous shrubs: 4-12 mg $CO_2 \cdot dm^{-2} \cdot hr^{-1}$ under conditions of light saturation, optimal temperature and moisture, and normal CO_2 concentration.

Figure 3-12 shows that of the three species, *L. tridentata* exhibited the least decrease in photosynthesis with increasing moisture stress. Barbour et al. (1974) examined concentration in more detail on the mesic range of -8 to -26 bars tissue water potential and gas exchange of some forty greenhouse-grown specimens of *L. tridentata, L. divaricata,* and *L. cuneifolia,* all of which were about six months old. Fluctuations within the range of -8 to -26 bars water potential had little effect on rates of photosynthesis or transpiration for any taxon. When water potential was dropped to an average of –45 bars, however, *L. tridentata* photosynthesis decreased by 8 percent while that of *L. divaricata* declined more drastically by 96 percent, and that of *L. cuneifolia* declined less drastically by 76 percent (Table 3-3). Although intraspecific variability precluded statistical separation of these three responses,

TABLE 3-3 *Transpiration and Net Photosynthesis of 6- to 8-Month-Old, Greenhouse-Grown* Larrea *Seedlings (from Barbour et al. 1974).*

Series and taxon	Tissue water potential (bars)	Transpiration ($g\ H_2O \cdot g\ dw^{-1} \cdot hr^{-1}$)	Photosynthesis ($mg\ CO_2 \cdot g\ dw^{-1} \cdot hr^{-1}$)
Mesic series			
L. tridentata (Sonoran)	-16.1	2.90	3.52
L. divaricata	-14.9	5.44	4.93
L. cuneifolia	-15.0	3.18	3.87
Xeric series			
L. tridentata (Sonoran)	-44.5	0.11	0.51
L. divaricata	-46.5	0.49	0.17
L. cuneifolia	-41.6	0.92	0.93

Note: Chamber conditions: 38° C, 19% RH, and 48,400 Lux.

the steep decrease by *L. divaricata* did correlate with its relatively mesic nature.

Water Use Efficiency

According to Bamberg et al. (1973), water use efficiency of in situ Mojave *L. tridentata* varies between 0.3 and 1.5 mg CO_2 incorporated per mg H_2O lost, depending on temperature and moisture status of the plant. These efficiencies are approximately equivalent to those shown by *Ambrosia dumosa, Lycium andersonii,* and *L. pallidum* when in leaf, but they were lower than those of *Krameria parvifolia.* Water use efficiency appeared to be correlated with soil moisture status: Drier soils correlated with lower efficiencies in *Larrea.* There was also an inverse relationship with temperature, the highest efficiency was reached below 20° C and the lowest above 45° C.

Diurnal and Seasonal Photosynthesis Patterns

The rate of photosynthesis is a function of many other environmental variables besides water availability. This section of the chapter examines the response to temperature and light.

Photosynthetic Response to Temperature

Another potential major stress on *Larrea* production is high tissue temperature. As previously stated, leaf and air temperatures are generally comparable.

Leaf temperatures of 42 to 46° C have been reported for Mojave *L. tridentata* on warm days by Wallace and Romney (1972), and similar high temperatures are probably experienced by other *Larrea* taxa as well.

Temperature optima for photosynthesis in *L. tridentata* are lower than might be expected from an examination of in situ tissue and air temperatures. Data of Bamberg et al. (1973) for Mojave *L. tridentata,* for example, indicate a temperature optimum of less than 25° C. Strain and Chase (1966), however, showed that preconditioning affects the temperature optima, as well as the rate of photosynthesis and the compensation temperature (Table 3-4). In connection with this and the preceding section, we should note that soil moisture level can also affect the compensation temperature. Plants growing in Mercury, Nevada, may show a natural upper compensation temperature above 50° C, but after experimental irrigation the high temperature compensation point may be reduced to 45° C (Bamberg et al. 1973).

Strain and Chase (1966) also examined respiration. They found that respiration rates were affected by temperature preconditioning (respiration at a given temperature decreased with increasing preconditioning temperature), but the Q_{10} remained constant. This response results in a homeostatic process that tends to minimize the fluctuations in CO_2 lost in dark respiration due to seasonal temperature changes. Later studies by Strain (1969) indicated that seasonal acclimation of photosynthesis and respiration occur in the field as well: At 25° C, Sonoran *L. tridentata* respiration rates were seen to be about 2.4 times higher during the winter than during the summer. Without acclimation, the Q_{10} respiration response to summer temperatures would normally cause higher respiration rates.

As evidenced by reports of positive photosynthesis at 50° C, *L. tridentata* seems well adapted to high tissue temperatures (Oechel et al. 1972a). In fact, there is considerable evidence that *L. tridentata's* range is limited by low rather than by high temperatures. For example, Shreve (1940) stated that death is caused by six consecutive days of below-freezing temperatures. Although low temperatures are important in limiting the distribution of *Larrea,*

TABLE 3-4 *Effect of Acclimation Temperature (°C) on Photosynthesis of Sonoran* L. tridentata *(from Strain and Chase 1966).*

Preconditioning temperature		T_{opt} for photosynthesis	P_{net} at T_{opt}	Upper compensation temp.
Day	Night		(mg CO_2 • g dw^{-1} • hr^{-1})	
15	7	15	2.6	32
30	15	15	4.4	40
40	25	25	3.4	>40

Note: Acclimation period varied from 7 to 17 days.

exceptions to this reaction are described by Wallace and Romney (1972), Beatley (1974), and Barbour (1967).

Photosynthetic Response to Light

Field light response curves performed on Sonoran *L. tridentata* by Oechel and Strain (*unpublished data*) indicate that terminal branches do not light saturate under normal irradiances or radiation intensities (in excess of 2,000 μei · m^{-2} · sec, or 12,000 ft-c, or approximately 120,000 Lux). The branches used, however, were placed in a cuvette in their natural orientation, so leaves were not oriented perpendicularly to the sun nor were they spread apart to avoid self-shading.

Barbour et al. (1974) examined the light response curves of six-month-old, greenhouse-grown individuals of Sonoran *L. tridentata, L. divaricata,* and *L. cuneifolia.* Branches were sandwiched between nylon meshes, the leaves were spread, and the whole was oriented at right angles to the light source. All three taxa showed the same general response curve and reached saturation at 800 μ Einsteins · m^{-2} · sec^{-1} (PhAR), a value well below full sunlight.

Metabolic Pathway of Photosynthesis

Sonoran *L. tridentata, L. divaricata,* and *L. cuneifolia* have recently been tested for pathway of photosynthesis by Barbour et al. (1974). The testing employed analysis of RuDP carboxylase/PEP carboxylase enzyme ratios in greenhouse-grown material, and analysis of $^{13}C/^{12}C$ ($=\delta^{13}C$) ratios in field collected material. Both series indicated that *Larrea* is a C_3 plant. Independent carbon isotope ratios have been performed by Bruce Smith at The University of Texas at Austin (*personal communication*), and his conclusions are the same. The only evidence to the contrary is a report by Wallace et al. (1971) who showed an enzyme ratio of approximately 1, thereby indicating equal inputs from C_3 and C_4 pathways, for Mojave *Larrea.*

CARBON ALLOCATION

The process of carbon gain by photosynthesis in *Larrea* has been discussed earlier in this chapter. Now we turn to the allocation of this carbon resource within the plant. Mooney (1972a) has pointed out that we do not have enough information to completely account for carbon allocation in any species. This observation certainly applies to *Larrea.* As a consequence we will only be able to broadly sketch an outline of *Larrea* carbon allocation (Figure 3-14). The dashed boxes represent pools of nonstructural carbohydrates that can potentially be used in synthesis of new organic compounds or respired to provide maintenance and construction energy. The solid boxes represent carbon that has been irretrievably committed to the development of new structures within the plant. The thin arrows illustrate possible pathways of carbon transfer within the plant. To simplify the diagram, the nonstructural carbohydrate pools all are shown to exchange with a common mobile pool. This arrangement avoids the complexity of connecting each nonstructural carbohydrate pool with each of the others and illustrates that mobilization of these reserves to supply any organ is possible. The heavy arrows indicate pathways by which the carbon gained by the plant is returned to the environment.

Figure 3-14 can serve as a guide for quantifying the description of carbon allocation. We should know the size of each of the structural and nonstructural carbon compartments and the rates of carbon movement between the compartments and from the plant to the environment. In addition, we should know the effects of the environment, phenology, and previous history of carbon gain and allocation on the compartment sizes and transfer rates. Although most of this information is not yet available, we can begin filling in this framework with the quantitative information available and ask where the important gaps in our knowledge lie.

The nonstructural carbohydrate pools are the reserve carbon resources

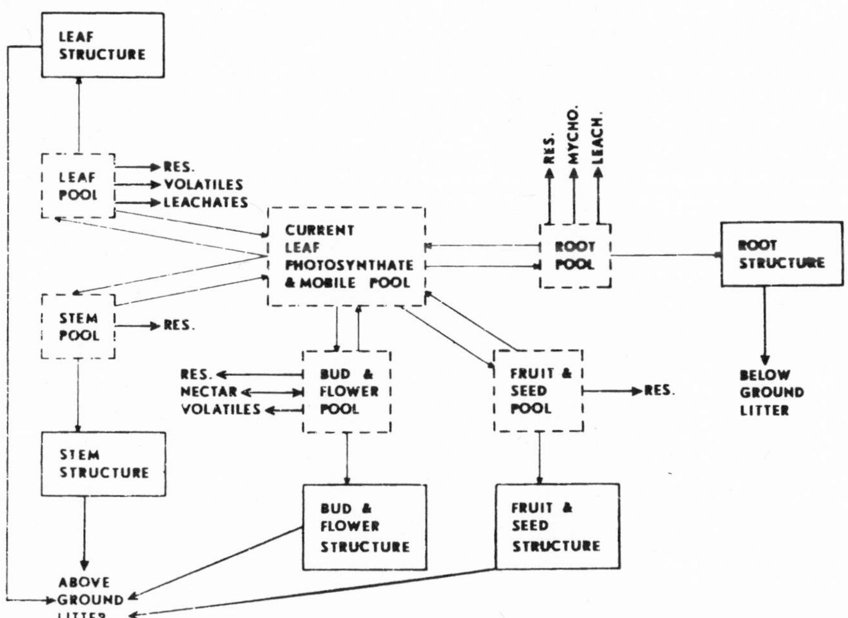

FIGURE 3-14. *Diagrammatic representation of potential fates of carbon fixed by* Larrea. *See text for details.*

that are available for construction of new tissues and organic compounds and for respiration to supply energy for metabolic processes. Strain (1969) measured the seasonal variation in alcohol soluble carbohydrates in leaves and stems of Sonoran *L. tridentata* growing in situ in the Colorado Desert of California. The stem bark soluble fraction varied only from about 12 to 19 percent of the alcohol insoluble dry weight. For leaves this value varied only between about 4 and 7 percent. This same pattern of relatively constant nonstructural carbohydrate pool size was found in *Acacia gregii,* another species that retains its leaves through the hot dry summer. Two drought deciduous species, *Hymenoclea salsola* and *Encelia farinosa,* showed much greater seasonal variations in nonstructural carbohydrate contents of leaves (45 to 8 percent) and stem bark (25 to 4 percent).

Oechel et al. (1972a) observed the seasonal variation of ^{14}C incorporation and redistribution in Sonoran *L. tridentata* individuals growing in situ in the Colorado Desert of California. They also found that the relative rate of incorporation in various nonstructural pools and structural components did not vary appreciably with season. They further concluded that incorporation of carbon into the various structural components occurred at the expense of currently gained carbon and was not the result of the plant drawing on nonstructural carbon reserves.

We can conclude that the levels of nonstructural carbon pools in *Larrea* are low. Further, reserve carbon pools apparently are not readily mobilized and translocated to different organs or tissues. These conclusions, however, are based on studies conducted in the Colorado Desert where *Larrea* appears to be capable of growth and photosynthesis throughout the year. Information of this type is needed from areas where *Larrea* shows more of a seasonal pattern of growth such as the Chihuahuan Desert of Arizona (Chew and Chew 1965) and New Mexico (Burk and Dick-Peddie 1973).

Allocation to Roots

Some information on the relative allocation of carbon to root structure can be gained by examining values of root-shoot ratios. These are ratios of standing crop biomass of roots and above ground vegetative portions of the plant. Therefore, their interpretation in terms of carbon allocation must be done with caution since production of above and below ground litter are probably not equivalent. In some cases differences in the amount of carbon in the mobile pools might also introduce some bias in estimating carbon allocation to root structure from root-shoot ratios. The small size of the nonstructural carbon pools probably reduces this error with *Larrea.*

Reported values of root-shoot ratios for *Larrea* are quite variable. Barbour (1967) found that forty-day-old seedlings had root-shoot ratios of 0.60. This value seems in good agreement with those obtained by Chew and Chew (1965) in southeastern Arizona. They found root-shoot ratios that varied from a high of 0.50 for one-year-old plants to a value of 0.23 for plants 25 to 65 years of age. A value of 0.30 has been reported for mature *L. tridentata* growing in a Mojave Desert wash (Garcia-Moya and McKell 1970).

These values are in striking contrast to average root-shoot ratios of 1.24 that have been observed on several sites in the Mojave Desert of southern Nevada (Bamberg, *personal communication*) or to those reported by Singh (1964) for mature *L. tridentata* shrubs in the Chihuahuan Desert of southern New Mexico. He excavated twenty shrubs growing on a single section and obtained values ranging from 0.64 to 6.78 (mean of 2.4).

Singh found no apparent correlation of root-shoot ratio with plant size, but Ludwig (1975) did. Ludwig analyzed thirteen excavated *L. tridentata* shrubs from a Chihuahuan Desert site in southern New Mexico and found a range of root-shoot ratios from 2.7 to 0.2 with a mean of 0.9. The two smallest plants had an average ratio of 0.31, whereas the seven largest plants had an average ratio of 0.95. This correlation is opposite to that reported by Chew and Chew (1965). Ludwig (1975) concluded that the root system size and form depends on the soil environment in which the plant has become established.

Greater allocation of the carbon resource to root structure has been widely believed to enhance the ability of desert shrubs to survive under conditions of low soil moisture. Barbour (1973) and Ludwig (1975) have examined the evidence upon which this belief is based and found it lacking. Certainly for *Larrea* in North America the extent of carbon allocation to root structure appears to be extremely variable even within a small area. More information is needed before conclusions can be drawn concerning carbon allocation to root structure. The possibility that ephemeral roots might be produced near the soil surface during rainy periods has not been examined for *Larrea*.

Allocation to Leaves

Monsi and Murata (1970) have pointed out the importance of carbon allocation to new leaf structure in determining the ability of the plant to maintain acceptable levels of photosynthesis. The reinvestment of photosynthetically gained carbon to leaf structure allows the plant to maintain or enhance the levels of carbon available for performing other functions and thus presumably increases its capacity to survive and reproduce.

Chew and Chew (1965) estimated the cumulative percentage of above-ground vegetative biomass that is allocated to leaves for various age *Larrea* plants growing in the Sonoran-Chihuahuan ecotone of southeastern Arizona. They found that approximately 68 percent of the above ground vegetative biomass was allocated to new leaves during the first year. This amount declined to a value of about 50 percent at an age of 30 to 32 years. Thereafter the percentage remained about the same up to age 65. In southern New

Mexico, Burk and Dick-Peddie (1973) found that during the period of their study, the percentage allocation to new leaves was about the same as measured by Chew and Chew. At the U.S. IBP Chihuahuan Desert validation site, new leaves compose approximately 47 percent of the total above ground vegetative production (Ludwig, *personal communication*).

In the Mojave Desert of southern Nevada approximately 66 percent of the above ground vegetative biomass increment of *Larrea* was in new leaves during the 1971 growing season. In 1972 the value was 61 percent (Bamberg, *personal communication*).

On the basis of these limited data, we might safely conclude that about 70 to 45 percent of above ground vegetative production will be allocated to new leaf structure, depending upon the age of the shrub and possibly site characteristics.

Allocation to Reproductive Structures

Recent research has shown that the proportion of the carbon resource that a plant allocates to reproduction can be very important in determining the survival of the population when it is faced with different types of selective pressures (Harper and Ogden 1970; Gadgil and Solbrig 1972; Abrahamson and Gadgil 1973). Populations that allocate more resources to reproduction appear to be more successful in situations where population size is regulated by density independent factors. Conversely, where the primary controls on population size are density dependent, a greater proportion of the resource pool is allocated to vegetative growth.

Current work on the relative allocation of carbon to vegetative and reproductive growth in *Larrea* indicates that the ratio of reproductive to vegetative growth can be quite variable. In general, when conditions are less favorable for total production, a greater proportion is allocated to reproductive growth. In the Chihuahuan Desert *Larrea* shrubs, which were growing on field plots where the soil moisture was maintained at or near the field capacity, were found to allocate only 0.5 percent of their total above-ground production to reproductive growth. In contrast, unwatered controls allocated 10 percent of their above-ground biomass to reproduction (Cunningham et al. 1974). (In absolute values, however, the total above ground production of the watered plants was 11.6 times as great as it was for the unwatered controls.)

Increased percent allocation to reproduction when total production is low has also been documented on the U.S. IBP Desert Biome Chihuahuan Desert site (Ludwig and Whitford 1975). In 1971, a year of low precipitation, total above-ground production was estimated at 350 kg dry wt · ha^{-1}. Of this total, 43 percent was allocated to buds, flowers, and fruits. In 1973, a year with slightly more precipitation, total above-ground production was 385 kg dry wt · ha^{-1} and reproductive allocation amounted to 31 percent of the total. In this case, absolute amounts of reproductive allocation were also greater in the dry year: 150 kg dry wt · ha^{-1} in 1971; 120 kg dry wt · ha^{-1} in 1973.

The percentage allocation of above-ground biomass to reproductive structures has thus been observed to vary from a low of 0.5 percent for well-watered shrubs to a high of 43 percent during dry periods. Other published values fall within this broad range (Bamberg, *personal communication*; Burk and Dick-Peddie 1973). *Larrea* appears to shift its allocation of resources toward greater reproductive effort under drier conditions, presumably when density independent factors are having the greatest control on the population.

Total Seasonal Productivity

Perhaps the best seasonal productivity study has been done for Mojave *L. tridentata* in Rock Valley, Nevada (*unpublished IBP data*). Table 3-5 summarizes monthly increments of photosynthate over the course of two years. The precipitation differed greatly during the two years; a 170 percent increase in precipitation brought an 80 percent increase in annual productivity. (The relative contribution of *Larrea* to total community productivity was less during the wetter years, thereby indicating that productivity of other plants increased even more).

Other unpublished data from Rock Valley reveal that the caloric value of *Larrea* tissue is remarkably similar for leaves, wood, seed, and flowers and averages 4,649 cal · g^{-1}. This finding agrees closely with calorimetry (4,611 cal · g^{-1}) for Silverbell bajada, Arizona (*unpublished IBP data* in Table 3-6 supplied by James MacMahon) and for a Chihuahuan Desert site (4,579 cal · g^{-1}; see Burk and Dick-Peddie 1973).

Respirational Carbon Loss

Evaluation of standing crop biomass gives only a relative indication of carbon allocation to various functions within the plant. The carbon loss back to the environment through respiration for maintenance and construction energy must also be evaluated to properly assess the total allocation.

Strain (1969) has reported dark respiration rates of *Larrea* leaves on plants growing in situ in the Colorado Desert of southern California. He found values of 0.43 and 1.02 mg CO_2 · gm dry wt^{-1} · hr^{-1} at 25° C in July and January, respectively. These values were not surprising in light of the previously reported temperature acclimation of respiration in greenhouse-grown *Larrea* (Strain and Chase 1966). These respiration rates are about half the values reported for the drought deciduous shrubs *Hymenoclea salsola* and *Encelia farinosa,* but about the same as the winter deciduous *Acacia greggii.*

TABLE 3-5 *Monthly Increment of Photosynthate (kg/ha) for Mojave* L. tridentata *at Rock Valley, Nevada (unpublished IBP data courtesy of Bamberg).*

Year	Total ppt. (mm)	Jan	Feb	Mar	Apr	May	Jun	Jul	Aug	Sep	Oct	Nov	Dec	*Larrea* total	*Larrea* as % of all spp.
1972	91	1.5	3.3	10.3	9.2	4.1	1.4	0.7	1.0	1.4	1.8	1.7	1.2	37.6	26
1973	247	1.1	1.2	2.6	10.1	22.1	17.5	4.5	1.7	2.5	2.4	1.4	1.2	68.1	13

TABLE 3-6 *Chemical Analysis of Sonoran* L. tridentata *from Silverbell Bajada, Arizona, Collected during Peak of Vegetative Growth in 1972 (unpublished IBP data).*

Part	Caloric content ($ca\ 1 \cdot g^{-1}$)	Ash (%)	Ash free ($cal \cdot g^{-1}$)	Protein (%)	Carbo-hydrate (%)	Fat (%)
Leaves	5060	5.57	5358	11.01	79.64	3.78
New wood	4851	4.56	5083	–	–	–
Roots	4420	7.74	4791	11.88	79.58	0.80
Old wood	4561	2.37	4672	6.65	89.79	1.19
Flowers	4406	8.50	4815	–	–	–
Seeds	4370	4.69	4585	14.68	77.63	3.00

Note: Each point is the mean of the three determinations.

When these respiration values for leaves are compared with respiration rates of reproductive structures, that reproduction can be quite costly in terms of respirational carbon loss becomes clear. At 25° C young buds respire at a rate of 30.15 mg $CO_2 \cdot$ gm dry $wt^{-1} \cdot hr^{-1}$. As the buds mature into flowers this rate increases to 78.28 mg $CO_2 \cdot$ gm dry $wt^{-1} \cdot hr^{-1}$. The rate then falls to 11.33 mg $CO_2 \cdot$ gm dry $wt^{-1} \cdot hr^{-1}$ in immature (green) fruits. Once the fruit is mature, no respirational carbon loss can be detected (Cunningham et al. 1973).

No information appears to be available at this time on respirational losses in stems and roots of *Larrea.* It can probably be assumed, however, that these losses are small compared to leaf and reproductive structure losses on a unit dry weight basis for short periods of time. However, their greater biomass and persistence throughout the year may combine to make their total respirational carbon demand quite significant. More quantitative information is needed.

Other Carbon Losses

Carbon is lost from plants in the form of organic molecules that are leached and volatilized from leaves and exuded from roots (Mooney 1972a; Tukey 1970). Little or no information is available on the quantitites of carbon allocated to these organic molecules in *Larrea.* Some carbon is probably lost by the plant in the support of mycorrhiza. This may be a significant portion of the total carbon resource, but no quantitative information is available. There are many secondary compounds which are produced in considerable amounts, but many of their roles are unclear (Mabry and Turner 1972; Saunier et al. 1968; Duisberg 1952a).

SUMMARY

Germination, seedling survival, stem and leaf anatomy, shrub architecture, photosynthesis, water relations, carbon allocation, phenology, and life span topics were reviewed for *L. cuneifolia* (including Monte and chaco ecotypes), *L. divaricata* (including Monte and chaco ecotypes), and *L. tridentata* (including Chihuahuan, Sonoran, and Mojave ecotypes). For many topics, ecotype data were not available.

Seed dispersal patterns and seedling density vary considerably from year to year, but survival is consistently low. Rainfall as low as 16 mm over a few weeks is sufficient to trigger germination, providing that minimum temperatures are above 15 to 20° C. Laboratory work shows the germination of *Larrea* to be relatively intolerant of moisture stress, high temperature, basic pH, and salinity; it has failed to substantiate field observations that allelopathy is involved in seedling survival, but it has implicated the importance of soil oxygen concentration.

Stem anatomy is highly specialized and there are minor differences between taxa. Chlorenchyma is present in young twigs. Leaf anatomy is typically isolateral, with large, thick-walled epidermal cells that were coated with a resin that does not, however, plug the stomata. There are minor differences between taxa here also, but their ecological significance remains obscure.

Shrub architecture differs considerably between the taxa, and greenhouse studies show the differences to be genetically based. In contrast to *L. cuneifolia* and *L. tridentata, L. divaricata* plants have rapid shoot growth that results in tall, spindly plants with less compact foliage. The root systems of all taxa reflect soil characteristics more than inherent genetic potential. *L. divaricata* can be phreatophytic.

Detailed phenological data are few, but recent short-term studies indicate that Sonoran *L. tridentata* and *L. divaricata* have similar patterns of flowering and fruiting. In addition, the period of maximum growth for *L. cuneifolia* and *L. divaricata* is September through May, which is equivalent and hence similar to the March to November activity period for *L. tridentata.* Within the latter species, Mojave populations show a major flowering peak in spring and sometimes a second peak in late summer; Sonoran and Chihuahuan populations show both peaks more consistently. The roles of moisture, temperature, and day length in regulating phenology are still unclear, and studies have suggested that rainfall above a critical level does not affect the intensity of a phenological event. The life span of *Larrea* is still unknown.

Larrea is able to tolerate tissue water potentials as low as -115 bars, though most field data show -65 bars to be a typical seasonal low. *Larrea* is able to maintain photosynthesis and cell division at lower water potentials than most other species. In addition to its simple tolerance of drought, *Larrea* shows a low cuticular transpiration rate and a reduction of transpiration surface of up to 80 percent. Leaf temperature is usually close to air temperature.

Under mesic conditions, this trait is due in part to evaporative cooling, but during drought conditions, it is mainly due to rapid loss of sensible heat across the thin boundary layer that results from the small leaf size. The photosynthetic rate drought stress is within the limits for other evergreen, sclerophyllous xerophytes. Rate of photosynthesis is most directly related to tissue water potential, although temperature acclimation tends to keep photosynthesis and respiration relatively uniform through the year. Whether, under stressed conditions, *Larrea* taxa differ significantly in transpiration and photosynthesis rates is still not clear. All taxa are C_3 plants.

Levels of nonstructural carbon pools appear to be low and not readily translocated, but more data are required. Carbon allocation to roots is extremely variable even within a small area; its amount seems to be determined by soil conditions. Allocation to new leaves varies from 45 to 70 percent of above-ground annual production, depending on shrub age. Allocation to reproductive structures varies from 0.5 to 43 percent, depending on moisture: The greater the precipitation, the *lower* the relative amount allocated. The caloric value of *L. tridentata* tissue is remarkably uniform over organ, space, and time; it averages 4,613 cal g^{-1}.

Respirational loss from reproductive structures (buds, flowers, green fruit) can be 10 to 150 times that of leaves. The amount of carbon lost from respiration of roots and stems, from the leaching or volatization of organic molecules, or from mycorrhizal associations, is not known.

RESUMEN

Se hizo un estudio de los siguientes tópicos: germinación, supervivencia de plántulas, anatomías caulinar y foliar, arquitectura arbustiva, fotosíntesis, relaciones hídricas, asignación de carbón, fenología y longevidad de *L. cuneifolia* (incluyendo los ecotipos del Monte y del Chaco), *L. divaricata* (incluyendo los ecotipos del Monte y del Chaco) y *L. tridentata* (incluyendo los ecotipos de los desiertos Chihuahuense, Sonorense y Mojavense). En muchos tópicos se careció de datos ecotípicos.

Los patrones de dispersión de semillas y de densidad de plántulas varían considerablemente año tras año, pero la supervivencia es consistentemente baja. Una precipitación pluvial de 16 mm en el período de unas pocas semanas es suficiente para iniciar la germinación, siempre que las temperaturas mínimas estén por encima de 15 a 20° C. Los estudios de laboratorio muestran que la germinación de *Larrea* es relativamente intolerante a restricciones excesivas de humedad, alta temperatura, alcalinidad y salinidad; dichos estudios no han podido confirmar las observaciones de campo que la alelopatía está involucrada en la supervivencia de plántulas, pero han puesto de manifiesto la importancia de la concentración de oxígeno en el suelo.

La anatomía caulinar está altamente especializada y hay diferencias menores entre los diferentes taxa. Hay clorénquima en las ramas jóvenes. La anatomía foliar es típicamente isolateral, con células epidérmicas grandes, de paredes gruesas. La epidermis se encuentra cubierta por una capa resinosa que sin embargo no obstruye a los estomas. También hay aquí diferencias menores entre los diferentes taxa, pero su significado ecológico permanece obscuro.

La arquitectura arbustiva difiere considerablemente entre los taxa y estudios de invernadero demuestran que las diferencias tienen base genética. En contraste con *L. cuneifolia* y *L. tridentata,* las plantas de *L. divaricata* tienen un cremimiento rápido, resultando plantas altas, espigadas, con follaje menos compacto. Los sistemas radicales de todas los taxa reflejan más bien características del suelo que potencial genético inherente. *L. divaricata* puede ser freatófita.

Hay pocos datos fenológicos detallados, pero estudios recientes, de corta duración, indican que *L. divaricata* y *L. tridentata* del Desierto Sonorense tienen patrones semejantes de floración y fructificación. Además, el período de máximo crecimiento de *L. cuneifolia* y *L. divaricata* es septiembre-mayo, equivalente y por lo tanto similar, al período de actividad marzo-noviembre de *L. tridentata.* En esta última especie, las poblaciones del Desierto Mojavense muestran un pico principal de floración en la primavera y, a veces, un segundo pico a fines del verano; las poblaciones de los desiertos Sonorense y Chihuahuense muestran ambos picos más consistentemente. Los papeles que desempeñan la humedad, la temperatura y la longitud del día son aun poco claros. Se ha sugerido que la precipitación pluvial por encima de un nivel crítico no afecta la intensidad de un evento fenológico. El período de vida de *Larrea* es todavía desconcido.

Larrea es capaz de tolerar potenciales de agua de tejidos tan bajos como -115 barios, aunque la mayoría de los datos de campo muestra que -65 barios es una baja estacional típica. *Larrea* es capaz de mantener fotosíntesis y división celular con potenciales de agua menores que los de la mayoría de otras especies. Además de la mera tolerancia a la sequía, *Larrea* muestra una tasa baja de transpiración cuticular y una reducción de la superficie de transpiración hasta de 80%. La temperatura foliar es, por lo general, cercana a la del aire; bajo condiciones mesofíticas, esto se debe, en parte, al enfriamiento por evaporación, pero, durante condiciones de sequía, se debe principalmente a la pérdida rápida de calor sensible a través de la delgada capa límite que resulta del pequeño tamaño de la hoja. La tasa fotosintética de sequía severa se encuentra dentro de los límites para otras xerófitas esclerófilas perennifolias. La tasa fotosintética está relacionada principalmente con el potencial hídrico de los tejidos, aunque la aclimatización a la temperatura tiende a mantener a la fotosíntesis y a la respiración relativamente uniformes durante todo el año. Todavía no está muy claro si, bajo severas condiciones, los taxa de *Larrea* varían significativamente en tasas de transpiración y de fotosíntesis. Todo los taxa son del tipo C_3.

Los niveles de almacenamiento de carbón no estructural parecen ser bajos y no fácilmente transportados, pero se necesitan más datos. La asignación de carbón a las raíces es extremadamente variable aun dentro de una pequeña area; la cantidad parece estar determinada por las condiciones del suelo. La asignación a las hojas nuevas varía de 45 a 70 percent de la producción anual sobre la superficie, dependiendo de la edad del arbusto. La asignación a estructuras reproductivas varía de 0.5 a 43 percent, dependiendo de la humedad: Mientras mayor sea la precipitación, *menor* es la cantidad relativa asignada. El valor calorífico del tejido de *L. tridentata* es notablemente uniforme en órgano, espacio y tiempo, promediando 4613 cal g^{-1}.

La pérdida respiratoria de estructuras reproductivas (botones, flores, fruto verde) puede ser 10 a 150 veces la de las hojas. Se desconoce la cantidad de carbón pérdido por la respiración de raíces y tallos, por lixiviación volatilización de moléculas orgánicas, o por asociaciones micorrízicas.

4

Reproductive Systems of *Larrea*

B. B. Simpson, J. L. Neff, and A. R. Moldenke

When we consider the diversity in morphology (see Chapter 2), physiology, and habitat preferences (see Chapters 3 and 9) of the five species of *Larrea,* finding that they also differ in their breeding systems and relationships with flower-visiting insects is no surprise. The reproductive systems and flower-insect associations of three of the taxa, *L. tridentata* (tetraploid), *L. divaricata,* and *L. cuneifolia,* have been studied in detail. Field observations have provided limited data for the other two species as well. Some of the features of the floral syndromes, breeding behaviors, and insect interactions reflect close evolutionary relationships between various taxa (see Chapter 2), while others appear to have resulted from convergent selection pressures in disjunct but similar habitats (see Chapters 3 and 9).

FLORAL MORPHOLOGY

The basic floral pattern of all species of *Larrea* is the same, but specific differences do occur. Figure 4-1 illustrates the general morphology of a *Larrea* flower using *L. tridentata* as a model. In all species, there are five free yellow petals and five partially fused smaller green sepals. The ten stamens have large basal scales that serve to cup nectar produced by a circular area of tissue at the base of the style. The ovary is globose, superior, supported by a short gynophore, and terminated by a single style and stigma. The ovary is usually divided into five locules, each of which contains seven to nine centrally attached ovules. Although more than one ovule in a locule may be fertilized and begin development, only one will mature. Consequently, a maximum of five seeds can be produced by a single flower. Frequently, however, flowers can be found with six-loculed ovaries. These flowers occasionally produce six seeds. Apomixis is not known in the genus, but varying amounts of vegetative reproduction have been reported. Barbour (see Chapter 3) points out that the lower branches of *L. tridentata* can take root if covered by soil. Vasek et al. (1975) have investigated the "fairy ring" type of concentric spreading of individual *Larrea tridentata* (hexaploid) plants in California. *Larrea ameghinoi* is known to spread by woody runners, a trait that appears

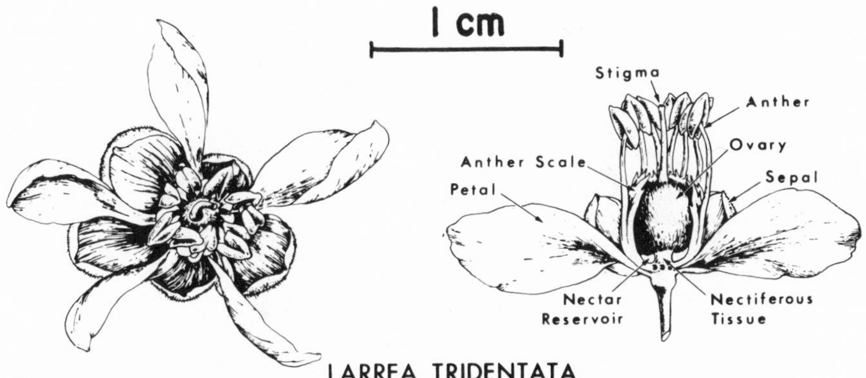

FIGURE 4-1. *Face view and cross section of a flower of* L. tridentata *from Silver Bell, Arizona.*

to persist in all its hybrid derivatives (Hunziker, *personal communication*). Some hybrid individuals resulting from crosses between *L. ameghinoi* and *L. divaricata* in southern Argentina have produced a series of independent shrubs from branches that became buried, sprouted, and were later severed from the parent plant by the death of the connecting tissue (Hunziker, *personal communication*). These reports imply that most species of *Larrea* are capable of vegetative reproduction by a phenomenon similar to branch layering.

When the flower first opens, the anthers rest horizontally cupped in the petals, or even hang slightly below the flower between the petals. Each flower lasts several hours to one day before drying. The anthers rise more or less sequentially, but there is a marked hiatus between the anthesis of the outer and the inner five anthers. The anther sacs are dorsifixed and dehisce longitudinally, exposing masses of orange pollen often mixed with globules of resin. Pollen grains are tricolporate, lightly reticulate, and between 21 and 26 μ long. Dehiscence is concentrated in the morning, but the anthers continue to shed during the day. The resultant continuous, if reduced, pollen supply throughout the day may encourage repeated visits to the same flower by pollen-collecting female bees, the most prominent visitors to the flowers of *Larrea* species. While a similar floral pattern and flower maturation occurs in the five *Larrea* species, the taxa differ in the amount of the expansion of the corolla and the extent to which the stamens become appressed to the style as they finish dehiscence.

Flowers of *L. cuneifolia* and some populations of *L. tridentata* appear to be protogynous, but Cocucci (*personal communication*) has found that the stigma is not receptive until the flower opens and anthesis begins. In *L. cuneifolia* the stamens are slightly shorter than the style (Figure 4-2), but in all the other taxa, they are more or less equal in height to the stigma (Figure 4-2). As the anthers finish dehiscing, they curl loosely about the style in *L. cuneifolia, L. divaricata,* and *L. tridentata,* but in *L. nitida* and *L. ameghinoi*

FIGURE 4–2. *Representative face views and side views of flowers of the South American species of* Larrea. L. cuneifolia *drawn from a specimen from Andalgalá.*

the anthers press more tightly around the stigma. In all species, therefore, and especially in the last two, a mechanical opportunity for self-pollination exists.

BREEDING SYSTEMS

All the species outcross, but as indicated by dissimilar floral morphologies they differ in the relative amounts of self-compatibility and/or facultative inbreeding. As an arbitrary designation, those species that produce (on the average) fewer than one seed per flower after persistent artificial self-pollinations are termed *weakly self-compatible.* Similarly those species that can naturally self-pollinate, but produce 10 percent or fewer seeds when sheltered from external pollen vectors, are considered to have low self-pollination. *Larrea divaricata* near Andalgalá, while not specifically tested for compatibility, exhibits a rather high degree of self-pollination. In contrast, *L. cuneifolia* is self-compatible, but has a low level of inbreeding. In this last species, the mechanical separation of the stigma and the anthers (Figure 4-2) undoubtedly helps to prevent self-pollination within a flower, but the patterns of insect foraging within a given shrub must often lead to self-pollination and inbreeding. Although *L. tridentata* (tetraploid) near Tucson has a relatively low amount of self-pollination, Raven has suggested (1963) on the basis of a report by Twisselmann (1956) that the hexaploid race in the Colorado Desert is self-compatible and normally produces abundant seed by self-pollinating.

These results, shown in Table 4-1, indicate there is a probability, although low in cases, of self-pollination and seed set without external agents in all of the species studied. Such a system of facultative inbreeding allows the production of some seed even in years when potential pollinators are absent or in low numbers. Species of *Larrea,* at least those of warm desert regions, are opportunistic bloomers. Although the cues used by *Larrea* to initiate a bloom are probably also used as emergence cues by many of the insects that visit *Larrea* flowers, the timing is not always perfectly synchronized. A case in point was the spring of 1975 when the coldest April on record near Tucson delayed the flowering of many of the desert shrubs. Toward the end of April, there was sufficient ground moisture, proper day length, and temperatures sufficiently warm for *Larrea* to bloom. However, temperatures were apparently warm enough earlier to trigger the emergence of a number of the *Larrea*-specific bees that were thus forced to wait, in a sense, two weeks for their pollen host to bloom.

Another side effect of the ability of *L. divaricata* to produce viable seeds from self-pollinations would be the ability to establish colonies from single seeds. Biosystematic evidence (see Chapter 2) indicates that *Larrea* dispersed from South America to North America, probably over large areas of unfavorable habitat. The ability to produce populations from a single, long-

TABLE 4-1 *Breeding Experiments with* Larrea *Species.*

Treatment	Mean number of fertilized ovules per fruit ± standard error of mean (% carpel fill)		
	L. tridentata[a]	*L. divaricata*[b]	*L. cuneifolia*[c]
Undisturbed, untreated flowers and plants	.72 ± .07 (14)[d] 1,86 ± .11 (37.2)[e]	2.63 ± .27 (52.6)	2.57 ± .16 (51.4)
Undisturbed flowers experimental plants	.79 ± .09 (21.2)	–	3.52 ± .22 (71.2)
Untreated, bagged	.41 ± .08 (8)	.95 ± .27 (19)	.36 ± .22 (7.2)
Selfed, bagged	.82 ± .19 (16.4)	–	1.61 ± .39 (32.2)
Crossed, bagged	2.89 ± .18 (57.8)	–	3.76 ± .18 (75.2)

[a]Includes only tetraploid plants from the Tucson region.
[b]Includes only diploid plants near Andalgalá.
[c]Data from diploid plants near Andalgalá.
[d]Data from April 1973.
[e]Data from August 1974.

distance-dispersed individual would support this theory of the original colonization.

Inbreeding appears to occur more commonly in *L. nitida* and *L. ameghinoi* than in the larger-flowered species of the genus (see Figure 4-2). Hybrid derivatives under cultivation produced by natural crosses between these two species are both self-compatible and generally self-pollinating, which thus suggests that the parental types may also produce seeds by self-fertilization. The morphological characters of the small, somewhat cup-shaped flowers and the clustering of the anthers around the style at anthesis (see Figure 4-2) are often associated with self-pollination in other plant taxa. The presence of naturally occurring hybrids between the two taxa (Hunziker et al. 1969), however, demonstrates that outcrossing occurs and that inbreeding must be facultative.

REWARD STRUCTURE

All species of *Larrea* provide both pollen and nectar that are gathered by flower-visiting insects, but they differ in the relative amounts produced on a per flower basis (Table 4-2). The closer evolutionary relationship of *L. divaricata* to *L. tridentata* with each other than of either to *L. cuneifolia* (see Chapter 2) is reflected in the similarities of their nectar and pollen production even though they are not structural equivalents in the two desert scrub areas (see Chapter 3). The blooming patterns of *L. tridentata* near Tuc-

TABLE 4–2 *Floral Characters of* Larrea *in South and North America.*

Species	Flower width, mm	Flower depth, mm	Flower dry weight, gm	Mean number of flowers–per shrub per year and floral biomass per shrub/year	Pollen size in μ	Mean pollen per flower, mg	Total sugar[a] per flower, mg
L. tridentata North America	21.23 (6.2,62)	9.71 (1.2,62)	.0204 (9×10^{-6},78)	2765.57 56.42 gms	ca 22	1.88	.65
L. divaricata South America	20.54 (8.4,84)	10.09 (1.6,84)	.0215 (10^{-5},84)	NOT DETERMINED	24–34	1.87	.50
L. cuneifolia South America	25.0 (3.3,117)	10.54 (1.33,117)	.0164 (10^{-5},117)	3457.84 56.71 gms	ca 22	.71	.88

Note: Localities for each sample are as in Table 4–1; the numbers in parenthesis are the variance and sample size, respectively.
[a]For *L. tridentata* at Silver Bell our analyses have shown the sugars to be primarily glucose mixed with smaller quantities of fructose. Total sugar calculated by multiplying nectar quantity by the sugar concentration.

son and *L. divaricata* near Andalgalá are similar in that both of these taxa have an initial spring blooming peak, but individuals of both taxa may continue to bloom, usually at a low level, for a prolonged period of up to several months in relatively mesic wash or upper bajada situations. *Larrea tridentata* in the Avra Valley generally has a major second bloom in the summer if there is rainfall in July. In contrast, *L. cuneifolia,* occurring predominantly in the dry lower bajada and playa habitats near Andalgalá, typically blooms in short, intense bursts following the summer rainstorms. This trait is clearly a facultative response to moisture availability, since scattered individuals occurring in more mesic habitats with *L. divaricata* or along the edges of large washes bloom continuously from October until February or March, typically with only a few (one to ten) flowers per shrub each day.

Despite the differences in blooming patterns however, calculations show that in comparable areas of habitat (pure *Larrea* flats) and comparable years, individuals of *L. tridentata* and *L. cuneifolia* produce an equivalent biomass of flowers (see Table 4–2). Calculations by Barbour et al. (see Chapter 3) have shown that in similar areas of desert scrub habitat, *L. tridentata* and *L. cuneifolia* have similar vegetative biomass on a per hectare basis. These similarities suggest that the two species of *Larrea* that occupy the same parts of the desert scrub ecosystems studied apportion energy similarly to vegetative and floral structures.

While the total energy (measured as dry weight of flowers) put into flowering appears to be roughly equivalent in *L. tridentata* and *L. cuneifolia,* the distribution of that energy within the flowers of the two species is quite different. Individual flowers of *L. cuneifolia* produce only half as much pollen as those of either *L. divaricata* or *L. tridentata,* but 1.3 times as much total sugar in the nectar (see Table 4–2). An explanation of the differences might lie, in part, in the blooming patterns of the two species and the reward structure of other members of the communities in which each species occurs. Possibly because of its brief and unpredictable blooming pattern, *L. cuneifolia* relies heavily on generalist bees for pollen transfer. Such generalist feeders visit a broad range of pollen and nectar hosts in addition to *Larrea,* even while it is in bloom. For example, an analysis of the desert scrub communities at Andalgalá (Simpson, *in preparation*) shows that *Cassia aphylla,* one of the dominant species, often blooms at the same time as *L. cuneifolia.* Like all species of the widespread genus *Cassia,* this yellow-flowered legume is exclusively a pollen plant. Being unable to compete in terms of pollen production with a taxon that puts all of its energy into pollen, *L. cuneifolia* may emphasize a large sugar supply as the primary attractant for insects on the lower bajadas and flats near Andalgalá.

In more southern areas of Argentina, where *L. divaricata* rather than *L. cuneifolia* is the dominant desert flat species and in the Sonoran Desert where *L. tridentata* occurs, most of the dominant, coexisting insect-pollinated perennials produce abundant nectar. In these areas, pollen appears to be as important as, or more important than, nectar as the primary *Larrea* pollen vector attractant.

FLOWER VISITORS

In both desert scrub areas, the dominance of *Larrea* (up to 6,000 plants per hectare in practically pure stands) makes it a major source of food for flower visiting insects. Table 4-3 gives the major groups of animals found visiting the flowers of *Larrea* in the two desert scrub ecosystems and assesses their relative effectiveness as pollen transfer agents. As can be seen, they range from nectar-sipping hummingbirds to a wide variety of insect species, including beetles, flies, butterflies, moths, wasps, and bees. Many of these groups are undoubtedly of only marginal significance as either pollen vectors or pollen and nectar consumers, because they occur only infrequently on the flowers. Other insect flower visitors destroy floral parts when they consume various flower tissues and thus counteract the beneficial effect of any inadvertent pollen transfer.

Hummingbirds, most Lepidoptera, and many wasp species are typically infrequent visitors to *Larrea* flowers. This low rate of visitation, coupled with poor floral constancy and few morphological or behavioral adaptations that favor the pollen transfer of creosote bush flowers, renders most members of these groups insignificant pollinators. However, short-tongued wasps such as *Plesiomorpha* spp. in northern Argentina and *Myzinum* spp. in Arizona are often important visitors during the summer bloom. Such wasps are morphologically and ethologically well suited for *Larrea* pollen transfer. Occasionally during years of population buildup (and subsequent migration), a variety of butterfly and moth species may play important roles in *Larrea* pollination due to their abundance and the opportunity they may provide for long-distance pollen transfer. Prominent among such species observed near Andalgalá were *Ascia manusta, Tatochile autodice,* and *Libytheana carinata.* No similar phenomenon of outbreaks of butterflies were seen during the three-year study period around the Arizona site, but similar migrations are known to occur in the deserts of the southwestern United States.

A variety of ants, beetles (primarily Tenebrionidae, Scarabaeidae, and Meloidae), and a variety of Hemiptera are often observed visiting the flowers of *Larrea* at night. Nectar-feeding ants probably have little effect on fertilization, except to accentuate self-pollination and possibly to reduce nectar supplies for "legitimate" pollinators. Of more serious consequence is the behavior of leaf-cutting ants (Attini) that strip all buds and flowers from individual *Larrea* shrubs in both Arizona and Argentina. Damage inflicted by Hemiptera feeding on the cell sap of ovaries and buds and by beetles that consume anthers, petals, or entire flowers will also overshadow any occasional pollen transfer to flowers that subsequently abort. Certain species of Mel-

TABLE 4–3 *Major Groups of* Larrea *Flower Visitors at Silver Bell and Andalgalá.*

Family	Species	Abundance on *Larrea* flowers	Purpose of floral visit	Role as pollinators
Hymenoptera				
Bees				
Colletidae	*Colletes salicola* (NA)	Typically most abundant group at all locations and during all flowering seasons.	Adults feed on nectar and, to lesser extent, pollen. Non-parasitic females collect pollen and nectar to provision nests. Mating on flowers common. Some (*Megachile* spp.) collect petals for nest construction.	Dominant pollinator group. Good anther/stigma contact, high rate of inter-floral and inter-plant movement, particularly by pollen collecting females of larger species. Floral host specificity high in many species (N.A. & S.A.).
Halictidae	*Pseudagapostemon pampeanus* (SA)			
Andrenidae	*Ancylandrena larreae* (NA)			
Melittidae	*Hesperapis larrae* (NA)			
Oxaeidae	*Protoxaea ferruginea* (SA)			
Megachilidae	*Heteranthidium larreae* (NA)			
Anthophoridae	*Centris brethesi* (SA)			
Apidae	*Bombus opifex* (SA)			
Wasps				
Vespidae	*Polistes buysonni* (SA)	Most groups infrequent visitors.	Adults feed on nectar and, to limited extent, pollen. Some social vespoids collect nectar for larval provisions.	Minor role in pollination due to low visitation rates, low floral constancy and paucity of body hairs to facilitate pollen transport.
Sphecidae	*Ammophila* spp. (NA or SA)			
Pompilidae	*Pepsis* spp. (NA or SA)			
Tiphiidae	*Plesiomorpha* spp. (SA)			
Scoliidae	*Campsomeris tolteca* (NA)			
Ants				
Formicidae	*Acromyrmex versivolor* (NA) *Camponotus blandus* (SA)	Infrequently observed, primarily nocturnal.	Workers collect nectar or honeydew from flower-feeding Hemiptera. Leaf-cutting ants (Attini) often gather flower parts or buds for utilization in the nest.	Ant mediated cross pollination probably very rare due to infrequency of inter-plant visitation. May facilitate self-pollination.
Diptera				
Long-tongued flies				
Bombyliidae	*Bombyliius* spp. (NA or SA) *Anthrax* spp. (NA or SA) *Pthiria* spp. (NA or SA)	Common—particularly during warmer parts or season of day.	Primarily nectar feeders but some pollen consumption.	Minor role as pollinators—particularly longer tongued species with minimal contact of anthers or stigma. Shorter tongued species probably more efficient (*Anthrax* spp.).
Short-tongued flies				
Syrphidae	*Eupeodes volucris* (NA)	Infrequent—but occa-	Adults of many species are	Important pollinators where

Tachinidae	*Archytas* spp. (NA)	sionally locally abundant, particularly during cool, early spring.	major pollen consumers as well as nectar feeders.	common. Good anther/stigma contact by larger species. Low floral constancy.
Lepidoptera				
Butterflies				
Lycaenidae	*Thecla eurytulus* (SA)	Infrequent but occasionally locally abundant.	Adults feed on nectar.	Minor role as pollinators due to low visitation rates and poor anther/stigma contact by most species. Low floral constancy.
Pieridae	*Tatochile autodice* (SA)			
Moths				
Noctuidae	UNIDENTIFIED	Infrequent but occasionally locally abundant, primarily nocturnal.	Adults feed on nectar. Larvae of some species feed on buds and flower parts.	As above.
Geometridae				
Coleoptera				
Beetles				
Meloidae	*Pyrota postica* (NA)	Common, frequently locally abundant. Some species primarily nocturnal.	Most adults feed on buds, flower parts and/or pollen.	Minor role as pollinators due to infrequent inter-floral and inter-plant movement as well as destructive feeding habits.
Melyridae	*Trichochrus* spp. (NA)			
Tenebrionidae				
Scarabaeidae	*Phyllophaga* spp. (NA)			
Hemiptera				
Bugs				
Miridae	*Phytocoris covilleae* (NA)	Common—often locally abundant.	Adults and immatures suck juices from buds, ovaries and developing fruits.	Minor role as pollinators due to infrequent inter-plant and inter-floral movement and destructive feeding habits.
Pentatomidae	*Dendrocoris contaminatus* (NA)			
Aves				
Hummingbirds				
Trochilidae	*Chlorostilbon aureo-ventris* (SA)	Very infrequently observed.	Feeding on nectar and/or hunting flower feeding insects.	Very minor due to rarity of visitation and low floral constancy.

Note: These are only a few examples of many more families and species.
SA = South American site; NA = North American site.

oidae are doubly harmful for successful pollination because the adults feed on floral parts and the larvae are parasitic on bees (larvae), the most important group of pollinators of *Larrea.*

Second in importance to the bees are a variety of flies (particularly Bombyliidae and Syrphidae), which are frequent visitors of *Larrea* at both the Arizona and Argentina sites. In the cool early parts of the spring, large pollen-eating syrphid flies (i.e., *Volucella* and *Eupeodes* spp.) may be locally abundant in either region. During the warmer parts of the blooming season, several species of long-tongued bee flies commonly collect nectar on *Larrea.* Because of their long mouth parts and ability to reach the nectar without coming into contact with either the style or the anthers, most bombyliids are probably ineffective agents of pollen transfer. In addition, like many of the Meloidae, the larvae of many bombyliids are parasitic on bee nests.

BEES ASSOCIATED WITH *LARREA*

In terms of the number of species, the number of individuals visiting flowers, the amount of contact with anthers and stigmas, and the frequency of movement from flower to flower and shrub to shrub, bees are clearly the most important group involved in the pollination of *Larrea.* In both North and South America, a number of species appear to restrict pollen collecting exclusively to *Larrea* flowers and hence, when abundant, are of particular importance for seed production. These species are known as *Larrea* oligoleges or specialists, whereas those that forage on a wide range of plant species are known as polyleges or generalist collectors.

In the southwestern United States a survey of museum collections and literature revealed that more than 140 species of bees have been recorded visiting the flowers of *Larrea.* A comparable list for northern Argentina is not available. However, collections (Neff, *unpublished;* Hurd and Linsley 1975) have shown, as pointed out by Hurd (in Raven 1963), that no native bee species has a distribution completely overlapping that of *Larrea* in either North and/or South America. At the species level, the bee faunas visiting *Larrea* on the two continents appear to be completely distinct. Yet, there are at least thirteen genera of bees that have species visiting *Larrea* flowers in both the Sonoran Desert and the Monte. These include *Colletes, Caupolicana* (Colletidae); *Protoxaea* (Oxaeidae); *Augochloropsis, Dialictus, Sphecodes* (Halictidae); *Megachile, Anthidium, Coelioxys* (Megachilidae); *Exomalopisis, Anthophora, Melissodes, Centris, Xylocopa* (Anthophoridae); and *Bombus* (Apidae). This list of shared genera will undoubtedly grow as more extensive collections are made in South America and near the southern limits of *Larrea* in North America. Nevertheless, the generic similarities of some of *Larrea*-visiting bee species should not be taken to imply that there was a "direct" overland migration of *Larrea* with an attendant bee fauna from South to

North America. Virtually all of the shared genera are comprised primarily of polylectic species, and most are quite widespread throughout the Americas or even other continents. In the few instances where the species of shared genera are oligolectic or show a preference for *Larrea* pollen (i.e., *Colletes, Anthidium* and possibly *Megachile*), the *Larrea* specialists occur on only one of the two western continents. In the case of *Colletes,* several of the North American species appear to be oligolectic on *Larrea,* while a South American species was observed to have a high preference for *Bulnesia retama,* a related member of the Zygophyllaceae. Since the species of *Colletes* involved are not closely related to one another, their preference for collecting the pollen of zygophyllaceous plants would seem to be the result of convergence.

The independent evolution of the *Larrea* bee faunas of North and South America can be seen in the current distributions and apparent areas of origin of the oligolectic bees associated with *Larrea* on the two continents. In North America, species of *Colletes* (Colletidae); *Ancylandrena, Megandrena, Nomadopsis* and *Perdita* (Andrenidae); *Hesperapis* (Melittidae); *Hoplitis* and *Heteranthidium* (Megachilidae) have evolved oligolectic relations with *Larrea* (Hurd and Linsley 1975). With the exception of the virtually cosmopolitan genus *Colletes,* none of these groups are known to occur in South America. *Nomadopsis* appears to be derived from South American relatives of the *Liopoeum-Acamptopoeum* group of "rabbit-tailed" panurgines (Rozen 1958; Shinn 1967), most of which appear to be polylectic and none of which are known to be oligolectic on any member of the Zygophyllaceae (Neff, *unpublished*). *Ancylandrena* and *Megandrena* are very small genera restricted to the arid regions of the southwestern United States and adjacent Mexico. The former appears to be most closely allied with the large holarctic genus *Andrena,* while *Megandrena* may be related to the *Nomadopsis-Calliopsis* group of panurgines (Zavortink 1974). *Perdita* is an extremely large genus of very small bees characterized by oligolectic behavior and occurring primarily in the arid regions of northern Mexico and the western United States (Timberlake 1954). Oligolectic relations with *Larrea* appear to have arisen independently in at least two and possibly three distinct subgenera of *Perdita* (*Perdita s.s., Perditella* and *Pseudomacrotera;* see Hurd and Linsley 1975). *Hesperapis* is a member of the Melittidae, a small, relictually distributed family that is totally absent in South America. Of the megachilids, *Hoplitis* is a member of a large, holarctic group of genera absent in South America, while *Heteranthidium* is another small genus restricted to North America.

In South America *Larrea* specialists are known to occur in *Bicolletes, Lonchopria,* and possibly *Oediscelis* (Colletidae); an undescribed panurgine genus of the *Psaenythia-Pseudopanurgus* complex (Andrenidae); *Anthidium* and apparently *Megachile* (Megachilidae). *Bicolletes* and *Lonchopria* are members of the Paracolletini, a large, primitive, austral tribe of colletids with an apparent Gondwanaland distribution (Michener 1965). The small, dark panurgine bee, common on *Larrea* throughout the Monte, appears to be most closely related to a group centered in southern Argentina and Chile and allied to the *Psaenythia-Pseudopanurgus* lineage, a group of apparent South American origin (Timberlake 1973). *Megachile* is an extremely large, virtually cosmopolitan genus, but the species believed to share a close association with *Larrea* belong to the subgenus *Dactylomegachile,* a large South American group. Several subgenera of *Megachile* have distributions that bridge the North-South *Larrea* disjunction, but none contain members with close relationships to *Larrea.* The closest link with the North American bee fauna among the South American *Larrea* oligoleges is *Anthidium,* a genus that may have entered South America from North America via a Cordilleran route. However, none of the North American species of *Anthidium* are known to have evolved as close a relationship with *Larrea* as *Anthidium friesei* in Argentina.

Species of *Larrea* are not dependent on any single species of bee (or insect) for successful pollination. In both North and South America the taxonomic composition of the bee fauna visiting *Larrea* may vary drastically from locality to locality, within microhabitats at a given locality, within and between seasons, or even during different parts of the day. In addition, bee densities may range from dozens of individuals foraging per shrub on isolated, luxuriously flowering plants in washes or along roadsides to extreme cases where there are fewer than 10 per hectare even though blooming *Larrea* plants may exceed 600 per hectare.

Given this range of variation, our discussion of pollinator interactions will be restricted to the IBP primary sites at Andalgalá and Silver Bell, which were intensively sampled from 1973 to 1975. We must stress that the interactions found in these two areas should not be considered as the sole sets of relationships that may pertain throughout the northern Monte and the northern Sonoran Desert, respectively. Such interaction will change with alterations in local climate, microhabitat, and the composition of the plant community at given sites.

LARREA BEE COMMUNITIES AT SILVER BELL AND ANDALGALÁ

Despite the lack of specific similarity between the bees visiting *Larrea* at the two desert scrub sites, several aspects of the bee faunas appear to have converged in the disjunct systems. The total numbers of bee species visiting *Larrea* at the two sites are both large: 41 at Andalgalá and 28 at Silver Bell. The higher number of species associated with *Larrea* at the Argentine site is somewhat surprising considering the higher total bee species diversity at Silver Bell relative to Andalgalá: 188 versus 116 species, respectively. At both sites, however, the majority of records represent rare observations and thus species of probable minimal importance in *Larrea* pollination.

The number of species known to collect *Larrea* pollen and considered to be major *Larrea* pollinators or pollen consumers are quite similar: 16 at Andalgalá and 13 at Silver Bell. The number of *Larrea* specialists at both sites is identical: 6 at both Andalgalá and Silver Bell. If two species–*Hoplitis biscutellae* and *Megandrena enceliae,* which were very scarce at Silver Bell, but known to be *Larrea* oligoleges–from collections at other sites are added, the number at the northern site increases slightly. Several species from Andalgalá are possible *Larrea* oligoleges but were locally too rare to make any firm conclusions as to feeding preferences.

As noted earlier, the primary *Larrea* bloom occurs during the spring in Arizona, but there is often a considerable hiatus (up to a month or more) between the cessation of the winter rains and the onset of the bloom. The prerequisite for spring flowering thus appears to be a combination of moisture and temperature. The spring bloom is the more predictable over a large number of years than the summer equivalent. However, it too may be reduced or absent if there is extended drought. Consequently, the evolution of bees appears to have led to their utilization of the same cues for emergence as *Larrea* uses for blooming, which is probably a widespread phenomenon in oligolectic desert bees (Hurd 1957). In general, use of these cues minimizes the possibility of emerging and finding no host plants. Since the spring bloom is both the most extensive and reliable, it is the peak of activity for the majority of *Larrea* specialists (Table 4–4). Of the six species of *Larrea* oligoleges occurring at Silver Bell, only one, *Heteranthidium larreae,* is sufficiently common to be considered a dominant pollinator. In the case of all of the specialists, the system of synchronized cues is far from perfect. As mentioned earlier, during the unusually cool spring of 1975, both sexes of *Heteranthidium larreae* were found nectaring on spring annuals over two weeks before the initiation of the *Larrea* bloom.

The relationship of *Heteranthidium larreae* with its host appears to be particularly close. Males regularly patrol *Larrea* shrubs, and mating commonly occurs on or about the flowers. In addition, the females commonly collect small balls of *Larrea* resin for use in nest construction (MacSwain 1946; Neff and Simpson, *personal observations*).

Other major *Larrea* pollinators include *Centris pallida* and *Nomia tetrazonata,* both of which are polylectic species. *Centris pallida,* a robust, hairy species, normally forages primarily on *Cercidium microphyllum, C. floridum,* and *Olneya tesota* (all Leguminosae), but when they are not in flower, it often frequents *Larrea* for nectar and pollen. Due to its large population sizes and frequent movements from flower to flower, *C. pallida* is clearly a major *Larrea* pollinator. It is particularly abundant on upper bajadas and near washes, the primary habitats of its preferred *Cercidium* hosts.

One of the most striking features of the spring Arizona *Larrea* bloom is the apparent rarity of all pollinator groups over large areas. Bee populations tend to be concentrated in a limited set of favorable microhabitats where

TABLE 4-4 *Major Pollen Collecting Species of* L. tridentata *at Silver Bell, Arizona.*

Family, species	Degree of pollen specificity	Relative abundance on *Larrea*[a] Summer	Summer/fall	Est. pollination efficiency[b]	Body length in mm[c]	Relative biomass[d]	Comments
Colletidae							
Colletes covilleae Timberlake	oligolege of *Larrea*	+		2	♀ 7.5 ♂ 9.5	30 63	Relatively uncommon vernal species of Sonoran and Mojave deserts.
Colletes salicola Cockerell	polylectic–emphasis on *Larrea & Prosopis*	+		2	♀ 7.5 ♂ 9.0	30 54	Common vernal species.
Andrenidae							
Ancylandrena larreae Timberlake	oligolege of *Larrea*	+		3	♂ 10.5 ♀ 11.0	105 148	Locally abundant vernal species of Sonorana and Mojave deserts.
Perdita larreae Cockerell	oligolege of *Larrea*	+	+++	1	♂ 3.0 ♀ 4.0	1 2	Widespread–primarily Sonoran and Chihuahuan deserts, nectars on many diverse, taxa.
Perdita n. sp. A.	oligolege of *Larrea*	+		1	♂ 5.0 ♀ 5.0	2 4	Locally common in southwest Arizona (Silver Bell to Ajo).
Oxaeidae							
Protaxae gloriosa (Fox)	polylectic		++	3	♀ 18.0 ♂ 17.0	648 612	Abundant summer species of Sonoran Desert.
Halictidae							
Nomia tetrazonata tetrazonata Cockerell	polylectic	++	+	3	♀ 9.0 ♂ 9.0	94 94	Widespread multivoltine species.

Melittidae							
Hesperapis larreae Cockerell	oligolege of *Larrea*	++		3	♂ 7.0 ♀ 9.0	21 54	Widespread, abundant, vernal species.
Megachilidae							
Heteranthidium larreae (Cockerell)	Oligolege of *Larrea*	+++		4	♀ 11.0 ♂ 12.0	99 144	Widespread, abundant, vernal species.
Megachile sidalceae Cockerell	polylectic	+	+	3	♂ 12.0 ♀ 13.5	126 213	Widespread, and abundant, not restricted to desert areas.
Anthophoridae							
Centris cockerelli resoluta Cockerell	polylectic	++		3	♀ 12.0 ♂ 12.0	330 300	Common oil-collecting vernal species of Mojave and Sonoran deserts.
Centris pallida Fox	polylectic	++		3	♀ 17.5 ♂ 15.0	735 450	Abundant vernal species primarily associated with *Cercidium, Olneya* and *Dalea.*
Centris rhodopus Cockerell	polylectic	+	+	3	♂ 11.0 ♀ 14.0	248 350	Common oil-collecting species of Chichuahuan and Sonoran deserts.

[a]By season: + = rare or infrequent; ++ = common; +++ = abundant.

[b]Based on combination of morphological and behavioral characteristics including frequency of shrub-to-shrub movements; the scale is one (1) to four (4) with one indicating lowest efficiency and four the highest.

[c]Rounded to nearest 0.5 mm.

[d]Biomass per individual based on crude volume.

flowering is probably most predictable. Large, pure *Larrea* stands are consistently characterized by low pollinator densities.

In Argentina, the pattern of pollinator visitation to *L. divaricata* is similar to that observed in *L. tridentata* at Silver Bell. Occurring primarily in relatively mesic wash and upper bajada situations around Andalgalá, *L. divaricata* has a major bloom in the early spring following a normally rainless, cold winter. As in the case of Silver Bell, this bloom is the greatest period of activity for *Larrea* specialist bees, but due to a number of differences in the overall phenological pattern of the Argentina *Larrea* community, the demarcation is less distinct than that observed near Tucson. The spring bloom of *L. divaricata* appears to be more predictable than that of *L. tridentata* in Arizona, which may explain the fact that there are consistently higher densities of bees during the spring bloom of *L. divaricata* than during the spring bloom of *L. tridentata.* The dominant specialist species observed in the Bolsón (Table 4-5) was *Anthidium friesei,* which, like *Heteranthidium larreae,* mates on the flowers of *Larrea.* Instead of collecting *Larrea* resin for nest building, this species clips the trichomes from the fruits and uses them as nest construction material. A number of *Megachile,* including *M. leucographa,* are known to use *Larrea* petals for lining their nests. Nesting biologies of other Argentine bees are either unknown or show no close relationship with *Larrea.* As in North America, the majority of the solitary bees are ground nesting.

Other major specialist pollinators include an undescribed *Lonchopria* (Colletidae) and *Megachile leucographa* in addition to dominant polylectic species such as *Centris brethesi, Xylocopa splendidula,* and *X. ordinaria.*

Later in the summer in Arizona, intense localized rainstorms may trigger a second, quite patchy, *Larrea* bloom. During this summer bloom of *L. tridentata* (tetraploid) in Arizona, the most prominent *Larrea* visitors are two robust polylectic species, *Protoxaea gloriosa* and *Centris rhodopus,* but neither is particularly abundant. Numerically, the most abundant summer bee visiting creosote bush is *Perdita larreae,* an extremely small (about 3mm long) *Larrea* specialist. Like many of the tiny species of *Perdita,* it carefully works each anther of the flowers of its host plant to extract pollen that is apparently unavailable to the larger, more widely ranging species. Despite its abundance, several characteristics–minute size, limited foraging range and infrequent contact with the stigma–would appear to limit severely its role as an agent of cross-pollination.

In the region of Andalgalá, the summer rains are heavy and extensive and comprise most of the yearly precipitation. These summer rains trigger the mass flowering of *L. cuneifolia,* the dominant species of *Larrea* on the lower bajadas and playas. This summer bloom is typically very brief–that is, often lasting less than a week on the flats, but longer in microhabitats where water accumulates or when unusual weather conditions prevail. Subsequent rains may lead to as many as three distinct blooms before the onset of the winter drought, if a sufficient period of time for fruit maturation occurs between the periods of precipitation. There is also a resurgence of flowering in *L. divaricata* during the summer, but the level of flower production is considerably lower than in the spring.

During the summer blooms of *L. cuneifolia,* the most prominent visitors in the Bolsón de Pipanaco were the same *Megachile* that visits *L. divaricata* in the spring: the *Bicolletes stilborhina* (Colletidae) and a small undescribed panurgine bee. Although they are locally abundant, the distribution of these species tends to be quite patchy with concentrations occurring near major washes and on the upper bajadas, which is a pattern similar to that found in Arizona. On the broad, extensive *Larrea* flats, the most commonly encountered species are the polylectic bees, *Centris brethesi, Xylocopa spendidula,* and *Alloscirtetica arrhenica* (Anthophoridae), but all of these species occur at low densities away from the upper bajadas and washes. Since the dry, open flats are the principal habitat for *L. cuneifolia,* obviously the majority of its potential pollinators are a limited set of generalist bees.

None of the South American *Larrea* specialists appear to be restricted to either of the two species of *Larrea* as their sole pollen hosts, but the difference in habitat (see Chapter 2) and flowering times (see Chapter 3) of the two species of jarilla presumably reduce any potential interspecific competition for pollinators. In washes and upper bajadas, where *L. divaricata* and *L. cuneifolia* do occasionally occur and flower together, the bees visit both species. Foraging under these conditions tends to be concentrated on the individual plants of either species—that is, on the species whose plants have the greatest concentration of fresh flowers. At a site in Río Negro, where *L. divaricata, L. cuneifolia, L. nitida, L. ameghinoi,* and a number of hybrids grow and flower together, foraging was clearly concentrated on *L. divaricata* and *L. cuneifolia.* However, these two species were in comparatively fresh bloom whereas *L. nitida* and *L. ameghinoi* were in later stages of flowering with many old flowers and maturing fruits. Consequently, a consistent preference for the former two species may not exist.

In addition to differences in seasonal foraging periods and microhabitat preferences, a number of factors may contribute to the coexistence of several *Larrea* specialist bees at a given locality. One such method is diurnal partitioning of *Larrea* resources. Assuming that different species of bees have different thermal optima for foraging, the broad range of diurnal temperatures in the spring (21 to 26° C difference between the warmest and coldest parts of the daylight hours) would allow a ready basis for such segregation. Such partitioned foraging times have been documented by the extensive research of Hurd and Linsley (1975) in the southwestern United States. Observations in Argentina were insufficient to document clearly cases of diurnal segregation of *Larrea* resources, but *Xylocopa, Caupolicana, Centris,* and *Lonchopria* exhibited a predominance of foraging in the morning. More extensive investigations may reveal a pattern similar to that found in North America.

TABLE 4-5 *Major Pollen Collecting Species of* L. cuneifolia *and* L. divaricata *in the Bolsón de Pipanaco, Catamarca.*

Family, species	Degree of pollen specificity	Relative abundance on *Larrea*[a] Spring	Relative abundance on *Larrea*[a] Summer/fall	Est. pollination efficiency[b]	Body length in mm[c]	Relative biomass[d]	Comments
Colletidae							
Colletes furfuraceus Holmberg	polylectic	+	+	2	♂ 8.5	51	Widespread, most common *Colletes* of northern Monte.
					♀ 10.5	126	
Lonchopria n. sp. A.	oligolege of *Larrea* and *Bulnesia*	++	+	3	♀ 10.5	110	Locally abundant throughout northern Monte.
					♂ 10.0	88	
Bicolletes stilborhina Moure	oligolege of *Larrea*	+	++	2	♂ 7.0	16	Abundant throughout Monte.
					♀ 7.0	21	
Bicolletes n.sp. A.	oligolege of *Larrea*	+	+	3	♂ 8.0	60	Widespread but uncommon in northern Monte.
					♀ 8.0	60	
Andrenidae							
Liopoeum mendocinum Joergenson	polylectic	+		1	♂ 7.0	42	Abundant and widespread.
					♀ 8.0	84	
Near "*Pseudopanurgus*" n. sp. A.	oligolege of *Larrea*		+++	2	♂ 3.0	2	Locally abundant throughout Monte; sea level to 3,000+ meters.
					♀ 4.5	7	
Oxaeidae							
Protoxaea ferruginea (Friese)	polylectic		+	3	♂ 16.0	528	Common summer species of northern Monte, infrequent on *Larrea.*
					♀ 17.5	634	
Halicitidae							
Dialictus sp. A.	polylectic	+	++	1	♂ 4.0	3	Widespread in Monte, possibly a variable complex of related species.
					♀ 4.0	3	

Megachilidae							
Anthidium friesei Cockerell	oligolege of *Larrea*	+++		4	♂ 13.0 ♀ 11.0	260 192	Common throughout Monte; primarily vernal; sea level to 3,200+ meters
Epanthidium sanguinum (Friese)	polylectic	+	+	2	♂ 7.5 ♀ 9.0	56 68	Common species occurring in many temperate habitats.
Megachile aff. *leucographa*	probable *Larrea* oligolege	+++	+++	4	♀ 11.0 ♂ 9.5	149 114	Locally abundant on *Larrea.*
Megachile aff. *albo-punctata*	polylectic	+	+	3	♂ 12.0 ♀ 14.0	189 280	Widespread, locally abundant on *Prosopis.*
Anthophoridae							
Alloscirtetica arrhenica (Vachal)	polylectic		++	3	♂ 9.5 ♀ 10.0	114 140	Common summer species.
Centris brethesi Schrottky	polylectic	+++	+++	3	♂ 12.0 ♀ 12.0	330 363	Most ubiquitous and abundant species of northern Monte.
Svastrides zebra (Friese)	polylectic	+	+	3	♂ 12.5 ♂ 13.0	210 358	Locally abundant, particularly on *Prosopis.*
Xylocopa ordinaria Smith	polylectic	++	+	3	♂ 28.0 ♀ 28.0	2772 2772	Common and widespread.
Xylocopa spendidula Lepeletier	polylectic	+	+	3	♀ 17.0 ♀ 17.0	701 561	Common and widespread.

[a]By season: + = rare or infrequent; ++ = common; +++ = abundant.
[b]Based on combination of morphological and behavioral characteristics including frequency of shrub-to-shrub movements; the scale is one (1) to four (4) with one indicating lowest efficiency and four the highest.
[c]Rounded to nearest 0.5 mm.
[d]Biomass per individual based on crude volume.

A second basis for coexistence of *Larrea* bee specialists may be differential foraging methods. These differences are, however, often related to differences in foraging times. Individuals of small-bodied species can visit and harvest resources from a smaller number of flowers than the larger bodied species since they require less pollen and nectar. They can also harvest or scavenge the remaining pollen and nectar from flowers that have been previously visited by large species, which tend to forage upon only the most easily harvested pollen and nectar. The observation that the large bodied species indeed tend to forage primarily in the relatively cool early hours when pollen and nectar is most abundant, while the smallest species (e.g., *Perdita, Dialictus*) may be found scavenging pollen from virtually bare anthers during the midday heat strongly suggests a system of physiologically determined foraging periods.

As mentioned earlier, despite the large number of oligolectic and generalistic bee species that visit *Larrea* in either of the desert scrub areas, visits to the flowers of *Larrea* are often very scarce at any time of day, particularly away from the predictable habitats such as washes and upper bajadas. It seems probable that the yearly and seasonal fluctuations in the timing and intensity of the *Larrea* blooms tend to prevent large stable populations of flower-feeding taxa. Therefore, during a favorable year for flowering when *Larrea* produces abundant pollen and nectar, the resources remain incompletely exploited.

Selection has apparently favored diurnal partitioning of resources (at least in North America) and a narrow range of temperatures during which a bee species most efficiently forages. Although species survival may be ensured in poor *Larrea* blooming years, the tradeoff is that in good years, many species may not be able to expand their thermal ranges and more fully exploit the abundant resources. In addition, the flowering period may simply be so short (perhaps a week near Andalgalá) that even with synchronized cues for blooming and bee emergence, there is still insufficient time in any given season for bees to mate, construct, and provision enough nests to produce a highly dense population. The result of both these factors is that in years of copious flowering, there is a low bee–flower ratio. In 1973 and 1975 in Arizona, although good *L. tridentata* blooms occurred in the spring, the majority of flowers were found to have never been visited (as indicated by uncollected pollen or nectar). Crossing experiments (see Table 4–1) have shown that both *L. tridentata* at Silver Bell and *L. cuneifolia* will produce a higher seed set under artificial cross-pollination than under natural circumstances. Since the number of potential pollinators relative to the number of *Larrea* flowers is higher in average or poor years, there should be more successful fertilization (and probably cross-fertilization) on a per flower basis in a poor rainfall year than in a good rainfall year.

The variation in average number of seeds produced per capsule under natural conditions is illustrated by the varying reports of Chew and Chew

(1965) for California, Valentine and Gerard (1969) for New Mexico, and those in Table 4-1 for *L. tridentata* in Arizona. Chew and Chew reported an average of 3.03 seeds per capsule (60.6 percent carpel fill) whereas Valentine and Gerard found an average of 1.76 seeds per fruit (35.36 percent carpel fill). In our studies (see Table 4-1), average seed set in nature was only 0.72 (14 percent carpel fill) in the abnormally wet, heavy blooming season of the spring of 1973. In the rather dry summer of 1974, during which there was sporadic blooming of *Larrea* near Tucson, the average number of seeds per capsule was 1.86 (37.2 percent carpel fill). All of these numbers are given on the basis of the number of seeds in fruits that matured and do not reflect the number of flowers that were produced since those that did not expand fruits were not counted.

The predominantly self-pollinating *L. nitida* and *L. ameghinoi,* which occur in a far more limited range of habitats than either *L. divaricata* or *L. cuneifolia,* are found primarily in the cold, windy areas of southern Argentina where pollinating insects of all types tend to be scarcer than in warmer climates. There is a definite selective advantage in turning to inbreeding and the attendant reduction of energetic costs for the attraction of pollinators.

SUMMARY

All five species of *Larrea* have the same floral pattern of cup-shaped yellow flowers with five free petals, ten anthers, and a superior globose ovary. They differ in the size of their flowers and the degree to which the anthers reach and are pressed against the stigmas. Experimental data and floral morphology suggest that these differences are related to the amount of natural self-pollination. Experiments have shown that all of the species are self-compatible, but that *L. tridentata* (tetraploid), *L. cuneifolia,* and *L. divaricata* exhibit an increasing series in their levels of natural self-pollination. Floral morphology of *L. nitida* and *L. ameghinoi* indicates that they depend heavily on self-pollination. The dominance of *Larrea* in New World warm desert scrub ecosystems and the resultant relative abundance of flowers make *Larrea* an important source of food for floral herbivores. Both pollen and nectar are offered by the five species as rewards for potential pollen vectors, but the relative amounts of each produced appear to depend on the rewards of the flowers of sympatric, synchronously blooming species. Although a variety of animals visit the flowers, bees are the most abundant and diverse group of floral visitors in all *Larrea* desert areas and are undoubtedly the most important pollinators of the creosote bush. At the two IBP desert scrub study sites, the *Larrea* bee faunas are, for the most part, taxonomically unrelated, but show convergence in the number of species considered to be major pollen vectors (16 in Andalgalá; 13 at Silver Bell) and in the number of obligate specialists on *Larrea* (6 in each area). In addition, the two bee faunas show convergence in temporal and behavioral foraging patterns that permit their coexistence on the same floral host.

RESUMEN

Las cinco especies de *Larrea* poseen el mismo patrón floral consistente en flores cupuliformes y amarillas, con cinco pétalos libres, diez anteras y ovario superior globoso. Difieren en el tamaño de las flores y en el grado de desarrollo y de contacto que alcanzan las anteras, en relación con los estigmas. Los datos experimentales y la morfología floral sugieren que estas diferencias están relacionadas con el grado de autopolinización natural. Se ha demostrado, por medio de cruzas experimentales, que todas las especies son autocompatibles, pero que *L. tridentata* (tetraploide), *L. cuneifolia* y *L. divaricata* muestran una serie decreciente en los niveles de autopolinización natural. Las morfologías florales de *L. nitida* y *L. ameghinoi* indican que estas especies dependen en gran parte de la autopolinización. La dominancia de *Larrea* en los ecosistemas de matorral de los desiertos cálidos del Nuevo Mundo y la resultante abundancia relativa de flores, hacen de *Larrea* una fuente importante de alimento para los herbívores florales. Los cinco especies proveen polen y néctar como recompensas para los vectores polínicos potenciales, pero las cantidades relativas producidas de cada uno perecen depender de las recompensas de las flores de especies simpátricas con floración sincrónica. Aunque una variedad de animales visita las flores, las abejas son el grupo más abundante de visitantes florales en todas las áreas desérticas de *Larrea* y son, sin duda, los polinizadores más importantes de este arbusto. En los dos sitios de estudio de matorral desértico del IBP, las especies de abejas de *Larrea* no están, en su mayoría, taxonómicamente muy relacionadas, pero muestran convergencia en el número de especies consideradas como principales vectores polínicos (16 en Andalgalá; 13 en Silver Bell) y en el número de especialistas obligados de *Larrea* (6 en cada una de las áreas). Además, las dos faunas de abejas muestran convergencia en los patrones temporales y de conducta en la colecta de alimento, lo cual permite la coexistencia en el mismo huésped floral.

5

The Natural Products Chemistry of *Larrea*

T. J. Mabry, D. R. DiFeo, Jr., M. Sakakibara, C. F. Bohnstedt, Jr., and D. Seigler

Because members of *Larrea* represent dominant shrubs in both the Arizonan and Argentine ecosystem sites as demonstrated in the previous chapters, *Larrea* was selected for comprehensive analysis of its natural products (waxes, volatiles, saponins, and especially phenolics, including notably flavonoid aglycones and glycosides and NDGA). The chemical studies were designed to establish not only the external and internal natural products (both qualitatively and quantitatively) elaborated by the *Larrea* taxa in the ecosystem sites, but also the patterns of variation throughout the ranges of these taxa in order to determine the role these substances play in the ability of *Larrea* to flourish in desert ecosystems.

Our chemical studies have concentrated upon the tetraploid *L. cuneifolia,* which dominates in the Argentine study site, and the South American-North American *L. divaricata-L. tridentata* complex, of which the tetraploid of the latter taxon dominates in the Arizona study site. The chemical analysis of the *L. divaricata-L. tridentata* complex was of particular interest, because these taxa represent one of the most puzzling examples of North American-South American disjuncts, and the chemical data were expected to aid in understanding the origin of the complex.

One of the first chemical investigations of any *Larrea* taxa was Waller and Gisvold's 1945 report of *L. tridentata*'s natural products:

> One, if not the most active, of the bacterial agents present in *Larrea tridentata* Cov. has been characterized as nordihydroguaiaretic acid, m. p. 184–185° C. This is the first recorded instance of the isolation of this compound in nature.
>
> A wax has been isolated that is composed of esters. Saponification yielded an acid and an alcohol fraction. The melting point of the acid fraction indicates it to be a mixture of C_{28} and C_{26} acids. The alcohol fraction appears to consist mainly of a C_{30} alcohol.
>
> The nonsaponifiable portion of the petroleum benzin extract yielded a small amount of a sterol fraction which melted at 126–128° C and was apparently a mixture.

A yellow flavonol with an auxochromic group in position 5 has been isolated and partially characterized.

An orange-colored flavonol that has an auxochromic group in position 5 has been isolated and partially characterized.

Although *Larrea tridentata* has a marked characteristic aromatic odor, only a very small amount of volatile oil has been obtained upon steam distillation (0.1%).

Although alkaloids have been purported to be present in *Larrea tridentata,* the usual alkaloidal tests failed to reveal the presence of alkaloids.

Sucrose was isolated and identified.

From this meager beginning, we now have knowledge of the detailed structures of over one hundred natural products from *Larrea* taxa from both North and South America and have considerable comparative data, both qualitative and quantitative, for many of the natural products elaborated by members of this genus.

In this account of the natural products chemistry of *Larrea* and related taxa, all comparative data that are available for the several taxa are presented along with isolated chemical results obtained for individual populations, ploidy levels, and species. In the final section of the chapter, the way these chemical data bear upon the controversy regarding the origin of the *L. divaricata–L. tridentata* complex are discussed briefly.

NORDIHYDROGUAIARETIC ACID (NDGA) AND RELATED LIGNANS

In terms of its natural products chemistry, *Larrea* is best known for the large quantities of nordihydroguaiaretic acid (1 in Figure 5-1) that are deposited on the external surfaces of the leaves (see Perry et al. 1972 and Thaker 1971 for physical properties of NDGA). Until recently, the creosote bush remained the best commercial source of this excellent antioxidant. We and others have found that approximately 5 to 10 percent of the dry weight of the leaves of *L. tridentata* consists of NDGA (see, for example, Chapter 6).

In an excellent account of the history, chemistry, and applications of NDGA that appeared in 1972 (Oliveto) was the notation that this powerful antioxidant was prepared for the first time in 1918 (Schroeter et al.) by reduction and demethylation of guaiaretic acid (2 in Figure 5-1), a constituent of guaiac gum (from *Guaiacum officinale* L., *G. sanctum* L., and *Bulnesia sarmientoi* Lor. ex Griseb.). The structure of NDGA was later confirmed by synthesis (Haworth 1934; Sugimoto and Okumura 1956). In the early 1940s NDGA was found not only to be the major constituent of the resinous exudate of *L. tridentata* (Waller 1942; Waller and Gisvold 1945) but also to be an excellent antioxidant for fats and oils (Lundberg 1944). The creosote

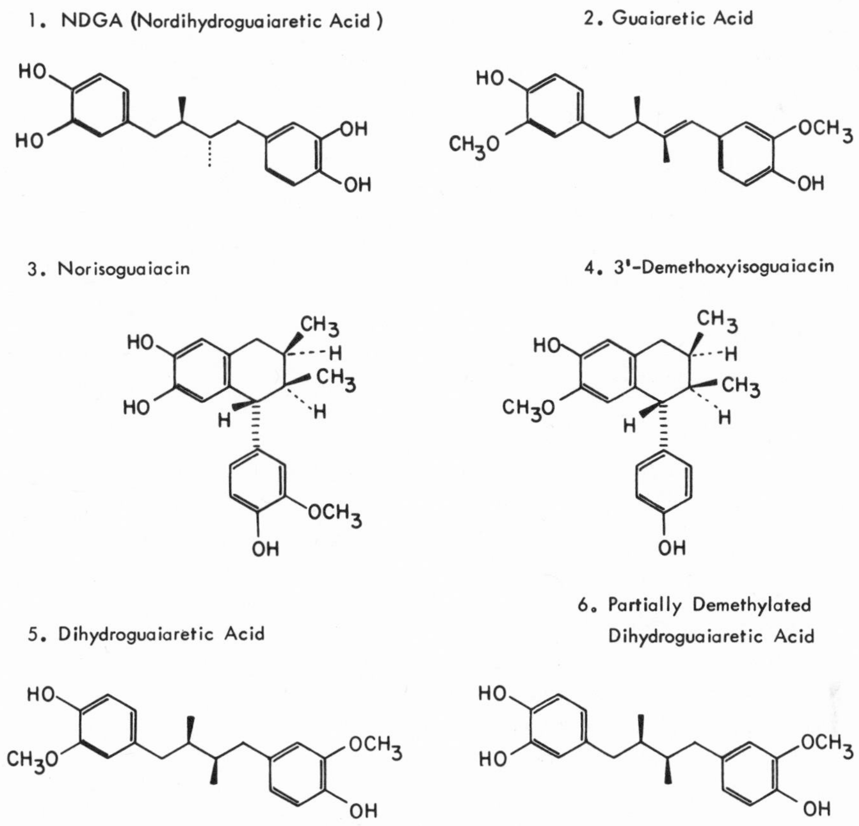

1. NDGA (Nordihydroguaiaretic Acid)

2. Guaiaretic Acid

3. Norisoguaiacin

4. 3'-Demethoxyisoguaiacin

5. Dihydroguaiaretic Acid

6. Partially Demethylated Dihydroguaiaretic Acid

FIGURE 5-1. *Lignans from* L. tridentata.

bush was the major source of NDGA for use as an antioxidant in foods (beginning in 1943) until a synthesis satisfactory for commercial purposes was described in 1972 (Perry).

The high reactivity of NDGA to oxygen and especially the high chemical reactivity of the oxidized NDGA (an ortho di-α-β-unsaturated quinone) to hydroxyl and amine groups probably accounts for its effectiveness as a defense substance against herbivores (see Chapter 6).

NDGA has been detected in all species of *Larrea.* Moreover, Gisvold and Thaker (1974) reported four lignans structurally related to NDGA: Norisoguaiacin (3 in Figure 5-1), 3′-demethoxyisoguaiacin (4 in Figure 5-1), dihydroguaiaretic acid (5 in Figure 5-1), and partially demethylated dihydroguaiaretic acid (6 in Figure 5-1) from a Tucson, Arizona, population of *L. tridentata.* The relative quantities of NDGA produced by all ploidy levels of *L. tridentata* is the same when bulk collections of plant material are used, but variation of the quantity in individual leaves (of different ages) can be detected (see Chapter 6).

FLAVONOIDS

The role most flavonoids play in plants is unknown; nevertheless, several functions have been established for flavonoids including notably the antimicrobial activity of many of them (see McClure 1975). Of interest is the fact that one dihydroflavanone and two dihydroflavonols were found to serve as primary attractants for the dark beetle, *Scolytus mediterraneus,* which attacks and inflicts much damage to deciduous fruit trees in Israel (Levy et al. 1974).

Flavonoid Aglycones

The natural products on the surface of fresh *L. divaricata* and *L. tridentata* leaves constitute about 14 percent of the weight of the leaves, and of this 14 percent at least 80 percent of the material can be accounted for in the phenolic fraction, with the major phenolic constituent being NDGA (1 in Figure 5-1). A complex array of 19 flavone, flavonol, and dihydroflavonol methyl ethers provide remarkable structural diversity to the phenolic material (Table 5-1 and Figures 5-2 and 5-3) and hence generalistic-defensive ability for the plant.

Despite reports of flavonoids in *L. divaricata* as early as 1945 (Waller and Gisvold 1945; Horn and Gisvold 1945), the first account of detailed structures of flavonoids in the genus was our 1972 description of the structures and properties of eleven flavonoid aglycones from *L. cuneifolia* (Valesi et al. 1972).

More recently, Chirikdjian (1973a, b) isolated and identified eight flavonoids from *L. tridentata.* As shown in the figures, five of these are aglycones: kaempferol (21), kaempferol 3-methyl ether (isokaempferid) (19), quercetin, isorhamnetin (16), and quercetin 3-methyl ether. Quercetin and quercetin 3-methyl ether have not yet been identified by our group from any species of *Larrea.*

Our flavonoid aglycone analysis of *Larrea* emphasized the species occurring in or near the primary study sites, namely *L. tridentata* (all three ploidy levels), *L. divaricata,* and *L. cuneifolia.* In addition, the two remaining species, *L. nitida* and *L. ameghinoi,* and several taxa closely related to this group were screened for their flavonoid patterns.

Nineteen flavonoid aglycones were isolated and fully characterized from the hexaploid race of *Larrea tridentata* (Sakakibara et al. 1976); three of the constituents, gossypetin 3,7,3′-trimethyl ether (7), gossypetin 3,7-dimethyl ether (8) and herbacetin 3,7-dimethyl ether (9), were recently described as new natural products from this taxon (Sakakibara et al. 1975; Sakakibara and Mabry 1975). Two other flavonols, quercetin 3,7,3′-trimethyl ether (11) and quercetin 7,3′,4′-trimethyl ether (12), were reported as new natural

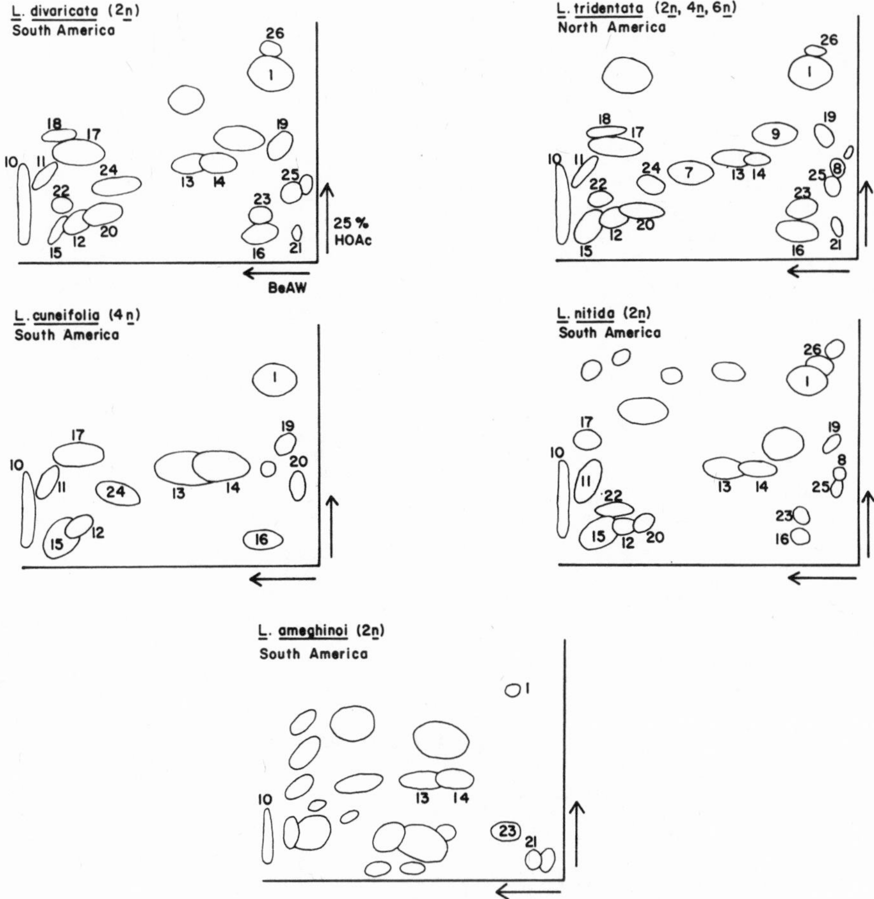

FIGURE 5-2. *Chromatographic profiles of flavonoid aglycones from* Larrea.

products from *L. cuneifolia* (Valesi et al. 1972). The remaining flavonoids were previously known.

No qualitative differences were observed for the flavonoid aglycones in the resin among the three ploidy races of *L. tridentata* that occur over a southeast-northwest range of more than a thousand miles in the United States and Mexico; moreover, the internal flavonoid glycoside patterns (see later comments on the glycosides), as determined by two-dimensional paper chromatography, were also identical except for a probably recently derived population in Querétaro, Mexico (150 miles northwest of Mexico City), which contained all the aglycones and all but two of the glycosides. Two of the three flavonols that are distinguished by having hydroxyl groups at the 8-position were also observed in *L. divaricata* from Peru, but not Argentina, which thus indicates more chemical variation in the resin of *L. divaricata* than

TABLE 5-1 *Flavonoid Aglycones of* Larrea.

	L.t.	L.d. (Arg.)	L.d. (Peru)	L.c.	L.n.[a]	L.a.[b]
7 Gossypetin 3,7,3′-trimethyl ether	+	–	–	–	–	–
8 Gossypetin 3,7-dimethyl ether	+	–	+	–	–	–
9 Herbacetin 3,7-dimethyl ether	+	–	+	–	–	–
10 Quercetin 3,7,3′,4′-tetramethyl ether	+	+	–	+	+	+
11 Quercetin 3,7,3′-trimethyl ether	+	+	–	+	+	o
12 Quercetin 7,3′,4′-trimethyl ether	+	+	–	+	+	o
13 Quercetin 3,7-dimethyl ether	+	+	–	+	+	+
14 Quercetin 3,3′-dimethyl ether	+	+	+	+	+	+
15 Quercetin 7,3′-dimethyl ether	+	+	–	+	+	o
16 Quercetin 3′-methyl ether	+	+	+	+	+	–
17 Kaempferol 3,7-dimethyl ether	+	+	–	+	o	o
18 Kaempferol 3,4′-dimethyl ether	+	–	+	o	o	o
19 Kaempferol 3-methyl ether	+	+	+	+	o	–
20 Kaempferol 7-methyl ether	+	+	+	–	+	o
21 Kaempferol	+	+	+	–	–	o
22 Luteolin 7,3′-dimethyl ether	+	+	–	–	+	+
23 Luteolin 3′-methyl ether	+	+	–	–	+	+
24 Apigenin 7-methyl ether	+	+	–	+	–	o
25 Apigenin	+	+	–	+	+	o
26 Dihydromyricetin 3′,5′-dimethyl ether	+	+	+	–	o	–

Note: + = present; – = absent; 0 = not detectable by paper chromatography.
[a]Compounds are determined by paper chromatography only; *L. nitida* contains 7 unknown spots besides the ones marked.
[b]Compounds are determined by paper chromatography only; *L. ameghinoi* contains 17 unknown compounds besides the ones marked.

in the resin of *L. tridentata* despite the fact that the latter contains three chromosomal races.

As we can see from these data, a greater overall difference of flavonoid aglycones exists between the Peruvian and Argentine *L. divaricata* than exists between the Peruvian *L. divaricata* and the North American *L. tridentata* or between the Argentine *L. divaricata* and *L. tridentata*. These data strongly suggest a more ancient isolation of this Peruvian population than the separation of the North American *Larrea* from the South American *Larrea*. The data also provide strong evidence against the "way-stations" of Raven (1963).

Another indication that more interpopulational chemical variation occurs in *L. divaricata* than in *L. tridentata* is the distributional data for kaempferol 3,4′-dimethyl ether (18), which is produced sporadically and in low quantity by *L. tridentata* and not at all by *L. divaricata* in Argentina; yet it is one of the major components in the Peruvian *L. divaricata*.

Our data show a close relationship between the Argentine *L. divaricata* and *L. tridentata* since there is a difference of only three of the twenty major flavonoid aglycone resin components. Comparison of the flavonoid aglycone

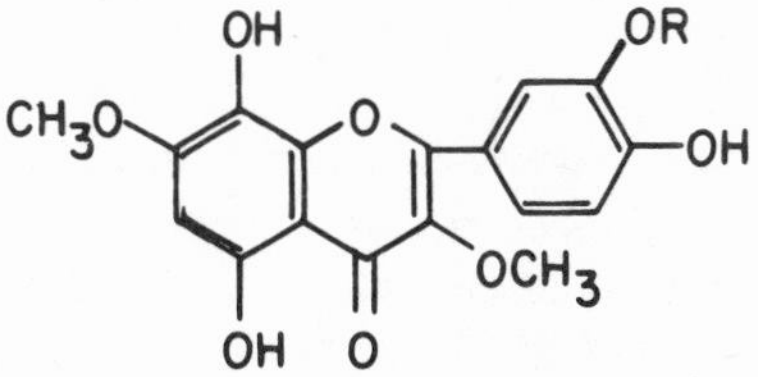

(7) R = CH_3
(8) R = H

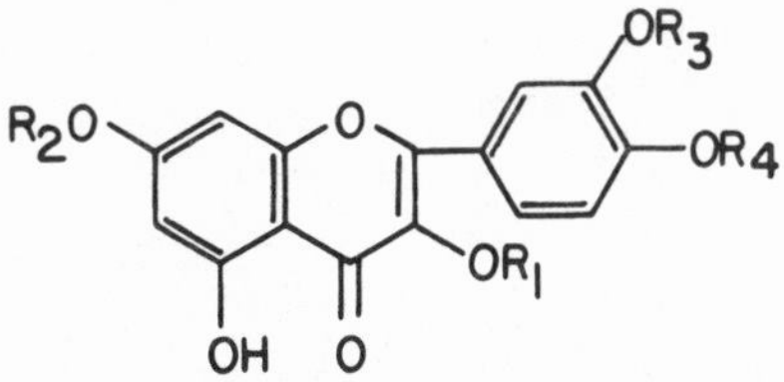

(10) R_1, R_2, R_3, R_4, = CH_3
(11) R_1, R_2, R_3, = CH_3 ; R_4 = H
(12) R_2, R_3, R_4, = CH_3 ; R_1 = H
(13) R_1, R_2 = CH_3 ; R_3, R_4 = H
(14) R_1, R_3 = CH_3 ; R_2, R_4 = H
(15) R_2, R_3 = CH_3 ; R_1, R_4 = H
(16) R_3 = CH_3 ; R_1, R_2, R_4 = H

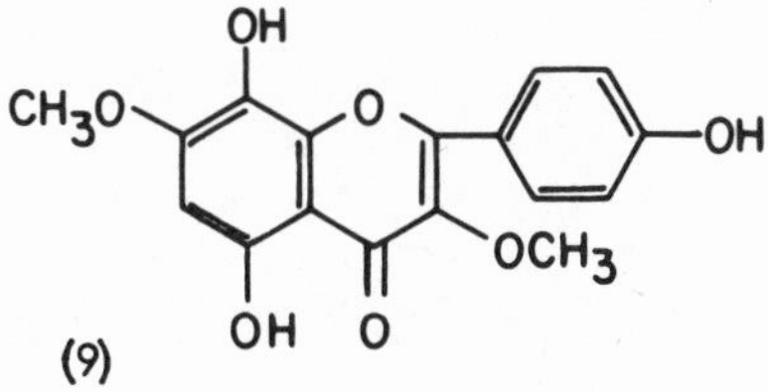

(9)

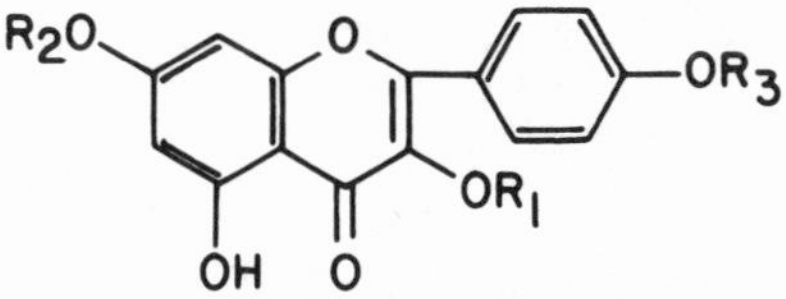

(17) R_1, R_2 = CH_3 ; R_3 = H
(18) R_1, R_3 = CH_3 ; R_2 = H
(19) R_1 = CH_3 ; R_2, R_3 = H
(20) R_2 = CH_3 ; R_1, R_3 = H
(21) R_1, R_2, R_3 = H

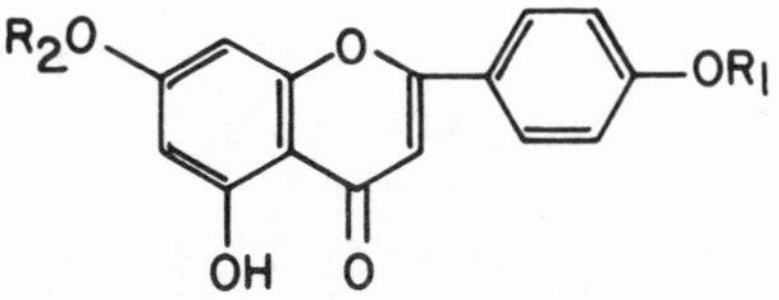

(24) R_2 = CH_3 ; R_1 = H
(25) R_1, R_2 = H

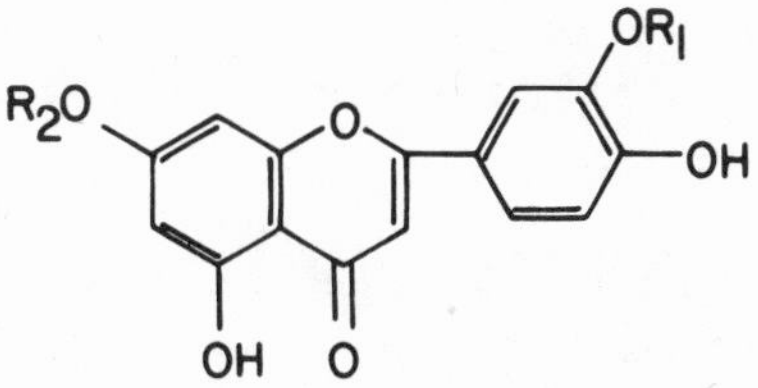

(22) R_1, R_2 = CH_3
(23) R_1 = CH_3 ; R_2 = H

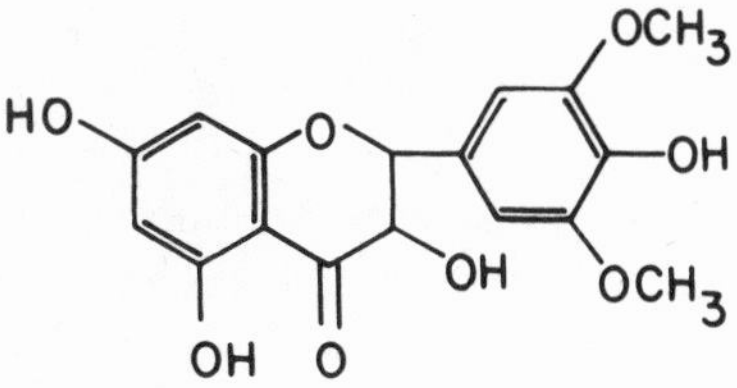

(26)

FIGURE 5-3. *Flavonoid aglycones from* Larrea.

data for *L. cuneifolia* with the more complex patterns detected in *L. divaricata* shows a difference of 8 compounds, primarily as a result of the absence of flavones and the 8-hydroxy flavonols in *L. cuneifolia.* Thus, at this time, our chemical data indicate that within section *Bifolium, L. divaricata* (n = 13) is closer to *L. tridentata* (n = 13, 26, 39) than to *L. cuneifolia* (n = 26), even though *L. cuneifolia* is an amphidiploid containing one genome of *L. divaricata* (see Chapter 2; see also Yang 1970; Hunziker et al. 1972b). Our preliminary chemical results for *L. nitida* and *L. ameghinoi* clearly distinguish them from section *Bifolium.*

These latter two species, *L. nitida* and *L. ameghinoi,* seem to form two distinct groups with the former being closer to section *Bifolium* since the latter produces the most distinct resinous coating, containing the lowest quantity of NDGA and having chalcones and aurones in addition to flavones and flavonols.

Several taxa closely related to *Larrea* were also examined for flavonoid aglycones. *Sericodes greggii,* the taxon from North America suggested to be most closely related to *Larrea* by Porter (1974), was found to be devoid of aglycones as were the South American taxa, *Bulnesia retama, B. schickendanzii,* and *Plectrocarpa tetracantha.*

Flavonoid Glycosides

The flavonoid glycosides produced by *Larrea* taxa represent a complex array of phenolic constituents occurring internally in the leaves (Table 5-2 and Figures 5-4 and 5-5). Unlike flavonoid aglycones, the glycosides are water soluble and are thus not suitable as an external resin; on the other hand, they are soluble in the cell sap and can be transported inside the cell. The chemical diversity afforded the leaves by these glycosides may represent a major defensive system against microorganisms.

A total of 18 flavonoid glycosides were detected by two-dimensional chromatography from all taxa of *Larrea.* Of these, 16 are found in *L. tridentata* and 17 in *L. divaricata.* The number of flavonoid glycosides in *L. cuneifolia, L. nitida,* and *L. ameghinoi* is 8, 7, and 8, respectively, with *L. cuneifolia* and *L. nitida* each producing one unique compound. Each pattern is species specific.

Kaempferol 3-rhamnoglucoside (nicotiflorin) (29), quercetin 3-O-glucoside (isoquercetrin) (30), and quercetin 3-O-rhamnoglucoside (rutin) (31) were isolated and identified by Chirikdjian (1973a, b) from *L. tridentata.* In addition to these, we have detected apigenin 6,8-di-C-glucoside (vicenin-2) (27), chrysoeriol 6,8-di-C-glucoside (28) and isorhamnetin 3-O-rhamnoglucoside (32) in *L. tridentata* (Mabry et al., *unpublished data*).

We have detected sulphated flavonoids (41, 43) in *L. tridentata* and *L. divaricata.* Since these compounds are apparently not produced by any of the other species, this finding indicates another chemical link between

TABLE 5-2 *Flavonoid Glycosides of* Larrea.

Spot no.[a]	*L. divaricata*	*L. tridentata*	*L. cuneifolia*	*L. nitida*	*L. ameghinoi*
27	+	+	+	+	+
28	+	+	–	–	–
29	+	+	–	–	–
30	+	+	–	–	–
31	+	+	+	+	+
32	+	+	+	+	+
33	+	+	+	+	+
34	+	+	+	+	+
35	+	+	+	+	+
36	+	+	+	–	–
37	+	+	–	–	+
38	–	–	–	–	+
39	+	+	–	–	–
40	+	+	–	–	–
41	+	+	–	–	–
42	+	–	–	–	–
43	+	+	–	–	–
44	–	–	–	+	–

Note: + = present; – = not detected.
[a]As compared to chromatographic profiles Figure 5-3.

L. tridentata and *L. divaricata.* In addition, we might note that this finding is also the first report of these unusual types of compounds in the Zygophyllaceae.

All taxa produce one or more members of each class of flavonoid (i.e., flavone O-glycoside, flavone C-glycoside, and flavonol O-glycoside) which thus indicates a similar biosynthetic capability in all taxa.

Population studies for flavonoid glycosides of *L. divaricata* from Argentina and *L. tridentata* from North America show no intrapopulational variation in the twenty populations examined over both ranges. Moreover, the glycosides of the Peruvian *L. divaricata,* unlike the flavonoid aglycones, are not different from those found in the Argentine *L. divaricata.* As mentioned earlier, minor variation was detected in one population of *L. tridentata* in an isolated valley in the state of Querétaro, Mexico; this probably recently derived population has lost the ability to produce (or accumulate) two flavone C-glycosides that are present in other populations of *L. tridentata.*

WAX ESTERS FROM *L. TRIDENTATA* AND *L. DIVARICATA*

The presence of a waxy material from *L. tridentata* was observed by Waller and Gisvold (1945) who reported some of its physical and chemical

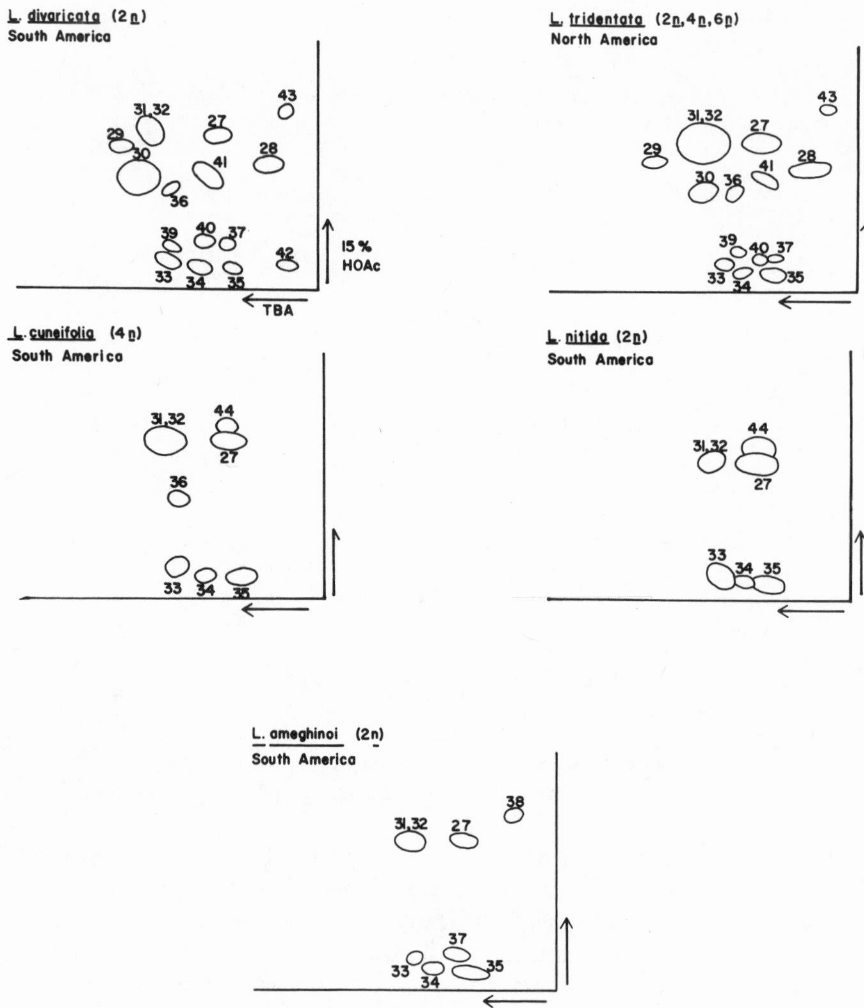

FIGURE 5–4. *Chromatographic profiles of flavonoid glycosides from* Larrea.

properties; the wax is, in many respects, similar to carnauba wax. Because these workers only saponified the wax and, on the basis of rather limited data (primarily melting points), concluded it was composed of C_{26} and C_{28} fatty acids and a C_{30} primary alcohol, the waxy material from the stems and leaves of *L. tridentata* was reinvestigated (Seigler et al. 1974). The yields of waxes from *L. tridentata* and *L. divaricata* are summarized in Tables 5-3 and 5-4. All samples examined contained a similar quantity of waxes—that is, approximately 0.1 percent dry weight of the stems.

The NMR and IR spectra of the recrystallized fraction obtained from the petroleum ether extract of *L. tridentata* stems showed no absorptions other

27. Vicenin ; R = H

28. Chrysoeriol 6,8 - di - C - glucoside ; R = OCH_3

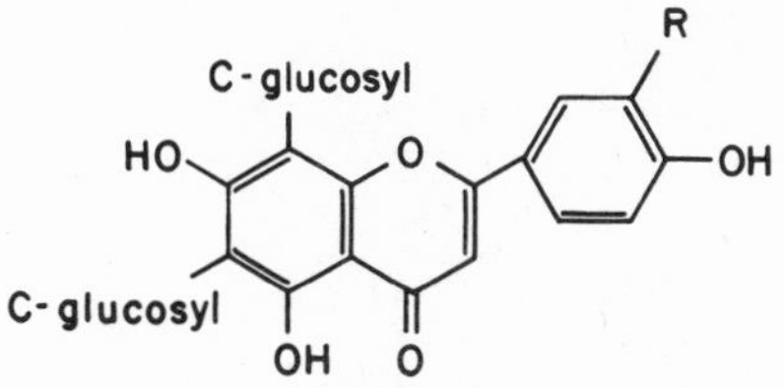

29. Kaempferol 3 - 0 - rhamnosylglucoside

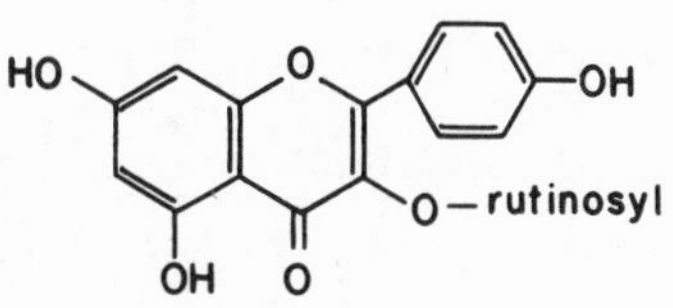

30. Isoquercitrin ; R_1 = glucosyl ; R_2 = H

31. Rutin ; R_1 = rhamnosylglucoside ; R_2 = H

32. Isorhamnetin 3 - 0 - rhamnosylglucoside ;
R_1 = rhamnosylglucoside ; R_2 = CH_3

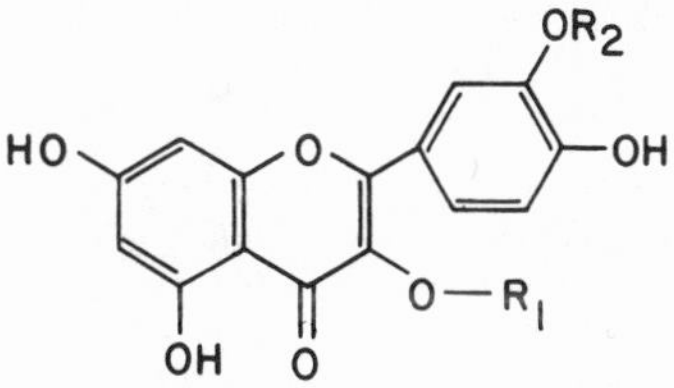

FIGURE 5-5. *Flavonoid glycosides from* Larrea.

than those corresponding to alkyl esters consisting of long chain primary alcohols and fatty acids. The protons in the NMR spectrum were assigned as follows:

$$\underset{d}{CH_3} - \underset{c}{(CH_2)_x} - \underset{a}{CH_2} - 0 - \overset{O}{\overset{\|}{C}} - \underset{b}{CH_2} - \underset{c}{(CH_2)_y} - \underset{d}{CH_3}$$

a = 4.10 ppm δ, overlapping triplets

TABLE 5-3 *Yield of Waxes from* L. tridentata *and* L. divaricata.

	Stems (g)	Wax esters (g)	% Yield
L. divaricata	50	0.081	0.16
L. tridentata			
diploid	440	0.470	0.11
tetraploid	78	0.081	0.10
hexaploid	370	0.479	0.13

b = 2.30 ppm δ, overlapping triplets
c = 1.27 ppm δ, broad, intense peak
d = 0.95 ppm δ, overlapping distorted triplets

On the basis of GC and MS data (using MS procedures described by Aasen et al. 1971), we concluded that the wax esters from *L. tridentata* are composed of several compounds, most of which correspond to those summarized in Table 5-5.

Comparative data for the wax esters of all *Larrea* taxa (Seigler et al., *un-*

TABLE 5-4 *Composition of the Wax Ester Extracts of* L. tridentata *and* L. divaricata.

m/e	Relative % *L. divaricata*	Relative % *L. tridentata* (2*n*)	Relative % *L. tridentata* (4*n*)	Relative % *L. tridentata* (6*n*)
564	0.8	1.0	0.5	0.9
592	1.8	0.6	0.7	0.6
606	–	0.9	0.5	0.4
620	15.3	1.9	2.6	1.6
634	2.9	1.3	1.2	1.2
649	24.8	9.5	15.1	10.9
663	3.2	2.3	2.6	2.4
676	24.8	25.3	26.4	21.9
690	2.4	3.8	3.5	3.2
704	13.9	25.3	26.4	32.8
718	1.0	3.4	3.3	3.6
732	5.7	15.8	11.3	13.7
746	–	1.2	1.4	1.4
760	2.4	5.1	2.6	4.0
774	–	0.6	0.5	5.0
788	0.8	1.5	2.3	0.7
816	0.4	0.3	0.9	0.4

TABLE 5-5 *Relative Percentage Composition of* Larrea tridentata (2n) *Wax as Calculated from GC and MS.*

Wax Ester	Acid	Alcohol	m/e	Relative Percentages (GC)	(MS)
C_{46}	C_{22}	C_{24}	676.7	4.8	
C_{48}	C_{22} C_{24}	C_{26} C_{24}	704.7	16.5	14
C_{50}	C_{22} C_{24} C_{26}	C_{28} C_{26} C_{24}	732.6	27.0	27
C_{52}	C_{22} C_{24} C_{26} C_{28}	C_{30} C_{28} C_{26} C_{24}	760.8	29.0	27
C_{54}	C_{24} C_{26} C_{28} C_{30}	C_{30} C_{28} C_{26} C_{24}	788.7	16.9	21
C_{56}	C_{26} C_{28} C_{30} C_{32}	C_{30} C_{28} C_{26} C_{24}	816.8	6.15	11

published) indicate no significant differences in the amount and chemical makeup of these surface substances. Basically, the data suggest that the genetic mechanism controlling production of waxes in *Larrea* was present in the pre-*Larrea* ancestor and is in accord with the view that the wax plays a role in the adaptation of the shrubs of *Larrea* to the arid climate it now occupies.

SAPONINS FROM *L. TRIDENTATA*

Saponins (nortriterpene glycosides) have recently been reported to represent about 10 to 15 percent of the dry weight of *L. tridentata* leaves. Moreover, the structures of two of the sapogenins that occur internally in the leaves as glycosides have been determined, namely, larreagenin A and larreic acid (Figure 5-6; see also Habermehl and Möller 1974).

The evolutionary importance of the production of saponins by *Larrea* as well as their potential importance for man have only now begun to be considered. At the time of preparation of this manuscript we have been unable to confirm the high saponin content in *Larrea;* reinvestigations of the Habermehl and Möller report are warranted.

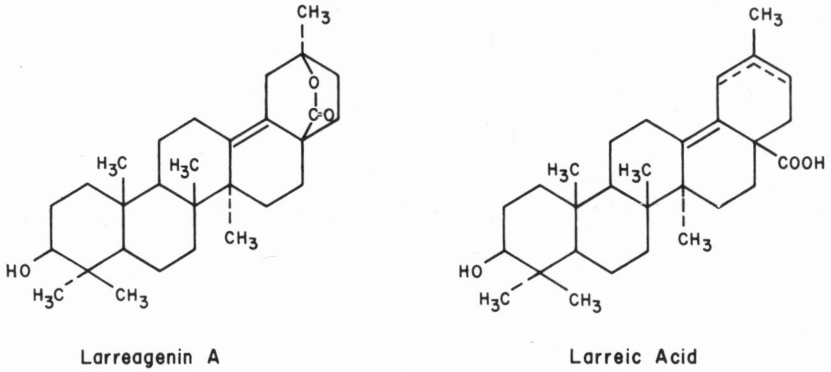

FIGURE 5-6. *Sapogenins from* L. tridentata.

VOLATILE CONSTITUENTS OF *LARREA*

Volatile constituents of plants function in a variety of ways including pollinator attractants (Dodson et al. 1969) and allelopathic inhibitors (Muller 1965; Muller and Moral 1966). In some instances, the volatile constituents also serve as cues to aid insects seeking feeding and breeding grounds (Rudinski 1966; Bedard et al. 1969).

Of the compounds listed in Table 5-6, the vinyl ketones have been detected as consistent major constituents in all taxa except *L. ameghinoi.* The highly volatile substances camphene, limonene, borneol, camphor, 2-dodecanone, and 2-undecanone have been detected in all taxa of *Larrea.*

In 1945 Waller and Gisvold reported that steam distillation of *L. tridentata* yielded a small amount (0.1 percent) of volatile oil. In our investigation we found that the steam distillation of fresh *Larrea* leaves affords 0.1 to 0.2 percent of a complex mixture of volatiles (Figure 5-7); the complexity of the pattern is much greater than evident from a single GC run since an individual GC peak often represents several compounds. Thus while a typical GC run exhibits about 100 peaks and shoulders, the actual number of compounds present is several hundred, of which about 100 account for more than 90 percent of the total oil.

The compounds that have been identified to date from *Larrea* (Table 5-6 and Figure 5-8) are differently derived from the isoprene, fatty acid, and shikimic acid pathways.

Comparison of the volatile constituents of *Larrea* species, ploidy levels of *L. tridentata,* and hybrids between various *Larrea* taxa indicates that all taxa of *Larrea* share much of their volatile chemistry. Of the compounds listed in Table 5-6 the monoterpene hydrocarbons, borneol, camphor, benzaldehyde and the 2-ketone compounds (2-dodecanone and 2-undecanone) have been detected in all three North American ploidy levels of *L. tridentata.* The South American taxa have the monoterpene hydrocarbons in common

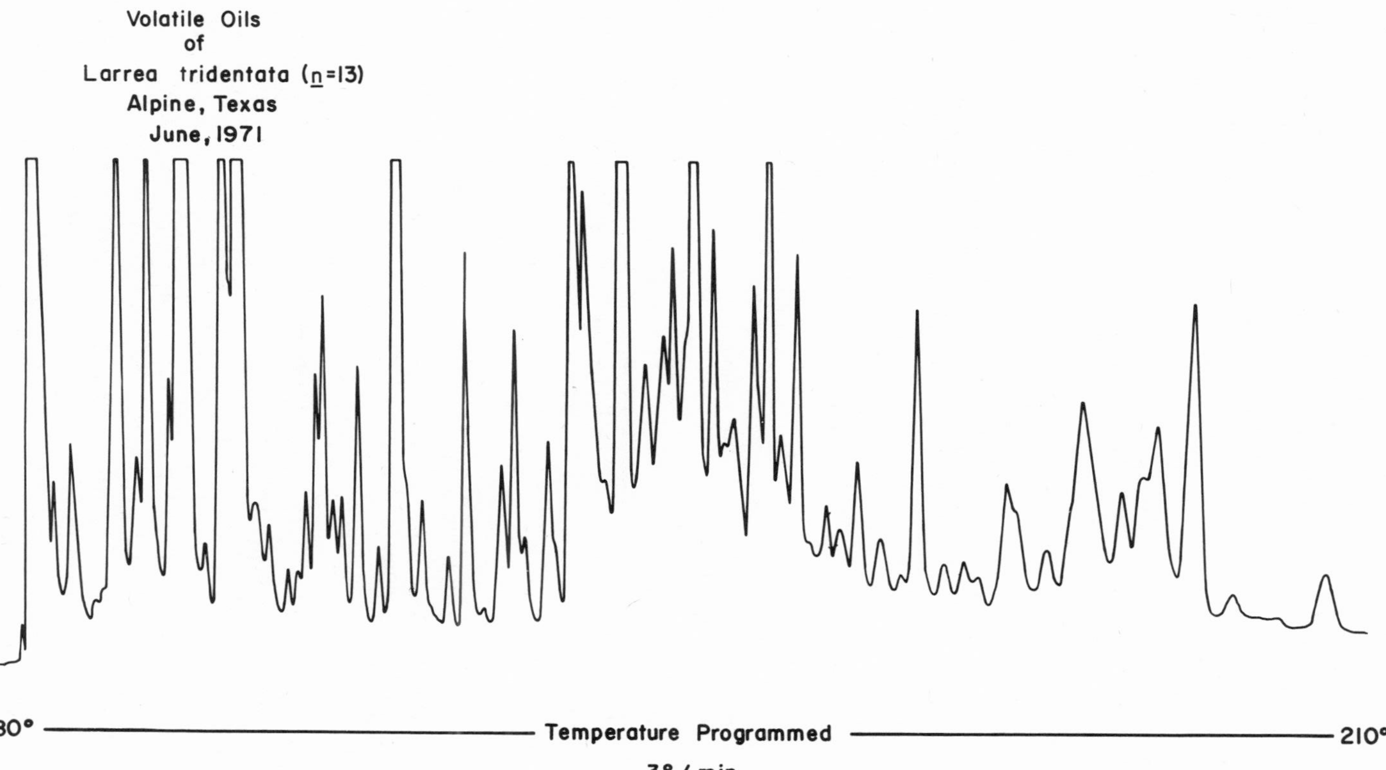

FIGURE 5-7. *GC pattern of volatiles from* Larrea.

TABLE 5–6 *Identified Volatiles of* Larrea.

Monoterpene hydrocarbons	*Aromatics*
α-pinene	benzaldehyde
Δ-3-carene	*p*-cymene
limonene	benzyl acetate
camphene	benzyl butanate
	o-methyl anisate
Oxygentated monoterpenes	ethyl benzoate
linalool	methyl naphthalene
borneol	1,2-dihydro-1,5,8-trimethyl-naphthalene
camphor	
bornyl acetate	*Miscellaneous*
Sesquiterpene hydrocarbons	*n*-tridecane
α-curcumene	*n*-tetradecane
calamenene	*n*-tricosane
β-santalene	2-heptanone
cuparene	2-nonanone
α-bergamontene	2-undecanone
edulane	2-dodecanone
	2-tridecanone
Oxygenated sesquiterpenes	2-tetradecanone
β-eudesmol	2-pentadecanone
farnesol	3-hexanone
α-agarofuran	3-hexanol
	hexanal
	3-hexen-1-yl acetate
	isobutyric acid
	1-hexen-3-one
	1-hepten-3-one
	1-octen-3-one

with the North American taxa. Apparently, the volatile chemistry, although very complex, is qualitatively rather similar throughout the genus and varies only quantitatively among the species.

COMPARATIVE DATA FOR TOTAL NATURAL PRODUCTS FROM *LARREA* AND RELATED TAXA

Comparative data for the amount and types of chemical constituents present in (and on) all taxa of *Larrea* have been obtained. The amount of resin obtained with diethyl ether on the external surface of the leaves ranges from 7.70 to 12.31 percent dry weight of the leaves; moreover, dry versus fresh material does not alter the quantities of extractable natural products

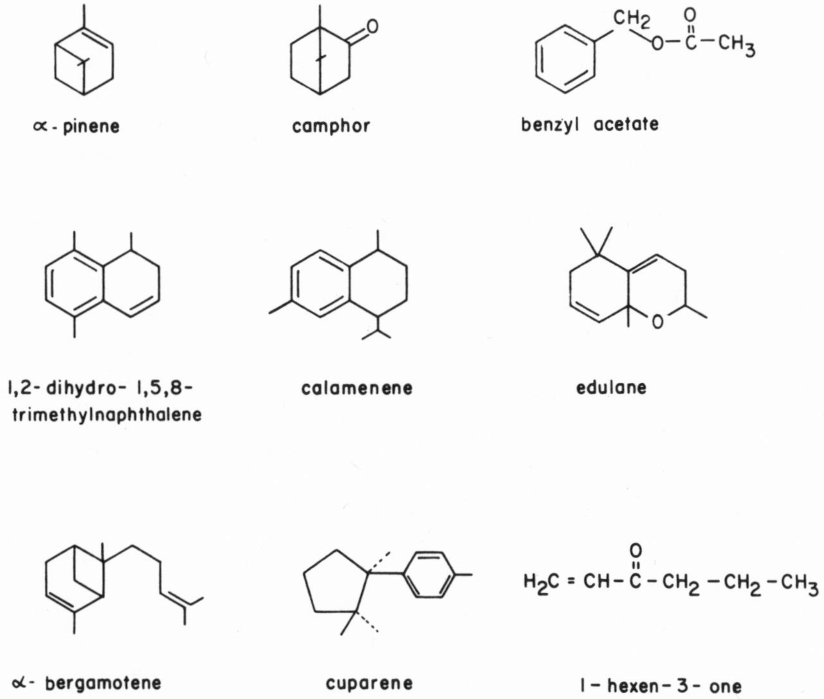

α - pinene

camphor

benzyl acetate

1,2- dihydro- 1,5,8- trimethylnaphthalene

calamenene

edulane

α- bergamotene

cuparene

$H_2C = CH-\overset{O}{\overset{\|}{C}}-CH_2-CH_2-CH_3$

1 - hexen- 3 - one

FIGURE 5-8. *Volatile structural diversity in* Larrea.

(Table 5-7). Other solvents afforded lower yields of compounds but more chlorophyll.

The extraction procedures remove the external resin and subdivide it into phenolics (e.g., flavonoids and NDGA), neutrals (e.g., waxes), basics (e.g., alkaloids), and acidics (e.g., phenolic acids) (Table 5-7). An interesting note is that *L. nitida* contains the highest quantity of resin (23 percent of the dry leaf material) and the prostrate cold-desert species, *L. ameghinoi,* the lowest (about 8 percent).

For all taxa the phenolic portion contains the largest amount of material ranging from 83 percent of the total extract in *L. ameghinoi* to 91 percent in the diploid *L. tridentata.* The phenolic material in all cases accounts for 83 to 91 percent of the external resin: (1) *L. tridentata,* diploid and hexaploid (91 percent in both cases); (2) *L. tridentata,* tetraploid, *L. divaricata,* and *L. cuneifolia* (86 percent, 89 percent and 89 percent, respectively), and (3) *L. ameghinoi* and *L. nitida* (83 percent in both cases).

A minute quantity of basic constituents (alkaloids and/or amines) is present in all plants, with extractable quantities ranging from 0.04 g to 0.05 g (0.2 to 0.5 percent of the total extract).

The neutral and acidic substances constitute only a slightly larger amount

TABLE 5-7 *Amounts of Compounds by Class Present on the External Leaf Surface of* Larrea.

Taxa	Phenolics	Neutrals	Basics	Acidics	Total Extract
North America					
L. tridentata					
diploid	16.50[a] (91.4%)[b]	0.80 (4.1%)	0.05 (0.3%)	0.70 (3.9%)	18.05
tetraploid	12.33 (86.3%)	1.35 (9.5%)	0.04 (0.3%)	0.57 (3.9%)	14.29
hexaploid	16.15 (91.2%)	0.90 (5.1%)	0.05 (0.3%)	0.60 (3.4%)	17.70
South America					
L. divaricata	13.80 (88.5%)	1.40 (9.0%)	0.04 (0.3%)	0.35 (2.2%)	15.59
L. cuneifolia	11.01 (88.9%)	0.92 (7.4%)	0.04 (0.3%)	0.42 (3.4%)	12.39
L. ameghinoi	6.43 (83.1%)	0.88 (11.4%)	0.04 (0.5%)	0.39 (5.0%)	7.74
L. nitida	19.40 (83.2%)	2.20 (9.4%)	0.05 (0.2%)	1.66 (7.1%)	23.31

[a]Percent of extract from dry leaf material.
[b]Percent of specific extract as related to total extract.

of the total resin than do the basic compounds. A striking feature of these neutral and acidic fractions is that *L. ameghinoi* produces a relatively higher percentage of both types of material when compared to its phenolic constituents and to its total extract, even though *L. nitida* produces more of both quantitatively (Tables 5-7 and 5-8).

The data indicate that the two study site species, *L. cuneifolia* and the tetraploid of *L. tridentata,* both produce almost the same amount of each type of material, while *L. ameghinoi* produces the lowest amount of each overall.

Our view is that while most of the structural nature of natural products produced by a plant depends upon its ancestry rather than the present ecosystem that it inhabits, its detailed qualitative and quantitative pattern of chemical components is associated with current pressures in the ecosystem.

ON THE ORIGIN OF *LARREA*

As to the origin of *L. tridentata* in North America, three different views are generally considered (see Chapter 2). Although our data do not fully resolve the controversy regarding the origin of *Larrea,* they do bear upon this question, as well as upon the nature of the polyploidy in *L. tridentata.* The lack of chemical differences between the diploid, tetraploid, and hexaploid races of *L. tridentata* in North America provides strong evidence that the latter two are autoploids. The detection in the South American taxa not only of essentially all the biosynthetic machinery found in the North American *Larrea* but also of many different compounds, as well as the lack of varia-

TABLE 5-8 *Relative Amounts of Ether and 85 Percent Aqueous Methanol Soluble Natural Products in* Larrea.

	External Et_2O extract	Internal Et_2O extract	Total Et_2O extract	85% aqu. MeOH extract after Et_2O extraction	Total extractable material
L. tridentata					
diploid	18.90[a]	1.39	20.29	17.45	37.83
tetraploid	15.25	1.48	16.73	17.69	34.42
hexaploid	18.40	1.50	19.90	18.79	38.69
L. divaricata	15.80	1.10	16.90	15.02	31.92
L. nitida	24.46	1.09	25.55	18.15	43.70
L. ameghinoi	8.60	2.39	10.99	20.15	31.14
L. cuneifolia	12.53	0.93	13.46	20.24	33.70

[a]As percent of plant material that is soluble.

tion in the flavonoid chemistry of *L. tridentata* and considerable variation of the flavonoids of *L. divaricata* from Peru and Argentina, suggests a relatively recent origin for the North American populations from a more ancient *L. divaricata*-like South American progenitor.

SUMMARY

The external resin chemistry of two of the South American *Larrea* species, *L. cuneifolia* and *L. divaricata,* and the North American ploidy complex (n = 13, 26, 39) of *L. tridentata* was established; the former two are dominant vegetational elements in the Monte, while the tetraploid of the latter occurs in the Silver Bell bajada site. In addition to the lignan NDGA (nordihydroguaiaretic acid), more than twenty flavonoid aglycones were found to be resin constituents. Moreover, various *Larrea* taxa were compared for their external wax chemistry and internal flavonoid glycoside patterns. The structures of a number of essential oils elaborated by several of the *Larrea* species along with two sapogenins from *L. tridentata* were described.

The available comparative natural products chemistry of *Larrea* is in agreement with cytological and morphological data that indicate that the genus originated and underwent species diversification in South America; the chemistry further suggests that *L. tridentata* is an autoploid complex derived from a South American *L. divaricata*-like progenitor. Finally, the chemical studies indicate that natural products patterns in this genus are evolutionarily conservative and may not directly reflect coevolution with other elements in presently occupied ecosystems.

RESUMEN

Se estableció la composición química de la resina externa de dos de las especies sudamericanas de *Larrea, L. cuneifolia* y *L. divaricata,* así como la del complejo poliploide (n = 13, 26, 39) de *L. tridentata* de Norteamérica; las dos primeras son elementos dominantes de la vegetación en el Monte, en tanto que el tetraploide de la última ocurre en el sitio de bajada Silver Bell. Se encontraron como constituyentes de la resina, además de lignano NDGA (ácido nordihidroguayarético), más de 20 agluconas de flavonoides. Por otra parte, se compararon entre sí las composiciones químicas de la cera externa de varios taxa de *Larrea,* al igual que los patrones internos de glucósidos de flavonoides. Fueron descritas las estructuras de varios aceites esenciales elaborados por varias de las especies de *Larrea,* así como dos sapogeninas de *L. tridentata.*

La información disponible comparativa de los productos naturales de *Larrea* se encuentra en concordancia con los datos citológicos y morfológicos que indican que el género se originó y sufrió diversificación de especies en Sudamérica; el estudio químico de los productos naturales sugiere además que *L. tridentata* es un complejo autoploide derivado de un progenitor sudamericano parecido a *L. divaricata.* Finalmente, los estudios químicos indican que los patrones de productos naturales en este género son, en el sentido evolutivo, relativamente conservadores y pueden no reflejar directamente coevolución con otros elementos en ecosistemas ocupados en la actualidad.

6

The Antiherbivore Chemistry of *Larrea*

D. F. Rhoades

A substantial literature has accumulated that implicates many plant secondary chemicals as defensive substances directed against herbivores, pathogens, and other plants (see Wallace and Mansell 1976; van Emden 1973; Schoonhoven 1972). Most work on antiherbivore chemistry has centered on substances with known or implied toxic effects on metabolic processes occurring within the herbivore. Alkaloids, isothiocyanates, nonprotein amino acids, hormone analogues, steroid glycosides, and cyanogenic substances, to name a few, are all thought to act in this way.

A notable exception to this approach has been provided by the work of Feeny (1970) on the interaction between the winter moth (*Operophtera brumata* L.) and the pedunculate oak (*Quercus robur* L.). Seasonal occurrence of winter moth larvae was correlated with the nitrogen and condensed tannin content of the oak leaves—that is, the larvae feeding in the early spring when leaf nitrogen content was high and tannin content low. Deleterious effects of condensed tannins on the larvae were postulated to occur by a complexing between the tannins and oak leaf proteins to disrupt proteolysis and reduce nitrogen availability. Thus, in this mode of defense the key chemical interaction occurs in a region that is topologically external to the herbivore (its gut), and the observed "toxic" effects are due to starvation. The widespread occurrence of tannins in the leaves and other tissues of woody perennial plants (Bate-Smith and Metcalf 1957) attests to the importance of digestibility reduction as a defense mode. Rhoades and Cates (1976) have calculated that ∿80% of woody perennial dicotyledonous plant species and ∿15% of annual and herbaceous perennial dicot species contain tannins.

The following studies on the antiherbivore defenses of *Larrea tridentata* of North America and *Larrea cuneifolia* of Argentina provide evidence that the resinous phenolic constituents of these plants deter grazing by their protein-complexing and digestibility-reducing properties in a fashion that is similar to tannin action. In addition, the phenoloxidase systems of these plants may enhance the digestibility-reducing capacities of the resins.

THE PHENOLIC RESIN OF *LARREA* SPECIES

Larrea tridentata and *L. cuneifolia* are characterized by the presence of diethyl ether-soluble phenolic resin on the surface of the leaves and terminal stems. Within the plants a concentration gradient of resin exists (see Tables 6-1 and 6-8) that decreases from young to mature leaves.

For preliminary work (see Tables 6-1, 6-2, 6-3, 6-4, and 6-8) leaves were divided into two age classes. Young leaves were defined as the youngest, terminal, still-folded leaf pair at the spray tip, and mature leaves were defined as the remaining leaves occurring at various node positions down the sprays, excluding senescent leaves. For later work (see Tables 6-9 and 6-15 and Figure 6-5) in which properties of leaves at individual node positions were investigated, the terminal, still-folded leaf pairs were defined as tips and the remaining progressively more mature leaves were labeled in terms of their node position by counting nodes back from the tip. Thus leaf pair 1 was defined as those leaves at node position 1, the first node below the tip. Leaf pairs 5-6 or 5-8, for instance, refer to leaves at both the 5th and 6th nodes from the tip or those at the 5th, 6th, 7th and 8th nodes from the tip, respectively.

In the case of *L. cuneifolia* (March 16, 1974, Andalgalá, Catamarca Province, Argentina) the young leaves contained 44 percent (d.w.) resin as opposed to 15 percent resin for mature leaves (see Table 6-8). In the case of *L. tridentata* (April 25, 1973, Avra Valley near Tucson, Arizona) the young leaves contained 26 percent resin versus 10 percent resin for mature leaves (Table 6-1).

Over 80 percent of the resin of both species is composed of phenolic aglycones, the major component of which is nordihydroguaiaretic acid, or NDGA (Figure 6-1), which is a lignan catechol (Duisberg et al. 1949). Total catechol content of the resin, estimated as molybdate-positive material and expressed as % NDGA by the method of Duisberg et al. (1949), averages 41 percent for leaf pairs tip-4 of *L. tridentata* and 31 percent for leaf pairs tip-6 of *L. cuneifolia*. The remainder of the resin is a complex mixture of partially O-methylated flavones and flavonols (see Figure 6-1) together with small quantities of other neutral, acidic, and basic materials (see Chapter 5).

The within-plant distribution of resin and catechols reported here appears to contrast with the findings of Duisberg (1952a) who found that the concentrations of 95 percent ethanol-soluble "resin" and "NDGA" were higher in "mature" (33.8 percent resin, 8.9 percent NDGA, dry weight), than in "young" growth (27.9 percent, 5.2 percent) of *L. tridentata* (diploid).

Two factors may contribute to this differrence. First, the "resin" and "NDGA" of Duisberg were determined as, or from, 95 percent ethanol-soluble material, as opposed to diethyl ether-soluble material in the present study. However, this fact is probably of secondary importance since positive correlation between amounts of ether and alcohol-soluble extractives can be expected.

TABLE 6-1 *Chemical Properties of Mature and Young Leaves of* L. tridentata.

Fresh weight % composition	Mature leaves	±S$\bar{x}$	Young leaves	±S$\bar{x}$	*n*	Mature / Young	W[a]	Significance[b]
Nitrogen	1.05	0.06	1.01	0.08	4	1.04	18	0.557
Water	61.0	0.9	60.6	0.4	4	1.01	19	0.443
Catechols	1.49	0.25	4.93	0.34	4	0.30	26	0.014
Resin minus catechols	2.61	0.39	5.39	0.30	4	0.48	26	0.014
Resin	4.09	0.64	10.32	0.63	4	0.40	26	0.014
Dry weight % composition								
Nitrogen	2.68	0.13	2.25	0.20	4	1.05	19	0.443
Catechols	3.82	0.65	12.51	0.87	4	0.31	26	0.014
Resin minus catechols	6.67	0.96	13.68	0.72	4	0.49	26	0.014
Resin	10.48	1.60	26.18	1.55	4	0.40	26	0.014

[a]W = higher rank sum.
[b]Significance of difference between properties of mature and young leaves; Wilcoxon Rank Sum Test (Hollander and Wolfe 1973).

Secondly, the leaf age classes of Duisberg were entirely different from those examined in the present study. The young leaves of Duisberg consisted of all leaves stripped from *entire sprays* emerging either as new spring growth or as growth from stumps that had been cut back to the ground. These young sprays were then compared to sprays of summer growth, or sprays from

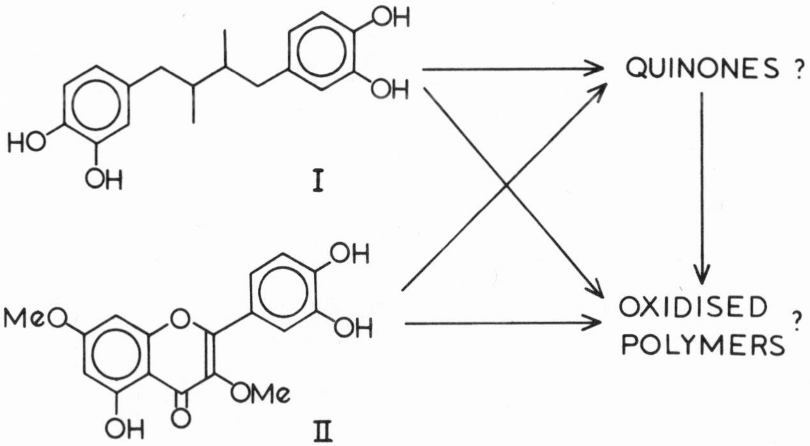

FIGURE 6-1. Larrea *resin components nordihydroguaiaretic acid (NDGA) (I), and a representative flavonoid quercetin 3,7-dimethylether (II). Quinones and oxidised polymers are possible products formed under the influence of* Larrea *phenoloxidase on maceration of the leaves.*

plants that had not been stump cut, respectively. In the present study, leaf age is defined on a *within-spray* basis.

PALATABILITY OF LOW AND HIGH RESIN LEAVES OF *LARREA* TO HERBIVORES

Field observations at Avra Valley indicated that a grasshopper, *Cibolacris parviceps,* and a geometrid moth larva, *Semiothisa colorata,* preferentially consumed the mature leaves and avoided the young leaves (as previously defined) of their host plant, *L. tridentata.* We therefore decided to investigate this preference more rigorously in the laboratory to ascertain whether the differential resin content of young and mature leaves contributed to grazing preference. To quantify this preference, insects were confined with *L. tridentata* sprays, and the numbers of young and mature leaves eaten during an experiment were recorded. Leaf palatability (P) was defined as the percentage of leaves of a given type that were consumed (Eq. 1). Relative palatability (PR) of mature to young leaves was defined as the palatability of mature leaves divided by that of young leaves (Eq. 2).

$$P = \frac{\text{amount eaten}}{\text{amount offered}} \times 100 = \frac{\text{number leaves eaten} \times \text{leaf size}}{\text{number leaves offered} \times \text{leaf size}} \times 100$$
$$= \frac{\text{number leaves eaten}}{\text{number leaves offered}} \times 100 \qquad (1)$$

$$PR = \frac{P\text{ (mature)}}{P\text{ (young)}} \qquad (2)$$

In this method, for equal palatability (PR = 1), tissues are eaten in the same proportion as that in which they occur. Differences in leaf size are immaterial (Eq. 1).

At the time of the study (April 1973), three insects were available at the Avra Valley site in numbers adequate for palatability determinations (Table 6-2). *Cibolacris* is a polyphagous grasshopper that utilizes *L. tridentata* and several species of grasses and forbs at the Avra Valley site (J. C. Schultz, *personal communication*). Schultz has raised juvenile *Cibolacris* to the adult stage in field cages on a mixture of *Lepidium* spp., *Sporalsia ambigua, Cryptantha racemosa, Plantago* spp., *Encelia farinosa, Gerea canescens,* and unidentified grasses and has shown that the insect is not dependent on *Larrea* for normal development. In addition, *C. parviceps* occurs outside the range of *Larrea* (Helfer 1963). *Semiothisa* is a monophagous insect restricted to *L. tridentata* (see Chapter 7). *Schistocerca americana,* a widely polyphagous grasshopper (Otte 1975), was not observed to utilize *L. tridentata* at the Avra Valley site during a three-year study (J. C. Schultz, *personal communication*).

TABLE 6-2 *Relative Palatability (PR) of Mature and Young Leaves of* L. tridentata *and* L. cuneifolia *to Leaf Chewing Insects.*

Insect species	Plant species	P_{mature}	$\pm S\bar{x}$	P_{young}	$\pm S\bar{x}$	n	PR	W[a]	Significance[b]
Cibolacris parviceps (Acrididae)	*L. tridentata*	40.49	6.47	0.50	0.08	4	81.0	26	0.014
Semiothisa colorata (Geometridae)	" "	44.78	8.61	1.27	0.26	4	35.3	26	0.014
Schistocerca americana (Acrididae)	" "	28.65	2.24	7.26	0.44	2	4.0	7	n.s.
Astroma quadrilobatum (Proscopiidae)	*L. cuneifolia*	22.81	5.66	6.92	2.65	7	3.3	70	0.013

[a] W = higher rank sum of P values.
[b] Significance of difference between P_{mature} and P_{young}; Wilcoxon Rank Sum Test (Hollander and Wolfe 1973); n.s. = not significant = >0.05.

All three insects strongly preferred to eat the mature leaves as opposed to the young leaves of *L. tridentata* (see Table 6-2).

J. C. Schultz (*unpublished*) has found that the grasshoppers *Bootettix punctatus,* a monophagous *L. tridentata* herbivore (see Chapter 7), and *Ligurotettix coquilletti,* an insect utilizing mainly *L. tridentata* at the Avra Valley site–but which has been reported to utilize *Atriplex polycarpa, Simmondsia* sp. and grasses in other areas of Arizona (Otte and Joern 1975)–also prefer the mature leaves of *L. tridentata* (PR>1, equations 1 and 2). The katydid *Insara covilleae,* a monophagous *L. tridentata* herbivore, may not discriminate between young and mature leaves (J. C. Schultz, *personal communication*), but this insect consumes only the petiole and a small basal portion of the leaf, whereas all other insects described above consume entire leaves. Therefore, all leaf-chewing insects tested that consume entire leaves prefer the mature leaves of *L. tridentata.*

Later in the study a similar preference for mature leaves was found for *Astroma quadrilobatum,* a proscopiid grasshopper, feeding on *L. cuneifolia* in the laboratory (Table 6-2). *Astroma* was the dominant insect herbivore on *L. cuneifolia,* in terms of biomass and numbers, at the Andalgalá site (see Chapter 7). In addition to *L. cuneifolia, Astroma* also utilized the leaves of four other desert woody perennials at Andalgalá: *L. divaricata* (Zygophyllaceae), *Bulnesia retama* (Zygophyllaceae), *Trichomeria usillo* (Malpighiaceae), and *Zuccagnia punctata* (Leguminosae).

Total leaf fixed nitrogen content, water content, and resin contents for young and mature leaves from the same plants used in the relative palatability determinations for *Cibolacris* and *Semiothisa* were measured (see Table 6-1). The resin extracts from each leaf type were analyzed for total catechol content. Thus nitrogen, water, resin, ether-soluble catechols, and the rest of the resin (resin minus catechols) were quantified for each leaf type.

Whether the chemical composition of plant material is best expressed in terms of leaf dry or fresh weight, when considering the possible effects of various leaf components on tissue preference by herbivores, is problematical. Arguments in favor of both dry and fresh weight expression can be advanced. If water is not limiting to the herbivore and if the processing and excretion of excess water is associated with a minimal metabolic cost, we can argue that expression of chemical composition on a dry weight basis is more appropriate, especially when a single putatively attractive component (e.g., nitrogen content) is being measured. However, we can also argue that since herbivores consume fresh leaves, expression of chemical composition and other leaf properties on a fresh weight basis is more appropriate. In addition, some variables (e.g., water content and leaf toughness) can only be meaningfully expressed on a fresh weight or fresh leaf basis. Thus, when correlating leaf preference with leaf properties, expressing all leaf properties on the same basis is often possible only if a fresh weight comparison is used. For these reasons leaf chemical composition will be expressed, whenever possible, in terms of both fresh and dry weight.

Although a marked preference was shown by insects for the mature leaves of *L. tridentata*, leaf nitrogen and water contents of young and mature leaves were not significantly different (see Table 6-1). On the other hand, total resin content and content of the two resin fractions, catechols and resin minus catechols, were all markedly and significantly higher in young leaves than in mature leaves. Thus we can conclude that a repulsive influence by resin or resin components on tissue preference by the herbivores was likely.

Resin was removed from *L. tridentata* sprays by ether wash, and the palatabilities of young and mature leaves of ether-extracted and fresh leaves were compared for *Cibolacris* and *Semiothisa* (see Tables 6-3 and 6-4). For *Cibolacris* (Table 6-3) the marked preference for mature leaves of fresh material (PR $\frac{\text{mature}}{\text{young}}$ = 123) disappeared for ether-extracted material PR $\frac{\text{mature}}{\text{young}}$ = 0.93 n.s.). Additionally, both mature and young leaves of extracted material became more palatable than the corresponding fresh leaves (PR $\frac{\text{extracted}}{\text{fresh}}$ = 5.08 and 672 for mature and young leaves, respectively). These results are consistent with a deterrent effect of leaf resin or resin components on grazing by *Cibolacris*.

For *Semiothisa* a more complicated picture emerged (Table 6-4). The preference of *Semiothisa* for mature leaves of fresh material (PR $\frac{\text{mature}}{\text{young}}$ = 68) disappeared for extracted material (PR $\frac{\text{mature}}{\text{young}}$ = 1.36, n.s.,), as with *Cibolacris*. For young leaves, extracted material became more palatable than fresh material (PR $\frac{\text{extracted}}{\text{fresh}}$ = 14.49), again as with *Cibolacris*. However, for the preferred leaf age class—mature leaves—palatability of extracted material was less than that of fresh material (PR $\frac{\text{extracted}}{\text{fresh}}$ = 0.29). These results are consistent with a deterrent effect by resin or resin components at high concentrations but an attractive effect at low concentrations on grazing by *Semiothisa*. Thus the possibility is that the monophagous *Semiothisa* has adapted to utilize resin or resin components as feeding cues, but remains deterred by these leaf components at high concentration, whereas the more generalized *Cibolacris* is deterred by resin or resin components at all concentrations.

TABLE 6-3 *Relative Palatabilities (PR) of Fresh and Extracted Leaves of* L. tridentata *to* Cibolacris parviceps.

	Fresh			Extracted			PR	
	$\bar{X}$	$\pm S\bar{x}$	n	$\bar{X}$	$\pm S\bar{x}$	n	$\frac{\text{extracted}}{\text{fresh}}$	Significance[a]
P_{mature}	5.418	0.929	45	27.52	4.48	45	5.08	0.01
P_{young}	0.044	0.044	45	29.57	5.32	45	672	0.01
PR $\frac{\text{mature}}{\text{young}}$	123			0.93				
Significance*	0.01			0.8				

[a]Student's *t*-test.

TABLE 6-4 *Relative Palatabilities (PR) of Fresh and Extracted Leaves of* L. tridentata *to Semiothisa colorata.*

	Fresh			Extracted			PR extracted/fresh	Significance[a]
	$\bar{X}$	$\pm S\bar{x}$	n	$\bar{X}$	$\pm S\bar{x}$	n		
P_{mature}	17.34	3.73	20	5.010	1.414	20	0.29	0.01
P_{young}	0.255	0.255	20	3.695	1.387	20	14.49	0.01
PR $\frac{mature}{young}$	68.0			1.36				
Significance	0.01			0.6				

[a]Student's *t*-test.

Ligurotettix coquillettii is a territorial grasshopper (Otte and Joern 1975) whose territory normally consists of a single *L. tridentata* bush. In a given area males occupy some bushes but not others. A study of 31 *L. tridentata* bushes occupied by *Ligurotettix* males and 40 sympatric unoccupied bushes showed that leaf pair 2, a preferred leaf tissue of *Ligurotettix,* of occupied bushes had a significantly (0.05, *t*-test) lower average resin content (7.8 ± 2.4 percent, $\bar{X} \pm Sx$, d.w.) than unoccupied bushes (9.2 ± 2.1 percent).

The relative palatability of young and mature leaves to insects, the effects of resin removal on leaf palatability, and *Ligurotettix* occupancy of low resin bushes all suggested a repellent influence by resin or resin constituents on herbivores. This finding led to an investigation of resin properties, the object of which was to determine properties that might render the resin objectionable to herbivores.

COMPLEXING OF *LARREA* RESIN WITH PROTEINS AND STARCH

Larrea tridentata and *L. cuneifolia* resins are moderately lipophilic substances, exhibiting high solubility in diethyl ether, acetone, ethanol, somewhat lower in chloroform, but having low solubility in water or petroleum ether. However, despite their low solubility in water, both resins are quite soluble in dilute (1 to 2 percent) aqueous protein solutions.

Extraction of *L. tridentata* resin (11.8 mg.) plus water (5 ml) with aliquots (15 ml) of ether results in ∿96 percent recovery of resin in the ether layers after three extractions (Figure 6-2; also see Table 6A-1). On the other hand, extraction of resin plus aqueous gelatin solution with ether results in recovery of only ∿56 percent of the resin after three extractions. Repeated extractions

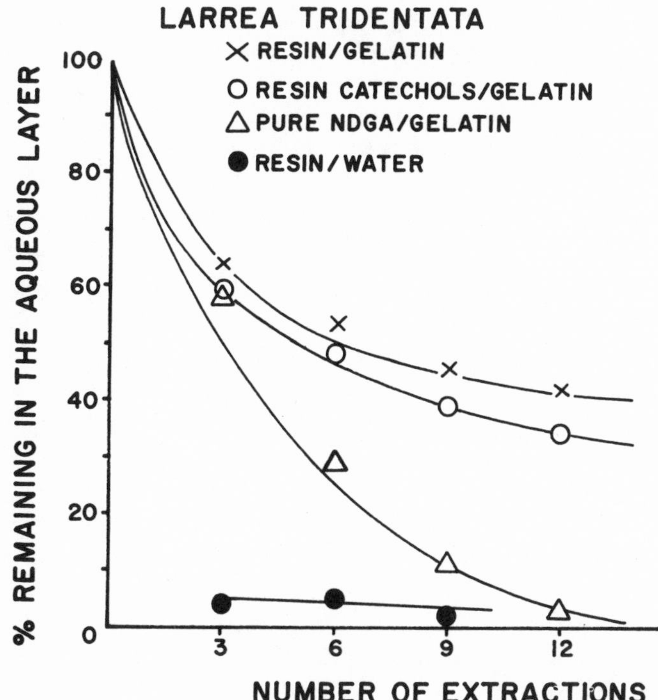

FIGURE 6-2. *Extraction of* L. tridentata *resin (X) and resin catechols (O) or pure nordihydroguaiaretic acid (NDGA)* (△) *from 1.5% gelatin solution with aliquots of diethyl ether.*

of the gelatin layer leaves ∿40 percent of the resin apparently permanently bound in the gelatin layer. Little fractionation of resin components occurs as shown by thin layer chromatography and catechol content of recovered fractions (see Figure 6-2 and Table 6A-1). These observations indicate that *Larrea* resin is a protein-complexing agent. Pure NDGA also complexes with gelatin but can be recovered by repeated extraction (see Figure 6-2 and Table 6A-1). The more rapid recovery of NDGA from pure NDGA-gelatin than recovery of total catechols from resin-gelatin is suggestive of cooperative action between the various resin components during complex formation.

Partition of *L. tridentata* resin between ether and buffered solutions of various solutes showed (Table 6-5; see also Rhoades and Cates 1976) that the resin complexes with gelatin (partly degraded collagen), casein (milk phosphoprotein), and edestin (hemp seed protein) were all very similar to a degree. Complexing also occurrs with α-chymotrypsin (bovine endopeptidase) and with starch, though more weakly than with the above proteins. Complexing with gelatin does not occur in the presence of urea at 8M concentration.

TABLE 6-5 *Partition of* L. tridentata *Resin Between Diethyl Ether and 1.5 Percent Solutions of Various Solutions in pH 7.0, 0.2 M Sodium Phosphate Buffer.*

Solute	pH of aqueous phase	% Resin in aqueous phase $\bar{X} \pm S\bar{x}$
–	7.03	3.0 ± 0.9
Gelatin	7.02	72.9 ± 0.7
Casein	6.98	66.4 ± 0.8
Edestin	6.92	68.5 ± 0.7
α - Chymotrypsin	7.00	39.0 ± 1.0
Starch	7.01	16.5 ± 0.8
Gelatin/8 M Urea	7.60	2.7 ± 0.5
Hydrolyzed Casein	6.89	2.8 ± 0.5
Dextrose	7.00	2.4 ± 0.8

This finding is consistent with stabilization of the complexes by hydrogen bonding. Complex formation does not occur with dextrose or hydrolyzed casein, which thus shows that stable complexes are formed only with the polymerized forms of these substances.

The resin is functionally a tannin, though it does not fall within the classic definition of tannin. Whereas the vegetable tannins are defined as polymeric, hydrophilic, phenolic compounds that precipitate proteins and starch from aqueous solution, the resin is composed of monomeric, moderately lipophilic phenols that form complexes with proteins and starch that are quite water soluble. This lack of a readily observable manifestation of the interaction is the probable reason that the protein- and starch-complexing property of *Larrea* resin has not been noted previously.

The tannin-like properties of *Larrea* resin suggested a possible mechanism for antiherbivore activity, namely, disruption of digestive processes. True tannins have long been known to inhibit a variety of digestive and non-digestive enzymatic processes (Van Sumere et al. 1975; Goldstein and Swain 1965). We therefore decided to investigate possible inhibition of in vitro proteolysis by *Larrea* resin.

INHIBITION OF PROTEOLYSIS BY *L. TRIDENTATA* AND *L. CUNEIFOLIA* RESINS

A method for studying the effects of plant extractives on proteolysis was developed, based on several in the literature (Soto-Ramirez and Mitchell

1960; Vogel 1968; Feeny 1969). The method consists of an assay of a free α-amino nitrogen released (Rosen 1957) after incubation of casein, gelatin, or some other protein substrate with a commercially available proteolytic enzyme such as erepsin (a crude mixture of porcine proteases) or chymotrypsin (bovine) for a given length of time under standard conditions of temperature and pH. The effect of added plant extractives on the rate of proteolysis can thus be measured by comparing the rate of α-amino nitrogen released from the test versus the control digestate. Substitution of herbivore gut extract for the standard proteolytic enzymes enables the effects of plant extractives on the performance of the proteolytic enzyme system of the particular herbivore under study to be easily measured. Figure 6-3 shows the action of *L. cuneifolia* resin on the digestion of casein by both erepsin and *Astroma* proteolytic enzymes at pH 7.0. In the range of resin-protein concentration found in *L. cuneifolia* leaves, both erepsin and *Astroma* enzymes are inhibited from 60 to 80 percent. The fact that the two inhibition curves are so similar suggests that *Astroma* enzymes are not specially adapted (relative to porcine enzymes) to carry out proteolysis in the presence of resin. This finding is somewhat surprising, but supports the hypothesis that the resin is a heterogeneous generalized protein-complexing agent against which specialized enzyme adaptations are at best difficult. Although *L. cuneifolia* is a major food plant for *Astroma,* the herbivore does utilize at least four other desert perennials, as previously described. Possibly the proteolytic enzyme systems of herbivores restricted to *Larrea* will show adaptations against resin action. Inhibition of casein-erepsin and casein-α-chymotrypsin proteolysis by *L. tridentata* resin was also demonstrated (Rhoades and Cates 1976).

EFFECT OF pH ON THE PROTEIN-COMPLEXING PROPERTY OF *L. TRIDENTATA* RESIN

Stability of protein-tannin complexes rapidly decreases above pH 8 (Loomis and Battaile 1966; Van Sumere et al. 1975). The same is true of gelatin-*L. tridentata* resin complexes. Using the aqueous gelatin-ether partition method (Rhoades and Cates 1976) has shown that the percent resin in the gelatine phase was independent of pH between pH 3 to pH 8.5 (Figure 6-4; also see Table 6A-2). Above pH 8.5 the percent resin in the gelatin phase decreases until at ∿ pH 10.5 (the pK_a of the resin), with the percentages of resin present in the gelatin phase and control buffer phase being approximately equal. This disappearance of the interaction on approaching the pK_a of the resin is consistent with stabilization of the complexes by phenolic OH groups that in their deprotonated form are no longer able to enter into hydrogen bonding. Examination of the gut pH ranges for *L. tridentata* herbivores showed that only one insect, *Semiothisa,* exhibited a gut pH (9 to 9.5) within the range of reduced protein-resin binding (see Figure

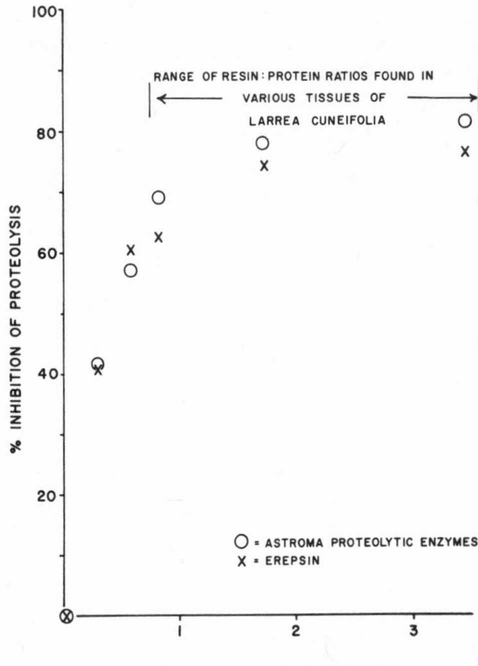

FIGURE 6-3. *Inhibition of casein proteolysis by* L. cuneifolia *resin. A comparison between inhibition of erepsin (X) and inhibition of the proteolytic enzymes of* Astroma quadrilobatum *(O).*

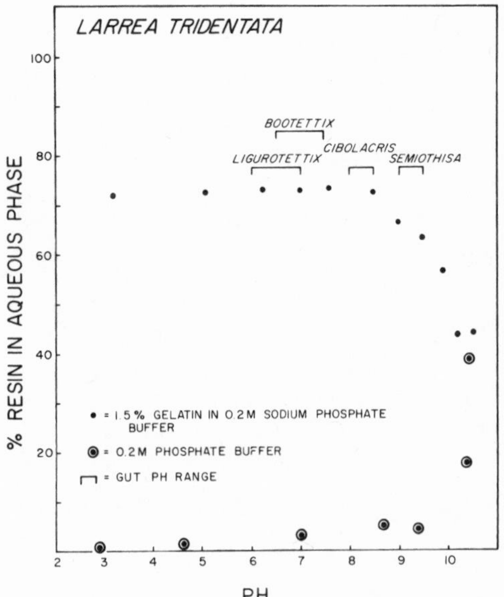

FIGURE 6-4. *Partition of* L. tridentata *resin between buffer* (⊙) *or 1.5% gelatin in buffer* (•) *and diethyl ether, as a function of pH. Gut pH ranges for* L. tridentata *herbivores are indicated.*

6-4). *Semiothisa* is a lepidopteran monophagous on *L. tridentata* and the high gut pH of this insect may represent an adaptation to minimize the protein-complexing property of *L. tridentata* resin. A similar function has been suggested (Feeny 1970) for the high gut pH of the winter moth to circumvent the action of tannin in oak leaves. The other orthopteran *L. tridentata* herbivores, *Ligurotettix, Bootettix,* and *Cibolacris,* all exhibit gut pH ranges below the range of apparent reduced protein-resin binding (see Figure 6-4). In addition, the gut pH of *Astroma quadrilobatum,* a *L. cuneifolia* herbivore, ranges between 6 and 7. *Bootettix* is monophagous for *L. tridentata,* and even *Ligurotettix* consumes largely *L. tridentata* at the Avra Valley site. If high gut pH represents an adaptation against resin action, why is high gut pH not exhibited by these other insects? The answer to this question is not known but may lie in physiological limitations imposed by high gut pH. For example, high gut pH may preclude the use of gut symbionts. High gut pH is common among Lepidoptera (Waterhouse 1949; House 1974b), and Lepidoptera commonly may not utilize gut symbionts (P. Feeny, *personal communication*). Orthoptera, some members of which are known to utilize gut symbionts (Wigglesworth 1972; House 1974a), commonly exhibit a neutral or mildly acidic gut pH (House 1974b).

THE PHENOLOXIDASE SYSTEM OF *LARREA*

During the later part of the work on selective grazing by *L. tridentata* herbivores, we discovered that *L. tridentata* possesses a powerful phenoloxidase (PO) system. Maceration of fresh leaves and terminal stems of *L. tridentata* in a VirTis homogenizer in the presence of air for 10 minutes results in ∿30 percent reduction in total resin recovery and in ∿60 percent reduction in ether-soluble catechol recovery (Table 6-6) relative to that obtained from leaves macerated under anaerobic conditions or in the presence of cyanide added to inactivate the phenoloxidase (Hughes 1973). Heat treatment of the plant material (100° C, 2 min) prior to maceration also results in an increase in recoverable resin and catechols. Thus, on maceration of fresh *Larrea* tissue in air, the phenolics are subject to an oxygen and metalloenzyme dependent reaction that results in reduced recovery. The principal products of plant PO activity are reactive *o*-quinones and polymeric material formed by oxidative coupling of phenolic residues (Hughes 1973).

The method of choice for assay of phenoloxidase activity (Mayer et al. 1966) measures the rate of oxygen uptake by a known mass of homogenized tissue. On this basis, a method was developed to compare the macerated tissue oxygen demand (MTOD) of *L. cuneifolia* with that of other Argentine desert plant species and to compare MTOD for *L. cuneifolia* leaves of various ages using an oxygen monitor (see Tables 6-7, 6-8 and 6-9). MTOD includes

TABLE 6-6 *Recovery of Total Resin and Ether-Soluble Catechols from* L. tridentata *Leaves and Terminal Stems Homogenized in Air (*A*), in the Presence of Air Plus Cyanide (*B*), and Under Anaerobic Conditions (*C*).*

Sample	H_2O%	Resin %(f.w.)	$\pm S\bar{x}$	*n*	Cathechols %(f.w.)	$\pm S\bar{x}$	*n*	Color of homogenate
A	56.8	4.68	0.06	3	1.34	0.02	3	dark brown
B	–	6.97	0.07	3	3.62	0.04	3	pale green
C	–	6.80	0.05	3	3.52	0.01	3	pale green
$\frac{A-B}{B} \times 100$		-32.9			-63.0			
$\frac{A-C}{C} \times 100$		-31.2			-61.9			

oxygen uptake due to any residual respiratory activity in addition to special processes such as phenoloxidase activity, and possibly the MTOD values for many of the plants listed (Table 6-7) are due mainly-perhaps entirely-to such residual respiration. Leaf pairs 1-3 of *L. cuneifolia* exhibited an MTOD of 0.421 ml O_2, g^{-1} d.w., min^{-1}, the highest value for any plant measured (see Table 6-7). For *L. cuneifolia* addition of excess NDGA substrate to the macerated leaves lead to an increase in oxygen uptake rate ranging between 37 to 108 percent, which demonstrates that for this plant the reaction is at least partially under substrate concentration control (see Table 6A-4).

Since the products of PO activity, particularly *o*-quinones, have been shown (Horigome and Kandatsu 1968; Allison 1971; Pierpoint 1969) to have a negative effect on biological value of plant proteins and the availability of amino acids in plant proteins, the effect of PO on digestibility reduction by *Larrea* resin was investigated. Ideally, "pure" enzyme would be isolated from the plant and added, together with resin, to the digestion mixtures, but this has not been accomplished so far. The difficulties involved in the extraction of proteins from plants containing large quantities of phenolic substances are well known (Loomis and Battaile 1966). Removal of the resin by solvent extraction (diethyl ether, acetone) prior to attempts at enzyme isolation causes extensive loss of PO activity. Nevertheless, results were obtained that are consistent with, but do not prove, an enhancing action by the *Larrea* PO system on digestibility reduction by the phenolic resin. In these experiments casein was digested by an *Astroma* gut preparation in the presence of *L. cuneifolia* resin and PO activity was introduced into the system by addition of a small quantity of homogenized *L. cuneifolia* leaves. Inhibition by resin and homogenized leaves was then compared to inhibition by the same amount of resin alone (taking into account resin introduced into the system by the

TABLE 6-7 *Macerated Tissue Oxygen Demand (MTOD) of Leaves of Some Argentine Desert Plants.*

	Plant Family	$H_2O\%$ $\bar{X} \pm S\bar{x}$		MTOD[a] $\bar{X} \pm S\bar{x}$		*n*
Woody perennials						
Jatropha macrocarpa	E	74.0	1.2	0.012	0.002	3
Trichomeria usillo	M	66.3		0.017		1
Prosopis nigra	L	51.2		0.019		1
Ximenia americana	O	56.9		0.025		1
Jatropha excisa	E	73.0		0.036		1
Zuccagnia punctata	L	52.0		0.047		1
Prosopis chilensis	L	67.1	1.8	0.052	0.003	3
Acacia furcatispina	L	55.9		0.062		1
Cercidium praecox	L	68.9		0.068		1
Mimosa farinosa	L	57.0		0.079		1
Senecio galsianus	C	78.9		0.093		1
Acacia aroma	L	65.4		0.138		1
Bulnesia retama	Z	68.1		0.234		1
Prosopis torquata	L	56.7		0.413		1
Larrea cuneifolia	Z	56.0	0.6	0.421	0.021	3
Herbaceous perennials						
Morrenia odorata	As	77.5		0.050		1
Mikania urticifolia	C	91.0		0.068		1
Annuals						
Allionia incarcerata	N	87.9		0.026		1
Gomphrena tomentosa	A	84.9		0.027		1
G. martiana	A	83.5		0.031		1
Euphorbia catamarcensis	E	76.8		0.034		1
Nicotiana noctiflora	S	79.4		0.036		1
Verbesina encelioides	C	85.0		0.053		1
Tribulus terrestris	Z	81.9		0.057		1
Ibicella parodii	M	79.0		0.067		1
Croton bonplandianus	E	78.6		0.087		1

Note: E = Euphorbiaceae; M = Malpighiaceae; L = Leguminosae; O = Olacaceae; C = Compositae; Z = Zygophyllaceae; N = Nyctaginaceae; A = Amaranthaceae; S = Solanaceae; M = Martyniaceae; As = Asclepiadaceae.

[a]ml O_2, g^{-1} d.w., min^{-1}.

leaves). Inhibitions of 2.6 percent, 38.3 percent, and 54.2 percent were obtained by leaf homogenate, resin and resin plus leaf homogenate, respectively (see Table 6A-5). There is thus a component of *L. cuneifolia* leaves that enhances the digestibility-reducing property of *L. cuneifolia* resin. This component could well be the PO enzyme.

More conclusive evidence was obtained for the enhancing action of commerical mushroom polyphenoloxidase on digestibility reduction by *L. triden-*

tata resin. In this case erepsin and casein comprised the enzyme-substrate system and inhibitions of 69.8 percent for resin alone and 81.8 percent for resin plus PO were obtained (see Table 6A-6).

In the light of the probable enhancing effect of the *Larrea* PO system on digestibility reduction by the resin, we decided to measure relative palatability of young and mature leaves of *L. cuneifolia* to *Astroma* and to examine correlations between leaf palatability and MTOD and other leaf properties, including leaf toughness, which was measured by a penetrometer method. As with the *L. tridentata* herbivores, *Astroma* prefers the mature leaves of *L. cuneifolia* (see Table 6-2). All leaf properties measured, except nitrogen content, show a significant difference between young and mature leaves (Table 6-8). Leaf toughness is significantly higher for mature leaves, but a positive effect of leaf toughness on palatability seems unlikely on theoretical grounds. Water content is significantly higher for the mature leaves and resin; resin components and MTOD are all significantly lower for mature leaves. These results are consistent with a negative effect of resin, resin components, or resin plus PO on leaf palatability to *Astroma.* An attractive influence by leaf water content is not excluded. But in the case of *L. tridentata,* there is no significant difference between the water contents of young and mature leaves, in spite of the large differences in palatability of young and mature leaves to herbivores (see Tables 6-1 and 6-2).

GROWTH RATES OF *ASTROMA* ON LEAF TISSUES OF *L. CUNEIFOLIA* VARYING IN MACERATED TISSUE OXYGEN DEMAND (MTOD) AND OTHER PROPERTIES

A preliminary study established that leaves from three bushes (A, B, and C in Table 6-9) could provide a suitable range of MTOD values. From these three bushes a total of seven leaf classes were chosen, each of which formed the diet for a group of eight juvenile *Astroma* females. Growth rates and survival over an eight-day period for each group of insects were then measured together with leaf MTOD, resin content, ether-soluble catechol content, resin minus catechol content, nitrogen content, water content, and leaf toughness. A wide range of both insect survival and growth rates were obtained (see Table 6-9). On leaves $C_{5\text{-}8}$ all insects survived, and an average growth rate of 6.45 percent fresh weight per day was obtained. This growth rate is equivalent to a mass doubling time of eleven days. On leaves A_{tip} only one insect survived, and a growth rate of -3.32 percent per day was exhibited by this insect. We should emphasize here that the quantities of leaves eaten varied considerably between groups, and group A_{tip} ate very little throughout the whole experiment. Thus, differences in survival and growth rates between groups are a product not only of the properties of ingested material but also of the amount of material ingested.

TABLE 6–8 *Properties of Mature and Young Leaves of* L. cuneifolia.

		Mature leaves		Young leaves					
		$\bar{X} \pm S\bar{x}$		$\bar{X} \pm S\bar{x}$		n[a]	Mature/Young	W[b]	Significance[c]
Properties expressed on a fresh weight or fresh leaf basis:									
Nitrogen	%	0.96	0.05	1.05	0.04	7	0.914	60	0.191
Water	%	56.3	1.1	50.0	1.3	7	1.13	73	0.003
Catechols	%	1.93	0.19	7.46	0.40	7	0.259	77	0.001
Resin minus catechols	%	4.76	0.43	14.50	0.46	7	0.328	77	0.001
Resin	%	6.69	0.61	21.96	0.76	7	0.305	77	0.001
MTOD	ml O_2, g^{-1}, min^{-1}	0.138	0.019	0.310	0.037	7	0.445	76	0.001
Toughness[d]	g	167	12	33	4	7	5.06	77	0.001
Properties expressed on a dry weight basis:									
Nitrogen	%	2.21	0.12	2.10	0.10	7	1.05	56	0.355
Catechols	%	4.38	0.34	14.90	0.54	7	0.294	77	0.001
Resin minus catechols	%	10.82	0.79	29.08	0.85	7	0.372	77	0.001
Resin	%	15.20	1.10	43.97	1.10	7	0.346	77	0.001
MTOD	ml O_2, g^{-1}, min^{-1}	0.311	0.038	0.615	0.061	7	0.506	76	0.001

[a] n = number of plants tested.
[b] W = higher rank sum.
[c] Significance of difference between properties of mature and young leaves; Wilcoxon Rank Sum Test (Hollander and Wolfe 1973).
[d] Mass in grams required to force a rod (0.8 mm diameter) through the fresh leaf.

TABLE 6–9 *Growth Rate and Survival of* Astroma quadrilobatum *Reared on Leaves of* L. cuneifolia *from Three Plants (A, B, and C) that Varied in Macerated Tissue Oxygen Demand (MTOD) and other Leaf Properties.*

Diet		A_{tip}	$A_{2,3}$	$A_{5\text{-}8}$	$B_{2,3}$	$B_{5\text{-}8}$	$C_{2,3}$	$C_{5\text{-}8}$
Δ % mass, fresh weight, per day		−3.32	−0.98	−1.22	3.97	4.30	2.98	6.45
# of survivors		1	5	6	7	8	8	8
Properties expressed on a fresh weight or fresh leaf basis:								
Nitrogen	%	1.46	1.49	1.31	1.61	1.32	0.90	0.85
Water	%	47.0	47.5	48.7	56.6	57.5	61.0	61.0
Catechols	%	10.81	1.78	1.58	1.74	1.03	1.75	1.01
Resin minus catechols	%	13.57	4.86	5.07	4.42	3.51	3.55	3.59
Resin	%	24.38	6.64	6.65	6.16	4.54	5.30	4.60
MTOD[a] ml O_2, g^{-1}, min^{-1}	$\bar{X}$	0.251	0.180	0.142	0.093	0.068	0.073	0.050
" " " " "	$S\bar{x}$	0.009	0.010	0.012	0.006	0.006	0.009	0.007
Toughness[b]	g $\bar{X}$	33	194	215	143	187	142	211
"	$S\bar{x}$	10	23	5	11	3	9	12
Properties expressed on a dry weight basis:								
Nitrogen	%	2.76	2.84	2.56	3.70	3.11	2.31	2.18
Catechols	%	20.40	3.39	3.08	4.02	2.43	4.50	2.59
Resin minus catechols	%	25.60	9.25	9.88	10.18	8.27	9.10	9.21
Resin	%	46.00	12.64	12.96	14.20	10.70	13.60	11.80
MTOD ml O_2, g^{-1}, min^{-1}	$\bar{X}$	0.473	0.342	0.276	0.214	0.161	0.186	0.127
" " " " "	$S\bar{x}$	0.018	0.020	0.024	0.013	0.015	0.023	0.017

[a] $n = 4$ (see Method 17 in Appendix 6A).
[b] $n = 5$ (see Method 17 in Appendix 6A).

Correlation between growth rates for the various groups of *Astroma* and properties of the leaf diets, expressed on both a fresh and dry weight basis, showed that only MTOD (fresh and dry) and water content exhibited significant correlations with growth rate (see Tables 6-9 and 6-10). The correlation of growth rate with MTOD (-0.942 fresh, -0.935 dry) was higher than that with water content (+0.928). To minimize the possibility that the higher correlation with MTOD than with other variables was due merely to a more linear relationship between growth rate and MTOD versus a more curvilinear relationship between growth rate and water content or other variables, correlation between growth rate and all the fresh weight and fresh leaf variables raised to higher powers were examined. All fresh weight and fresh leaf variables were raised to the following powers: x^{-3}, x^{-2}, x^{-1}, $\sqrt[2]{x}$, $\sqrt[3]{x}$, x^2, x^3 and regressed against growth rate. The two transformed variables most highly correlated with growth rate were $\sqrt[3]{\text{MTOD}}$ and (water content)$^{-3}$ (Table 6-10). Again MTOD showed a higher correlation with growth rate than did water content. These results are consistent with a negative effect of the products of *L. cuneifolia* phenoloxidase activity on growth rate of *Astroma.*

TABLE 6-10 *Correlation between Growth Rate (Δ % Mass Day*$^{-1}$*) of* Astroma quadrilobatum *and Properties of the* L. cuneifolia *Leaf Diet.*

		r[a]	Significance[b]
Properties expressed on a fresh weight or fresh leaf basis:			
Nitrogen	%	-0.512	n.s.
Water	%	+0.928	0.01
Catechols	%	-0.667	n.s.
Resin minus catechols	%	-0.731	n.s.
Resin	%	-0.701	n.s.
MTOD	ml O_2, g^{-1}, min^{-1}	-0.942	0.01
Toughness	g	+0.466	n.s.
$\sqrt[3]{\text{MTOD}}$		-0.964	0.01
(Water)$^{-3}$		+0.943	0.01
Properties expressed on a dry weight basis:			
Nitrogen	%	+0.007	n.s.
Catechols	%	-0.635	n.s.
Resin minus catechols	%	-0.642	n.s.
Resin	%	-0.640	n.s.
MTOD	ml O_2, g^{-1}, min^{-1}	-0.935	0.01

[a]r = correlation coefficient.
[b]n.s. = not significant = > 0.05.

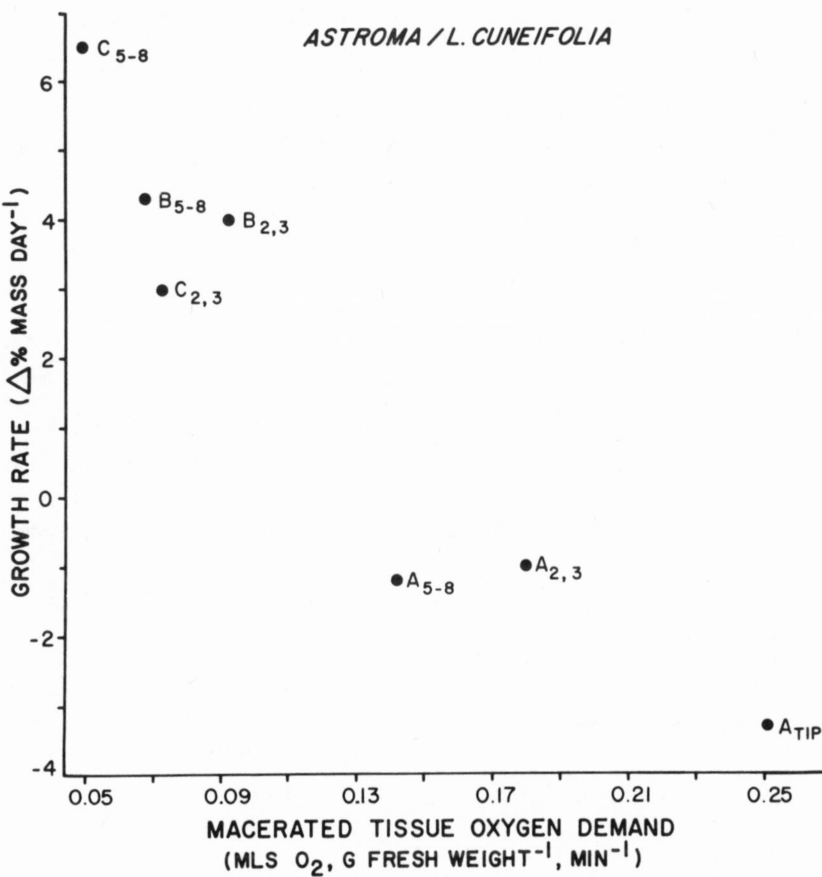

FIGURE 6–5. *The relationship between growth rate of juvenile* Astroma quadrilobatum (△% *mass day*$^{-1}$) *and the macerated tissue oxygen demand (MTOD) of the* L. cuneifolia *leaf diet. Each leaf diet is defined by plant* (A, B *or* C) *and leaf node position, counting nodes back from the tip of the spray.*

The relationship between growth rate of *Astroma* and leaf MTOD is shown in Figure 6–5.

MECHANISM OF ACTION OF RESIN AND PHENOLOXIDASE AS AN ANTIHERBIVORE SYSTEM

Evidence has been presented that (1) insects preferentially consume *Larrea* leaves of low resin content, (2) the resin complexes with starch and complexes with and reduces the digestibility of proteins, (3) a phenoloxidase system present in the leaves probably enhances the digestibility-reducing action of resin on proteins, and (4) growth rates of juvenile *Astroma* are negatively correlated with leaf macerated tissue oxygen demand, a composite measure dependent upon both phenoloxidase activity and the concentration of resin components.

We therefore propose that both the resin and the phenoloxidase of *Larrea* exhibit antiherbivore properties. The proposed mechanism of antiherbivore activity is as follows: Maceration of leaves by the herbivore leads to the formation of complexes between the resin, leaf proteins, and starch. These complexes are resistant to degradation by herbivore digestive enzymes. The herbivore enzymes may also be complexed since they themselves are proteins. The complexes are probably stabilized by hydrogen bond formation between phenolic hydroxyl groups and, in the case of protein-resin complexes, peptide carbonyl as has been shown to be the mechanism of protein-tannin complex formation (Gustavson 1956). This mechanism is essentially the same as that proposed by Feeny (1970) for the antiherbivore action of the condensed tannin fraction of oak leaves. In addition a phenoloxidase enzyme is present in the leaves, but isolated from the resin in the intact leaf. When a leaf is chewed, the phenoloxidase causes oxidation of part of the resin to substances that have more effective digestibility-reducing properties than native resin. This result may occur through the formation of reactive orthoquinones that cross-link the resin-protein complexes by covalent bonds or alternatively oxidative coupling of resin components may take place to give polymers of the condensed tannin type (see Figure 6-1). There is no reason why this defensive system should not also be active against pathogens since phenol-phenoloxidase systems have been implicated in such roles (Levin 1971).

The proposed antiherbivore system is not necessarily the only such system possessed by *Larrea.* A direct toxic action (as previously defined) by resin components, or other compounds present in the plant, on herbivores is possible, though presently little evidence exists for other antiherbivore systems. Of possible significance in connection with this last point is the fact that on several occasions we noticed that if *Semiothisa* larvae were confined in polyethylene bags with large quantities of *L. tridentata* sprays for periods of 2 to 3 hours, the larvae died. Although *Larrea* contains only 0.1 to 0.2 percent fresh weight of volatile components, many of the volatile compounds present (see Chapter 5) have known toxic and repellent effects on insects (Rodriguez and Levin 1976). Smith (1961) has shown that the volatile fraction of pine resin, which contains some of the same compounds present in *Larrea* volatiles, is toxic to bark beetles, especially to those beetle species not highly coevolved with the pine species from which the resin was obtained.

REASONS FOR THE WITHIN-PLANT DISTRIBUTION OF RESIN AND PHENOLOXIDASE

Both resin concentration and MTOD are higher in young leaves than in mature leaves (see Tables 6-1 and 6-8). This distribution presents an interesting contrast with that shown by tannin distribution within oak (*Quercus*), bracken fern (*Pteridium*), toyon (*Heteromeles*), and domestic plum (*Prunus*). In all these plants tannin concentration is low in newly initiated leaves, but increases as the leaves mature (Table 6-11). However, the apparently divergent defensive strategies of *Larrea* and these other plants can be unified if we assume that the level of defense exhibited by a plant tissue is directly related to the predictability and availability of that tissue as a food resource to herbivores. The leafing phenology of oak, bracken, toyon, and plum (and of temperate broad-leaf deciduous trees in general) is epitomized by that of oak. Oaks leaf out rapidly and, within a single tree, synchronously (Feeny 1970), and young leaves are available to herbivores for only a few weeks. In addition, the timing of bud burst varies as much as two weeks between individual trees and also in an unpredictable fashion from year to year, which thus renders locating the young leaves both in time and space difficult for herbivores. The average annual mortality of the winter moth between the time that the overwintering eggs are laid in the late fall and a new population of larvae is established in the spring is approximately 90 percent, largely caused by asynchrony between bud burst and egg hatch (Feeny 1970), thereby demonstrating the importance of "escape in space and time" from grazing for young oak leaves. Mature oak leaves, on the other hand, are a highly predictable resource to herbivores. Low levels of defensive substances in young leaves and high levels in mature leaves can thus be seen as an optimal defense strategy for oaks since sequestration of defensive chemicals in plant tissues, especially in rapidly growing and differentiating tissues, is very probably costly to the energy budget of the plant (Orians and Janzen 1974). In young leaves, where the escape component of defense is important, low levels of defensive substances are optimal. Conversely, in mature leaves, the escape component is low, and investing heavily in defensive chemicals is advantageous for the plant.

The leafing phenology of *Larrea* contrasts with that of oak (see Chapter 3). During moist periods leaves mature in sequence from the growing tips of the plant to give an array of leaves of various age classes down the sprays. As young leaves unfold and mature, they are immediately replaced by still younger leaves at the tip. During dry seasons, which occur in the early summer and fall in North America and during midwinter in Argentina, mature leaves are progressively shed (Morello 1955): the oldest first, until in the periods of drought only the youngest leaves at spray tips remain (Runyon 1934). The young leaves of *Larrea* can thus be considered to be the most predictable leaf resource on the plant since they are always present, and during very dry spells they are the only leaf age class present. It follows that the optimal defense strategy for *Larrea* is to load the growing tips with higher concentrations of defensive chemicals while lower, but still considerable, concentrations are optimal in the mature leaves.

An alternative, less parsimonious explanation involves both tissue predict-

TABLE 6-11 *Within-Plant Distribution of Digestibility-Reducing Substances.*

	Leaf age						Plant species	Growth form	Source
	Young		Intermediate		Mature				
	T	T/P	T	T/P	T	T/P			
Tannins	0.5	0.017	1.2	0.085	5.0	0.35	*Quercus robur*	WP	1
	2.0	0.083	2.5	0.21	4.5	0.91	*Pteridium aquilinum*	HP	2
	7.0	0.5	10.5	1.7	11.0	1.7	*Heteromeles arbutifolia*	WP	3
	Low				High		*Prunus domestica*	WP	4
	R	R/P	R	R/P	R	R/P			
Phenolic Resin	26.2	1.64	12.3	0.70	8.4	0.52	*L. tridentata*	WP	
	44.0	3.35	19.7	1.44	12.2	0.88	*L. cuneifolia*	WP	

Note: T = Tannin content; R = Resin content; P = Protein (crude) content (dry weight percentages); WP = Woody perennial; HP = Herbaceous perennial. *Low* and *High* refer to relative levels of procyanidins (condensed tannins).
Sources: 1 = Feeny 1968; 2 = Lawton, *in press*; 3 = Dement and Mooney 1974; 4 = T. Swain, *personal communication.*

ability and value. We can argue that young leaves are more valuable to plants than mature leaves since damage to the youngest leaves and buds should result in greater loss in plant fitness than an equal amount of damage to mature leaves (McKey 1974). Therefore, all other things being equal, plants should invest more heavily in defense of the growing tips and youngest leaves than in defense of mature leaves. Departures from this rule, such as exhibited by the tanniniferous plants in Table 6-11, should then only take place when the young leaves already have a large measure of protection due to escape in space and time or some other effect. In the case of *Larrea* the youngest leaves do not escape so they are more heavily defended by resin-PO than mature leaves, because they are more valuable than mature leaves. The author prefers this second explanation.

POSSIBLE DEACTIVATION OF THE PHENOLOXIDASE SYSTEM BY *ASTROMA*

We reasoned that if the phenoloxidase system of *Larrea* exhibited an enhancing effect on digestibility reduction by the resin, *Larrea* herbivores may possess systems to inhibit the PO system or to inactivate it in some way. Accordingly, the MTOD of foregut contents of *Astroma,* which had previously been feeding on *L. cuneifolia* leaves, was investigated and found to possess a high MTOD value that was increased 115 percent by addition of excess NDGA, which thus indicates high PO activity (see Table 6A-8). Comparison of the MTOD of foregut contents plus excess NDGA with that of leaf diet plus excess NDGA revealed that the MTOD of foregut contents, measured over the initial three minutes of oxygen uptake, was 2.52 times higher than that of an equal dry weight quantity of leaf diet (Figure 6-6; also see Table 6A-10). In addition, the low decay rate for the gut oxygen uptake curve gave an almost linear approach to anaerobic conditions, while the uptake curve for diet approached 100 percent saturation loss in asymptotic fashion (see Figure 6-6). Apparently, therefore, *Astroma* possesses an intrinsic foregut PO system differing quantitatively and perhaps also kinetically from the leaf PO system. The low decay rate for the gut oxygen uptake curve versus that of diet indicates that the *Astroma* PO system may be a more effective oxygen scavenger at low oxygen concentrations than is the leaf PO system. Thus, by competing with the PO system of the plant for available oxygen, the PO system of *Astroma* may effectively neutralize this portion of the plant's defensive system, at least for leaf tissues of low PO activity. The products of *Astroma* PO activity are presumed to be innocuous to the digestive process and could be high molecular weight polymers as suggested by Miles (1969) (see below). To further demonstrate that *Astroma* foregut possesses an intrinsic PO system, not associated with leaf material in the gut, the MTOD of whole empty foreguts from animals that had been starved for 22.5 hours was measured both without the presence of NDGA (MTOD = 0.078 ml O_2,

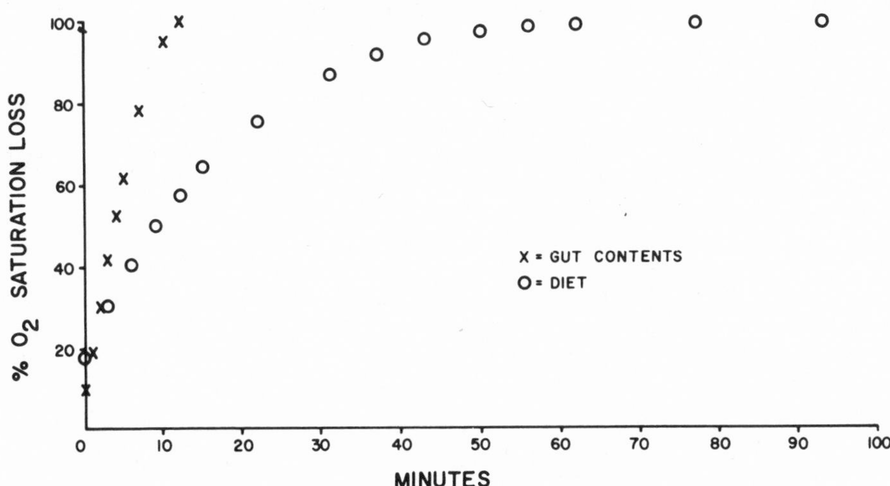

FIGURE 6-6. *Comparison of oxygen uptake by* Astroma quadrilobatum *foregut contents (X) with that of an equal dry weight quantity of the* L. cuneifolia *leaf diet (O).*

g^{-1} d.w., min^{-1}) and in the presence of excess NDGA (MTOD = 0.559). This last finding provides evidence against an alternative explanation for the increased MTOD of gut contents versus that of diet in which the increase is itself part of the plant's defensive system. In this alternative scheme the plant PO system undergoes modification on ingestion of the leaves, perhaps under the influence of herbivore digestive enzymes, to a state of higher activity than that present in native leaves.

The oxygen demand of *Astroma* oral regurgitate, the well-known "tobacco juice" emitted when many Orthoptera are disturbed, was measured in the presence of excess NDGA and found to possess a high value (0.735 ml O_2, ml^{-1}, min^{-1}; dry matter content of regurgitate was not measured).

Intrinsic PO activity has been reported in the salivary secretions of phytophagous Hemiptera (Miles 1969). Miles suggested that these secretions may be adaptations by the insects to circumvent defensive plant reactions in a similar fashion to that proposed here for *Astroma* PO. He proposed that phenols released by the plant into tissue injured by the probing activities of the bugs were defensive in nature and under the influence of the insect's salivary PO were oxidized to innocuous high molecular weight polymers.

SUMMARY

Evidence has been presented that the resinous coating on the leaves of *L. tridentata* and *L. cuneifolia* repels leaf-chewing insects that, in cases studied, prefer to eat leaves of low resin content.

Composed mainly of phenolic aglycones, the resin exhibits tannin-like protein-complexing and starch-complexing properties and in addition reduces the in vitro digestibility of protein. A phenoloxidase (PO) system present in the leaves, activated on leaf maceration, probably enhances the digestibility-reducing action of resin on protein and growth rates of *Astroma quadrilobatum* (Orthoptera:Proscopiidae), which are negatively correlated with resin–PO activity as measured by macerated leaf oxygen demand.

The high oxygen demand of *Astroma* foregut contents, higher than can be explained as due to macerated *Larrea* leaf diet present in the gut, possibly represents a counteradaptation of the insect in which a PO system, intrinsic to the insect, competes with the plant PO system for available oxygen. This arrangement could lead to partial deactivation of the plant's defense system in leaves of low PO activity.

Resin concentration and macerated leaf oxygen demand, which are both higher in young than in mature leaves, show an inverted within-plant distribution when compared to the concentration of tannin in the leaves of oak, toyon, bracken fern, and plum. The apparently divergent defense strategies of *Larrea* and the tanniniferous plants can be unified if we assume that the level of defense by tannin or tannin-like digestibility-reducing systems exhibited by a plant tissue is largely determined by the predictability and availability of that tissue as a food resource to herbivores.

RESUMEN

Se he presentado evidencia de que la capa resinosa de las hojas de *L. tridentata* y *L. cuneifolia* repele a insectos masticadores de hojas, los cuales, en los casos que han sido estudiados, prefieren comer aquéllas con contenido bajo de resina.

Esta resina, compuesta principalmente por agliconas fenólicas, forma complejos con proteínas y almidones, propiedades éstas similares a la de los taninos y, aun más, reduce la digestibilidad in vitro de proteínas. Un sistema de fenoloxidasas (PO) presente en las hojas, activado por la maceración de éstas, probablemente favorece la acción reductiva de digestibilidad de la resina sobre la proteína y se ha encontrado que las tasas de crecimiento de *Astroma quadrilobatum* (Orthoptera:Proscopiidae) se encuentran inversamente relacionadas con la actividad de PO de la resina, medida por la demanda de oxígeno en hojas maceradas. La alta demanda de oxígeno del contenido del intestino anterior de *Astroma*—mayor de la que puede explicarse como debida a la dieta de hojas maceradas de *Larrea* presente en el intestino—posiblemente representa una contraadaptación del insecto en el cual un sistema PO, intrínseco al insecto, compite con el sistema PO de la planta por oxígeno disponible. Esto podría conducir a una desactivación del sistema defensivo de la planta en hojas con baja actividad PO.

La concentración de resina y la demanda de oxígeno en hojas maceradas, ambas mayores en hojas jóvenes en adultas, muestran una distribución invertida dentro de la misma planta, si se compara con la concentración de tanino en las hojas de encino, *Heteromeles arbutifolia, Pteridium aquilinum* y ciruelo (*Prunus* sp.). Las estrategias defensivas, aparentemente divergentes, de *Larrea* y de las plantas taníferas, pueden unificarse si se asume que el nivel de defensa por medio de sistemas de taninos o similares que reducen la digestibilidad, exhibidos por un tejido vegetal, está determinado en gran parte por la predictibilidad y disponibilidad de este tejido como recurso alimenticio de herbívoros.

APPENDIX 6A
MATERIALS, METHODS, AND EXPERIMENTAL RESULTS

Materials

Plant Material

Larrea tridentata was collected at Avra Valley near Tucson, Arizona, and was of the tetraploid race. *Larrea cuneifolia* was collected from the Bolsón de Pipanaco, Andalgalá, Catamarca Province, Argentina. Collection methods were as follows:

Frozen: sprays from 5 *L. tridentata* plants collected (April 27, 1972) into polyethylene bags, placed on ice in the field, stored on ice for 48 hours, and then stored at -20° C until use;

Bag: sprays collected into polyethylene bags, shielded from direct sunlight, and stored at ambient temperature for no longer than 6 hours;

Water: the stems of sprays cut under water and allowed to remain in water until use;

Greenhouse: young plants (15 to 35 cm) collected from Avra Valley (August 1972) and grown in a greenhouse in Seattle, Washington, until use;

Terminal stem portions: the distall 5 cm of stem material.

Insects

Cibolacris parviceps, Semiothisa colorata, Schistocerca americana, Ligurotettix coquilletti, Bootettix punctatus, and *Insara covilleae* were studied at or collected from Avra Valley, near Tucson, Arizona. *Astroma quadrilobatum* was studied at or collected from Andalgalá, Catamarca Province, Argentina.

Methods

1. Resin Content of Larrea *Tissues*

A known mass of fresh plant material was soaked in diethyl ether at room temperature for 2 to 12 hours. A soak of 30 minutes removes 92 percent of the ether-soluble material obtainable by a soak of 18 hours. The resin solution and washings were decanted into a tared flask and rotary evaporated (80° C, 29″ Hg, 2 min). Lower evaporation temperatures result in the retention of ether and water in the resin.

2. Water Content of Larrea *Tissues*

A known mass of fresh material was dried at 60° C for 5 to 24 hours in an oven, unless otherwise stated.

3. Diethyl Ether-Soluble Catechol Content of Larrea *Tissues*

Resin was extracted as of Method 1 and dissolved in 95 percent ethanol. Catechol content of this solution was determined by the ammonium molybdate method of Duisberg et al. (1949). All compounds with at least two vicinal phenolic hydroxyl groups should be molybdate positive. Such compounds present in the resin include NDGA, other minor lignan catechols, and many of the flavonoids (see Chapter 5). Results were calculated from the colorimetric data by using a standard curve of pure NDGA and expressed as percent NDGA. The noncatecholic portion of the resin (resin minus catechols) was then calculated by subtracting catechol content from resin content.

4. Nitrogen Content of Larrea *Tissues*

Total fixed nitrogen content of dried material was determined by the Dumas combustion method.

5. Relative Palatability (PR) of Mature to Young Leaves of L. tridentata *for* Cibolacris *and* Semiothisa *(Table 6-2) and Determination of the Chemical Properties of These Leaves (Table 6-1)*

Sprays of *L. tridentata* from 4 plants were cut under water and kept immersed during transportation and during the experiments (April 25, 1973). Adult female *Cibolacris* and *Semiothisa* larvae (9 to 15 mm) of unknown sex were collected, stored on *Larrea* sprays (bag) and used within 6 hours.

Thirty *Cibolacris* were confined in a cage for 13.5 hours with four sprays, one from each plant. The experiment was conducted in a darkened room under the illumination of a 7.5 watt incandescent bulb suspended directly over the sprays, which were arranged in a square formation. The experiment was designed to simulate nighttime conditions, since in the field *Cibolacris* grazes on *Larrea* only at night. Young and mature leaves present on each spray were counted both before and after the experiment. In the case of partially eaten leaves the percent eaten was visually estimated to the nearest 5 percent. Thus for each spray the number of young and mature leaves eaten and initially present were determined. Relative palatability of mature to young leaves (PR) was then calculated for each spray as previously described (Table 6-2). In a parallel experiment PR values for mature to young leaves for *Semiothisa* were determined (Table 6-2). Four sprays, one from each plant, were clumped together to form a composite "bush" upon which 70 caterpillars were placed in random fashion. The experiment was conducted in total darkness for 13.5 hours.

During the experiment young and mature leaves were collected (water) from sprays of each of the four plants for determination of resin, catechol, water, and nitrogen contents (Table 6-1).

6. Relative Palatability (PR) of Mature to Young Leaves of L. tridentata *to* Schistocerca *(Table 6-2)*

The stem of a *L. tridentata* spray (water, April 11, 1972) was inserted through plastic netting into a layer of water at the bottom of a glass jar (1 L). Two *Schistocerca* adults, one male and one female, were placed in the jar (96 hours) with the lid lightly screwed on. The experiment was repeated (72 hours) using fresh animals. PR values were determined as in Method 5.

7. Relative Palatability (PR) of Fresh L. tridentata *Leaves to Diethly Ether-Extracted Leaves for* Cibolacris *and* Semiothisa *(Tables 6-3 and 6-4)*

Sprays were all collected (bag, April 12-15, 1972) from the same plant. Some sprays were soaked in ether (10 min), dried in sunlight (8 hr, ∿32° C) and humidified in polyethylene bags containing water-soaked paper (3 hr). Adult female *Cibolacris* and *Semiothisa* larvae (9 to 15 mm) of unknown sex were collected and stored on *L. tridentata* (bag) until use (<12 hr). One spray each of extracted and fresh material, stems immersed in water, were simultaneously presented to the insects in glass jars (24 hr) as in Method 6. In the case of *Semiothisa* the two sprays were clumped together, touching each other in many places to facilitate transfer of larvae between sprays. Two insects were placed in each jar, one on each spray. PR values (Tables 6-3 and 6-4) were determined as in Method 5.

8. Maceration of L. tridentata *in the Presence of Air, Air and Cyanide, and under Anaerobic Conditions (Table 6-6)*

Leaves and terminal stems (4.25 g, 8 plants pooled, greenhouse, July 26, 1976) were homogenized (10 min) with buffer (40 ml, 0.2 M sodium phosphate, pH 7.0) in a homogenizer vessel (125 ml) with a large air space (85 ml). The macerate was brought briefly to boil to terminate enzyme activity, cooled, and shaken with ether (400 ml, 5 min) in a separatory funnel. After separation of the layers (2 hr) an aliquot of the ether layer was evaporated for determinations of extractable resin and catechols. A second sample (4.47 g) was similarly homogenized with 0.128 percent sodium cyanide in buffer; termination and extraction were as above. A third sample was similarly homogenized under anaerobic conditions in a homogenizer vessel equipped with a sidearm through which helium gas was admitted during the homogenization. The buffer solution had previously been out-gassed with helium. Termination and extraction were as above.

The use of borate buffers for this experiment or any other experiment involving *Larrea* should be avoided since TLC indicates that compounds not present in native resin (probably borate esters) are formed.

9. Ether Extraction of L. tridentata *Resin, Resin Catechols and NDGA from Aqueous Gelatin Solution (Figure 6-2)*

Larrea tridentata leaf (bag, one plant, April 22, 1973) resin (11.8 mg) in ether (1 ml) was shaken by hand (5 min) with a solution of gelatin (5 ml, 1.5 percent in distilled water) in a volumetric flask. Additional ether (14 ml) was added and the mixture shaken (2 min). After the layers had separated (2 min) the ether layer was decanted. The extraction was repeated with additional 15 ml aliquots of ether. Extracts were pooled in groups of three and evaporated for determination of recovered resin and catechols (Table 6A-1). The procedure was repeated substituting distilled water (5 ml) for the gelatin solution. Recovery of pure NDGA (21.9 mg) from 1.5 percent aqueous gelatin was determined by an identical procedure.

10. Partition of L. tridentata *Resin Between 1.5% Gelatin in Buffer (pH 3.20–10.52) and Ether, and Measurement of Gut pH of Herbivores (Figure 6-4)*

The method of Rhoades and Cates (1976) was followed by using resin

TABLE 6A-1 *Ether-Extraction of* L. tridentata *Resin, Resin Catechols, and NDGA from Aqueous Gelatin Solution.*

# Extractions	% Remaining in the aqueous layer: Resin-water Resin	Resin-gelatin Resin	Resin-gelatin Catechols	NDGA-gelatin NDGA
3	4.1	64.0	59.5	58.2
6	6.1	53.4	49.5	29.5
9	2.5	45.4	40.1	11.4
12		43.0	36.0	3.2

(24.75 mg) obtained from frozen leaves and terminal stems, partitioned between ether (15 ml) and buffer (5 ml) or between ether (15 ml) and gelatin solution (5 ml, 1.5 percent in buffer) to give the data in Table 6A-2.

Gut pH ranges for herbivorous insects (Figure 6-4) were measured using indicator paper and thus represent only approximate values. Live animals (N = 3) were collected from *L. tridentata* in the field, dissected within 1 hour, and the pH of the fore-, mid-, and hindgut of each replicate recorded to the nearest 0.5 pH unit. Gut pH ranges (Figure 6-4) represent the highest and

TABLE 6A-2 *Partition of* L. tridentata *Resin between 1.5% Gelatin in in Buffer and Ether.*

pH[a]	% Resin in buffered gelatin solution $\bar{X}$	$\pm S_{\bar{x}}$	*n*	% Resin in buffer[b] $\bar{X}$	$\pm S_{\bar{x}}$	*n*
2.92				0.9	–	1
3.20	72.0	0.6	3			
4.65				1.5	–	1
5.08	72.6	1.0	3			
6.25	73.1	0.6	3			
7.02	72.9	0.3	4			
7.03				3.0	–	1
7.62	73.5	0.4	3			
8.49	72.5	0.5	3			
8.71				4.0	–	1
9.01	66.5	0.8	3			
9.40				4.2	0.9	3
9.49	63.6	0.1	2			
9.90	56.7	0.6	2			
10.18	43.6	1.1	3			
10.40				17.6	0.9	3
10.45				38.9	1.0	3
10.52	44.3	0.3	3			

[a]Measured pH of aqueous phase.
[b]0.2 M sodium phosphate buffer.

lowest values recorded for each insect species. Little variation in pH between fore-, mid-, and hindgut compartments was noted.

11. Inhibition of Proteolysis by L. cuneifolia *Resin (Figure 6-3)*

A suspension of erepsin (0.100 g/100 ml) in buffer (0.1M, pH 7.0, sodium phosphate) was stirred (∿30 min) and centrifuged at low speed to remove suspended material. Pooled whole guts (1.607 g f.w., fore-, mid-, and hindguts) dissected from 10 *Astroma* females (3rd and 4th instars) that had been starved for two days were homogenized (2 min) in buffer (40 ml), and the homogenate was filtered. Both enzyme preparations were used within 30 minutes.

Fresh *L. cuneifolia* leaves (bag, leaf pairs 2-3 from a single plant, March 11, 1974) were soaked in ether (12 hr) and aliquots of the resin solution evaporated into tared flasks.

A solution of casein (0.833 percent) in buffer was briefly boiled and cooled to room temperature. Casein solution (6 ml) was added to each flask containing resin (B) and also to control flasks containing no resin (A). The flasks were heated (∿90° C, 3 min) while swirling to dissolve the resin, cooled to room temperatures and chloroform antiseptic was added (5 drops) followed by enzyme preparation (erepsin or *Astroma,* 2 ml). Digestion was allowed to proceed (18.25 hr) at 37° C in a shaker bath under aerobic conditions. Termination was achieved by addition of trifluoroacetic acid (TFA) (0.5 ml), after which precipitated protein was removed by filtration and the free α-amino nitrogen content of the filtrate was assayed (Rosen 1957). To account for ninhydrin-positive substances present in the starting materials (mainly in the enzyme preparations), the α-amino nitrogen content (AB) of undigested control solutions and of undigested solutions containing resin (BB) were assayed. This was accomplished by addition of the TFA prior to addition of the enzyme preparation. Controls (A, AB) were performed in triplicate and averaged. Single replicates of test determinations (B, BB) were carried out. The α-amino nitrogen assays were performed in triplicate on all solutions and averaged.

Evaporation of 2 ml of the erepsin and *Astroma* enzyme preparations showed a solids content (other than buffer salts) of <2.5 mg in both cases. Total protein content of digestion solutions were thus 50 mg (casein) + <2.5 mg.

Inhibition of proteolysis was calculated as follows. The resulting data are shown in Table 6A-3. If the α-amino nitrogen contents of solutions *A, B, AB,* and *BB* = *A, B, AB* and *BB,* respectively,

$$\% \text{ inhibition} = \frac{(A - AB) - (B - BB)}{(A - AB)} \times 100.$$

TABLE 6A-3 *Inhibition of Proteolysis by* L. cuneifolia *Resin.*

Resin added / Casein present	% Inhibition of proteolysis	
	Erepsin	*Astroma* proteases
0.0	0.0	0.0
0.287	41.5	41.6
0.574	60.3	57.1
0.860	62.7	69.2
1.720	74.5	78.0
3.440	77.0	81.4

12. Macerated Tissue Oxygen Demand (MTOD) for Leaves of L. cuneifolia *(Tables 6-7, 6-8, and 6-9) and Other Desert Plants (Table 6-7)*

For determinations in Table 6-7, bagged plant material was used, from which leaves of "intermediate" age were picked. For most plants these leaves consisted of those at nodes 1, 2, and 3 behind the growing tip, which had lengths at least half that of the largest leaves on the plant. In the case of scapose plants, leaves of intermediate size were used. For determinations on *L. cuneifolia* leaves (Table 6-8 and 6-9) stems were cut under water. All MTOD determinations were performed within 5 hr of plant collection.

Fresh leaves (0.1 to 0.15 g) were weighed and homogenized (aerobic, 2 min, ∿32°C) with buffer (20 ml, 0.1M, pH 7.0, sodium phosphate). An aliquot (2 ml) of homogenate was rapidly (∿30 sec) transferred to the sample chamber of the oxygen monitor containing preequilibrated buffer (5 ml, 37° C) and the oxygen electrode was inserted. Oxygen saturation loss (%) was recorded after known time intervals. A leaf sample was dried to determine leaf dry matter content.

MTOD was calculated over the first 5 min of oxygen uptake, assuming a saturated oxygen content for the buffer of 5.13×10^{-3} ml ml^{-1} at 32-37° C.

A = % saturation loss in time interval B minus % saturation loss at time = 0
B = time interval (5 min unless otherwise stated)
C = oxygen content of buffer = 5.13×10^{-3} ml^{-1}
D = total volume of buffer = 7 ml
E = fresh weight of leaves homogenized
F = % dry matter content of leaves
G = fraction of macerate added to chamber (0.1 unless otherwise stated)

$$\text{MTOD (dry)} = \frac{A \times C \times D}{B \times E \times F \times G}$$

ml O_2 absorbed per gram dry weight of tissue per minute

$$\text{MTOD (fresh)} = \frac{A \times C \times D}{B \times E \times 100 \times G}$$ ml O_2 absorbed per gram fresh weight tissue per minute

13. Influence of Excess NDGA or Sodium Cyanide on MTOD of L. cuneifolia *Leaves*

MTODs of 5 leaf types (Table 6A–4) from 3 plants (bag, March 10, 1974) were determined (Method 12). The experiments were repeated with a large excess of finely ground (mortar and pestle) NDGA added to the sample chamber prior to addition of the leaf macerates. In a separate experiment of oxygen demand of a large excess of NDGA alone, due to autoxidation, was measured and found to be negligible. In the case of leaves $A_{2,3}$, sodium cyanide was added to the sample chamber prior to addition of the macerate.

14. Influence of Homogenized L. cuneifolia *Leaves on Inhibition of Proteolysis by* L. cuneifolia *Resin*

A solution of *L. cuneifolia* (bag, leaf pairs 1,2 from 3 plants, pooled, March 18, 1974) leaf resin in ether (18 hr soak) was evaporated into tared flasks C, CB, D, DB (below). Buffer (pH 7.0) and casein solution (1.0 percent in buffer) were prepared as in Method 11. Whole gut extract of starved (2 day) *Astroma* females (3rd and 4th instar) was prepared as in Method 13 (10 animals, 1.937 g f.w. guts, 40 ml buffer). A sample of the leaves (1.000 g f.w. 45.1 percent H_2O, 9.78 percent f.w. resin) was homogenized (5 min) with buffer (30 ml). One ml of this homogenate thus contained 33.3 mg leaf material and 3.3 mg resin.

The following solutions were prepared:

A = 5 ml 1% casein + 5 ml buffer + 5 drops $CHCl_3$
AB = A + 0.5 ml TFA
B = 1 ml leaf homogenate + 5 ml 1% casein + 5 ml buffer + 5 drops $CHCl_3$
BB = B + 0.5 ml TFA
C = 21.2 mg resin + 5 ml 1% casein + 5 ml buffer + 5 drops $CHCl_3$
CB = C + 0.5 ml TFA
D = 17.9 mg resin + 1 ml leaf homogenate + 5 ml 1% casein + 4 ml buffer + 5 drops $CHCl_3$
DB = D + 0.5 ml TFA

Resin was dissolved in the casein solution (C,CB,D,DB) prior to addition of the other ingredients as in Method 11. All solutions were then incubated (37° C, 20 min, aerobic) after which time erepsin solution (2 ml, 0.1 percent prepared as in Method 11) was added to all samples. Digestion was allowed to proceed (aerobic) at 37° C for 19.75 hr after which time TFA (0.5 ml) was

TABLE 6A–4 *Influence of Excess NDGA or Sodium Cyanide on MTOD of* L. cuneifolia *Leaves*

Plant #	A		B		C
Leaf age	2,3	6,7	2,3	5–8	5–8
Resin present (mg) in the chamber	0.72	0.60	0.68	0.60	0.61
MTOD (dry)	0.1203, 0.1057	0.0684, 0.0738	0.2261, 0.2711	0.2357, 0.2083	0.1430, 0.1198
$\overline{X}$	0.1130	0.0711	0.2486	0.2220	0.1314
NDGA added (mg)	6.3	7.2	7.8	7.5	5.5
MTOD (dry)	0.1394, 0.1692	0.0896, 0.1074	0.5143, 0.5185	0.3300, 0.2958	0.1674, 0.2060
$\overline{X}$	0.1543	0.0985	0.5164	0.3129	0.1867
Δ MTOD %[a]	+36.5	+38.5	+107.7	+40.9	+42.1
NaCN added (mg)	1.0				
MTOD (dry)	0.0143				
Δ MTOD %[b]	–87.3				

[a]% change in MTOD due to addition of NDGA.
[b]% change in MTOD due to addition of NaCN (no NDGA present).

added to A, B, and C to terminate the reaction. Three replicates of each determination were carried out. Inhibition of proteolysis was calculated as in Method 11. (See Table 6A-5).

15. Influence of Mushroom Polyphenoloxidase on Inhibition of Proteolysis by L. tridentata *Resin*

A solution of *L. tridentata* leaf and terminal stem (frozen) resin in ether was evaporated into tared flasks, B, BB, C, CB. Buffer (pH 7.0) casein (1 percent in buffer) and erepsin (0.1 percent in buffer) were prepared as in Method 11. Mushroom polyphenoloxidase 0.1 percent in buffer was prepared by dissolution at room temperature.

The following solutions were prepared:

A = 3 ml 1% casein + 1 ml buffer + 5 drops $CHCl_3$

AB = A + 0.5 ml TFA

B = 18.9 mg resin + 3 ml 1% casein + 1 ml buffer + 5 drops $CHCl_3$

BB = B + 0.5 ml TFA

C = 18.9 mg resin + 3 ml 1% casein + 1 ml 0.1% polyphenoloxidase solution + 5 drops $CHCl_3$

CB = C + 0.5 ml TFA

Resin was dissolved in the casein solution (B, BB, C, CB) prior to addition of the other ingredients as in Method 11. All solutions were then incubated (37° C, 20 min, aerobic) after which erepsin solution (2 ml) was added to each sample. Digestion was allowed to proceed (aerobic) at 37° C for 2.0 hr after which time TFA (0.5 ml) was added to A, B, and C to terminate the reactions. Three replicates of each determination were carried out. Inhibition of proteolysis was calculated as in Method 11. (See Table 6A-6.)

TABLE 6A-5 *Influence of Homogenized* L. cuneifolia *Leaves on Inhibition of Proteolysis by* L. cuneifolia *Resin.*

Additive	% Inhibition of proteolysis $\bar{X}$	± $S_{\bar{x}}$	n
Leaf homogenate	2.6	1.5	3
Resin	38.3	1.2	3
Leaf homogenate + resin	54.2	1.1	3

TABLE 6A-6 *Influence of Mushroom Polyphenoloxidase on Inhibition of Proteolysis by* L. tridentata *Resin.*

Additive	% Inhibition of proteolysis		
	$\bar{X}$ ±	$S\bar{x}$	n
Resin	69.8	2.5	3
Resin + polyphenoloxidase	81.8	1.7	3

16. Relative Palatability (PR) of Mature to Young Leaves of L. cuneifolia *for* Astroma *(Table 6–2) and Determination of Leaf Properties (Table 6–8)*

Sprays of *L. cuneifolia* (March 16, 1974) from 7 plants were collected (water) and presented to juvenile *Astroma* females (10.25 hr, 150 insects, 3rd and 4th instar) in a similar fashion to that described for *Cibolacris* in Method 5. Relative palatability (PR) of mature to young leaves of each spray were calculated as in Method 5. Water, nitrogen, resin, ether-soluble catechol, resin minus catechol contents, and MTODs were determined for young and mature leaves of sprays collected (water) from each of the 7 bushes at the same time that the palatability determination sprays were collected. Leaf toughness of each leaf type was determined by using a penetrometer method as follows: A fresh leaf was clamped in a plexiglass sandwich equipped with a hole (3 mm) through which a cylindrical rod (flat, smooth-ended, 0.8 mm diameter) rested on the leaf surface. A test tube, surrounded by a clamped sleeve, rested in turn upon the rod. Mercury was added dropwise to the tube until the rod penetrated the leaf surface. Each leaf toughness value (Tables 6–8 and 6–9) is the mass in grams required to force the rod through the leaf. Five leaves of each type were tested.

17. Growth Rates of Juvenile Astroma *on* L. cuneifolia *Leaves Varying in MTOD and Other Properties (Figure 6–5 and Table 6–9)*

Sprays of *L. cuneifolia* were collected (water, March 6–14, 1974), trimmed to single leaf age classes (Table 6–9), and the stems were placed in glass jars containing water. Each jar containing an individual spray was surrounded by a tube of plastic netting to prevent escape of the insects. Plugs of netting were inserted into the jar mouths to prevent access of the insects to and subsequent drowning in the water. Small sticks were arranged around each spray between the floor and the leafy portion of the spray so that insects falling below could readily climb back up. Juvenile *Astroma* females (56 insects, 3rd and 4th instars) were collected and randomly assigned to 7 groups. Each group was weighed and placed on a particular leaf tissue type. Sprays were replaced every 2nd day—on the 3rd, 5th and 7th days of the experiment—and any dead insects were removed. An excess of leaves was always present and in no case did the insects consume greater than 75 percent of the leaves offered. MTOD values of samples of each leaf type were measured initially and at the time of each spray change. These values were then averaged (N = 4) to give the MTOD values in Table 6-9. Weighed samples of leaves from each of the initial sprays and each of the replacement sprays were (1) extracted with ether (12 hr) for determination of resin, ether-soluble catechol and resin minus catechol contents and (2) dried for determination of water and nitrogen contents. Values (Table 6-9) for resin, catechol, resin minus catechol, nitrogen, and water contents are from single determinations carried out on the pooled samples from the initial sprays and the 3 replacement sprays. Thus, although these values are averaged over the 4 sprays presented to each *Astroma* group, the variance is unknown. Leaf toughness was determined (Method 16) only for the second replacement sprays. Each toughness value value (Table 6-9) is the average of 5 replicates.

On the 9th day the total mass of surviving insects (fresh weight) in each group was determined. From the initial and final total masses, the average initial mass per insect and the average final mass per survivor was calculated for each group. From these figures the average growth rate of surviving insects (Δ% mass per day) over the eight-day period was calculated; this equals the change in fresh weight mass per surviving insect per day over the eight-day period, compounded daily.

18. Oxygen Uptake of Astroma *Foregut Contents with and without Addition of Excess NDGA and Excess NDGA plus Sodium Cyanide*

Live *Astroma* (3 insects, 3rd or 4th instar females), which had been feeding on fresh *L. cuneifolia* leaves in polyethylene bags for 5 hours since capture, were dissected. The pooled foregut contents (A) were weighed, homogenized with buffer (0.1M, pH 7.0, sodium phosphate) and an aliquot (2 ml) added to the sample chamber of the oxygen monitor as in Method 12. The experiment was repeated with addition of excess NDGA (B) and also with addition of both excess NDGA and sodium cyanide (C) to the sample chamber prior to addition of homogenate. The dry matter contents of a further three pooled foregut contents were determined (110° C, 30 min). MTOD values were calculated as in Method 12. (See Tables 6A-7 and 6A-8).

TABLE 6A-7 *Contents of the Test Samples for Oxygen Uptake by* Astroma *Foregut Contents with and without Addition of Excess NDGA and NDGA plus Sodium Cyanide.*

	A	B	C
Gut contents homogenized (g f.w.)	0.3234	0.3015	0.3125
Dry matter (%)	34.8	34.8	34.8
Fraction added to chamber	0.0333	0.0357	0.0345
Gut contents added to chamber (g d.w.)	0.00375	0.00375	0.00375
NDGA added to chamber (mg)	0	12.5	12.3
NaCN added to chamber (mg)	0	0	1.1

TABLE 6A-8 *Oxygen Uptake by* Astroma *Foregut Contents with and without Addition of Excess NDGA and NDGA plus Sodium Cyanide.*

	% saturation loss		
Time (min)	A	B	C
0	15.0	12.5	10.0
1		27.5	
2	36.0	49.5	
3	41.5	65.5	
4		77.0	
5	49.5	87.0	11.5
6	52.5		
7	54.5		
10	60.0		
15	66.0		
MTOD (dry)	0.661	1.428	0.029
Δ MTOD %	–	+115.2	-95.6

TABLE 6A-9 *Contents of the Test Samples for Comparison between Oxygen Uptake of* Astroma *Foregut Contents and That of* L. cuneifolia *Leaf Diet.*

	Foregut contents	Diet
Tissue homogenized (g f.w.)	0.3816	0.2490
Dry matter (%)	28.7	45.5
Fraction added to chamber	0.0333	0.0322
Tissue added to chamber (g d.w.)	0.00365	0.00365
NDGA added to chamber (mg)	8.5	9.7

TABLE 6A-10 *Oxygen Uptake of* Astroma *Foregut Contents and of* L. cuneifolia *Leaf Diet.*

Time (min)	% Saturation loss	
	Foregut contents	Diet
0	10.5	18.0
1	19.5	
2	30.5	
3	42.0	30.5
4	52.5	
5	62.0	
6		40.5
7	78.0	
9		50.0
10	95.0	
12	100.0	57.5
15		64.5
22		75.5
31		87.0
37		92.0
43		95.5
50		97.5
56		98.5
62		99.0
77		99.5
93		99.75
MTOD (dry)[a]	1.034	0.410
Relative MTOD[a]	2.52	1.00

[a]Measured over the first 3 minutes.

19. Comparison between Oxygen Uptake of Astroma *Foregut Contents and that of the* L. cuneifolia *Leaf Diet (Figure 6-6)*

Astroma (3rd or 4th instar females) were allowed to feed (bags, 24 hr) on sprays of *L. cuneifolia* from a single bush from which all leaves other than those at nodes 5-8 had been removed. Oxygen uptake curves for 3 pooled foregut contents in the presence of excess NDGA and an equal dry weight quantity of the *L. cuneifolia* leaf diet in the presence of excess NDGA were then measured as in Method 12. Three pooled foregut contents and a leaf sample were dried (110° C, 30 min) to determine dry matter content. (See Tables 6A-9 and 6A-10).

7

Larrea as a Habitat Component for Desert Arthropods

J. C. Schultz, D. Otte, and F. Enders

Because *Larrea* is a numerical and biomass dominant over a great portion of both the Sonoran Desert of North America and the Monte of South America, we might expect it to be an important habitat component for a variety of arthropods in these deserts. Studies of arthropods on *L. cuneifolia* near Andalgalá and on *L. tridentata* near Silver Bell confirm this expectation. At least twenty-five species in six orders of insects have been found in association with *L. cuneifolia* near Andalgalá, and thirty species in five orders have been found associated with *L. tridentata* near Silver Bell during the present study. Some twenty-three species of spiders are found associated with *L. cuneifolia* and twenty-six species with *L. tridentata* (not including ground-dwelling species) in the two deserts. As many as thirty species of bees may use *L. cuneifolia* flowers in northwestern Argentina; perhaps a similar number utilize *L. tridentata* in Arizona (see Chapter 4).

Insect-plant interactions of several types have varying degrees of fidelity. Some arthropods are specific to *Larrea,* while some use other plant or habitat components. Arthropods may be only partially restricted to *Larrea,* such as *Astroma quadrilobatum* (Orthoptera:Proscopiidae), which feeds mainly or exclusively on *L. cuneifolia* but oviposits in the ground. Other species may use *Larrea* in more than one mode—for example, *Insara covilleae* (Orthoptera: Tettigoniidae), which feeds and oviposits on *L. tridentata.*

There are four main ways arthropods use plants: (1) as a source for water and other nutrients, (2) as a place to hide, (3) as a place to hunt (in part confounded with first use), or (4) as a location for reproductive activities. How do the characteristics of *Larrea* influence its use in these ways? What patterns of use can actually be discerned? This chapter provides tentative answers to these questions because the answers are necessarily based on work recently completed and only partly analyzed.

LARREA AS A NUTRIENT AND WATER SOURCE

Arthropod herbivores require at least four basic kinds of substances from plants: protein for growth, vitamins, sterols, and an energy source (Southwood 1973). Arthropods of several orders have overcome evolutionary hurdles to exploit the variety of complex and energy-rich compounds produced by plants. In addition, since water must be present for photosynthesis to occur, plants provide good water sources for many herbivores.

The distribution of nitrogen and water within *Larrea* shrubs has been investigated by Rhoades (see Chapter 6) who found insignificant differences among leaves of different ages. Differences in toughness and resin content were more significant among the same tissues. Burk and Dick-Peddie (1973) have shown that there is little or no significant difference in caloric value among leaves, stems, flowers, and fruits of *L. tridentata.* Although both phloem and xylem may be under considerable negative pressure, they can be expected to serve as adequate water sources (Halvorson and Patten 1974).

The availability to arthropods of nutrients and water from *Larrea* seems to vary little temporally. Of course, strong seasonality in flower and fruit production may be observed, but *Larrea* tissues show relatively low seasonal variation in carbohydrate and sugar content, since *Larrea* is "almost evergreen" (Halvorson and Patten 1974; Strain 1970). This low variation factor seems true for both the North and South American species, and if it is so, we can expect production of nutrients and availability of water in *Larrea* to exert relatively little influence on the seasonality of associated arthropods.

The availability of nutrients and water from *Larrea* to herbivorous arthropods is strongly regulated by the plant's defenses. These defenses have been characterized (see Chapter 6) and consist primarily of a phenolic resinous coating on the leaves, which disrupts digestive processes in a fashion similar to that exhibited by the vegetable tannins. A phenoloxidase system present in the plant is also involved in antiherbivore defense. Spatial, temporal, and individual variation in the strength of this effect have been observed. Newer, rapidly growing tissues (e.g., young leaves) seem most heavily defended while protection of other tissues declines with age. There is thus an indirect relationship between expected income value to the plant and degree of protection among *Larrea* leaves, in which the most "valuable" tissues are best protected. At the earliest stages of development, flower buds are well defended; however, mature flowers and fruits are low in resin. Fine hairs that develop on the fruits as they mature may deter small insect (e.g., mirid bugs). That any of the plant's defenses serve adequately to reduce water loss to arthropods, except as they deter attack in general, is doubtful.

Differences in nutrient availability between *L. cuneifolia* and *L. tridentata* appear minimal, although direct comparisons are few. Mabry et al. (see Chapter 5) find resin content to be much higher by dry weight in *L. cuneifolia.* The results of these incomplete surveys could reflect seasonal, habitat, and/or even random variation in the populations sampled. Apparently, the basic antiherbivore mechanisms of the two species function quite similarly and affect nutrient availability in similar ways.

Seasonality of production in the two species of *Larrea* is quite different due to the lack of substantial winter rains at the Andalgalá site (see Chapter 3). Hence *L. cuneifolia* exhibits a single main peak in production, flowering, and fruit set, while *L. tridentata* at Silver Bell exhibits both a winter and a summer peak of growth. A single, one-season arthropod community might have been anticipated associated with South American *L. cuneifolia* at Andalgalá (summer) and possibly two arthropod communities associated with *L. tridentata* at Silver Bell (winter and summer), depending on the distinctness of these peaks.

Also, *L. tridentata* in Arizona shows a drop in defensive capabilities (defined by resin and catechol concentrations) from late afternoon until midnight, while this drop is much less distinct for Argentine *L. cuneifolia* (Table 7-1). Insects feed on both plants primarily during this period (evening), and casual observation suggests that feeding intensity drops after eleven in the evening at Silver Bell. Data are inadequate for a close comparison between the *Larrea* species in terms of this effect. Arachnid diet cycles are similar in the two deserts.

Thus, each species of *Larrea* presents herbivorous arthropods with a mosaic of tissue types that differ spatially and temporally in defense (resin content) and spatially in morphology and toughness. There appears to be only small quantitative differences between the two *Larrea* species in defense, primarily by virtue of a greater dry weight percentage of resin in *L. cuneifolia.*

Utilization of *L. cuneifolia* as a Nutrient and Water Source

Finding that a number of insect species in several orders use *Larrea* for nutrients and/or water is not surprising. Most distinguishable tissue types are consumed by at least one species of herbivore. These herbivores range from polyphagous species for which *Larrea* is but one of a wide range of foods to monophagous *Larrea* specialists (Table 7-2). Interestingly, the degree of specialization (judged by the proportion of monophagous species) of the North American *L. tridentata* herbivores appears to be higher than that of the South American *L. cuneifolia* herbivores. The evolutionary reasons for this are not clear, although a complex interaction of effects among utilization of the plant as food and as a predation-avoidance substrate and history are probably involved (Cates et al. 1977).

Of the eighteen chewing insect species using *L. cuneifolia* for food near Andalgalá, five appear to be monophagous, three oligophagous, and seven polyphagous. Of these species the dominant in terms of biomass, conspicu-

TABLE 7-1 *Diurnal Resin Variation of Leaf Pair 2 in* L. cuneifolia *and* L. tridentata.

	Night		Early morning		Midday		Afternoon	
	L.c.	L. t.	L. c.	L. t.	L. c.	L. t.	L. c.	L. t.
% Resin dry wt.	12.81 ± 1.06	14.61 ± 3.21	13.48 ± 1.64	13.30 ± 2.70	12.92 ± 0.82	12.65 ± 3.38	13.16 ± 1.99	11.32 ± 2.78
Resin mg/10 lvs	8.24 ± 1.53	9.13 ± 2.33	7.80 ± 1.32	8.05 ± 2.09	7.73 ± 1.28	8.10 ± 2.28	7.58 ± 1.14	6.18 ± 1.27
Resin catechols % dry wt	4.04 ± 0.62	4.16 ± 1.40	4.60 ± 1.0	4.36 ± 1.03	4.03 ± 0.37	4.11 ± 1.26	4.36 ± 1.05	3.94 ± 0.76
Resin catechols mg/10 leaves	2.61 ± 0.62	2.79 ± 0.94	2.67 ± 0.66	2.87 ± 0.87	2.41 ± 0.45	2.71 ± 1.09	2.50 ± 0.57	2.16 ± 0.49

TABLE 7-2 *Characteristics of Insects Associated with* L. cuneifolia *at Andalgalá, Catamarca, Argentina.*

Taxon	Season	Diet breadth	Food	Mouth parts	Hiding substrate	Pred.-av. guild	Oviposition site
Orthoptera							
Proscopiidae							
Astroma quadrilobatum	summer	oligoph	yng leaves	chewing	old-yng stems, old leaves	8	ground
Tettigoniidae							
Tetana grisea	spr/sum	oligoph	flowers	chewing	mid-old stems	1	leaves
Mantidae							
Stagmomantis sp. 1	summer	predator	predator	chewing	all tissues	5	old stems
Stagmomantis sp. 2	summer	predator	predator	chewing	all tissues	3	old stems
Coleoptera							
Meloidae							
Pyrota sanguinothorax	spr/sum	monoph	flowers	chewing	leaves	6	? ground
Glaphyrolytta viridipennis	spr/sum	monoph	flowers	chewing	leaves	5	? ground
Scarabaeidae							
Co-14	spring	monoph	leaves	chewing	ground	9	ground
Co-38	spring	oligoph	flowers	chewing	ground	9	ground
Tenebrionidae							
Co-5A	spr/sum	polyph	flowers	chewing	mid-yng stems	3	? off bush
Co-5B	spr/sum	polyph	flowers	chewing	mid-yng stems	3	? off bush
Co-29	summer	monoph	yng stems	chewing	old stems	4	?
Co-183	summer	polyph	old leaves	chewing	mid-yng stems	5	? off bush
Buprestidae							
Chalcopoecila ornata	summer	monoph	old leaves	chewing	new leaves	3	old stems
Psiloptera baeri	summer	monoph	yng stems	chewing	old-mid stems	1	mid stems
Curculionidae							
Naupactus sulfureosignathus	summer	polyph	mid leaves	chewing	all tissues	6	? off bush

Pantomorus viridosquamosus?	summer	polyph	buds, flowers, old leaves	chewing	lvs, flowers, yng-mid stems	6	? off bush
Co-17	spr/sum	monoph	old leaves	chewing	upper stems	3	? off bush
Heteroptera							
Miridae							
He-1	spr/sum	oligoph	buds, imm. fruits	sucking	buds, old lvs, imm fruits	6	yng stems
He-50	spring	oligoph	lvs, imm frts, buds, stems	sucking	yng leaves	1	leaves or stems
He-52	spr/sum	monoph	flowers, imm fruits	sucking	old leaves, stems	3	leaves or stems
Pentatomidae							
He-51	summer	monoph	fruits, stems leaves	sucking	leaves	5	stems, leaf surface
Homoptera							
Cicadellidae							
Ho-19	summer	monoph	yng leaves, stems	sucking	yng leaves, stems	3	yng leaves
Lepidoptera							
Geometridae							
Lp-60	summer	monoph	yng leaves	chewing	leaves, stems	1	leaves

Note: Spp. total = 21 (2 predators and 19 herbivores). Monoph = monophagous (eating only *Larrea* tissues); oligoph = oligophagous (eating two to four species of plants); polyph = polyphagous (eating more than four species of plants).

ousness, and damage to the plant is a grasshopper in the South American family Proscopiidae, *Astroma quadrilobatum* (Mello-Leitao). Populations of this branch-mimicking species may reach densities of fifty to one hundred large adult insects on a small- to medium-sized bush of *Larrea*. Populations of this grasshopper frequently defoliate *Larrea* bushes of average size (height: 1 meter, volume: 2 to 3 m^3). They prefer younger leaves but will eat leaves of all ages, flowers, and flower buds. No other single species of chewing or sucking herbivore has ever been observed in this study to reach such damaging densities on any species of *Larrea*.

Several species of insect herbivores prefer flowers and/or buds to other tissues of *L. cuneifolia*. Among these insects are the conspicuous meloid beetles *Pyrota sanguinithorax* and *Glaphyrolytta viridipennis*. The only orthopteran other than *A. quadrilobatum* associated with *L. cuneifolia* at Andalgalá is *Tetana grisea* (Tettigoniidae), which also strongly prefers flowers, but tends toward cannibalism during laboratory trials and is able to survive flowerless periods in the field while refusing to eat leaves.

A number of beetles feed extensively on *L. cuneifolia:* several scarabs (leaves or flowers), several tenebrionids (leaves or flowers), and two buprestids (leaves or young stems). These feeding records are the results of extensive field observations and of laboratory preference tests using fresh plant material.

The appearance on *L. cuneifolia* at Andalgalá of most of the chewing herbivores follows the beginning of summer rains fairly closely, usually in early January. *Astroma* eggs will hatch in November if sufficient rain falls to soak the ground. The nymphs mature even in a dry December and reach adulthood in January. More commonly, eggs hatch in January and adults are observed by the end of February. Active adults have been found as late as June (J. leClaire, *personal communication*), but none have been seen in August.

The two meloid beetles also may appear if there is sufficient flowering by either *L. cuneifolia* or *L. divaricata* in November. Otherwise they too appear after the first heavy rains of January, when *L. cuneifolia* flowering is strongest.

Two curculionid weevils, *Pantomorus* sp. (prob. *viridosquamosus*), and an unidentified otiorhynchine (collection no. Co-17) may be found during November, but few were collected. An as yet undertermined scarabaeid beetle (collection no. Co-38), "close to *Phyllophaga*"–USNM) regularly appears in November and occurs into January when it becomes less common. It feeds on flowers of *L. divaricata* and *L. cuneifolia*.

Flowers may also be taken by fungus-growing ants (Hymenoptera:Formidae) in the genera *Acromyrmex* and *Trachymyrmex*. These "leaf-cutter" ants have only rarely been seen cutting leaves from *L. cuneifolia,* but they stripped flower buds from plants that were watered during the dry season. Seeds and seed husks may also be collected by these genera as well as by harvester ants, *Pogonomyrmex,* and scavengers, *Camponotus* sp. Various Homoptera are tended by ants on this bush. No specific coadapted relationships have been studied involving ants and *L. cuneifolia.*

As is common among insects everywhere but in cold climates, the feeding activities of most of these *Larrea* associates are limited to crepuscular or nocturnal hours. Exception include the two meloid species, which feed actively through the morning hours, all of the Heteroptera, which can be found feeding both day and night, and perhaps some Orthoptera. In both deserts feeding activity is rare during the hot afternoon hours. At the Argentine site, activity of insect herbivores extends well past midnight.

Of the six species of sucking insects found feeding on *L. cuneifolia,* three are monophagous, and three are oligophagous and feed only on Zygophyllaceae. The two oligophagous mirid bugs (as yet undertermined) are not particularly selective for tissues pierced, although one (collection no. He-1) prefers flower buds while the other will feed on leaves and young stems as well as on flower buds and fruits. Both species appear to be facultative predators. Feeding differences between these sucking types appear to be based on frequency distributions of tissues in their diets rather than any strict tissue preferences. Young, growing stems are the common feeding locus for *Protargionia larreae,* the coccid scale insect associated with *Larrea* (at least *L. cuneifolia* and probably *L. divaricata*) in Argentina according to MacGillivray (1921).

The sucking insects differ somewhat from chewers in seasonality of occurrence in that the three mirids appear in November and remain into summer. One pentatomid (collection no. He-51) and a common cicadellid (collection no. Ho-19) appear only after summer rains.

Utilization of *L. tridentata* as a Nutrient and Water Source

In south-central Arizona, the community of insect herbivores on *L. tridentata* is not dominated by any single species; rather it consists of a variety of insects that are frequently common, but not extremely abundant. Of the fifteen chewing insects using *L. tridentata* at Silver Bell, eleven are monophagous, none are oligophagous, and four are polyphagous species (Table 7-3).

The Orthoptera are represented by six regularly occurring species in four families, including a walking stick (Phasmidae) and a katydid (Tettigoniidae). Four of these species exhibit fairly specific tissue preferences on the bush and are limited to *L. tridentata.* One acridid species, *Cibolacris parviceps,* utilizes annual plants as well, especially in early spring. Another acridid, *Melanoplus lakinus,* is polyphagous (Caplan 1966) and only occasionally includes *Larrea* in its diet. The importance of the inclusion of winter annuals in the diet of *Cibolacris* is perhaps indicated by the virtual absence of this species from the Silver Bell study sites during the summer of 1974; this period followed a win-

TABLE 7–3 *Characteristics of Insects Associated with* L. tridentata *at Silver Bell, Arizona.*

Taxon	Season	Diet breadth	Food	Mouth parts	Hiding substrate	Pred-av. guild	Oviposition site
Orthoptera							
Acrididae							
Ligurotettix coquilletti	summer	monoph	old leaves	chewing	old stems	3	ground
Bootettix punctatus	summer	monoph	yng leaves	chewing	yng leaves	1	ground
Cibolacris parviceps	win/sum	polyph	old leaves, flowers	chewing	ground	3	ground
Melanoplus sp.	summer	polyph	old leaves	chewing	ground, stems	3	ground
Tettigoniidae							
Insara covilleae	summer	monoph	tips, resin glands	chewing	yng leaves	3	inside leaves
Phasmidae							
Diapheromera covilleae	summer	monoph	yng stems, tips	chewing	old stems	1	ground
Mantidae							
Stagmomantis limbata	summer	predator	predator	chewing	leaves	5	stems
S. californica	summer	predator	predator	chewing	leaves	3	stems
Coleoptera							
Meloidae							
Epicauta lauta	summer	monoph	flowers	chewing	flowers, lvs	6	flowers
Pyrota postica	summer	oligoph	flowers	chewing	flowers	6	ground
Scarabaeidae							
Diplotaxis sp.	summer	monoph	yng leaves	chewing	ground	4	ground
Curculionidae							
Eupagoderes marmoratus	winter	polyph	old leaves, flowers	chewing	old stems	5	? off bush
E. decipiens	winter	monoph	old leaves	chewing	stems	3	? off bush

Chrysomelidae							
Pachybrachis mellitis	summer	monoph	old leaves	chewing	mid stems	3	?
Heteroptera							
Miridae							
He-2	winter	monoph	flowers, buds	sucking	leaves	3	inside yng stems
He-4	winter	monoph	fruits	sucking	leaves	3	inside yng stems
Pentatomidae							
Thyanta pallidovipens	summer	monoph	buds, leaves, ovaries, stems	sucking	yng-old leaves	5	leaves
Dendrocoris contaminatus	summer	monoph	buds	sucking	old leaves	5	leaves
Reduviidae							
Zelus soccus	summer	predator	predator	sucking	mid stems	3	?
Homoptera							
Membracidae							
Multareoides bifurcatus	winter	monoph	leaves, yng stems	sucking	yng leaves	3	inside stems
M. digitatus	winter	monoph	leaves, yng stems	sucking	yng-mid stems	3	inside stems
Centrodontus atlas	winter	monoph	yng stems, leaves	sucking	yng-mid stems	1	inside stems
Lepidoptera							
Geometridae							
Synglochis perumbraria	winter	monoph	yng leaves	chewing	yng stems?	1	leaves
Semiothisa colorata	winter	monoph	yng leaves	chewing	yng leaves, yng-mid stems	1	leaves
Psychidae							
Thyridopteryx meadi	winter	monoph	leaves	chewing	–	4	inside case

Note: Spp. total = 25 (3 predators and 22 herbivores). Monoph = monophagous (eating only *Larrea* tissues); oligoph = oligophagous (eating two to four species of plants); polyph = polyphagous (eating more than four species of plants).

ter in which drought had drastically reduced the number and diversity of winter annuals (C. H. Lowe, *personal communication*). Species like *Bootettix punctatus* and *Ligurotettix coquilleti,* which are dependent solely on *Larrea* from winter hatching through the summer, appeared to be as common during the summer of 1974 as any previous years.

These five orthopteran species occur together commonly in south-central Arizona, although *Diapheromera covilleae* (Phasmidae) may be more common to the east while *Ligurotettix coquilleti* (Acrididae) is near the eastern edge of its range at Tucson. The Tucson area represents the center of the ranges of *Cibolacris parviceps* and *Insara covilleae* (Tettigoniidae). *Clematodes larreae* (Acrididae), another *Larrea* specialist, occurs in extreme southern and eastern Arizona and Chihuahua, Mexico, but is rare (Ball et al. 1942; Helfer 1963; Otte, *personal observation*). None were observed during these studies.

Feeding segregation on the basis of tissues among the five orthopteran species feeding on *Larrea* is relatively minor among the acridids, but noticeable between the acridids and the other two families represented. *Diapheromera* (Phasmidae) shows clear preference for young growing stem tips and green stems and frequently ignores leaves, while *Insara* (Tettigoniidae) eats exclusively the petiole and resin gland portion of the leaves. Among the acridids, all of which feed on leaves or flowers, *Bootettix* prefers young leaf tissues (leaf pair number two, numbering from stem tip) while *Ligurotettix* prefers slightly older leaf pairs (numbers three and four). *Cibolacris,* the more generalized feeder, prefers the oldest leaves it can find (pairs number four and older). These rather fine discriminations are probably based on the chemical composition of the leaves and the fact that much overlap occurs (see Chapter 6).

Unlike the herbivore community of *L. cuneifolia* in Argentina, the community of *L. tridentata* has a conspicuous lepidopteran component. The feeding of these lepidopterans is limited to the leaves of *L. tridentata,* and the preference of *Semiothisa colorata* is for young tissues, usually leaf pair number one (see Chapter 6). Feeding observations are insufficient to describe the tissue preferences of the psychid larva and of *Synglochis,* both of which are rare at the study site.

Flower feeding on *L. tridentata* in Arizona is apparently the domain of the Meloidae (Coleoptera) and one acridid grasshopper, *Cibolacris parviceps.* In addition to the two meloid species (*Epicauta lauta* and *Pyrota postica*) other beetles feed on *L. tridentata* flowers but prefer leaves. These include a cryptocephaline chrysomelid, *Pachybrachis* prob. *mellitis* (monophagous), at least two curculionid weevils, *Eupagoderes marmoratus* and probably *E. decipiens,* which are both probably polyphagous, and a scarab, *Diplotaxis* sp. (monophagous). A buprestid, *Hippomelus* sp., is reportedly associated with the flowers, but insufficiency of observations prevented confirmation. (There may be more than two species of weevils associated with *L. tridentata,* but determinations of the species involved have not yet been completed.)

As is the case in Argentina, no specific relationships seem to have evolved between *L. tridentata* and any ant species. Species in the harvester genera *Pogonomyrmex, Veromessor,* and *Aphaenogaster* may collect seeds as may *Camponotus,* a scavenger. *Acromyrmex versicolor* has been reported taking leaves of creosote bush (F. G. Werner, *personal communication*), but it is very rare in our study site, in contrast to Argentine *Acromyrmex.*

Of the orthopteran species feeding on *L. tridentata,* all but *Cibolacris* hatch in early spring (February to April) and develop slowly into adults by July or August. *Cibolacris* adults are common by April, but slowly taper off in numbers through the summer (Ball et al. 1942). Some staggering of developmental stages among species occurs—for example, *Insara* hatches and matures slightly later than *Bootettix.*

The two geometrid species reach peak abundances in March and April, but they may persist through the summer. *Synglochis perumbraria* appears to be the more seasonal of the two species (F. G. Werner, *personal communcation*).

All of the Coleoptera species found on *L. tridentata* are of summer occurrence with the exception of the weevils, which are most numerous in March, April, and May, although they may be present in reduced numbers through the summer. The two meloid species appear during the July flowering period and are occasionally very numerous in restricted areas (J. L. Neff, *personal communication*).

All eight principal species of sucking insects occurring on *L. tridentata* are limited to the plant. Very occasionally other accidental species in the Pentatomidae or Miridae will be found on *Larrea,* but no other regular feeding associations have been observed.

The two mirids most common on creosote bush (collection nos. He-2 and He-4) show slightly different feeding preferences. One (He-2) is most frequently found feeding on flower buds; the other (He-4), on immature fruits. Each insect can be found occasionally on the other's preferred tissue. Another heteropteran, *Geocoris* sp. (Lygaeidae), is a facultative predator, but may be casual on *L. tridentata* in sampling leaves, young stems, buds, and fruits. The two pentatomid species, *Thyanta pallidovirens* and *Dendrocoris contaminatus,* also segregate with respect to food with the former preferring flower buds and the latter, the fruits.

Three species of membracids (Homoptera), *Centrodontus atlas, Multareoides bifurcata,* and *M. digitatus* all feed on young stems and occasionally on leaves.

Three species of lac insects (Homoptera:Lacciferidae) infest *L. tridentata,* but their patterns of utilization on the plant are not well studied. They tend to congregate near growing tissues, particularly on young stems, as is frequently the case among the Homoptera (Kennedy and Fosbrooke 1973; Painter 1953).

MacGillivray (1921) lists three species of scale insects (Homoptera:

Coccidae) from *Larrea* in North America, one of which is recorded only from New Mexico. Tissue preferences for these species have not been studied.

All of these sucking insects appear in the winter and reach peak abundances during the period from March through May (with the possible exception of *Geocoris,* observed only in August 1973 by Schultz). The two pentatomid species may remain fairly numerous through the summer months, as they continue to feed on flower buds and fruits during the second flowering period. The membracids are also present at least through September, although in reduced numbers.

Daily feeding patterns that exist among these North American herbivores are similar to those found in South American species: Chewing insects tend to restrict their activities to hours after sundown (*Cibolacris*) or at night, except for the two meloid species which feed on flowers during the day; the sucking insect types may be found feeding day or night, although they are more likely to be found feeding at night.

LARREA AS A HIDING SUBSTRATE

Visually hunting predators can shape adaptive phenotypes of arthropods (Kettlewell 1961; Rand 1967; Ricklefs and O'Rourke 1975; Cates et al. 1977; Schultz, *in preparation*).

Superficially, *L. cuneifolia* and *L. tridentata* are similar in appearance. Both branch almost immediately from the rootstock into a shrub approaching an inverted cone in shape. The bottom portion of this cone is largely leafless and consists of grey or reddish-grey stems numbering from two or three to a dozen or more and having age-related diameters ranging from 0.3 to 3 centimeters. Although leaf shapes are different, the basic tissue structures are quite similar, and the same tissue types are possessed by both species (Table 7-4).

TABLE 7-4 Larrea *Tissues Utilized in Crypsis and Their Colors.*

	L. cuneifolia		*L. tridentata*	
Tissue	Color	Munsell code	Color	Munsell code
young leaves	yellow-green	2.5GY 5-6/8	yellow-green	2.6GY 5-6/6
old leaves	green	2.5GY 5/4	green	2.5GY 6/4-5
young stem	green	2.5GY 6/5	green	2.5GY 6-7/4
intermediate stem	red-brown	7.5YR 4-5/4	red-brown	2.5YR 4.5/4
old stem	brown-grey	2.5YR 6/0.5	red-grey	5R 5/1-2
flower petals	yellow	5Y 6/6	yellow	5Y 8.5/11
fruit	yellow-green	7.5YR 5/4	yellow-green	2.5GY 7/6
senescent leaves	yellow-brown	2.5YR 4-5/4	yellow-brown	2.5Y 7/8

Note: Key to Munsell Color Code is Hue-Value/Chroma.

Source: Munsell Color Charts for Plant Tissues, Munsell Color Co., Inc. Baltimore, Maryland, 1968.

The ranges of colors existing in *L. cuneifolia* and *L. tridentata* are similar; different colors are actually present (see Table 7–4). Also the proportions of color and tissue types appear to differ between the North and South American species. The absolute amounts and/or proportions of various backgrounds that may be utilized by cryptic arthropods may set a limit on the numbers of such prey and influence community structure (Rand 1967; Ricklefs and O'Rourke 1975; Cates et al. 1977). In *L. tridentata* and *L. cuneifolia* the most recent stem growth is green in color and is separated from the older, grey stem by a band of intermediate-aged stem that may be brown or red-brown. This band is broader and more prominent in *L. cuneifolia.*

Frequently in *L. cuneifolia* a proportionately greater length of major stem carries leaves or leaf-bearing branches. In comparison *L. tridentata* gives the appearance of possessing long naked stems with terminal tufts of green leaves, since proportionately less of each main stem bears leaves. This difference is in part because *L. tridentata* only retains about four pairs of leaves during growing seasons, while *L. cuneifolia* may retain as many as six to ten leaf pairs and has a slightly different branching pattern.

Differences in branching patterns also result in differences in planarity between the two *Larrea* species. *Larrea cuneifolia* presents the leaf blade surfaces in a strongly east-west orientation, probably to reduce heat load on the broader, less-dissected leaves (see Chapter 3). *Larrea tridentata* leaves tend to be oriented more randomly. Thus *L. tridentata* presents a less planar, more three-dimensional array of structures than does *L. cuneifolia.*

The possible importance of such morphological characteristics lies in (1) the limitation of hiding substrates for cryptic arthropods and (2) the influence of bush form on the effectiveness of various types of foraging strategies utilized by visual predators, mainly birds. For example, the visual penetrability of *L. cuneifolia* appears to be low compared to that of *L. tridentata,* thereby limiting the effectiveness of foraging strategies based on perusing and detecting prey at some distance through the bush (Schultz, *unpublished data*).

Utilization of *L. cuneifolia* as a Hiding Substrate

An organization of *Larrea*-inhabiting arthropods into predator-avoidance guilds is proposed (Cates et al. 1977) and classified according to this system (Table 7-5). The dominant herbivore at Andalgalá, *Astroma quadrilobatum,* is classified in the class-eight combination syndrome due to results of aviary experiments with native Argentine birds in which *Astroma* was found to be of low preference compared to other insects of similar size and taxon. Birds that commonly encountered *Astroma* in their foraging activities avoided instars 4, 5, and 6, even when they were quite conspicuous, and performed time- and energy-consuming gutting activities.

For example, two species of warbling finches that forage more as war-

TABLE 7–5 *Predator-Avoidance Guilds.*

Description	Effects on predator's foraging success	Pattern of occurrence
1. *Primary crypsis:* only defense is morphological and/or behavioral mimicry of substrate.	Reduces probability of encounter by reducing apparent density of prey.	Requires sessile lifestyle, more common among specialist feeders consuming tissues which are expensive to digest.
2. *Escape:* only defense is rapid exit from substrate upon encounter with predator.	Reduces probability of pursuit given encounter or probability of capture given pursuit by reducing apparent or real value of prey.	Rapid movement may attract attention, hence precludes 1° crypsis. Expected among species whose activities make them conspicuous or predictable either by foraging across several substrates or on predictable or "spotlight" substrates (e.g., flowers), or by performing some other conspicuous activity (e.g., reproduction). Species which do not invest heavily in digestion may use this syndrome.
3. *Escape with 2° crypsis:* rapid exit is combined with a non-specific cryptic coloration or form.	Reduces probability of pursuit given encounter and/or probability of capture given pursuit by reducing value and apparent density of prey.	Expected in species as above whose escape movements carry them to and from substrates similar in appearance. General resemblance of these substrates makes it difficult for predators to follow and find prey during and after movement. Conspicuousness of movement precludes close substrate mimicry or 1° crypsis.
4. *Defense:* toughness of body, resistance, or chemical defense exclusive characteristics of this syndrome.	Reduces probability of pursuit given encounter and probability of capture given pursuit by increasing handling time and reducing prey value.	Expected in species which are conspicuous and/or easily found. Sequestering toxins may occur among these species, in which case they may invest heavily in digestion. This ought not to be the case when physical resistance is used.

5. *Defense + 2° crypsis:* one of the defensive characteristics above is combined with a general substrate resemblance, usually just in terms of color.	Raises handling cost and/or value of prey, hence reducing probability of pursuit or capture given encounter while lowering encounter rate also.	Occurrence as above, in cases where substrates encountered are similar. Also may be evolutionary step in development of toxin sequestering and aposematism.
6. *Aposematism:* defense capability is combined with warning coloration.	Signal that value of prey item is low reduces probability of pursuit given encounter as well as cost of trial and error with predator's learning.	Expected in situations as above, especially when toxins are sequestered or produced.
7. *Escape and defense:* some defensive characteristic (e.g. toughness) combined with exit from substrate.	Value of prey is lowered by defense and exit from substrate is successful because of poor reward for predator for following. Reduces probability of pursuit given encounter.	Expected where defense used is energetically inexpensive as perhaps in body toughness (e.g. beetles which drop from branch). Useful when probability of encounter is fairly high.
8. *Escape with defense and 2° crypsis:* a combination of 7 above with general substrate resemblance.	Operates as 7 above but reduces probability of pursuit thereby making it difficult for predator to follow exit successfully.	This syndrome may be viewed as a variation on the above with improvement of escape success as in syndrome 3.
9. *Refugia:* predator-resistant physical structure is used or constructed.	Reduces probability of encounter if refuge is hidden (e.g. in ground) or probability of capture or pursuit if refuge is exposed but difficult to penetrate. This second case is probably more common.	Energy investment in travel to refuge or in its construction ought to limit this syndrome to species which need not expend a great deal of energy in feeding/digestion.
10. *Batesian mimicry:* character convergence by undefended species with an aposematic species.	Deceit reduces probability of pursuit and capture given encounter.	Really a special case of 4 above, species which possess this syndrome may not invest heavily in feeding and are subject to the population constraints imposed by learning by the predators (cannot be too common). This syndrome expected when species must be conspicuous to feed or reproduce.

blers, *Poospiza ornata* and *P. torquata,* each spent up to four minutes in handling an individual 4th instar *Astroma* in the aviary and refused adult (6th instar) *Astromas. Poospiza torquata* gutted the grasshoppers by running the grasshopper back and forth lengthwise through the bill, squeezing out the gut contents, then beating the grasshopper against a plant stem. This action served to remove the head from the insect's body and emptied much of the abdominal cavity. In contrast, *P. ornata* held the insect down against some solid substrate with its feet while pulling the grasshopper's head off the body with its bill. Then the body cavity of the insect was carefully "cleaned" by probing with the bill and dropping the contents on the ground. After this operation, the whole remaining grasshopper was consumed. Large preying mantises were observed to eat entire *Astroma* individuals in the field and carefully leave the head, thoracic exoskeleton, and the digestive tract intact. These dried remains could often be found on the ground under *Larrea* bushes, and several were collected. The constancy of this behavior in the mantis was verified through feeding observations in the lab. *Astroma* instars younger than five were usually consumed completely. These observations suggest that contents of the insect's gastrointestinal tract plays a strong role in reducing the value of this prey item (Schultz, *in preparation*). This result is somewhat surprising considering the human observation that *Astroma* appears fairly well-hidden and has a pronounced escape response (leaping).

The other *Larrea* arthropods possess more straightforward predator-avoidance syndromes. *Naupactus sulfureosignathus* (Coleoptera:Cucurlionidae) possesses bold, high-visibility yellow stripes and appears to be aposematic. It is of low preference in aviary tests. Another weevil, *Pantomorus viridosquamosus,* may also be aposematic.

An important note is that only three species associated with *L. cuneifolia* at Andalgalá appear to depend exclusively on crypsis to avoid predators (primary crypsis). The katydid, *Tetana grisea,* has an irregular body-wing outline, is colored grey to match *Larrea* stem color closely, and rests head down on old stems with the abdomen elevated from the stem during the day. The geometrid larva (collection no. Lp-60) matches closely the color of young *Larrea* leaves in ground color and has a yellowish longitudinal stripe that gives the impression of a leaf edge when the caterpillar takes up its typical curved posture. Old *Larrea* stems have pronounced annulae that are somewhat darker than surrounding stem surface. A common species of mirid bug (collection no. He-52) rests almost exclusively on these annulae (which it matches closely in color) during daylight hours. None of these cryptic species has any well-developed behavioral response to threat from predators; they depend exclusively on these plant tissue resemblances. Clearly, *Larrea* shrubs comprise more substrates than these, and more "escape space" (Ricklefs and O'Rourke 1975) is available than is being used.

Most of the other herbivores combine some active escape response with secondary crypsis or are difficult to handle (defense) and secondarily cryptic.

The two *Phyllophaga*-type scarabaeid beetles feeding on *L. cuneifolia* at Andalgalá utilize the refuge of spending daylight hours buried in the soil and emerge each night to feed and copulate.

Among the noninsect arthropods, the thomisid spider, *Misumenops lenis,* appears cryptic on flowers. However, this species, like the rest of the spiders on the shrub, combines a well-developed escape response with this crypsis. Salticids, which are brightly colored, may be aposematic, but no good data concerning this possibility exist. Syndromes other than primary crypsis are to be expected among arthropods that must traverse various substrates during daily activities (e.g., hunting), which are located on highly conspicuous tissues (flowers), or that necessarily expose themselves to predation by tending webs. In keeping with this trend, two species of *Stagmomantis* and of *Stagmotoptera* (Orthoptera:Mantidae) that coexist on creosote bush near Andalgalá utilize either escape or threat responses upon disturbance by predators.

Utilization of *L. tridentata* as a Hiding Substrate

Four of the herbivorous insect species associated with *L. tridentata* at Silver Bell can be classified as primary cryptics. *Diapheromera covilleae* mimics older stems, *Bootettix punctatus* matches closely the color patterns of younger leaves, including the shininess of the resin coating, while *Semiothisa colorata* curls its body to resemble leaves and/or young stems and has brown spots resembling resin accumulations. A second morph of this species resembles intermediate-aged stems and uses a twig-imitating behavioral syndrome, while a third morph is grey and resembles still older twigs. *Centrodontus atlas* is colored and shaped much like the resin gland of young and intermediate-aged stems. None of these species demonstrates escape responses that reduce the effect of their plant mimicry. Observations are insufficient to classify *Synglochis* with certainty.

Insara covilleae, although closely resembling *Bootettix punctatus,* has a well-developed flight response upon being disturbed that frequently carries the individual to a new bush. *Bootettix* and *Insara* feed on different parts of the plant as well and can be found resting in different sections of the bush during the day.

Nine other residents of *L. tridentata* can be found utilizing escape with secondary crypsis as a major predator avoidance syndrome. *Ligurotettix coquilleti,* the "desert clicker grasshopper," appears to be a conspicuous member of the creosote bush community because of its loud, frequently continuous stridulation. When approached, the grasshopper slips around the lower stems of a *Larrea* bush where it most commonly rests during the day, and when disturbed it frequently flies to the ground where it is almost as hard to see as it is on the original stem. Usually only one male of this species may be found per *Larrea* individual, since they are territorial and may defend a bush against other males (Otte, 1975).

A similar strategy is exhibited by *Melanoplus lakinus,* which may rest on almost any part of the bush, and by *Cibolacris,* which rests on the ground but ascends the bush at night to feed. These species display a short, rapid evasive flight response when disturbed.

Pachybrachis mellitis does not strongly resemble any particular structure on *Larrea,* but its body color matches closely that of yellow senescent leaves or parts of leaves. It is an active and rapid flier.

The smaller of the two mantids commonly found on *L. tridentata, Stagmomantis californica,* is a fast runner that frequently leaves the bush via stems or by flying when disturbed. Its green coloration generally resembles foliage. The larger species, *S. limbata,* uses its yellow wings in a visual display when disturbed.

The two species of *Multareoides* (Membracidae) found on *L. tridentata* resemble thorns (of which there are none on *Larrea*) and fly readily when disturbed. The mirid bugs on *Larrea* are generally green and brown colored and are ready fliers.

The meloid beetle, *Epicauta lauta,* appears to bear no particular resemblance to any part of *Larrea,* but may be chemically defended as is common among the members of the family (Werner et al. 1966). It is thus classified as having a defense-type predator-avoidance syndrome. The other meloid found on *L. tridentata, Pyrota postica,* is colored yellow with black spots and hence generally matches the flowers on which it feeds, but it probably also possesses distasteful or poisonous properties. No direct chemical data are available for either species. Both pentatomid species appear to be chemically defended as well, and they resemble green (*Thyanta*) or brown (*Dendrocoris*) leaves.

Thyridopterix meadi (Psychidae) encloses its larval (feeding) stage in a very tough coccoon that offers considerable resistance to predators. The larvae are, however, quite susceptible to parasites and are frequently attacked by a pterimid wasp (F. G. Werner, *personal communication*).

Both weevils found on *Larrea* at Silver Bell generally resemble old stem bark in color and are found mostly on these tissues during the day. Both are very hard-bodied and drop to the ground or cling tightly to the stem when disturbed. They thus possess defensive, escape, and secondary cryptic characteristics.

The two common scarabaeid beetles that feed on *L. tridentata* do so only at night; they bury themselves in the soil by day, thus utilizing a refuge.

As is the case for the *L. cuneifolia* community, the spiders found on the shrubs either traverse a variety of substrates while hunting at night or tend a web, thus exposing themselves to predation. The result is that a preponderance of escape-secondary crypsis strategies exists among the spiders of *L. tridentata.* Species of *Misumenops* (Thomisidae), which frequent flowers and thus are found in conspicuous, predictable places, also combine crypsis with an escape response.

LARREA AS A HUNTING SUBSTRATE

Obviously, both species of *Larrea* provide essentially the same set of substrate types to arthropod predators as to arthropod prey. Arthropod predators range along stems of all ages, across leaves, and on flowers. Final identification of prey by most arthropod predators is more often tactile or chemosensory rather than visual, so that crypsis as a defensive strategy is not effective against these predators. One consequence of this is the observation that arthropod predator–prey interactions tend not to be very substrate specific, except for substrates that have especially high or predictable prey concentrations, such as flowers.

Because both *Larrea* species are essentially evergreen, the only significant change in hunting substrate availability during the year relates to flowering. We might expect flower-specific predators to appear during the flowering season. Other less-specific predators ought to follow the seasonality of their prey.

The prey available to arthropod predators consists of the herbivorous and predaceous species discussed above, as well as flower visitors and transient species.

Both *Larrea* species offer sufficient three-dimensional complexity and rigidity to support the webs of web-building spiders. *Larrea cuneifolia* has a more planar structure than *L. tridentata* and may be subjected to more consistent winds at Andalgalá than is *L. tridentata* at Silver Bell (Schultz, *personal observation*). No formal measures of rigidity have been made, but the devotion of a greater proportion of branch length to leaves in *L. cuneifolia* may make the bush more compact and/or more rigid.

Utilization of *L. cuneifolia* as a Hunting Substrate

Both web-building and solitary hunting spiders are common predators occurring on *L. cuneifolia* near Andalgalá (Table 7-6). Especially common among the former is a species of *Dictyna* (Dictynidae) that constructs a nebulous webbing about the leaf pairs and entraps small insects.

One species of the desert endemic genus *Diguetia, D. catamarquensis,* constructs a typical vertical silk tube over a maze of thread, especially in lower parts of the bush. The web includes a tubular refuge covered with bits of plant and other materials. Four or five species in the Theridiidae (including three species of *Latrodectus*) build cobwebs in *L. cuneifolia,* and as many as six species of orb-web spiders (Araneidae) may be found in *L. cuneifolia* bushes.

Among solitary hunters the Oxyopidae is represented by a single uncommon species, *Oxyopes nigromaculata* (Mello-Leitao), which hunts mostly on leaves. One or two species of clubionids (*sensu lato*) may be found hunting

TABLE 7-6 Larrea *Associated Spiders.*

L. cuneifolia	*L. tridentata*
Dictynidae	Dictynidae
Dictyna sp.	*Dictyna reticulata*
Diguetidae	Diguetidae
Diguetia catamarquensis	*Diguetia canities*
	D. imperiosa
	D. albolineata
	D. signata
Theridiidae	Theridiidae
Latrodectrus geometricus	*Latrodectrus hesperus*
L. #1	
L. #2	
Anelosimus sp.	*Euryopsis* sp.
Araneidae	Araneidae
Mastophora sp.	*Argiope trifasciata*
Metepeira labyrinthea	*Metepeira arizonica*
Neosconella candida	*Neosconella oaxacensis*
Parepeira deliciosa	*Eustala* sp.
Wixia rubelulla	*Larinia* sp.
Oxyopidae	Oxyopidae
Oxyopes nigromaculata	*Oxyopes tridens*
	Hamatalixa grisea
	Peucetia viridans
Clubionidae	Clubionidae
Clubiona sp.	*Unide* sp.
Xenoctenus marmoratus	
Thomisidae	Thomisidae
Misumenops lenis	*Misumenops coloradensis* and other congeners
Paracleonemis apostolis	*Ebo* sp.
P. termalis	*Titanebo* sp.
	Apollophanes texanus
Salticidae	Salticidae
Sitticine sp.	*Phidippus* orange leg
Cerionesta sp.	*P.* black leg
Dendryphantine #1	*Sassacus papenhoei*
D. #2	*Pseudicius piraticus*
Phiale pantherina	*Pellenes hirsutus*
Evophrys sutrix	*P. signatus*
Anyphaenidae	Mimetidae
Anyphaena sp.	*Mimetus* hesperas

on stems of *L. cuneifolia* at night and retreating to a refuge web, probably off the bush, by day.

The Salticidae are represented by seven species in five genera. Most range along stems of all sizes and hunt by day.

Five species in the Thomisidae (crab spiders) occur on *L. cuneifolia* near Andalgalá, with *Misumenops lenis* a flower-residing species.

Relatively little is known about the differences among these species in utilization of *L. cuneifolia,* except that the "sit-and-wait" thomisid spiders may be fairly tissue specific. Most, if not all, of the species in the groups mentioned are relatively nonspecific with respect to choice of plant, although some seem to prefer the "*Larrea* flat" habitat.

Many of the species respond to environmental cues so they take advantage of the coincidence of potential prey. Watering individual *L. cuneifolia* shrubs can induce the appearance of prey and of certain spider predators weeks before normal rainfall occurs in Argentina (Enders, *in preparation*).

A conspicuous and probably very important group of predators foraging on *L. cuneifolia* is the Solifugae. Three species in the Ammotrechidae may be found foraging at night in *Larrea.* These animals hunt by running along branches from base to tip and back while feeling for prey with pedipalps and tactile hairs. The three species (*Oltacoloa gomezi, Mummucia* sp., and *Pseudocleobis* sp.) are of different sizes, and all are common in various shrubs and trees.

Two species of the mantid genus *Stagmomantis* commonly occur in *L. cuneifolia.* They are of different body sizes and the larger of the two is dimorphic in color, with the forms being grey or green. This largest species also has greatly reduced wings. A third species, probably *Stagmotoptera precaria,* which frequents larger tree species such as *Prosopis* or *Acacia,* is more casual on *Larrea.* These mantids are active during the day and range across most substrates on a variety of shrubs in the South American desert. *Stagmotoptera* appears to prefer wetter habitats and is common in towns.

Various casual predators that forage on *Larrea* include species in the Reduviidae (*Apiomeris* sp.), the Pentatomidae, the Miridae, the Asilidae (Diptera) and the Coccinillidae (Coleoptera). None of these visitors demonstrate any special relationship with *Larrea* or more than the slightest fidelity to the shrub.

Utilization of *L. tridentata* as a Hunting Substrate

Among the web-building spiders using *L. tridentata* at Silver Bell (see Table 7-6), *Dictyna reticulata* is prominent, similar to the *Dictyna* species found at Andalgalá.

Two pairs of species of *Diguetia–D. signata* and *D. albolineata,* and *D. imperiosa* and *D. canities*–construct their webs-with-retreat in *L. tridentata,* with the latter pair particularly doing so in low parts of the bush. The form of the web is essentially as described for *D. catamarquensis,* but the vertical stratification is not seen in Argentine *Diguetia.*

One species of Theridiidae builds nebulous webs in creosote bush: *Latrodectus hesperus* webs are located mostly in lower, central portions of the shrub in contrast to the vertical stratification of Argentine *Latrodectus.* One theridiid (*Euryopsis* prob. *texana*) is a vagrant anteater.

Five species of orb-weavers place their webs in *L. tridentata,* usually in middle to upper portions of the shrub.

None of these web-building species is limited to *Larrea,* although *Dictyna* and *Diguetia* are more often associated with the plant than with others.

Among the solitary hunters, the same basic groups of spiders are represented on *L. tridentata* in Arizona as are found on the *Larrea* species at Andalgalá.

The oxyopids are somewhat more diverse, with three species found associated with creosote bush: *Oxyopes tridens, Hamataliwa grisea,* and *Peucetia viridans. Oxyopes tridens* hunts in the early evening on leaves, especially their undersides, while the other species range mostly along branches.

A single clubionid hunts on stems, and the otenids are unrepresented in collections from the Arizona creosote bush. *Mimetus hesperus* (Mimetidae) eats spiders and is found in Arizona *Larrea.*

Eight species of jumping spiders, the Salticidae, may be found on *L. tridentata,* including three species of *Phidippus.* These seven species range across stems and leaves, although they may concentrate their hunting activities near flowers (Enders, *personal communication*).

Again, none of the hunting spiders are limited to *Larrea* or to any substrate type thereon with the possible exception of members of the Thomisidae, which await prey on flowers (*Misumenops,* three species). One genus in this group may be limited to *Larrea* (*Ebo* sp.).

Occasionally individuals of unidentified species in the Solifugae may be found on *L. tridentata,* but the arboreal habits seem less well developed among North American Solifugae.

Among arthropod predators associated with *Larrea,* two species in the Mantidae (Orthoptera) are prominent: *Stagmomantis californica* and *S. limbata. Stagmomantis limbata* is the larger of the two and tends to hunt by day by hanging upside down under the leafed terminal stem areas. *Stagmomantis californica* ranges more freely and actively across upper leaf surfaces and stems. Both are found commonly on other plants, as is *Litaneutria minor,* a much smaller species that hunts along the ground and ascends the lower stems of many shrub species.

As with *L. cuneifolia* in Argentina, various other predators may be found occasionally on *L. tridentata,* including coccinellid bettles, reduviid bugs (*Apiomeris* sp.), asilid flies, pentatomid bugs, and mirid bugs. One reduviid species, *Zelus soccus,* occurs with great regularity on *L. tridentata* and is frequently seen hunting on older stems.

LARREA AS A REPRODUCTIVE SUBSTRATE

A plant may be of importance to the reproductive activities of an insect by serving as a substrate for mating activities and even as an attractant to bring together individuals of the two sexes of a species. Oviposition may take place on or in the tissues of the plant, as may pupation. Holometabolous insects may pass larval life stages on the plant and adult stages elsewhere, or vice versa.

Larrea appears to be in no way unique with respect to this interaction. However, since it is essentially evergreen, the younger leaves are available year around and thus may be depended upon during the reproductive cycle of an arthropod. Leaves that are dropped during the year would not be suitable oviposition sites.

Utilization of *L. cuneifolia* in Reproduction

First-hand observations of oviposition or pupation by residents of *L. cuneifolia* are uncommon. Only seven species of the insects using *L. cuneifolia* near Andalgalá are known to oviposit on the bush itself (see Table 7-2). All of these that oviposit on *Larrea* are specific in food choice to the same shrub. The remaining ones oviposit on the several plant species they use for food or in the ground. The oviposition sites of several species are known.

The oviposition activities of three species may be harmful to their host plant. *Tetana grisea* inserts eggs into leaves and thus possibly impairs photosynthetic activity. Two buprestids oviposit and spend larval stages in the internal portions of stems. The larger of the two appears to prefer dead or dying wood, but the smaller, *Psiloptera baeri,* prunes the ends of younger stems and inserts eggs in the end of the severed branch. This behavior frequently results in the loss to the plant of as many as ten to twelve photosynthetic leaves. The three mirid species probably insert eggs into soft tissues, young stems, or leaves, which may also have deleterious effects (Miller 1956).

Apart from the two buprestid species, the only other insect that passes a larval lifestage on *L. cuneifolia* is the geometrid moth that is regular but uncommon near Andalgalá. Eggs are placed by the adult moth on leaves after rains in January or February, and the larvae feed through much of the summer. Pupation occurs in the soil beneath the bush.

Adults of all the insect species listed as using *L. cuneifolia* have been observed copulating on the plant. However, some may be observed copulating elsewhere as well. These species are usually feeding–hiding generalists (oligophagous or polyphagous). The trend among most species is to copulate at night, but the two meloids, the two buprestids, and all of the hemipterans frequently copulate during daylight hours. Only *Tetana grisea* stridulates to attract mates. The scarabaeids (Co-14 and Co-38) copulate at night while the female continues to feed.

Copulation of many "specialist" feeders tends to occur on or near the hiding substrate for diurnal copulators and on or near feeding substrates for nocturnal copulators.

All of the spiders utilizing *L. cuneifolia* may copulate and rear young on the plant, but they will also do so on any plant that they occupy. No other arthropod species is known to use *L. cuneifolia* for reproductive activity in any preferential manner.

Utilization of *L. tridentata* in Reproduction

Oviposition has been observed or deduced among thirteen of the twenty-four insect species listed to use *Larrea* for other purposes. Of these, only the two mantids oviposit on other plants as well as *Larrea.* Tissues utilized include surfaces of leaves and young stems (pentatomids, geometrids) and interiors (mirids, membracids). The psychid *Thyridopterix meadi* deposits eggs in the female's sac in which the larva has been living while feeding. The female is flightless and remains in this bag as an adult. Oviposition by insertion into leaves that is performed by *Insara covilleae* may damage the bush, as may insertion in leaves and stems by mirids and membracids.

Two geometrid species live and feed on the plant as larvae. No actual observations of buprestid larvae in the stems have been made, although such use is typical.

All the Orthoptera oviposit in the soil, except for *Diaphermoera,* which drops eggs singly or in groups into the ground (F. G. Werner, *personal communication;* Ball et al. 1942). We are not sure where most of the Coleoptera lay eggs, but we presume that the scarabs (*Diplotaxis* sp.) oviposit in the ground. *Epicauta lauta* drops eggs on the ground, and the larvae are predators on acridid eggs. The larval food and oviposition sites for *Pyrota postica* are unknown. *Pachybrachis mellitis* (Chrysomelidae) larvae are presumed to be parasites on Hymenoptera and may oviposit on the ground.

All of the insect species listed as using *L. tridentata* have been observed copulating on the plant. Among the Orthoptera, stridulation is a common behavioral phenomenon bringing the sexes together to this end, and this behavioral technique is utilized by *Ligurotettix coquilleti, Bootettix punctatus, Melanoplus lakinus, Cibolacris parviceps,* and *Insara covilleae. Melanoplus* and *Cibolacris* stridulate only while on the ground during daylight hours.

Adult geometrids of both species found on *Larrea* may be found copulating on or near flowers in both spring and summer. *Diplotaxis* sp. copulate while the female feeds at night. The only species that commonly copulate by day on the bush are the two meloids, the two mirids, and the two pentatomids. Any of the insects for which *L. tridentata* is only a part of their plant resource (generalists) may be found copulating elsewhere: On the ground (acridids) or on other plant species. This pattern extends to the spiders, which may copulate and rear young on *Larrea* or on the other plants with which they are associated. No particular tissue preferences are known, other than those relating to web placement for web-building spiders.

In Arizona copulation of many "specialists" tends to occur on or near the preferred food tissue for nocturnally copulating species; however, it occurs at or near the hiding site for diurnal copulators.

DISCUSSION AND CONCLUSIONS

If convergent evolution has occurred in widely separated habitats under very similar physical conditions, then we might expect to find that similar functional relationships have evolved independently among unrelated organisms. The physical and biological circumstances surrounding the arthropod faunas of the two species of *Larrea* in the Argentine and Arizona deserts clearly are not identical. They differ in seasonality of rainfall (bimodal in Arizona; more unimodal at Andalgalá) and geomorphology (height of surrounding mountains and slope exposures of the study sites), as well as in certain biotic factors (composition of the plant community and morphological differences between the two species of *Larrea*).

Still, we observe a number of functional similarities between the two faunas in their utilization of these shrubs. Most tissues are used in similar ways by both divergent and parallel arthropod groups in the two deserts. The Coleoptera contribute the bulk of the leaf-chewing species on *L. cuneifolia* at Andalgalá (six of eight) while only two of the nine leaf chewers on *L. tridentata* at Silver Bell are beetles. The Orthoptera and Lepidoptera dominate this group on the Arizona *Larrea.*

Each species of *Larrea* has a pair of meloid beetle species feeding on flowers. In addition, *L. cuneifolia* flowers are attacked by a katydid (*Tetana grisea*), several tenebrionid beetles, and occasionally a weevil (*Pantomorous* sp.). In contrast, the only other flower chewer observed on *L. tridentata* at Silver Bell during the study was *Cibolacris parviceps,* an acridid grasshopper.

Larrea cuneifolia and *L. tridentata* stems are consumed in each desert, but by members of quite unrelated groups. At Andalgalá, a buprestid beetle and a tenebrionid beetle each chew stems, while in Arizona *L. tridentata* stems are eaten by a species of walkingstick (Orthoptera:Phasmidae).

The taxonomic constituents of the sucking insects on the two species of *Larrea* are similar with the exception of the complete absence of the Membracidae (Homoptera) on the South American *Larrea.* But notably at Andalgalá an extremely abundant cicadellid (Homoptera) feeds on the tissues preferred by the membracids on North American *Larrea* and performs similarly in predator-avoidance situations.

Use of the two *Larrea* species as predator-avoidance substrates shows similar patterns. In general, most of the same tissues are similarly used as models for primary or secondary crypsis, but again, by some distinct insect groups.

Each species has an orthopteran mimic of older stems: on *L. cuneifolia*, the common *Astroma quadrilobatum* female (Proscopiidae), and on *L. tridentata*, the rare walkingstick *Diapheromera covilleae* (Phasmidae). The *Astroma* male strongly resembles young stems, a role taken by a geometrid moth larva (*Semiothisa colorata*) on *L. tridentata* at Silver Bell. Imitation of leaf coloration and reflectivity is achieved by a beetle (*Chalcopoecila ornata*) on *L. cuneifolia* and by an acridid grasshopper (*Bootettix punctatus*) on *L. tridentata* in Arizona. *Ligurotettix coquillettii* (Orthoptera:Acrididae) on *L. tridentata* at Silver Bell and *Psiloptera baeri* (Coleoptera:Buprestidae) on *L. cuneifolia* are rather similar in hiding on and resembling older stem tissue, despite the beetle's greater tendency to depend exclusively on the deception of predators by crypsis.

A slightly greater proportion of the resident species of *L. tridentata* use primary or secondary crypsis in predator avoidance than do the resident insect species of *L. cuneifolia* (twenty-one of twenty-five versus sixteen of twenty-two). Taking into account polymorphisms, there are more tissue-specific interactions of this sort on *L. tridentata* (thirteen tissue–insect associations versus four). This observation is similar to that made for feeding strategies and thus may reflect slightly greater specialization on the part of the Arizona *Larrea* fauna. Four of the resident insect species of *L. cuneifolia* are presumed or have been shown to be aposematic while only two species in the fauna of *L. tridentata* probably use this strategy. We should note that only the North American *Larrea* has an associated species that constructs a refuge (*Thyridopteryx meadi*).

A positive correlation exists between hiding substrate availability and the number of cryptic herbivore species coexisting on a plant species at the Argentine site (Cates et al. 1977). *Larrea cuneifolia* supports a somewhat lower number of cryptic species than expected, based on the number of available colors and substrates. This finding may be due to the optically dense, closely-packed, planar leaf and branching arrangement that favors escape strategies other than crypsis (Schultz, *in preparation*). *Larrea tridentata,* when compared with the Argentine community, supports about as many species of cryptic arthropods as we might expect.

In both faunas there appears to be a correlation between feeding on well-defended tissues (high resin, polyphenoloxidase content) and utilizing crypsis in a predator-avoidance syndrome. Presumably this pattern is the result of evolutionary tradeoffs based in part on the energetic costs involved in digesting well-defended tissues (Cates et al. 1977).

Astroma quadrilobatum presents an interesting picture as an herbivore that consumes well-defended (younger) tissues, yet does not specialize on

L. cuneifolia, but will eat *L. divaricata, Bulnesia retama* (Zygophyllaceae), *Zuccagnia punctata* (Leguminosae), and *Tricomaria usillo* (Malpighiaceae) as well. *Astroma* is able to defoliate *Larrea* as no other herbivore in either desert can and exceeds all other herbivores studied in total biomass.

Both *Larrea* species have predator faunas showing relatively little specificity either with respect to tissues on the plant or with respect to plant species; both are hunting substrates for a variety of generalized hunters.

Slightly less than half of the insect species associated with each *Larrea* species oviposit or pass larval life stages on the plant, and the tissue utilization pattern for this reflects parallel evolution between related groups. Data are scanty for adequate comparisons.

The pattern of herbivore community structure, then, is as follows. The *L. tridentata* herbivore biomass is taxonomically and functionally dissected compared to that of *L. cuneifolia* with a relatively even distribution of biomass among taxa and of taxa among tissues. At the Argentina site, one chewing herbivore, *Astroma quadrilobatum,* is a numerical and biomass dominant. Further, the degree of dietary specialization (by plant taxon) of the North American herbivores is greater than that of the South American *L. cuneifolia* herbivores; also the development of host-specific predator-avoidance adaptations is slightly more evident in North America. With the exception of seasonal differences, many of the functional relationships (feeding and predator-avoidance) between host plant and herbivores in each desert are very similar and thus frequently invite comparison of widely separated taxa; convergence is evident between different orders.

Larrea-associated predators in the two deserts demonstrate less host-specific adaptation and more taxonomic affinity than is shown by *Larrea* herbivores. This finding may be due to our failure to perceive details of plant–predator interactions, but it also suggests a reduced role for coevolution in these interactions. If so and if the host-specific adaptations observed among herbivores are consequences of a coevolutionary history, then the differences noted between the North and South American *Larrea* faunas present an interesting dilemma.

Southwood (1961) and Janzen (1973) have suggested that the number of herbivores associated with a plant species should accumulate through time, as herbivores species encounter and coevolve with the host species. Herbivore species may accumulate until some plateau of species numbers or saturation point is reached. This limit to the number of species associated with the host plant would be a function of the number of ways in which the herbivores can partition the plant and the amount the action of all herbivores removes from the plant's energy budget. At this point, competitive assortment may occur, with ongoing species turnover, much as in models of island colonization (Janzen 1973; MacArthur and Wilson 1967).

On the other hand, Strong (1974a, b) presents data that suggest that the number of insect species associated with host plant species may accumulate much more rapidly and reach a species number asymptote over what he, instead of evolutionary time, refers to as "ecological" time. Such terminology is confusing, since "evolutionary" time may be of almost any duration, as long as natural selection is strong enough to drive evolutionary processes. Hence "evolutionary" time for codling moths (*Laspeyresia pomonella*) coevolving with their host plants may be on the order of two or three moth generations, or less than a year (Philips and Barnes 1975). Strong (1974a) does not describe the nature or degree of coevolution between and among the "pest" species inhabiting cacao, and we know nothing of the functional or evolutionary natures of these associations or associations between British trees and their insects (Southwood 1961). Until such comparative information is available, we cannot generalize about coevolutionary rates, coevolutionary equilibria, or rates of competitive assortment among herbivores. All of the associations documented here have significant functional and evolutionary bases. However, data are insufficient for comparison of the herbivore faunas over the entire ranges of the different *Larrea* species. Such data are sorely needed, since *Larrea*'s disjunct distribution, colonization history, and different-sized populations present good opportunity to assess how appropriately island biogeography theory may be applied to natural plant and herbivore populations.

Nonetheless, for the comparison at hand the number of summer-only *Larrea* herbivore species is similar between the two deserts. The degree of host specificity is somewhat greater in North America. Yet new evidence suggests that *Larrea* may be a recent invader in North America (Wells 1977). If these coevolutionary relationships require evolutionary time to develop, then the *Larrea* use patterns do not follow from current assumptions. Either *L. tridentata* has had a longer coevolutionary history with its herbivores than has *L. cuneifolia* with its herbivores, or there has been stronger selection for herbivore adaptation to *L. tridentata* in North America.

This strong selection may have come about by virtue of the unique nature of *L. tridentata* among other plant taxa of the Sonoran Desert. There are no other shrubby species of zygophylls in the Arizona desert (Kearny and Peebles 1951), and the only two common genera in the family other than *Larrea* are trailing annuals. The chemistry of these other genera has not been studied extensively, but none is particularly noted for possessing *Larrea*-type resins. As *Larrea* invaded North America, it must have represented an expanding, major food resource for herbivorous insects. However, it also represented a secondary chemistry and morphology quite unlike other desert plant species. Hence, as a resource for these herbivores, it became abundant but very coarse-grained, which are two characteristics favoring specialization (Strong 1974b; Levins 1967). Strong selection would have been exerted on insects attempting to exploit this resource, in terms of both digestive adaptation and predator-avoidance adaptations. Dietary specialization should be observed on the basis of the amount of divergence from other digestive systems in the same environment that is necessary to be able to feed on *Larrea*. Perhaps an interesting note is that two of the *Larrea*-specific insect species that feed on very heavily defended tissues (*Insara covilleae* on petioles and stipules; *Diapheromera covilleae* on stem tips and stems) are close congeners of species that feed on plant species defended by protein-complexing systems (D. F. Rhoades, *personal communication*).

Insara elegans, closely related to *Larrea*-specific *I. covilleae* (Ball et al. 1942; T. Kohn, *personal communication*), is found primarily on *Olneya tesota* (Leguminosae) in the Avra Valley and on *Prosopis juliflora* in southeastern Arizona (Ball et al. 1942; Schultz, *personal observation*). The morphology and color patterns of the two *Insara* species are nearly identical; however, the yellow-green ground color of *I. covilleae* is replaced by blue-green in *I. elegans.* This blue-green coloration resembles much more closely the greyish blue-green of *Olneya tesota* leaves and of *P. juliflora* leaves. Widely-distributed *Diapheromera femorata* is closely related to *D. covilleae* and can be found in oak-juniper woodlands of southeastern Arizona, but it prefers oak leaves and differs in morphological details that aid it in its resemblance to oak stems.

In Argentina, *L. cuneifolia* coexists with as many as three other species of *Larrea* over much of its range and with one of these near the study site. Furthermore, *Bulnesia retama* is a common confamilial shrub at the study site and appears to possess a protein complexing defense, as does *Zuccagnia punctata,* a legume growing near Andalgalá (D. F. Rhoades, *personal communication*). Hence there are at least three common shrub species at the Argentine site that resemble *L. cuneifolia* in chemical defense and somewhat in morphology (especially *L. divaricata* and *Zuccagnia*). Several of the *L. cuneifolia* herbivores include one or more of these alternate hosts in their diets. Hence *L. cuneifolia* is not as unique in its community as is *L. tridentata* in Arizona. Through evolutionary time, colonization of *L. cuneifolia* may have proceeded via "island hopping" (Janzen 1973; MacArthur and Wilson 1967), thereby allowing herbivores with prior evolutionary experience to gain early advantage. The genus *Astroma* belongs to a grasshopper family widely distributed through the New World tropics. This genus possesses a distribution that follows closely that of *Larrea* in South America. Alternate hosts for *Astroma quadrilobatum* tend to be woody plants with widespread or predominantly tropical distributions. *Astroma* may be a genus with enough prior evolutionary experience to have developed a "predilection" for colonizing *L. cuneifolia* (Southwood 1961). Thus, the dominance of *Astroma* at Andalgalá may be the consequence of biochemical preadaptation.

Predator-avoidance patterns in the two deserts appear more comparable, which suggests that the shrubs are saturated with respect to this use. Morphological and behavioral characteristics relating to predator-avoidance were measured for each insect species resident on *L. tridentata* and *L. cuneifolia,* and mean similarity coefficients among all pairwise comparisons were calculated by using a numerical taxonomy technique designed by Colless (1967) and described by Ricklefs and O'Rourke (1975). The mean similarity among species and the average nearest neighbor distances among species were very similar for the inhabitants of each shrub (Schultz, *in preparation*). This finding suggests that the geometry of the shrubs and selection by predators on the insects within that geometry determine the array of predator-avoidance strategies found on each *Larrea* species. The geometry of *L. cuneifolia* is such as to give advantage to predator-avoidance strategies other than primary crypsis, since most predator–prey encounters will tend to occur at close distances. Only at very short distances does crypsis have the least escape advantage. Primary crypsis is more likely to be a viable strategy on *L. tridentata*, which is a more open, visually penetrable shrub. This observation and the numerical success of *Astroma* at Andalgalá suggest that *Astroma* could not be a primary cryptic, even though it resembles *Larrea* branches remarkably well. Because search image formation is facilitated by high prey densities (Tinbergen et al. 1966), *Astroma* could not be as abundant as it is and be a primary cryptic. In fact, the grasshopper appears to be of low preference for birds, and the adults are beyond the size range of all but the larger bird species.

In general we can say that the arthropod faunas of *L. cuneifolia* at Andalgalá, Argentina, and of *L. tridentata* near Silver Bell, Arizona, show similar patterns of utilization of their host plants with respect to the several ways in which the shrub may be considered a habitat component. The fauna of *L. tridentata* exhibits slightly more specialization in at least two utilization modes (food and predator-avoidance substrate), thereby suggesting either a longer coevolutionary history for this plant and its herbivores, or stronger selection for adaptation by the herbivores. Apparently, coevolution between plant and arthropod has proceeded in a convergent fashion between the two desert systems. However, details differ between the two sets of plant–arthropod associations as a consequence of subtle differences between the two *Larrea* species in the structure and availability of predator-avoidance substrates.

SUMMARY

Host plants provide arthropods with four main habitat components: a food-water source, an arena for interactions with predators, a reproductive substrate, and a hunting substrate for arthropod predators. The qualities of *L. tridentata* and *L. cuneifolia* are discussed with respect to these uses by arthropod residents. The value of *Larrea* as food for herbivores is most strongly determined by the plant's chemical defense. Both *Larrea* species are similar in this regard and should also be adequate water sources. The kinds of interactions likely between predators and arthropod prey on *Larrea* shrubs are to some extent predictable from the structures of the plants. *Larrea tridentata*

may be a more optimal habitat for cryptic prey species because of its open geometry. There appear to be no important differences between the two *Larrea* species in available reproductive substrates or hunting substrates.

The resident arthropod species studied in association with *L. tridentata* at Silver Bell, Arizona, and with *L. cuneifolia* at Andalgalá, Argentina, are listed, and their use of the shrubs as food, predator-avoidance substrates, reproductive substrates, and hunting substrates is described. Convergent patterns of utilization are noted in feeding and predator-avoidance strategies, often among arthropods from different orders. Arthropod predators tend to show parallel evolution in these respects.

The problem of differences in degree of coevolution between plant and arthropod for the two *Larrea* species (arthropods on *L. tridentata* appear more specialized) is discussed in the light of evidence that *L. tridentata* may be a very recent invader in North America. We suggested that *L. tridentata* presents a greater biochemical and morphological contrast with its surrounding plant community in Arizona than does *L. cuneifolia* in Argentina, where as many as three *Larrea* species plus related genera and hybrids may coexist. Since *L. tridentata* is a coarse-grained, abundant resource in the North American desert, natural selection could favor more specialization among arthropods using *L. tridentata* than among those using *L. cuneifolia.*

RESUMEN

Las plantas huéspedes suministran a los artrópodos cuatro principales componentes del habitat: una fuente de alimento/agua, una arena para interacciones con predadores, un substrato reproductivo, y un substrato de caza para artrópodos predadores. Se discuten las cualidades de *L. tridentata* y de *L. cuneifolia* con respecto a estos usos por los artrópodos residentes. El valor de *Larrea* como alimento para herbívoros está determinado principalmente por la defensa química de las plantas. Ambas especies de *Larrea* son similares en este renglón y también deberían ser fuentes adecuadas de agua. Las clases de interacciones probables entre artrópodos predadores y presas en arbustos de *Larrea* son hasta cierto punto predecibles por las estructuras de las plantas. *Larrea tridentata* puede ser, por su geometría abierta, un habitat más óptimo para especies de presa con coloración protectora. Parece no haber diferencias de importancia entre las dos especies de *Larrea* en cuanto a substratos disponibles reproductivos o de caza.

Se hace una lista de las especies de artrópodos residentes estudiados en asociación con *L. tridentata* en Silver Bell, Arizona, y con *L. cuneifolia* en Andalgalá, Argentina; se describe la utilización de los arbustos por estos artrópodos, como alimento, substratos para evitar predadores, substratos reproductivos y de caza. Se hacen notar patrones convergentes de utilización en estrategias de alimentación y desánimo de predadores, a menudo entre

artrópodos de diferentes órdenes. Los artrópodos predadoes tienden a mostrar evolución paralela en estos aspectos.

El problema de las diferencias en el grado de coevolución entre planta y artrópodo en las dos especies de *Larrea* (los artrópodos en *L. tridentata* parecen ser más especializados) se discute a la luz de la evidencia que *L. tridentata* puede ser un invasor muy reciente en Norteamérica. Se sugiere que *L. tridentata* presenta un mayor contraste bioquímico y morfológico con la comunidad vegetal circundante en Arizona que el que presenta *L. cuneifolia* en Argentina, donde coexisten hasta tres especies de *Larrea,* además de géneros relacionados e híbridos. Como recurso de grano grueso y abundante en el desierto norteamericano, la selección natural podría favorecer más especialización en artrópodos que usan *L. tridentata* que en los que utilizan *L. cuneifolia.*

8

Patterns of Some Vertebrate Communities in Creosote Bush Deserts

M. A. Mares and A. C. Hulse

All deserts are arid, although there are various climatic types represented among the deserts of the world. Some deserts are at high latitudes or altitudes and are considered "cold deserts," while others are at lower latitudes and elevations and are termed "hot deserts." Hot deserts place the more extraordinary climatic demands on animals.

Rainfall may vary from practically no precipitation in one year to more than 300 mm in another. Generally, there is no free water available to most of the fauna of desert regions during most of the year. Temperatures are also quite variable (e.g., from below freezing in winter to over 54° C in summer at Greenland Ranch in Death Valley). These and other environmental factors pose severe challenges to an organism successfully inhabiting the desert.

Many of the climatic extremes of desert regions can be modified somewhat by behavioral adaptations such as restricting activity to the cooler nighttime hours or choosing microhabitats that shield an animal from some of the more pronounced climatic variables. A gully forest, for example, offers shaded areas where some vertebrates may be active even during warmer parts of the day. Other habitats modify only slightly, if at all, the general climate of an area. A sand dune area is one such habitat, and a creosote bush (*Larrea*) flat is another. Both habitats are quite sparse floristically. Because of its leaf and stem alignment, a creosote bush produces practically no shade during the full desert sunshine (Figure 8-1). The low ground cover, and low shrub profile, only slightly disrupt the drying winds that are common in such flats. Often, few other plant species are represented in this habitat, and the only major food source available to a herbivore is creosote bush itself, a plant renowned for the number and types of toxic chemicals contained in its stems and leaves (see Chapters 5 and 6). Since the plant contains such a large number of chemical defenses, the total number of insects found in a *Larrea* flat may also be reduced (see Chapter 7), thus affecting the numbers and types of insectivorous vertebrates that may be supported in that community.

Since the *Larrea*-dominated community is such a harsh habitat, examining

FIGURE 8-1. *Shade of* L. cuneifolia *in the Monte Desert near Andalgalá, Catamarca Province, Argentine. Because of the small leaf size and leaf and stem alignment,* Larrea *provides only minimal shade during the full desert sunshine.*

the evolutionary process as it has molded the faunas that have adapted to desert life in that environment is of interest. How many species have managed to succeed in this community, and how does the diversity of its fauna compare with that of a more beneficent desert environment, such as a gully forest? Do the same types of vertebrate niches seem to be filled in different *Larrea* areas? In other words, are there only a very limited number of ways to be a vertebrate that lives in a creosote bush flat? In this chapter, vertebrate communities in different *Larrea* areas in North America, as well as the disjunct, phylogenetically distantly related faunas that live in *Larrea* areas in South America are compared. The research is primarily limited to *Larrea* flats in the Sonoran Desert of the southwestern United States and the Monte of northwest Argentina.

Larrea probably evolved in South America and has only entered North America since the Pleistocene (see Chapter 2). If this is indeed the case, we might expect to find more animals specialized on *Larrea,* or occurring in *Larrea*-dominated communities, in the southern desert. Logically, since this plant taxon is toxic to many herbivores and is found in areas that are climatically very challenging to vertebrates, long time spans would be necessary for animals to adapt to become able to coexist with creosote bush. Distinguishing between species that are really utilizing a resource offered by *Larrea* and species that seem to exist in such habitats in spite of *Larrea* is of course necessary.

REPTILES AND AMPHIBIANS

Reptiles and amphibians, like most terrestrial vertebrates, are usually not intimately associated with a specific plant taxon; however, they sometimes are restricted to specific plant communities. In the Monte, only the small gekkonid lizard, *Homonota underwoodi,* is limited to *Larrea* flats. Most of the other lizards forage in both the *Larrea* areas and the bordering wash communities (*Prosopis-Acacia* areas). This pattern is not unlike that found for the northern desert where five species of lizards and one species of snake are restricted to *Larrea* flats. (These lizards are *Dipsosaurus dorsalis, Uta stansburiana, Crotophytus wislizenii, Coleonyx variegatus, Phrynosoma m'calli,* and the snake is *Crotalus cerastes,* which also occurs in sand dune areas.) Of all species restricted to the *Larrea* flat, only *Dipsosaurus dorsalis* is an obligate herbivore. When *Larrea* is in flower, the diet of *D. dorsalis* consists almost entirely of flower parts of the plant (Norris 1953). In addition, Pianka (1971) states that seasonal activity of *D. dorsalis* is positively correlated with the availability of *Larrea* flowers as a food source. Northern limits of the range of *D. dorsalis* approximate the northern limits of *Larrea* in the Sonoran Desert. Seemingly, at least in part of its range, *D. dorsalis* is dependent upon *Larrea* flowers as a food source and other flowering plants will not suffice. No equivalent situation with a lizard in the Monte has been discovered.

The chuckwalla, *Sauromalus obesus,* is a large herbivorous iguanid lizard found primarily along rocky hillsides where *Larrea* is often present, but seldom abundant. Nagy (1973) found that *S. obesus* feeds to some degree on the fruits and flowers of *Larrea,* but is not as intimately associated with it as is *Dipsosaurus dorsalis,* since the former also feeds upon the flowers of most other desert shrubs as well. *Phymaturus palluma,* a medium-sized iguanid lizard of the southern Monte, is similar to *Sauromalus obesus* in morphology and habitat (Mares et al., *in preparation*). Both are stout-bodied, short-legged species that inhabit rocky hillsides. In both species the tail is short, stout, heavily spined, and in *S. obesus,* at least, tail autotomy is not well developed. Coloration in both species is similar, and both are sexually dimorphic. Females of the two species are uniformly olive brown dorsally with a salt-and-pepper venter and darkened gular region. In males, the head is black with a light-colored body. *Phymaturus palluma* is also an obligate herbivore and probably utilizes the fruits and flowers of *Larrea* in its diet. Although information is lacking for the Monte species, both northern desert herbivorous lizards eat the fruits and flowers of *Larrea,* but not the leaves.

As noted above, only *Homonota underwoodi* is restricted to *Larrea* flats in the Monte, while several lizard species in the Sonoran Desert are limited to that plant community. The reasons for these differences are not known, but one possibility is that insects are less diverse and/or less abundant in the southern desert (see Chapter 7) and that insectivorous lizards are thus forced to forage in both the *Larrea* areas and outlying wash communities.

Urosaurus graciosus is a small arboreal iguanid of the Sonoran Desert that uses *Larrea* as a perch site. The species is found in *Larrea* flats and in wash communities; however, when present in an interwash area (i.e., *Larrea*) it is found almost exclusively on creosote bush. It is a thin lizard with a brownish dorsal background color and with dark brown-to-black blotches. When resting on a *Larrea* stem, it is quite cryptic.

In addition to utilizing *Larrea* as a food source or a perch site, several desert reptiles and amphibians preferentially inhabit burrows placed under the plants where they hibernate or estivate, avoid excessive daytime temperatures, or evade predators. Several species of desert toads–including *Scaphiopus,* one of the most highly desert-adapted amphibians (Bragg 1950)–burrow into the soil adjacent to, or directly beneath, *Larrea* bushes. Most flatland desert lizards frequent burrows that they dig themselves or find abandoned by other vertebrates; these are generally under *Larrea* bushes in a creosote bush flat. The following lizard species have been shown to use this type of burrow: *Cnemidophorus tigris, Uta stansburiana, Dipsosaurus dorsalis,* and *Callisaurus draconoides* of the Sonoran Desert; and *Cnemidophorus longicaudus, Teius teyou* and *Liolaemus darwinii* of the Monte. Since these burrows are clustered under *Larrea* bushes, selection must act to avoid burrow placement in the open desert microhabitats. The slight amount of shade offered by a *Larrea* bush could allow burrows to be placed at shallower depths and still remain within the range of temperature fluctuations tolerated by the animals. The extra energy spent in digging deep burrows could then be shunted to other uses. The protection against predators offered by *Larrea* stems as an animal dashes for its burrow is also likely to be an important factor in burrow placement.

LIZARD COMMUNITY STRUCTURE

Lizard community structure was examined for two warm desert *Larrea* flats. The South American site was located just west of Andalgalá, Catamarca, and the North American site was located north of Mesa, Arizona. Both sites are interspersed with dry washes that flow after heavy rainfall. In the flatland desert *Larrea* is the dominant plant form (*L. cuneifolia* in South America and *L. tridentata* in North America). In both regions the washes are dominated by species of *Prosopis, Cercidium,* and *Acacia.*

Lizard faunal diversity was measured simply as the number of species present on each of the sites, with no reference made to relative or absolute densities. However, we feel this approach to be an adequate measure of ecological complexity. Table 8-1 lists the lizard species found in each of the communities. A total of nine species are present in the Sonoran Desert and

TABLE 8–1 *Lizard Species Found in the Two* Larrea *Communities*

Arizona	Argentina
Coleonyx variegatus (Gekkonidae)	*Homonota underwoodi* (Gekkonidae)
Heloderma suspectum (Helodermatidae)	*Homonota horrida* (Gekkonidae)
Uta stansburiana (Iguanidae)	*Liolaemus darwinii* (Iguanidae)
Callisaurus draconoides (Iguanidae)	*Teius teyou* (Teiidae)
Crotaphytus collaris (Iguanidae)	*Cnemidophorus longicaudus* (Teiidae)
Gambelia wisleizeni (Iguanidae)	
Phrynosoma solare (Iguanidae)	
Dipsosaurus dorsalis (Iguanidae)	
Cnemidophorus tigris (Teiidae)	

five in the Monte. Therefore, on the basis of sheer numbers the northern fauna is almost twice as diverse as the southern fauna. When higher taxonomic units are examined, the diversity is still greater in the northern desert. The Monte fauna is represented by three families and four genera, while the Sonoran fauna is represented by four families and nine genera with none of the species being congeneric. These data again provide an indication of a more complex, older faunal assemblage in the north.

Ecological diversity in the two communities was examined for several basic niche components, such as time of activity, place of activity, and diet. The temporal component was broken down into diurnal, nocturnal, and crepuscular. In both deserts the majority of species are diurnal, with the Sonoran Desert having one crepuscular and one nocturnal species. The Monte lacks any crepuscular species, but has two nocturnal species (Table 8–2).

With regard to place of activity, all species in both deserts are terrestrial. In other regions of the Sonoran Desert the iguanid lizard *Urosaurus graciosus* forms an arboreal component of the *Larrea* community; however, in the vicinity of Phoenix, Arizona, *U. graciosus* is restricted to riparian situations

TABLE 8–2 *Activity Time in the Two Lizard Communities*

Activity	Arizona	Argentina
Diurnal	*Dipsosaurus dorsalis*	
	Uta stansburiana	*Liolaemus darwinii*
	Crotaphytus collaris	*Teius teyou*
	Callisaurus draconoides	*Cnemidophorus longicaudus*
	Gambelia wislizeni	
	Phrynosoma solare	
	Cnemidophorous tigris	
Crepuscular	*Heloderma suspectum*	
Nocturnal	*Coleonyx variegatus*	*Homonota underwoodi*
		Homonota horrida

where it is present on trees, such as *Prosopis* and *Acacia,* and does not appear to venture into the open *Larrea* community.

The Monte fauna is strictly insectivorous, whereas the Sonoran fauna is more diverse in dietary habits (Table 8-3). One species, *Dipsosaurus dorsalis,* is herbivorous and three species are carnivorous. *Heloderma suspectum* feeds mainly on young mammals and ground nesting birds and their eggs. The other two species, *Crotaphytus collaris* and *Gambelia wislizeni* are primarily lizard eaters, but will consume large insects as well (Stebbins 1954). The rest of the Sonoran species are insect generalists, except for *Phrynosoma solare,* which is a specialist that eats ants. Although ants are an abundant food source in the Monte, no lizard has specialized to feed only on them.

After having examined these basic niche components, some value judgements can be made concerning ecological equivalents in the two *Larrea* communities. Ecological equivalents are listed in Table 8-4. One Monte and six Sonoran species have no equivalents.

Ecological diversity for the lizard fauna was also examined on the basis of morphological characteristics. Since form has long been assumed to have function, morphological characters (*after* Sage 1973) relating to patterns of behavior have been examined to give graphically a planar representation of niche diversity. The first character, head width to head length (*HW*/*HL*), relates to feeding behavior. An animal with a long narrow head is capable of swinging it rapidly from side to side to obtain food items; a long narrow head can also be used for entering crevices or as a lever to overturn small rocks and pieces of bark while searching for food. A short broad head cannot be moved about as rapidly, and it is not designed for overturning objects but is so designed that it has great crushing force. This type of jaw structure is better suited for capturing hard-bodied prey or prey that is large in relationship to the predator. The second character, length of fore leg to length of hind leg (*FL*/*HL*), relates to the lizard's mode of movement. Slow-moving or arboreal lizards tend to have fore and hind legs more equal in length, with both pair of legs more or less equally involved in movement–the fore legs pull and the

TABLE 8–3 *Dietary Habits in the Lizard Communities*

Diet	Arizona	Argentina
Herbivorous	*Dipsoaurus dorsalis*	
Insectivorous	*Uta stansburiana* *Coleonyx variegatus* *Callisaurus draconoides* *Phrynosoma solare** *Cnemidophorus tigris*	*Homonota underwoodi* *Homonota horrida* *Liolaemus darwinii* *Teius teyou* *Cnemidophorous longicaudus*
Carnivorous	*Heloderma suspectum* *Crotaphytus collaris* *Gambelis wislizeni*	

TABLE 8-4 *Equivalent Species Pairs in the Two Communities*

Arizona	Argentina
Coleonyx variegatus	*Homonota underwoodi* *Homonota horrida*
Uta stansburiana	*Liolaemus darwinii*
Cnemidophorus tigris	*Teius teyou*

hind legs push—whereas fast-moving or bipedal species tend to have shortened fore legs that contribute little to rapid movement.

Measurements of these characters were plotted on Figures 8-2 and 8-3 for the two lizard communities. *Heloderma suspectum* and *Dipsosaurus dorsalus* are missing from Figure 8-2 and *Cnemidophorous longicaudus* from Figure 8-3. *Cnemidophorous longicaudus* is a small teid with dimensions similar to *Teius teyou. Heloderma suspectum* is a large, squat, terrestrial lizard found in the Sonoran desert while *Dipsosaurus dorsalis* is a large fast-moving herbivorous lizard of the Sonoran desert.

The Sonoran fauna (see Figure 8-2) sorts out into basically nonoverlapping units, many of which can be correlated with the known ecologies of the species. Most of the lizard species have relatively longer hind legs than front legs, which fits in with the open habitat that they generally inhabit. The two notable exceptions are *Phrynosoma solare* and *Coleonyx variegatus.* Both of these lizards are of low agility. The one, *C. variegatus,* is a nocturnal ground forager, and the other, *P. solare,* is an ant specialist that positions itself in the vicinity of openings of any hills and captures ants as they enter or leave the colony. Probably *Heloderma suspectum* also fits into this category since it is crepuscular and a predator on nestling birds and mammals. Two species have very short fore legs when compared to hind legs. These are *Crotaphytus collaris* and *Gambelia wislizeni;* both are predaceous and utilize lizards as a main source of food. The species are basically equally divided on head conformation. The three species with short broad heads are *P. solare, C. collaris,* and *Callisaurus draconoides.* As mentioned earlier, *P. solare* feeds on hard-bodied ants and *C. collaris* on lizards. *Callisaurus draconoides* is mainly a predator of beetles and other hard-shelled insects, although flies and spiders are also taken.

The situation in the Monte is somewhat different (see Figure 8-3). Overlap does occur in the Monte; however, it is between the two sympatric species of *Homonota.* Both are terrestrial with relatively equal hind and fore legs, and both tend to have elongate snouts. This pair of characteristics correlates with their nocturnal habits and diet. The overlap is not as significant as may first appear due to the difference in size between the two species. *Homonota underwoodi* is a small species seldom exceeding 45 mm snout-vent length,

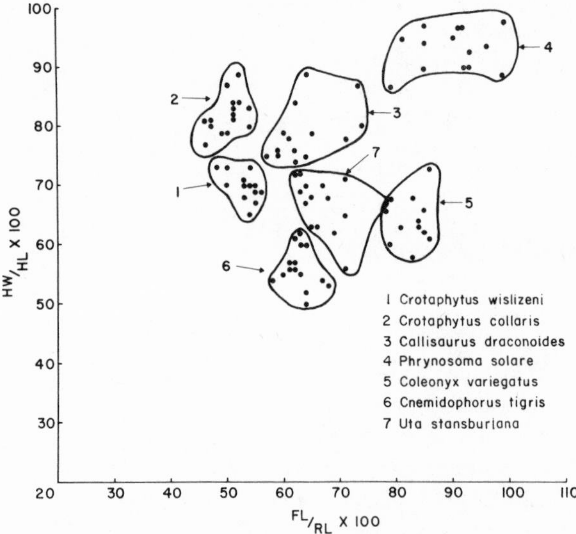

FIGURE 8-2. *Morphological space inhabited by seven species of Sonoran Desert lizards. HW/HL indicates head width /head length; FL/RL indicates from leg length/rear leg length.*

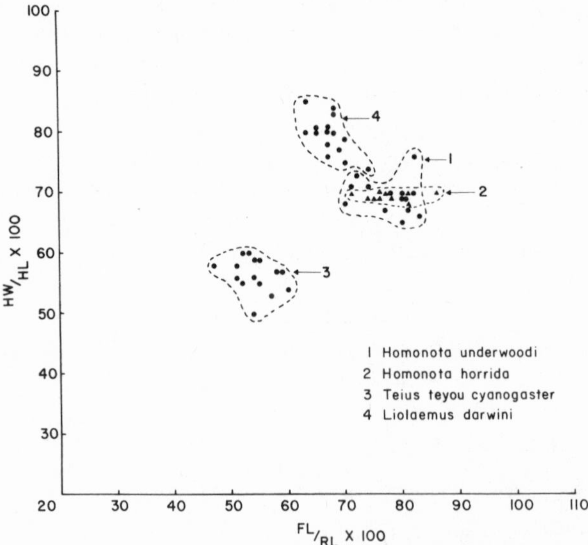

FIGURE 8-3. *Morphological space inhabited by four species of Monte Desert lizards. HW/HL indicates head width/head length; FL/RL indicates front leg length/ rear leg length.*

whereas *H. horrida* is considerably bigger and reaches 65 or 70 mm snout-vent length. In all likelihood, if *Cnemidophorous longicaudus* were figured, it would greatly overlap with *Teius teyou.* However, again the size difference between the two species is great: *C. longicaudus* seldom exceeds 70 mm, and *T. teyou* reaches 120 mm and more.

A measure of total niche utilization for the two lizard faunas can be obtained by comparing the total area utilized by the two faunas (Figure 8-4). Comparison shows that the Sonoran Desert fauna utilizes a larger area of its habitat than does the Monte. The reason for this remains unknown.

MAMMALS

Desert mammals include species that possess great vagility and can travel freely from one habitat type to another–for example, bats and carnivores–and more sedentary species that may have home ranges of only a few acres or less. This latter group is of particular interest when information requiring adaptation to a specific habitat or plant community is required. Individuals existing in the middle of an extensive *Larrea* flat may never encounter another plant community during their lives, and selection will act to favor adaptations that are conducive to existence in that harsh environment. Rodents in particular exemplify the nonvagil category of mammals that must either adapt to a specific habitat type or become extirpated from the area.

The small mammals of a number of North and South American desert and semidesert *Larrea* areas are listed in Tables 8-5 and 8-6. The species are grouped into size categories (<20g, 21-40g, 41-60g, 61-80g, 81-100g, 101-500g, >500 g), trophic categories (granivore, herbivore, insectivore, omnivore), and adaptational assemblages (ground dwelling, scansorial, quadrupedal saltation, dipedal saltation, fossorial, cursorial). Clearly there are a greater number of small mammals inhabiting the North American *Larrea* areas than there are in the southern desert. Mares et al. (*in preparation*) noted that there was a

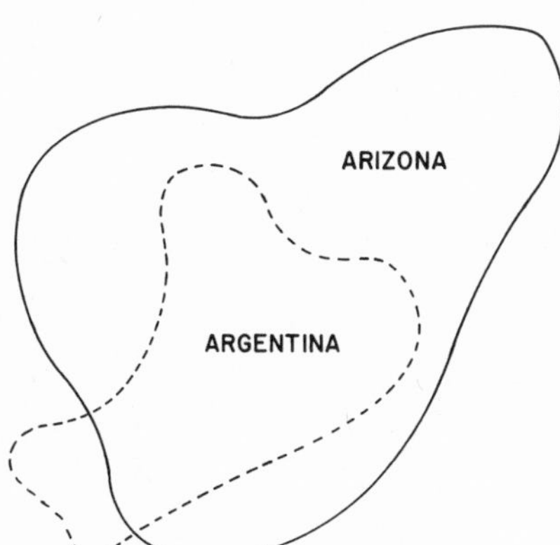

FIGURE 8-4. *Comparison of morphological space utilized by the lizard elements of the Monte and Sonoran deserts.*

TABLE 8-5 *Small Mammal Species of Creosote Bush (*Larrea*) Flats and Mesquite (*Prosopis*) Communities in the Northern Monte of Argentina (data from Mares 1973).*

Creosote bush	Mesquite
(I) Andalgalá region (Catamarca Prov.)	(M) Andalgalá region (Catamarca Prov.)
Eligmodontia typus (0,1,3)[a]	*Phyllotis griseoflavus* (0,4,2)
Ctenomys fulvus (H, 6, 5)	*P.* sp. (0,2,2)
Dolichotis patagonum (H, 7, 6)	*Galea musteloides* (H, 6, 2)
(J) Valle de la Luna (San Juan Prov.)	*Microcavia australis* (H, 6, 2)
Eligmodontia typus	*Dolichotis patagonum*
Dolichotis patagonum	*Ctenomys fulvus*
(K) Mendoza City region (Mendoza Prov.)	(L) Ñacuñan region (Mendoza Prov.)
Eligmodontia typus	*Phyllotis griseoflavus*
Ctenomys sp.	*Eligmodontia typus*
Dolichotis patagonum	*Galea musteloides*
Marmosa pusilla (I, 1,2)	*Microcavia australis*
	Dolichotis patagonum
	Lagostomus maximus (H, 7, 1)
	Ctenomys mendocinus (H, 6, 5)
	Marmosa pusilla

[a]Categories for niche parameters are, respectively: Food Habits; Granivore (G), Herbivore (H), Insectivore (I), Omnivore (O). Body Size: < 20 g (1), 21–40 g (2), 41–60 g (3), 61–80 g (4), 81–100 g (5), 101–500 g (6) > 500 (7). Adaptation: Ground Dwelling (1), Scansorial (2), Quadrupedal Saltation (3), Bipedal Saltation (4), Fossorial (5), Cursorial (6).

tendency for greater small mammal species diversities to occur in the more mesic desert tall-shrub communities than in the more xeric localities. This trend is not apparent with *Larrea* mammals. The semidesert New Mexico site (Blair 1943a) supported eleven species, as did the more arid Mojave study area of Ryan (1968). The lowest diversity found in three disparate regions (a Mojave site, an area near Superior, Arizona, and a site near Yuma, Arizona) was six species. In each of these three sites, the types of species supported were variable, but comparable. Each area contained two large cursorial herbivores (the jackrabbit, *Lepus californicus*, and the desert cottontail, *Sylvilagus audubonii*), one or two medium-sized granivores (*Dipodomys*), an insectivore (*Onychomys*) and/or a ground squirrel (*Spermophilus*), and at least one small granivore (*Perognathus*) or a microomnivore (*Peromyscus*). Thus, even at the lowest diversities, a rather large number of niche-types are represented. Interestingly, none of the species found in *Larrea* areas depend on *Larrea* exclusively for food. Indeed the majority of the species do not feed upon *Larrea* at all. Some creosote bush seeds are harvested by heteromyids (Chew and Chew 1970), and some bark and branches are browsed by leporids (Hayden 1966), but most species feed on the seeds of other plants, such as annuals, common

TABLE 8-6 *Small Mammal Species of Creosote Bush (*Larrea*) Flats and Mesquite (*Prosopis*) Communities in Desert Regions of North America.*

Creosote bush	Mesquite
(A) Colorado Desert (California)[a]	(B) Colorado Desert (California)[a]
Ammospermophilus leucurus	*Spermophilus tereticaudus*
Spermophilus tereticaudus	*Perognathus penicillatus*
Thomomys bottae (H,6,5)	*Dipodomys merriami*
Perognathus formosus	*D. deserti*
P. fallax	*Peromyscus maniculatus*
Dipodomys merriami	(N) Tucson area (Arizona)[b]
Peromyscus maniculatus	*Spermophilus tereticaudus*
P. eremicus	*Perognathus baileyi*
P. crinitus	*Perognathus penicillatus*
Neotoma lepida	*Dipodomys merriami*
Lepud californicus	*Reithrodontomys megalotis* (0,1,2)
(C) Yuma area (Arizona)[b]	*Peromyscus eremicus* (0,2,2)
Spermophilus tereticaudus	*Sigmodon hispidus* (H,6,1)
Perognathus amplus	*Neotoma albigula*
Dipodomys deserti (G,6,4)	*Lepus californicus*
D. merriami	*Sylvilagus audubonii*
Lepus californicus	(O) Superior area (Arizona)[g]
Sylvilagus audubonii	*Perognathus penicillatus*
(D) Yuma area (Nevada)[c]	*Dipodomys merriami*
Ammospermophilus leucurus (0,6,2)	*Onychomys torridus* (I,2,2)
Perognathus longimembris (G,1,3)	*Peromyscus eremicus*
P. formosus (G,1,3)	*Neotoma albigula*
Dipodomys merriami	*Lepus californicus*
Peromyscus maniculatus	*Sylvilagus audubonii*
P. eremicus	(P) Tulorosa Basin (New Mexico)[f]
P. crinitus (0,2,2)	*Spermophilus spilosoma*
Onychomys torridus	*Perognathus flavus*
Neotoma lepida (H,6,2)	*P. penicillatus*
Lepus californicus	*Dipodomys ordii*
Sylvilagus audubonii	*D. merriami*
(E) Portal area (Arizona)[d]	*Peromyscus maniculatus*
Spermophilus spilosoma	*Onychomys leucogaster*
Ammospermophilus harrisi	*Neotoma micropus*
Perognathus baileyi	*Lepus californicus*
P. penicillatus	*Sylvilagus audubonii*
P. flavus	(Q) Colorado Desert (California)[a]
Dipodomys merriami	*Spermophilus tereticaudus*
Peromyscus maniculatus	*Perognathus penicillatus*
P. eremicus	*Lepus californicus*
Onychomys torridus	*Sylvilagus audubonii*
Reithrodontomys megalotis	
Neotoma albigula	
Lepus californicus	
Sylvilagus audubonii	

(continued)

TABLE 8-6 (Continued)

Creosote bush	Mesquite
(F) Mojave Desert (California)[e]	(R) Tularosa Basin (New Mexico)[h,i]
Ammospermophilus leucurus	*Notiosorex crawfordi* (I,1,1)
Perognathus longimembris	*Spermophilus variegatus*
P. fallax (G,1,3)	*S. spilosoma* (0,6,2)
Dipodomys merriami	*Cynomys ludovicianus* (H,2,1)
Peromyscus eremicus	*Thomomys baileyi*
Onychomys torridus	*Perognathus baileyi*
Reithrodontomys megalotis	*P. flavus* (G,1,3)
Neotoma lepida	*Dipodomys ordii*
Lepus californicus	*D. merriami*
(G) Tularosa Basin (New Mexico)[f]	*Peromyscus maniculatus*
Spermophilus variegatus (0,6,1)	*P. leucopus* (0,2,2)
Thomomys baileyi	*P. eremicus*
Perognathus penicillatus	*Onychomys torridus*
Dipodomys merriami	*O. leucogaster* (I,2,2)
D. ordii	*Reithrodontomys megalotis*
Peromyscus maniculatus (0,2,2)	*Neotoma micropus*
P. truei	*N. albigula*
Onychomys torridus	*Sigmodon hispidus* (H,6,1)
Neotoma micropus (H,6,2)	*Lepus californicus*
Lepus californicus	*Sylvilagus audubonii*
Sylvilagus audubonii	
(H) Tucson area (Arizona)[b]	
Spermophilus tereticaudus (0,6,2)	
Ammospermophilus harrisi (0,6,2)	
Perognathus baileyi (G,2,3)	
P. penicillatus (G,1,3)	
P. amplus (G,1,3)	
Dipodomys merriami (G,3,4)	
Neotoma albigula (H,6,2)	
Lepus californicus (H,6,2)	
Sylvilagus adubonii (H,7,6)	

Sources: [a]Ryan 1968; [b]Mares 1973; [c]Bradley and Mauer 1973; [d]Chew and Çhew 1970; [e]Chew and Butterworth 1964; [f]Blair 1943a; [g]Bateman 1967; [h]Blair 1943b; [i]Blair 1941.

to *Larrea* areas or upon insects or small vertebrates that may frequent *Larrea* areas. Woodrats (*Neotoma*) may inhabit *Larrea* flats, usually when cacti (*Opuntia*) are also abundant in the area. Lee (1963) showed that most *Neotoma lepida* offered a diet of *L. tridentata* in the laboratory (with no free water available) lost weight rapidly, although a few individuals were able to maintain body weight. No indication was given of extensive consumption of *Larrea* by *Neotoma* in the field. None of the North American mammals seem to be specialists on *Larrea* although they may preferentially utilize the plant for nest placement (*Spermophilus tereticaudus,* for example, which in some areas must either place its burrow under *Larrea* or in the open without any ground cover at all) or may occasionally forage on some part of the bushes.

The situation in the Monte is quite distinct from that of the northern deserts. In three widely-spaced Monte localities, Mares (1973) found that small mammal diversity in a *Larrea* flat varied from two to four species. More extensive field work might eventually reveal that each locality supports the same species. Niche-types represented in the Monte include a large cursorial herbivore (*Dolichotis*), a fossorial herbivore (*Ctenomys*), a small micro-omnivore (*Eligmodontia*), and a small marsupial insectivore (*Marmosa*). No obligate granivores are found in the Monte, and while fossorial herbivores are common in North America (gophers), they are not common in *Larrea* flats. *Dolichotis,* while common in *Larrea* areas, can travel extensive distances to riparian gully forests. Indeed they appear to be more common in *Larrea* areas that border such forests than they are in the midst of extensive *Larrea* flats. Where *Dolichotis* is found at great distances from more mesic habitats, its occurrence is probably limited to *Larrea* areas with many succulents (cacti) present that serve as both a food and water source. *Eligmodontia,* while inhabiting pure stands of *Larrea,* is not common in such habitats. Only *Ctenomys,* the gopher-like tuco-tuco, seems to have a predilection for *Larrea* flats and for *Larrea.*

Ctenomys is an herbivore and spends the great majority of its time within complex burrow systems excavated in areas where soils are neither extremely rocky nor too shallow. Apparently soil depth is an important factor in determining whether or not a habitat is suitable for tuco-tucos (Mares, *unpublished*). Nevertheless, of all desert mammals inhabiting *Larrea* communities in the Western Hemisphere, only *Ctenomys* feeds extensively on creosote bush. As noted above, during much of the year the only plant found in many desert flats is *Larrea.* Since the movements of *Ctenomys* are essentially determined by the burrow system, the animals are highly localized with a particular microhabitat, and herbivorous food, of necessity, consists of *Larrea.* Individuals will burrow to the base of a *Larrea* bush and open their burrows near the trunk. They will then leave the burrow and proceed to gnaw through stems a few inches above the soil surface (Figure 8-5). The stems are then pulled into the burrow system (they may be gnawed into smaller sections) where they are eaten. An entire plant may be leveled in this manner (Figure 8-6), and if many *Ctenomys* are active in an area they can cause extensive openings in the midst of a *Larrea* community (Figure 8-7). Whether or not the leaves are eaten is not known, although Mares found no *Larrea* leaves in a number of excavated burrows. Stem and bark are eaten and bits of twigs are often encountered underground where they may be stored.

Ctenomys are caviomorph rodents, a group that has inhabited South America since about the Oligocene (Patterson and Pascual 1972). They were probably present when the Monte began to form, and their ability to utilize

FIGURE 8-5. Larrea cuneifolia *eaten near ground level by a tuco-tuco* (Ctenomys fulvus). *Note the plugged burrow entrances that were opened near the base of the bush when the fossorial rodent was foraging.*

FIGURE 8-6. Larrea cuneifolia *almost entirely cut back to ground level by foraging activities of tuco-tuco.*

FIGURE 8-7. *An opening in a* Larrea *flat caused by decimation of plants by tuco-tucos. The stumps of former bushes are visible, as are the numerous burrows of the rodents.*

Larrea as a food resource may account, at least in part, for the abundance of tuco-tucos in the desert. North American gophers (*Thomomys*) occur in desert populations occasionally, but they are not nearly as abundant in deserts as are *Ctenomys*.

By using methods similar to Fleming (1973), the mammals listed in Table 8-5 can be compared for diversity within the three ecological parameters noted above (body size, food habits, and adaptation). These measures transcend mere species richness (i.e., the number of species represented in an area) and examine various ecological attributes of species inhabiting a particular locality. As with most diversity measures, the more unpredictable a situation, the greater its diversity. Thus, if four species are distributed among four trophic categories in one area, and a second site also has four species but they represent only one trophic category, then the fauna of the first area is more diverse than that of the second. The chances of predicting which type of food specialist might be encountered in a random sample of the first areas is lower (1/4 or 25 percent) than predicting which type of food specialist will be encountered in the second area (100 percent).

The distribution of small mammal faunas of various North and South American *Larrea* areas (see Tables 8-5 and 8-6) along three different axes of ecological diversity are shown in Figure 8-8. The great differences in diversities (particularly body size and food habits) between Sonoran and Monte faunas are evident. Two of the three Argentine faunas, while containing fewer species than their northern counterparts, have their species distributed fairly evenly into adaptational categories. However, even the least diverse northern fauna (area C in Figure 8-8, near Yuma, Arizona) is much more diverse in food habits and in body size diversity. New Mexico semidesert area (area G) studied by Blair (1943b) is the most diverse *Larrea* area, although its separation from other very diverse *Larrea* sites is due to its greater adaptational diversity. In food habits and body-size diversities, it is quite comparable to more xeric *Larrea* localities.

Figure 8-9 demonstrates the ecological diversities among the same three niche parameters for the small mammal faunas of the same *Larrea* sites plus the faunas of a number of North and South American desert forest communities (*Prosopis-Acacia*) (see Tables 8-5 and 8-6). No definite differences in diversities exist between the habitats compared, although there may be a trend for *Prosopis* areas to support more diverse faunas than *Larrea* sites. However, as fewer *Prosopis* areas were examined and as the sites are not really comparable as to locality, climate, or other important variables, discerning any real trends in diversity patterns is not possible. Interestingly, the most diverse fauna in an Argentine locality (area L in Figure 8-9) and the least diverse North American area (area Q) are both *Prosopis* communities. Generally, species diversity of mammals is higher in *Prosopis* habitats in the Monte than it is in neighboring *Larrea* flats. In North America this is not necessarily true. *Larrea* flats may support more species of small mammals than a nearby

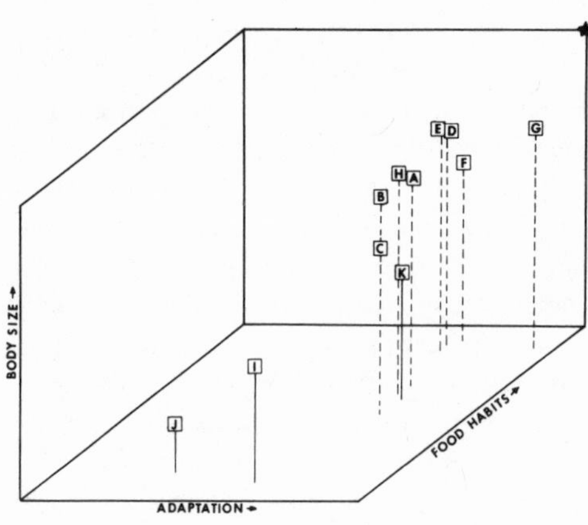

FIGURE 8-8. *Diversity of food habits, body size, and adaptation of rodents of creosote bush flats in North and South America. Maximum diversity occurs at the star (upper righthand corner of figure). Note that North American* Larrea *areas are much more diverse in all aspects than are those of the Monte. North American sites are indicated by a dashed line, while Monte localities are noted by a solid line. Abbreviations for each area are from Tables 8-5 and 8-6. See text for further explanation.*

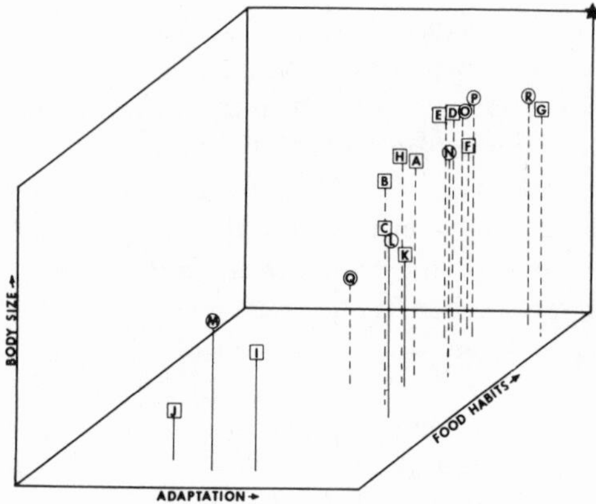

FIGURE 8-9. *Diversity of food habits, body size, and adaptation for rodent communities of* Prosopis *(circles) and* Larrea *(squares) habitats in North and South America. Symbols are as in Figure 8-8. From Mares et al.* (in preparation).

wash community, and vice versa. One cannot generalize about different species diversities in these two North American habitat types at present, although different small mammal species often prefer one or the other habitat. Mares (1973, 1975) has shown that Monte rodents are more restricted to mesic situations than are the rodents of the North American deserts. He felt that this restriction was due to the fact that most Monte species (i.e., noncaviomorphs) represent a relatively recent invasion of the desert and have not yet evolved the complex adaptive mechanisms that are demanded for a water-independent desert existence (and that are possessed by most North American desert rodents). Northern rodents have probably been present since the arid areas began to form in the Miocene. They have thus evolved along with the desert grassland, thorn scrub, and more xeric habitats and now fill many highly specialized desert rodent niches.

SUMMARY

Creosote bush desert flats exhibit wide climatic extremes and often lack a high diversity of vegetation. Communities of lizards and small mammals inhabiting *Larrea* flats in North and South America were examined, and some patterns of adaptation and distribution between these groups for each continent were compared. The Sonoran Desert creosote bush lizard fauna is more diverse than is that of the Monte: Five species are restricted to *Larrea* habitats in the north, whereas only one species is so limited in the south. Time of activity is similar for lizards in both deserts (most are diurnal), and most are terrestrial. Food habits of Sonoran lizards are more diverse than are those of lizards of the Monte (all of which are insectivorous). Morphological attributes of lizards in both deserts were compared, and we suggested that the lizard fauna of the Sonoran Desert is more morphologically and ecologically diverse.

Small mammal communities were compared from *Larrea* habitats throughout the southwestern United States and the Monte of northwestern Argentina. Greater species diversity (expressed as number of species per area) is found in the North American desert system. Small mammal faunas were compared for diversity patterns within three ecological parameters (body size, food habits, and adaptation). Greater overall diversity was demonstrated by North American desert faunas, whereas Monte faunas were of relatively low diversity. Small mammals of Monte *Prosopis* communities (a fairly diverse tree-shrub habitat) are more diverse overall than those of Monte *Larrea* areas, which thus suggests that the more mesic tree habitat is a more beneficent environment and more exploitable by Monte mammals that do not exhibit extreme desert adaptations. The only mammal that eats significant amounts of *Larrea* in either desert is the gopher-like tucotuco (*Ctenomys*) of the Monte.

RESUMEN

Los llanos desérticos de *Larrea* muestran amplios extremos climáticos y a menudo carecen de gran diversidad de vegetación. Se han estudiado comunidades de lacertílidos y pequeños mamíferos habitantes de llanos de *Larrea* en Norte y Sudamérica y se han comparado algunos patrones de adaptación y distribución entre estos grupos en cada continente. La fauna lacertilidiana de *Larrea* en el Desierto Sonorense es más diversificada que la del Monte; cinco especies se encuentran restringidas a habitats de *Larrea* en el norte, en tanto que solamente una especie tiene tales restricciones en el sur. Las horas de actividad de las lagartijas en ambos desiertos son similares (son principalmente diurnas); la mayoría son terrestres. Los hábitos alimenticios de las lagartijas del Desierto Sonorense son más diversificados que los de las lagartijas del Monte (todas las cuales son insectívoras). Se comparan atributos morfológicos de lagartijas de ambos desiertos y se sugiere que la fauna lacertilidiana del Desierto Sonorense tiene mayor diversidad morfológica y ecológica.

Se comparan comunidades de pequeños mamíferos de habitats de *Larrea* en el sudoeste de los Estados Unidos y en el Monte del noroeste de Argentina. La mayor diversidad de especies (expresada en número de especies por área) se encontró en el sistema desértico norteamericano. Se compararon faunas de pequeños mamíferos con respecto a patrones de diversidad de tres parámetros ecológicos (tamaño corporal, hábitos alimenticios y adaptación). La mayor diversidad se encontró en faunas de desiertos norteamericanos, en tanto que las faunas del Monte fueron de una diversidad relativamente baja. Los mamíferos pequeños de comunidades de *Prosopis* del Monte (habitat de árbol-arbusto bastante diverso) son más diversificados que los de áreas de *Larrea* del Monte, sugiriendo que el habitat más mesofítico de árboles en un medio ambiente más benéfico y más explotable por mamíferos del Monte, los cuales no exhiben adaptaciones extremas para condiciones desérticas. En ambos desiertos el único mamífero que ingiere cantidades significantes de *Larrea* es el tucotuco (*Ctenomys*) del Monte.

9

The Structure and Distribution of *Larrea* Communities

M. G. Barbour, J. A. MacMahon, S. A. Bamberg, and J. A. Ludwig

Species of *Larrea* so thoroughly dominate the warm deserts of North and South America that if we were truly to discuss *Larrea* communities in this chapter, we would find doing so a lengthy and difficult task. Such a task would also be beyond the basic objectives of this volume. Our purpose in this chapter is to review recent IBP research. Vegetation on IBP study sites is emphasized. The IBP data are supplemented with data from other, earlier studies only in a limited number of instances.

LARREA COMMUNITIES IN THE MOJAVE DESERT

Of the three North American warm deserts, the Mojave Desert overall shows the lowest diversity in the perennial flora. Frequently, *Larrea* alone or with a single associate dominates Mojave communities. *Larrea tridentata* and *Ambrosia dumosa* form the most characteristic association in the Mojave. In the northern Mojave, transitional to the Great Basin, Beatley (1969) recognized six *Larrea* dominated associations, with the most widespread being *Larrea-Lycium andersonii-Grayia.*

Larrea tridentata dominates on well-drained sandy flats, bajadas, and upland slopes throughout much of the Mojave, from below sea level in Death Valley to about 1,500 m elevation elsewhere. In other situations, such as washes, outcrops, and steep slopes, *L. tridentata* is present but not dominant. It is excluded only on dense soils in and around playas or other areas of high salt concentration (Wallace and Romney 1972; Lunt et al. 1973). The northern distribution limit of *Larrea* generally follows a broad area in California, southern Nevada, and Utah. In this zone, basin elevations rise from 600 to 1,000 m in the northern Mojave to 1,500 to 1,800 m in the Great Basin. Severity of winter frost is usually cited as the prime limiting factor here, but Beatley (1974) has recently theorized that excessive rainfall during the winter period may be of key importance.

Larrea tridentata has been most extensively studied on the Nevada Test Site, a transitional area between the Mojave and Great Basin deserts (Beatley 1965, 1969, 1974; Wallace and Romney 1972). Since 1971, one of the IBP Desert Biome validation sites, Rock Valley, which is in the Nevada Test Site, has been under additional intensive investigation (Turner 1973). Much of the material in this section comes from work done at the Nevada Test Site.

The contribution of *Larrea* to a number of Mojave sites is summarized in Table 9-1. Woodell et al. (1969) have shown that *Larrea* density generally increases with increasing annual precipitation, as one might expect; but Table 9-1 reveals that the relationship is not a close one. For example, Mercury Valley, Rock Valley, and Randsberg all experience nearly the same rainfall, yet *Larrea* density ranges from 178 to 1,003 shrubs per ha, and total shrub density ranges from about 3,000 to 11,000 per ha. Note also the biomass differences between Mercury and Rock Valleys. Clearly, other environmental factors are involved in determining shrub density.

Although the density of other shrubs may be moderately high, their diversity is usually not. In the homogeneous zones of Rock Valley, for example, five to eight major species typically occur in association, giving H′ = 0.67–0.81 diversity indices as calculated by the formula of Pielou (1969).

Characterization of Population Age Structure

As discussed by Barbour et al. (see Chapter 3), several investigators have attempted to age *Larrea* shrubs by correlating shrub volume or height to ring count. Barbour (1967) found that within small stands, height did correlate with ring count, and he prepared frequency diagrams for shrub heights that he claimed were indicative of age structure. Figure 9-1 shows diagrams for six

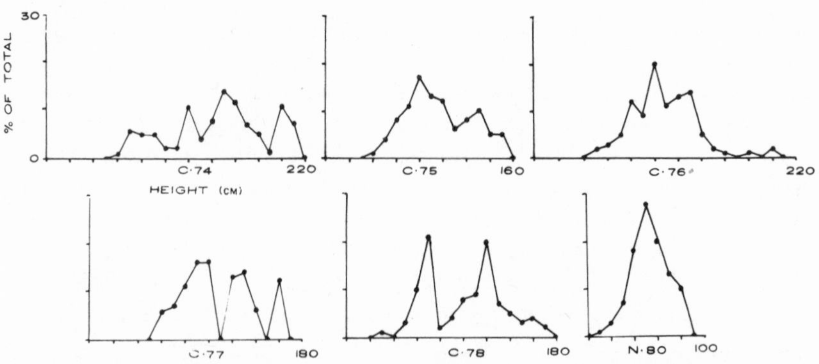

FIGURE 9-1. *Height (age) frequency diagrams for Mojave Desert* L. tridentata *populations. One-hundred shrubs selected by a restricted random method are summarized in each graph. From Barbour (1967).*

TABLE 9-1 *Density, Cover, and Biomass of* Larrea *and Other Perrenial Species for Selected Mojave Desert Sites.*

Site	Annual ppt. (mm)	*Larrea* dens. (shrubs/ha)	Other shrub dens.	*Larrea* cover (%)	Total cover (%)	Biomass (kg/ha)
Death Valley[a]	40–60	285	1,611	1.8	5.1	60
Death Valley[b]	40–60	393		6.2	14.0	
Stovepipe Wells[c]	40	60	47			
Inyokern[c]	91	262	7,439			
Cantil[c]	100	207	744			
Emigrant Spring[c]	111	262	763			
Mojave[c]	128	495	138			
Frenchman Flat[d]	132	614		7.8	18.0	
Jackass Flat[d]	138	797		7.3	18.7	
N-80[a]	140(?)	1,790		4.0	11.0	
Haiwee[c]	143	299	5,450			
Randsburg[c]	150	178	2,795			
Mercury Valley[a]	155	695	10,293	2.9	19.2	299
Rock Valley[a]	162	1,003	7,941	4.3	20.1	122
Yucca Flat[d]	166	398		4.6	27.0	
Wildrose Canyon[c]	207	538	10,223			
Morongo Valley[c]	218	488	574			

Note: Some data are means of more than one sample.
Sources: [a]Wallace and Romney 1972; [b]Barbour 1967 and 1969a; [c]Woodell et al. 1969; Beatley 1974.

Mojave populations (sites): C-74 through C-78 were at increasing elevations along Death Valley bajada; N-80 was about 30 km north of Pahrump, Nevada.

The Death Valley populations typically showed two or more peaks of size (age) and very few shrubs smaller than 40 cm. Barbour interpreted this data to mean that mass germination and establishment is a rare but recurring event. These populations lack the large number of young that traditionally characterize stable or expanding populations; however, in view of *Larrea*'s presumed long life span (see Chapter 3), the populations shown in Figure 9-1 should not necessarily be viewed as senescent.

Association and Pattern

The shrubs in the southern Mojave Desert are often widely spread and appear to be regularly patterned (Went 1955), but in the northern Mojave Desert, in the Nevada Test Site region, most shrubs are so closely associated with other species or other members of the same species that they occur in clumps with overlapping canopies. In Rock Valley 66 percent and in Mercury Valley 89 percent of *Larrea* shrubs occur in group associations instead of as solitary plants. Table 9-2 summarizes associations of some twenty-eight spe-

TABLE 9-2 *Degree of Association for All Possible Pairs of 28 Perennial Species at Mercury, Nevada (from Wallace and Romney 1972).*

	Number of other species		
Species	Positively associated with	Negatively associated with	Mutually exclusive with
Larrea divaricata	12	1	7
Acamptopappus shockleyi	3	8	5
Atriplex confertifolia	8	1	11
Cacti (mixed species)	13	0	8
Coleogyne ramosissima	1	0	20
Dalea fremontii	0	2	20
Encelia virginensis	3	0	24
Ephedra funerea	14	0	8
E. nevadensis	14	0	8
Eurotia lanata	13	4	2
Franseria (Ambrosia) dumosa	17	2	3
Grayia spinosa	12	1	9
Hilaria rigida	3	2	14
Hymenoclea salsola	3	0	21
Krameria parvifolia	13	1	2
Lepidium fremontii	6	0	9
Lycium andersonii	19	1	4
Machaeranthera tortifolia	13	0	6
Menodora spinescens	3	0	17
Oryzopsis humenoides	10	0	8
Prunus fasciculata	3	0	20
Psilostrophe cooperi	1	0	23
Salazaria mexicana	11	0	9
Sphaeralcea ambigua	10	1	3
Stephanomeria pauciflora	4	0	19
Stipa speciosa	6	0	11
Thamnosma montana	1	0	23
Yucca schidigera	13	0	7

Note: The nonsignificant interactions for each species are not tallied; their number equals the total of the three entries subtracted from 28.

cies in Mercury Valley (Wallace and Romney 1972). The method used involved circular plots 30.5 m in diameter and analysis of data by contingency table and calculation of chi-square values for each pair of species. *Larrea* does not appear to exhibit an unusual number of positive or negative associations, compared to the other species. In Table 9-2, "mutually exclusive" means that two species were never encountered in the same quadrat; hence it is an extreme form of negative association that was not statistically analyzed.

Even in the more arid portions of the Mojave Desert, *Larrea* shrubs may show a clumped or random pattern, rather than a regular pattern (Woodell et al. 1969; Anderson 1971; Barbour 1973, 1974; King and Woodell 1973). Seemingly, the desert surface is much less homogeneous than it at first appears. Pattern on a local scale can be related to very small washes, gravel pavement, depth to caliche, burrow systems of rodents, and small topographic differences. The uniformity in spacing predicted by Cody (1974) is not found in most of the Mojave Desert.

Density and pattern of *Larrea* has been attributed to differential seedling survival, because of competition for moisture near established shrubs or allelopathic substances given off by established shrubs (Went 1955; Sheps 1973). The importance of these factors is still unresolved. Clumps of *Larrea* appear to be of the same size (age), as though they had arisen as a clump of seedlings, but the observations of several workers indicate that such clumps arise from asexual reproduction—that is, a splitting of the root crown (Wallace and Romney 1972; Barbour 1969a; Muller 1953). Certainly, the data in Tables 9-1 and 9-2 indicate that the density of *Larrea,* and possibly its pattern, is independent of density and pattern of other species.

In Death Valley the low plant densities seem to preclude much association. Only about 10 percent of *Larrea* and 40 percent of *Ambrosia* shrubs grow in clumped associations. Distance to nearest neighbor (separate *Larrea* shrubs) average 5.2 m in contrast to 2.0 m for Mercury Valley and Rock Valley. In order to adequately sample *Larrea* density in Death Valley, a minimum rectangular strip 300 m long or a square plot 300 m on a side should be used.

LARREA COMMUNITIES IN THE SONORAN DESERT

For the Sonoran Desert, Yang (1970) points out that *Larrea* populations are generally tetraploid. The distribution of tetraploid individuals coincides with the usual interpretation of the eastern boundary of the Sonoran Desert at just west of Safford, Graham County, Arizona. For our purposes, however, we favor the suggestion of Lowe (1955), based on animal data, and Benson and Darrow (1954), based on the distribution of an aggregation of Sonoran Desert shrubs and subtrees, of extending the limit of the Sonoran Desert eastward, entering New Mexico in Grant and Hidalgo counties. Obviously, the Sonoran Desert by this definition includes both diploid and tetraploid *Larrea* populations. This admixture is consistent with the view of the Deming Plain as being a dispersal route for the meeting of Chihuahuan and Sonoran biotic elements (Findley 1969).

To the south, in mainland Mexico, the distribution of *Larrea* extends to the area of the Rio Mayo, Sonora. This area marks an appropriate terminus for the Sonoran Desert as it meets the thorn scrub (Gentry 1942). We must emphasize that the desert-thorn scrub vegetation interface is complex and not easily definable. We expect this complexity and difficulty in defining, since many "indicator" species of the Sonoran Desert are derived from the thorn forests of Latin America (Whittaker and Niering 1964).

General Vegetation Characteristics

Shreve (1951) recognized seven Sonoran Desert provinces based on component plant species. These divisions are useful, but hardly precise in nature. The maps of Hastings et al. (1972) show few species whose boundaries coincide with provincial limits. In addition, there is a great deal of heterogeneity in plant communities within the provinces. These variations are caused by local edaphic factors, history of man's use, and the myriad of other factors affecting vegetation composition, including a rich flora. The Sonoran Desert is generally conceded to be the richest, most diverse of all the North American desert types, due to the large number of species–over 3,000 according to Solbrig (1972)–and the great diversity of life forms–25 are recognized by Shreve (1942, 1951).

A map of perennial species density for the Sonoran Desert, based on the maps of Hastings et al. (1972) is shown in Figure 9-2. The map is necessarily general and at a rather large scale, but it serves to indicate the richness of the Sonoran Desert as contrasted to the Mojave. Most of the Sonoran exhibits about fifteen species in any one small region, and some localities exhibit more than twice that number.

Also, in contrast to the Mojave Desert, the Sonoran clearly has three vertical synusia of perennial plants at many localities (Figure 9-3). For a site in the Santa Catalina Mountains–perhaps no less typical a Sonoran site than the one used for Figure 9-2–there are 38 percent therophytes, 30 percent chaemophytes, 27 percent phanerophytes, and small percentages of hemicryptophytes and geophytes (Whittaker and Niering 1964). Synusial complexity may be most closely related to soil characteristics (Yang and Lowe 1956).

The Sonoran Desert in Arizona generally has a biseasonal rainfall pattern, which introduces an additional complexity–that is, the presence of a mix of summer and winter annuals in various proportions and the possibility of differential response of shrubs to one or the other season of rainfall. The extent of biseasonality decreases and shifts to a winter peak as one moves north or west from southern Arizona. As one moves south or east of southern Arizona, summer rainfall predominates. The two rainy seasons are themselves different in intensity and duration of rainfall events. Detailed analyses of these patterns are given by Bryson (1957) and Hastings and Turner (1965).

The point of this general introduction is that the biota and environment of the Sonoran Desert are varied. Therefore, generalizing is difficult. We shall

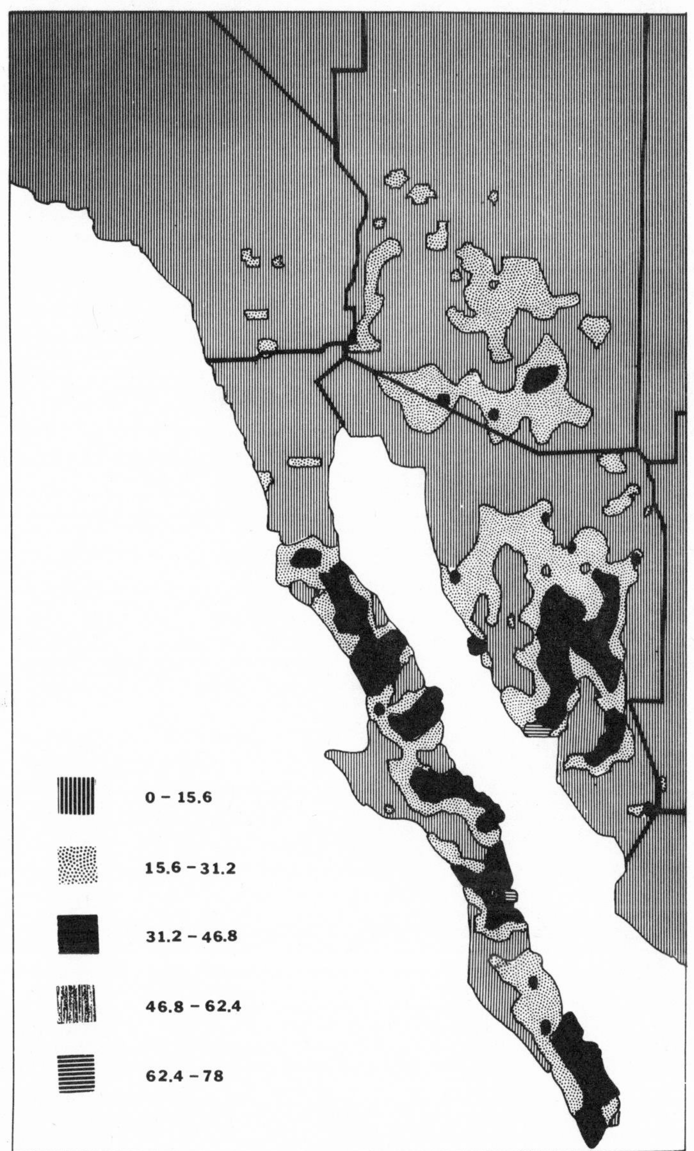

FIGURE 9-2. *Density of perennial plant species in the Sonoran Desert. Data were collected by overlaying each of the distribution maps of Hastings et al. (1972) with a grid of 40 × 40 km cells and counting the number of species in each cell. The results were then plotted and species density isophenes drawn with the Harvard computer program, SYMAP.*

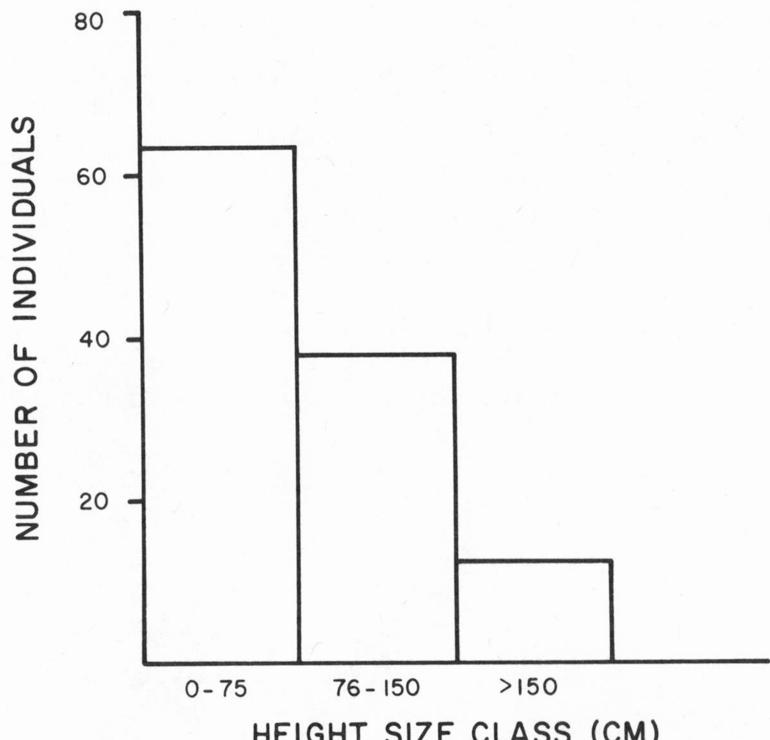

FIGURE 9-3. *Height class histogram for all perennial plants at the Sierra Estrella site, 12.5 km northwest of Maricopa, Pinal County, Arizona. Unpublished IBP data courtesy of MacMahon.*

discuss data for some Sonoran Desert stands; these may represent a broader area, but this is by no means certain.

Specific Site Data

Data presented in this section emphasize two main sites. Both sites fit the southwestern desert scrub-lower Sonoran-paloverde-sahuaro community of Lowe (1964).

The first is the U.S. IBP Desert Biome Sonoran Desert validation site, situated about 54 km northwest of Tucson, Arizona. The site is on the Silver Bell bajada and will be referred to as Silver Bell. Dr. John Thames, University of Arizona, the principal investigator for this site, is responsible for the collection of much of the Silver Bell data presented herein.

The second site is on the south end of the Sierra Estrella, 12.5 km northwest of Maricopa, Pinal County, Arizona. This site contains plots that one of us (MacMahon) has studied for several years, including a 1 ha plot on which every plant has been mapped and measured. Constance Braun, a former student of MacMahon's, assisted with field measurement and data analysis for this site.

Density, Cover, and Biomass

Data on density and cover of *Larrea* for twenty-seven Sonoran sites are summarized in Table 9-3. Many of the sites were analyzed by Barbour and

TABLE 9-3 *Density and Cover of* Larrea *in Selected Sonoran Desert Sites.*

Site	Annual ppt. (mm)	*Larrea* dens. (shrubs/ha)	*Larrea* cover Absolute (%)	*Larrea* cover Relative (%)
Niland[a]	48	86		
C-70[b]	65	130	11	50
C-71[b]	65	830	15	68
ARIZ-010[c]	70	215	< 1	6
ARIZ-011[c]	85	189	5	57
ARIZ-012[c]	95	338	4	92
Yuma[a]	91	108		
ARIZ-013[c]	103	266	6	63
ARIZ-014[c]	113	403	7	47
ARIZ-015[c]	185	670	9	59
ARIZ-016[c]	198	787	9	76
Organ Pipe[d]	205	667	6	28
ARIZ-017[c]	218	1,131	20	86
ARIZ-018[c]	218	1,118	9	96
ARIZ-019[c]	218	953	8	49
Sierra Estrella[e]	220	438	6	30
ARIZ-020[c]	225	1,066	20	100
ARIZ-001[c]	245	1,086	20	97
Silverbell[e]	245	188	3	
A-70[b]	245	187	1	2
A-71[b]	245	112	11	31
ARIZ-007[c]	275	1,378	29	83
ARIZ-004[c]	275	3,770	32	57
ARIZ-008[c]	275	462	7	19
ARIZ-009[c]	275	579	17	42
Cabazon[a]	299	239		
Semidesert[f]	439	4,460	17	

Sources: [a]Woodell et al. 1969; [b]Barbour 1967 and 1969a; [c]Barbour and Diaz 1973; [d]McCleary 1968; [e]unpublished IBP data courtesy of MacMahon; [f]Chew and Chew 1965.

Diaz (1973). They concluded that *Larrea* cover, *Larrea* density, and total ground cover increased with increasing moisture. The data in Table 9-3 reveal that this conclusion is only approximately correct (compare, for example, A-70 and A-71 near Tucson with identical rainfall and elevation but different abundance of *Larrea*).

In general, total shrub biomass (*Larrea* plus others) increases with rainfall, as might be expected (Figure 9-4), but how is the biomass distributed: many small shrubs, a few large shrubs, or something intermediate? Figure 9-5 depicts density and biomass for the major perennials on Mojave, Sonoran, and Chihuahuan sites. *Larrea* is indicated with arrows. On the Sonoran site (Tucson, 245 mm), *L. tridentata* has very low density and total biomass, with an average of about 2 kg per shrub. On the Mojave site (Rock Valley, 162 mm), *L. tridentata* has moderate density but still a low total biomass, for an average of only 0.3 kg per shrub. On the Chihuahuan site (Jornada bajada, 390 mm), *L. tridentata* has both the highest density and the highest total biomass, for an average of 0.7 kg per shrub. These biomass differences more or less match the differences in *L. tridentata* height that Barbour (1967) reported for the three deserts and reflect some of the physiognomic differences between the races of *L. tridentata.*

We have less information for below-ground biomass. Figure 9-6 is an attempt to estimate the vertical distribution of root biomass at the Silver Bell site. The curves were derived by counting hits with a pin frame in a vertical section of soil and then recording root size class. Data were then transformed to biomass and scaled up on an aerial basis.

The curves suggest a slight vertical stratification of the root mass of the species shown. The preliminary curve for *Larrea* fits between *Ambrosia* and *Cercidium.* Note the lack of roots in the upper 10 cm of soil, which may be the result of avoidance of a zone of high heat flux. The finding that the mass of *Larrea* roots are in the zone of from 10 to 45 cm depth (which is also true for excavation data for Sierra Estrella–not shown) agrees with observations by earlier workers (Cannon 1911; Chew and Chew 1965; Garcia-Moya and McKell 1970). Additional information on root systems of *Larrea* appears in Chapter 3.

Association and Pattern

By using continuum methodology (McIntosh 1967), the importance value (IV) was calculated for each perennial species along a North to South gradient of eighteen sites. The sites extend from Cave Creek, north of Phoenix, to Organ Pipe National Monument, Arizona. The data were then ordinated by using *Larrea* as one polar species and *Eriogonum fasciculatum* as the other (Figure 9-7).

An interesting note is that *Larrea* IVs are the complement of those of

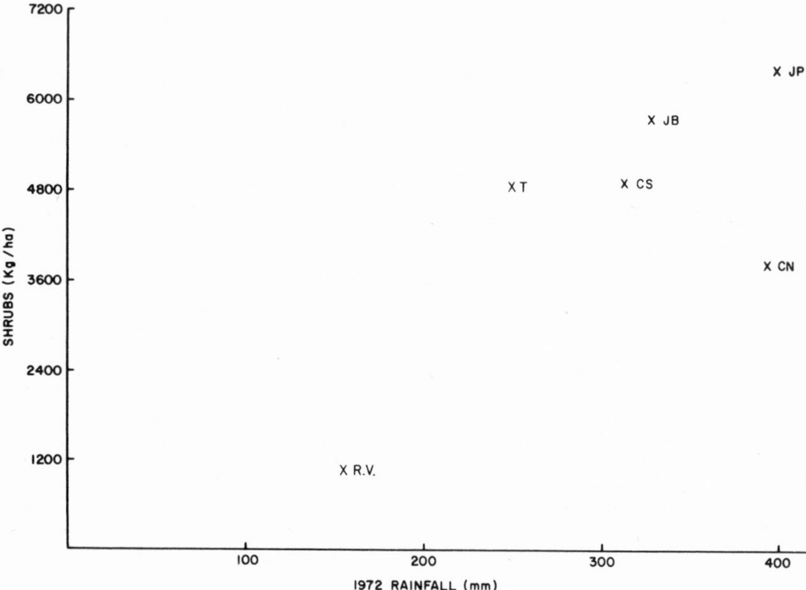

FIGURE 9-4. *Relation between above-ground biomass (all shrubs) and rainfall for U.S. IBP Desert Biome sites. RV indicates Rock Valley, a Mojave site; T is Silver Bell bajada, near Tucson, a Sonoran site; JB and JP are Jornada bajada and Jornada playa, Chihuahuan Desert sites; CS and CN are Curlew Valley north and south in the Great Basin near Snowville, Utah.*

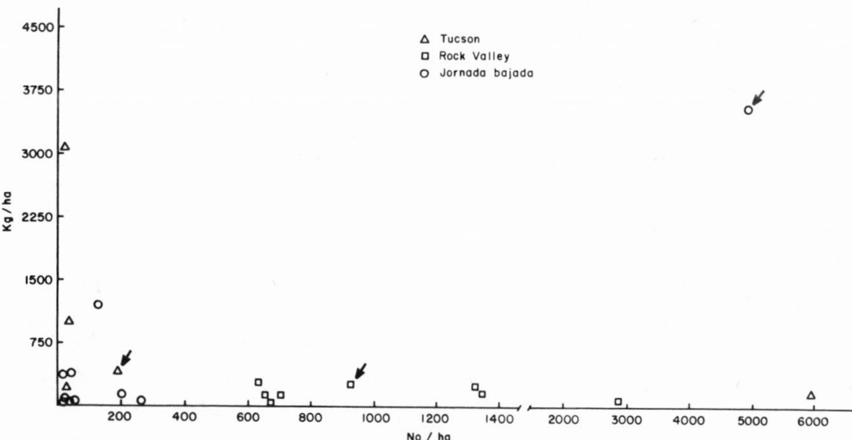

FIGURE 9-5. *Relation between plant numbers and above-ground biomass for major shrub species at U.S. IBP Desert Biome sites.* Larrea *is indicated by arrows. Unpublished IBP data courtesy of MacMahon.*

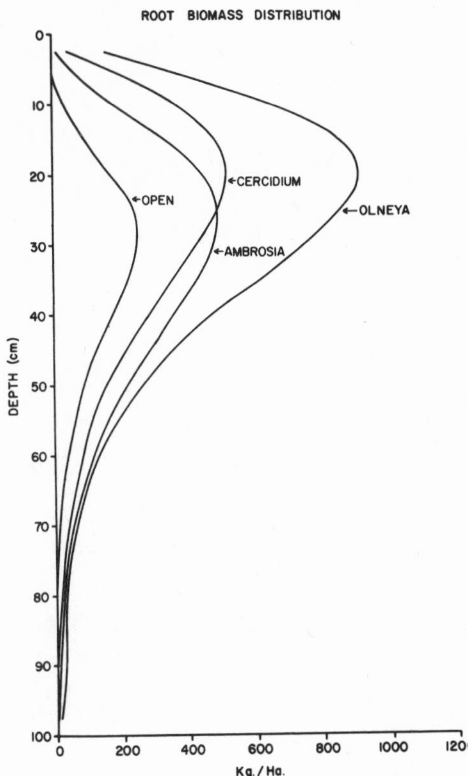

FIGURE 9-6. *Distribution of root biomass under various shrub species and in the open on the Silver Bell bajada. Unpublished IBP data courtesy of MacMahon.*

Ambrosia deltoidea, and to some extent *A. dumosa,* though these three species are together considered indicators of Sonoran Desert and the vegetation type is often referred to as a *Larrea–Ambrosia* association (Shelford 1963). Spalding (1909) also alluded to such an inverse relation between *Larrea* and *Ambrosia. Larrea* and *Ambrosia* frequently show a high degree of aggregation in local areas, however. The aggregation pattern of desert plants at a fine level of resolution is highly complex, and one hypothesis is that microsite patterning may be influenced by soil texture, microtopography, and soil organic content, or a combination of these factors. All three factors may also affect soil moisture availability.

A controversy exists as to the type of dispersion pattern represented by *Larrea* (Barbour 1973; Woodell et al. 1969; Anderson 1971; King and Woodell 1973). This chapter is not the place to elucidate all the problems of dispersion pattern measurement; however, a few comments are in order. Whether the plants are clumped, regular, or random, in part depends on plot size, the specific site studied, and the mathematical measures employed. Table 9-4 shows the problem. Three indices of dispersion are calculated for the Sierra Estrella enumeration plot. Every index value shows statistically significant

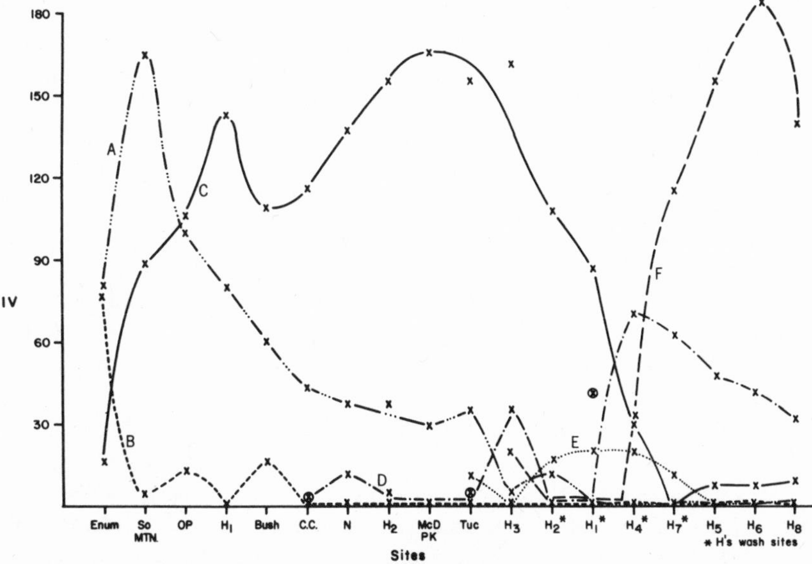

FIGURE 9-7. *Importance values and ordination of eighteen Sonoran Desert sites.* A *indicates* L. tridentata; B *is* Ambrosia dumosa; C *is* A. deltoidea; D *is* Simmondsia chinensis; E *is* Acacia constricta; F *is* Eriogonum fasciculatum. *Sites marked* H *were sampled by T. Halvorson and are used by permission of Duncan Patten, Arizona State University. Others are from unpublished IBP data courtesy of MacMahon.*

departure from a random shrub distribution. The problem is that values of the Hopkins (1954) and Pielou (1959) indices indicate a high degree of aggregation and that of Clark and Evans (1954) indicates an equally significant regular pattern.

The solution is in what the statistics measure. As Pielou (1969) points out, these indices measure two things: intensity and grain. *Intensity* is the

TABLE 9–4 *Pattern Analysis Data of Six Species of Shrubs, Using Three Methods of Analysis (data from Sierra Estrella).*

Species	Hopkins	Pielou	Clark & Evans
Larrea tridentata	8.8602	5.4633	1.9590
Encelia farinosa	8.2653	3.9321	1.8116
Ambrosia deltoidea	4.1585	2.5413	1.5156
Ambrosia dumosa	4.6798	5.0884	1.8458
Hymenoclea monogyra	60.6432	13.8709	3.2150
Lycium andersonii	5.5148	2.9301	1.6251

Note: All are significant at $p < 0.001$.

spatial variation in density; *grain* refers to the dispersion of density in an area. Thus Clark and Evans measure density of clumps and in this instance indicates regular pattern in the clump. The other two indices measure overall pattern and indicate aggregation. The problem is not only one of scale but our ability to perceive it, which is more fully discussed by Braun and MacMahon (1975).

The comments so far have dealt with *Larrea* in relation to other perennials. *Larrea* is frequently so aggregated with other *Larrea* individuals that the unit looks like a single plant. The problem is discussed by Wright (1970). He attributes the aggregation to root sprouting and crown splitting rather than to pattern of germination. Annuals also clump around *Larrea* (Muller 1953). Duncan Patten of Arizona State University has unpublished data showing that the density of annuals under Sonoran Desert shrubs (*Larrea, Ambrosia,* and *Cercidium*) at Cave Creek, Arizona, is a function of the amount and aspect of shrub cover, with the north sides of canopies having greater annual biomass than south sides. Increased organic matter and shading are at least two of the factors creating this pattern. One of us (MacMahon) has noted that in low rainfall years nearly all of the annuals that bloom are under shrubs, as opposed to wet years where intershrub spaces may be covered by blooming herbs. *Larrea* architecture funnels intercepted rain down the main trunk to the soil around it (Wallace and Romney 1972), and this probably contributes to such an herb pattern.

Larrea has many associates, depending on the site being considered. There is little reason to list codominant species from throughout the Sonoran Desert; Shreve (1951) lists many such species groupings.

LARREA COMMUNITIES IN THE CHIHUAHUAN DESERT

Plant community data for the Chihuahuan Desert apparently does not exist to the same degree of detail or volume as data for the other two warm deserts. Gardner's examination of *Larrea* in the Rio Grande Valley (1951) and the recent IBP work on the Jornada bajada site (about 40 km north of Las Cruces, Desert Biome Research Memorandum 73-4) particularly stand out. The relatively recent and apparently continuing invasion of *Larrea* and other shrubs into what had been grassland in New Mexico and Texas has attracted the attention of many more investigators (Bray 1901; Branscomb 1958; Lesueur 1945; Valentine and Norris 1964; York and Dick-Peddie 1969). Waterfall (1946) has pointed out *Larrea*'s avoidance of gypsum soils.

Species diversity and growth form diversity are relatively high, compared to the other warm deserts, but the Chihuahuan lacks the prominent arboreal element of the Sonoran Desert. Diversity changes dramatically when annual and perennial forbs are abundant. If we take the Jornada site as representa-

TABLE 9-5 *Densities of Shrubs, Succulents, Forbs, and Grasses in a* Larrea*-Dominated Ecosystem of the Chihuahuan Community (unpublished IBP data courtesy of Ludwig, from Jornada site, 40 km north of Las Cruces, New Mexico).*

Life form	Species or group	Density (shrubs/ha)
Shrubs	*Larrea divaricata*	4,844
	Prosopis glandulosa	27
	Xanthocephalum sarothrae	261
	Flourensia cernua	196
	Parthenium incanum	32
	Zinnia pumila	29
	Ephedra trifurca	24
	Fallugia paradoxa	19
Succulents	*Yucca elata*	123
	Yucca baccata	33
	Opuntia sp.	86
Grasses	*Aristida* sp.	31
	Muhlenbergia porteri	97
	Erioneuron pulchellum[a]	600
Forbs	Annual forbs[a]	102,500
	Perennial forbs[a]	15,590

[a]Based on a survey taken May 5, 1973.

tive, we see that its diversity index (H′, Pielou 1969) ranges from 0.35 to 0.98, depending on season. Table 9-5 summarizes the Jornada site in some detail.

Density of *Larrea* is much greater in Chihuahuan sites than in the other two warm deserts (Table 9-6). In other respects, however, the three deserts are quite similar. There is a general tendency for *Larrea* density to increase with increasing annual precipitation, but local edaphic factors may have overriding importance. Compare, for example, the six sites analyzed by Burk and Dick-Peddie (1973), all of which are located in the same general region and share the same climate and elevation (see Table 9-6): Edaphic differences caused *Larrea* density to vary from 2,800 to 8,400 shrubs per ha.; absolute cover, relative cover, and biomass showed similar large fluctuations. In this case, the major soil difference was presence or absence of a caliche hardpan 15 to 35 cm below the surface. Jornada 2, Picacho 1, and Picacho 2 all had the hardpan, and they exhibited the highest *Larrea* densities but the lowest relative and absolute cover by *Larrea*. Evidently, the size of *Larrea* decreased on these sites at the same time that diversity of other species increased. Cunningham and Burk (1973) examined the role of caliche on *L. tridentata* water relations.

TABLE 9-6 *Density, Cover, and Above-Ground Biomass of* L. tridentata *in Selected Chihuahuan Desert Sites.*

			Larrea cover		
Site	Annual ppt. (mm)	*Larrea* dens. (shrubs/ha)	Absolute (%)	Relative (%)	Biomass (kg/ha)
T-76[a]	90	3,230	15	23	
T-77[a]	90	3,260	6	46	
NM-74[a]	95	230	2	5	
T-70[a]	110	3,630	18	58	
T-71[a]	110	1,730	13	24	
T-72[a]	110	1,820	13	22	
T-73[a]	110	3,030	26	44	
T-74[a]	110	2,390	12	92	
T-75[a]	110	6,190	24	73	
NM-72[a]	107	3,830	15	100	
NM-70[a]	120	1,230	1	2	
NM-71[a]	120	7,460	9	47	
NM-73[a]	180	1,760	5	8	
Jornada[b]	390	4,844	24		3,520
Jornada 1[c]	441	3,455	18	88	3,263
Jornada 2[c]	441	8,420	12	41	1,010
Picacho 1[c]	441	4,104	12	50	1,354
Picacho 2[c]	441	3,686	8	49	848
Fillmore 1[c]	441	2,824	23	96	4,095
Fillmore 2[c]	441	3,574	31	89	6,505

Sources: [a]Barbour 1967 and 1969a; [b]unpublished IBP data courtesy of Ludwig; [c]Burk and Dick-Peddie 1973.

Barbour (1967) has examined the age structure of several Chihuahuan populations of *Larrea,* by correlating height with age (Figure 9-8). His graphs show a much more even distribution of shrubs over all heights (age), with many small shrubs; Barbour interpreted this finding to mean that germination and survival took place much more often in the Chihuahuan Desert than in either the Sonoran or Mojave Desert.

L. CUNEIFOLIA COMMUNITIES IN ARGENTINA

This is very little synecological data on communities dominated by *Larrea* in South America. Morello's important Argentine studies (1955, 1956, 1958) stand out in isolation. Unfortunately, these papers emphasize plant morphology and autecology. Community descriptions are rather superficial. Some of the author's conclusions appear to lack documentation—that is, the support-

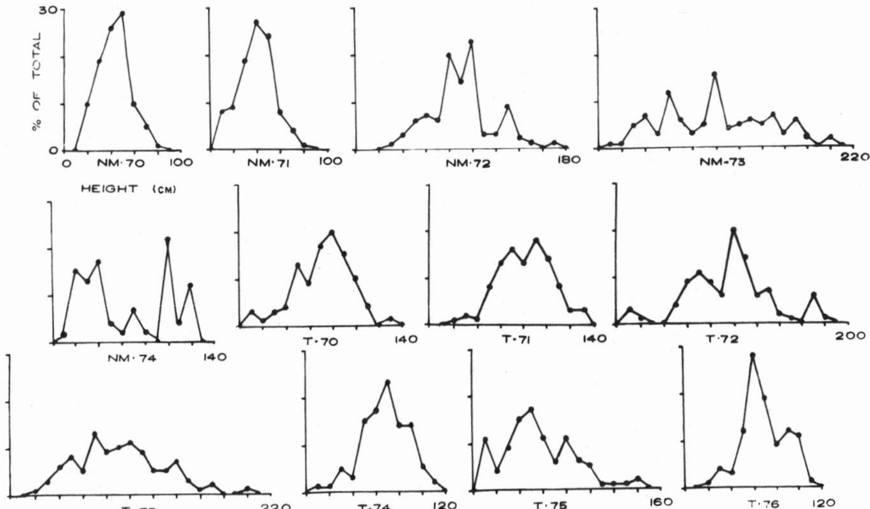

FIGURE 9-8. *Height (age) frequency diagrams for Chihuahuan Desert populations of* Larrea. *One hundred shrubs selected by a restricted random method are summarized in each graph (from Barbour 1967).*

ing data are not included or cited. Nevertheless, Morello's papers serve in fact as classics because of their wealth of information.

Morello points out that *L. cuneifolia,* rather than *L. divaricata,* is the appropriate analog to *L. tridentata* of North America. *Larrea cuneifolia* dominates the driest areas of the Monte. It occupies well-drained sites and avoids drainages or low-lying areas that may become periodically inundated. Its elevational limits are lower than those of *L. divaricata:* In the north *L. cuneifolia* extends up to 2,700 m and in the south up to 1000 m, while *L. divaricata* in both cases is able to reach 100 to 200 m higher.

Larrea divaricata, in comparison, is a relative mesophyte and a weed; it is able to invade areas where vegetation has been partially or totally destroyed. As summarized in Figures 9-9 and 9-10, *L. divaricata* becomes a widespread dominant only in areas outside the Monte—that is, areas with annual precipitation above 200 mm. Within the Monte, *L. divaricata* is riparian, and *L. cuneifolia* is the dominant taxon. The highest precipitation sites reported for *L. cuneifolia* are at 450 mm; the highest for *L. divaricata* are at 700 mm. *Larrea divaricata* is more tolerant of saline soils and soils with low oxygen content; it can live in (but is not restricted to) areas where a water table is constantly present 10 to 30 m below the surface. In this respect, *L. divaricata* is more of a phreatophyte, as *Prosopis* is in North America.

Consequently, we shall not discuss *L. divaricata*-dominated communities in this chapter. Other South American species of *Larrea* will also be ignored because they are largely outside the boundaries of the IBP study, which forms the central theme of this volume.

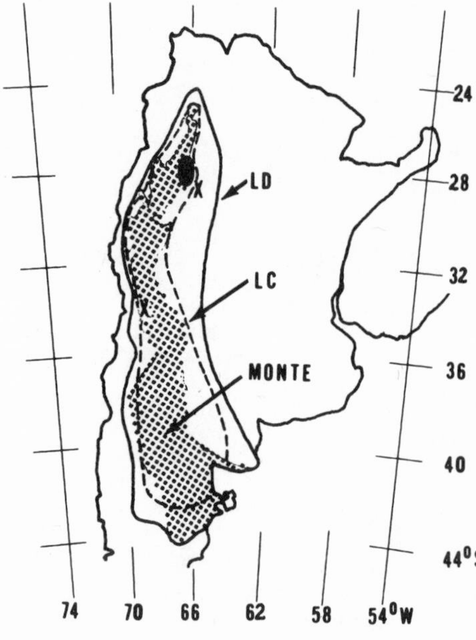

FIGURE 9-9. *Outlines of the Argentine Monte (dotted) and the range limits of* L. divaricata *and* L. cuneifolia. *Based on maps and text by Descole (1943), Gracia et al. (1960), and Morello (1955, 1958). The closed circle indicates the location of the Bolsón de Pipanaco; the two* X's *mark ecotone sampling locations.*

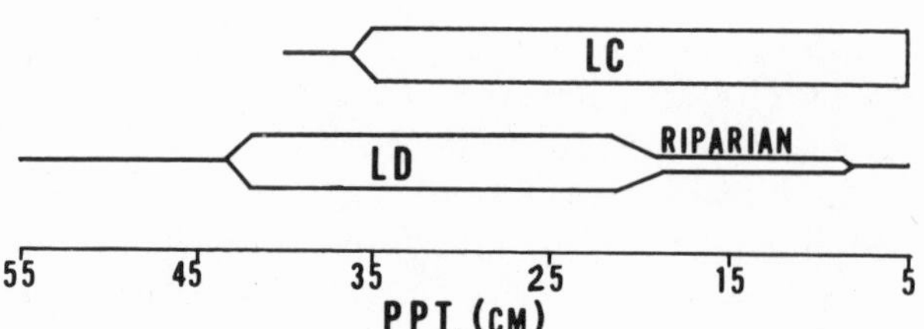

FIGURE 9-10. *The relative abundance or dominance of* L. divaricata *and* L. cuneifolia *in Argentina as a function of annual precipitation. Based on data by Lowe et al. (1973), Morello (1955, 1958), and Barbour* (personal observation).

IBP Investigations

Lowe et al. (1972, 1973), Morello (1972), Barbour and Diaz (1973), and Barbour et al. (1974) altogether have sampled about twenty-five *L. cuneifolia* dominated communities in Argentina, mainly in the northwestern portion (see Figure 9-9) that exhibits vegetational and floristic similarities with the North American Sonoran Desert.

Lowe et al. (1972, 1973) sampled eleven sites along a bajada about 50 km south of Andalgalá, in the Bolsón de Pipanaco. Elevation along that transect rose from 860 m to about 1100 m; precipitation rose from 165 mm to an estimated 215 mm. *Larrea cuneifolia* dominated all but the uppermost site. The authors found sixty perennial species along the transect, with alpha species diversity and percent ground cover increasing with elevation. The underlying causal factor for changes in species diversity and cover was thought to be soil texture, especially the percent rock and gravel, which increased with elevation. They found a similar pattern along a Sonoran bajada.

Barbour and Diaz (1973) sampled portions of the same bajada and generally reported similar patterns. The number of perennials increased from three to four species at the bajada bottom to fourteen near the top (Table 9-7), and total ground cover increased from 6 percent to 37 percent. Their surface soil samples (to a depth of 10 cm), however, did not show a peak in rock and gravel at the upper part of the bajada, where cover and density peaked. They also found a peak in density and cover of *L. cuneifolia* in the middle of the transect. Height frequency diagrams (possibly related to age frequency diagrams) did not appear to change with elevation. There were many small (young) shrubs and a wide range of heights (ages), thereby indicating a possibly high probability of seedling establishment any given year.

Barbour and Diaz (1973) sampled twenty other *L. cuneifolia* sites along a moisture gradient, within the Bolsón de Pipanaco, which ranged from about 75 mm to an estimated 270 mm. Elevation, however, was generally within ± 100 m for all sites. They concluded that as moisture increased, so did total cover, absolute *Larrea* cover, and *Larrea* shrub density (Table 9-8). Major exceptions to these trends were associated with sites not dominated by *Larrea*—that is, sites where the relative cover of *L. cuneifolia* was less than 40 percent, as is ARG-002, ARG-012. They pointed out that paired Sonoran sites, with similar rainfall, showed similar figures for total cover, relative *Larrea* cover, and *Larrea* density.

Species diversity did not correlate with rainfall. Sites with both low and high precipitation could be species poor (e.g., two species each in ARG-018 and ARG-016), and sites with similar precipitation could exhibit greatly different species richness (compare ARG-020 with six species and ARG-019 with one). Barbour and Diaz (1973) agreed with Lowe et al. (1972, 1973) that coarseness of soil texture affected species diversity much more than precipitation, with the diversity increasing with increasing percent of rock and gravel. Finding nearly pure *L. cuneifolia* communities under the highest rainfall regimes was possible, but these sites were on relatively level, fine-textured substrates.

Barbour and Diaz (1973) further reported that the pattern of *Larrea* shrub distribution seemed independent of rainfall; it was regular at one site with low rainfall (ARG-021, 75 mm), but either random or clumped at all other sites. Height frequency diagrams, however, did show a correlation with rainfall. In dry sites the distributions tended to have one pronounced peak and a relatively narrow range of overall heights; in wetter sites they tended to have many peaks and a very wide range of heights. If height does

TABLE 9-7 *Community Data of* L. cuneifolia *for Bajada Sites in the Bolsón de Pipanaco (from Barbour and Diaz 1973).*

Code	Elev. (m)	Slope and aspect	Gravel (%)	Total cover (%)	*Larrea* cover (rel)	No. spp.	*Larrea* den. (shrubs/ha)	Pattern
ARG- 004	859	1° W	2.9	6.2	6.2 (100.0)	3	816	Clumped[a]
007	833	0°	14.4	12.4	8.6 (68.7)	4	533	Clumped[a]
005	924	7° W	33.1	27.4	16.0 (58.4)	10	1027	Clumped[a]
006	1000	6° W	36.6	30.8	25.0 (76.0)	5	2280	Random
008	1076	8° SW	14.8	36.6	10.9 (28.0)	14	780	Clumped

[a]Nonhomogeneous stand; pattern data may not be accurate.

TABLE 9–8 *Community Data for Sites along a Moisture Gradient in the Bolsón de Pipanaco (from Barbour and Diaz 1973).*

Code	Est. ppt. (mm)	Elev. (m)	Slope and aspect	Gravel (%)	Total cover (%)	*Larrea* cover (rel)	No. spp.	*Larrea* den. (shrubs/ha)	Pattern
ARG- 017	75^-	1067	1° N	45.7	12.2	3.5 (20.7)	8	288	Random[a]
021	75	840	3° W	5.4	31.2	9.3 (29.8)	10	1177	Regular
019	100	818	2° NW	3.6	14.5	14.5 (100.0)	1	787	Clumped[a]
020	115	880?	2° SW	8.2	12.9	11.7 (90.7)	6	1300	Random
018	140	885	2° W	1.7	12.5	12.5 (100.0)	2	1320	Clumped[a]
009	155	885	1° W	1.5	14.8	14.8 (100.0)	4	953	Clumped
004	165	861	1° W	2.9	6.2	6.2 (100.0)	3	816	Clumped
002	215	788	1° W	2.8	42.0	13.0 (31.0)	9	469	Clumped[a]
010	220	824	2° W	7.4	23.3	21.1 (90.6)	6	527	Random
011	250	748	0°	4.2	25.4	23.8 (98.4)	4	1853	Clumped
001	260	1015	2° W	18.5	34.0	33.0 (97.1)	6	2541	Random[a]
012	280	1015	2° NW	9.0	49.6	5.2 (10.5)	16	351	Clumped
003	280^+	1100?	0°	16.1	46.0	23.0 (50.0)	14	2058	Random[a]
014	320	1140	0°	0.4	18.8	18.4 (97.9)	5	2405	Clumped[a]
016	330	1170	2° NW	1.8	34.8	34.8 (100.0)	2	•3003	Clumped[a]
015	370	1279	2° NE	0.4	79.7	77.3 (97.0)	7	5722	Random

[a]Pattern data may not be accurate.

correlate with age, this trend is to be expected, for with increasing moisture the probability of seedling establishment every year should become greater, and the standing population of shrubs should exhibit many age categories.

Ecotone Sites Between *L. cuneifolia* and *L. divaricata* Communities

Barbour et al. (1974) sampled two ecotone sites; one near the Bolsón de Pipanaco and the other near Mendoza, approximately 600 km south (see Figure 9-9). The northern site was a narrow ecotone in a level area (elevation 450 m, precipitation 260 mm). This site showed an interfingering of sharply demarcated communities, one of which was dominated by *L. cuneifolia* with almost no *L. divaricata,* and the other just the reverse. A control site dominated by *L. cuneifolia* was also selected only 300 m away from the ecotone site. Near Mendoza, topography gently rises west to the Andes, and the *L. divaricata*-dominated communities are generally higher in elevation than *L. cuneifolia*-dominated communities. The ecotone site and its paired *L. cuneifolia*-dominated site were located within 1.5 km of each other at an elevation of about 1,160 m with an annual precipitation of 250 mm.

TABLE 9-9 *Cover and Presence of Perennial Species in Four Argentina Sites (from Barbour 1974).*

Species	Catamarca		Mendoza	
	Ecotone	Control	Ecotone	Control
Larrea cuneifolia Cav.	11.3(3,055)	34.0(6,522)	16.4(1,125)	23.5(2,249)
L. divaricata Cav.	15.7(3,380)	0.8 (21)	7.0 (422)	
L. putative hybrids	+ (46)		0.4 (13)	
Mimozyganthus carinatus (Griseb.) Burk.	28.1	16.8		
Prosopis torquata (Lag.) DC				
P. nigra (Griseb.) Hieron.				
Aspidosperma quebrachoblanco Schlech.	7.4	7.0		
Cassia aphylla Cav.	5.8	1.2		
Ximenia americana L.	1.9	3.5		
Atamisquea emarginata Miers.	0.8			
Trichomeria usillo Gill. ex Hook. et Arn.	+	1.6		
Bulnesia schickendanzii Hieron. ex Griseb.	+	+		
Maytenus viscifolia Griseb.	+	0.5		
Tillandsia xiphioides (Morr.) Ker.-Gawl.	+	+		
T. pediciellata (Mez.) Castell.	+	+		

TABLE 9-9 (Continued)

Species	Catamarca		Mendoza	
	Ecotone	Control	Ecotone	Control
T. myosura Griseb.		+		
Prosopis flexuosa DC	0.8	2.3		+
Opuntia sulphurea Gill. ex Don.	0.4	0.8		1.2
O. glomerata Castell.	+	+		0.3
O. aoracantha Lem.			+	
O. sp.		0.5		
Gymnocalscium sp. aff. *sterium*	+	+		
Echinopsis sp.	+	+		
Cereus/Trichocereus sp. #1	+	+		
Cereus/Trichocereus sp. #2		+		
Trichocereus strigossus (SD) Britt. et Rose				+
T. sp.			+	0.4
Cereus aethiops Haworth			+	
Unknown shrub			0.4	
Zuccagnia punctata Cav.			18.3	14.8
Verbena aspera Gill. ex Hook.			8.6	10.5
Lycium chilense Miers.				
L. tenuispinosum Miers.				+
L. sp.	+	+		
Acantholippia seriphioides (A. Gray) Mold.			0.8	
Atriplex lampa Gill. ex Moq.			0.4	+
Philibertia giliesii Hook. et Arn.			0.4	+
Monttea aphylla (Miers.) Benth. ex Hook.			+	+
Gochnatia glutinosa Don.				+
Neobouteloua lophostachya (Gris.) Gould				+
Thymophylla belenidium Cabr.			+	
Pappophorum caespitosum R. Fries			+	
Condalia microphylla Cav.			+	
Tweedia brunonis Hook. et Arn.			+	
Psittacanthus cuneifolius (R. et P.) Blume			+	
Ephedra triandra Tulasne amended by J. H. Hunz			+	
Grabowskia obtusa Arn.			+	
Cercidium praecox (R. et P.) Harms.	5.5	0.8		
Total species	23	24	21	15

Note: + = species present but not contributing to ground cover; figures in parentheses for *Larrea* only = shrubs per hectare; all other figures = absolute percent ground cover.

The northern ecotone site showed nearly equal cover and density by both *Larrea* species (Table 9-9). Pattern analysis revealed that *L. cuneifolia* and *L. divaricata* were each clumped at all block sizes, and there was no association between the two taxa. Height (age) frequency distributions for both taxa were very similar; hence the authors concluded that periods of germination and establishment were similar. There were few differences in associated species between the ecotone and its control site, and the total density of *Larrea* shrubs was almost equal. The two taxa, then, seemed compatible and appeared not to have influence on each other or on associated species.

The Mendoza ecotone site, however, did not show equal shrub density for the two taxa, and contingency table analysis indicated that the two species were negatively associated. Furthermore, the control site showed many differences in species composition (coefficient of community, *sensu* Sørensen, of 39). Barbour et al. (1974) concluded that in this region species replacement could be due to biotic interactions. They went on to state:

> In the field one had the impression of being in a completely different desert from that near Catamarca and in the Bolsón de Pipanaco. One might experience the same degree of change in North America by moving from the Sonoran to the Chihuahuan Desert. We understand (personal communication) that Dr. Morello is considering a formal division of the monte into two or more subregions; certainly our limited field experience supports his decision. Pairs of Catamarca and Mendoza sites had a CC [coefficient of community] of 21 or less.

Morello (1955) has distinguished a "chaco" and a "Monte" ecotype of *L. cuneifolia,* but apparently there are not comparable "north" and "south" ecotypes.

SUMMARY

The structural contribution of *L. tridentata* to Mojave, Chihuahuan, and Sonoran communities and of *L. cuneifolia* to Argentine communities was summarized in terms of *Larrea* density, absolute, and relative cover, and biomass. These parameters in general were correlated to site annual precipitation, but local factors—especially those related to soil—could completely mask that relationship.

The pattern of *Larrea* shrub distribution was shown to include regular, random, and clumped types. Asexual reproduction could create tight clumps of shrubs. The causes of larger-scale pattern were attributed to nonuniformity of habitat, type of sampling method and data analysis used, and seedling survival.

The population age (size) structures showed more than one age (size) peak and an absence of young (small) shrubs in arid sites, in contrast to a single peak, or no peak at all, and many young (small) shrubs in mesic sites.

In Argentina, *L. cuneifolia*—rather than the relatively more mesophytic, weedy, phreatophytic *L. divaricata*—was shown to be the ecological analog of Sonoran *L. tridentata.* The relationship of site precipitation and soil texture to *L. cuneifolia* cover, density, pattern, and age structure was shown to parallel the pattern shown for Sonoran *L. tridentata.*

RESUMEN

Las contribuciones estructurales de *L. tridentata* a las comunidades Mojavense, Chihuahuense y Sonorense, y de *L. cuneifolia* a las comunidades argentinas se resumieron en términos de densidad, coberturas absoluta, y relativa, y biomasa de *Larrea.* Estos parámetros estuvieron correlacionados en general con la precipitación anual del sitio, pero factores locales—especialmente aquellos relacionados con el suelo—podrían enmascarar completamente esa relación.

Se encontró que el patrón de distribución de arbustos de *Larrea* incluye tipos regulares, al azar y agrupados. La reproducción asexual podría crear grupos compactos de arbustos. Las causas de los patrones de mayor escala se atribuyeron a la disuniformidad del habitat, el tipo de método de muestreo y el análisis de datos empleados, y a la supervivencia de plántulas.

Las estructuras de la edad de la población (tamaño) mostraron más de un pico de edad (tamaño) y la ausencia de arbustos jóvenes (pequeños) en sitios áridos, en contraste con un solo pico o ninguno, y muchos arbustos jóvenes (pequeños) en sitios mesofíticos.

En Argentina, *L. cuneifolia*—en vez de *L. divaricata,* más mesofítica, ruderal y freatofítica—probó ser en análogo ecológico de *L. tridentata* Sonorense. Las relaciones de precipitación en el sitio y textura del suelo con cobertura, densidad, patrón y estructura de edades de *L. cuneifolia* demostraron ser paralelas a los patrones mostrados por *L. tridentata* Sonorense.

10

Practical Uses of *Larrea*

B. N. Timmermann

For more than half a century, *Larrea divaricata* ("jarilla") and *L. tridentata* ("creosote bush," "gobernadora," "hediondilla") have commanded ecological, distributional, and chemical, as well as systematic studies from many investigators, as is exemplified by this volume.

In this chapter, the different practical uses that man has given to *Larrea* will be described. *Larrea* has been used by man in many ways for different purposes. A phenolic compound, nordihydroguaiaretic acid (NDGA), extracted from the plant has many applications and thus gives the plant economic importance. Creosote bush is also used as a whole plant as a livestock feed, as a medicinal plant, as firewood, or as a roofing material for adobe houses in western Argentina. An important factor in the possible exploitation of *Larrea* is the fact that it covers extensive areas on the order of thousands of square miles with an abundance of 90 percent or more (see Chapter 2).

The comprehensive chemical investigation shows that *Larrea* is very rich in natural products. Creosote bush has many phenolics (including especially the flavonoids and NDGA), volatile oils, waxes, saponins and free steroids (see Chapter 5).

NORDIHYDROGUAIARETIC ACID (NDGA)

Larrea is best known for the large quantitites of NDGA deposited on the external surface of the leaves and stems. In 1942 Waller reported that the leaves of creosote bush contained this phenolic compound. It is reported to be present in all the species and their hybrids (see Chapter 5; see also Ruth 1946, 1947a, b; Laban 1950; Mizrahi 1967).

Many works have been published about the presence, extraction, and isolation of NDGA (Gisvold 1945, 1946, 1947a, b, 1948; Ruth 1946, 1947a, b; Laban 1950; Page 1951, 1955).

Duisberg (1949, 1952a) and Botkin (1949) studied the factors that affect the NDGA content in the creosote bush. They also determined a simple and rapid method for the determination of NDGA in the plant (Duisberg et al. 1949).

Pure NDGA is prepared by crystallization from the extract of the plant material. It can be also prepared by chemical synthesis. Recently, a new synthesis was described that can produce NDGA of high quality (Oliveto 1972).

In 1944, Lundberg and coworkers deduced on the basis of the polyphenolic structure of NDGA that it might have antioxidant properties.

NDGA as an Antioxidant for Foods and Pharmaceuticals

Several biochemical studies have shown that NDGA inhibits numerous enzyme systems (Tappel and Marr 1954)–for example, lipoxidase. This enzyme is involved in the autooxidation of unsaturated fatty acids in vegetable and seed oils during their processing. NDGA inhibits the oxidation of linolate by the lipoxidase (Tappel et al. 1952, 1953; Tappel and Marr 1954; Siddiqi and Tappel 1957). Siddiqi and Tappel (1957) have shown that NDGA is a competitive inhibitor of the enzyme. Among the phenolic antioxidants used for stabilizing foods that contain unsaturated fats and undergo deterioration, NDGA was shown to have the greatest inhibitory effect.

NDGA also protects refrigerated or frozen foods, particularly meat, poultry and fish (Tappel and Marr 1954). It also has been used successfully in retarding the rancidity in lard (Higgins and Black 1944; Lundberg et al. 1944), bacon and salt-cured fish, in retarding the oxidation of esters of fatty acids (Stirton et al. 1945), in stabilizing carotene in vegetable oils (Richardson and Long 1947), and in retarding oxidative changes in vegetable oils (Matill et al. 1944) and dairy products (Stull et al. 1948a, b). The addition of NDGA to homogenized milk prevents the development of an activated flavor after exposure to solar radiation (Weinstein and Trout 1951).

Vitamin A was shown to be stabilized by NDGA (Dassow and Stansby 1949). NDGA was found to be very effective in protecting vitamin A in air-packed dry milks, particularly nonfat dry milk solids, and also to retard vitamin A destruction in fluid milks (Cox et al. 1957). The effectiveness of this antioxidant as a protector of vitamin A in ice cream and butter was demonstrated by Krukovsky et al. (1949). NDGA has also been used in pharmaceutical preparations that contain vitamin A and reserpine.

Oliveto (1972) did an excellent review on NDGA. Some of the following uses and properties are referred to in his work.

NDGA as an Antioxidant in Industrial Applications

NDGA has been used as a stabilizer of polymers, lubricants, rubber, perfumery oils, olive husks, and furfural. It was also employed as a developer in photography and can prevent metals from rusting (Oliveto 1972).

NDGA against Microorganisms and on Enzyme Systems

This compound was reported to be very effective against molds, *Salmonella* and *Penicillium* (Oliveto 1972). The toxicity of NDGA to *Tetrahymena pyriformis* was studied by Epstein et al. (1967).

NDGA acts as a competitive inhibitor of many enzyme systems including catechol O-methyl transferase, liver and serum esterases, phenylalanine hydroxylase, mitochondrial NADH oxidase, and succinoxidase (Oliveto 1972).

NDGA against Tumors

Plant tumors caused by *Agrobacterium tumefaciens* are known to be inhibited by NDGA. However, of more interest to man is the report that NDGA sensitizes certain tumor cells to X-ray irradiation (von Ardenne et al. 1969).

NDGA has been shown to have antitumor activity in vivo and in vitro. It is a powerful cancer antimetabolite producing in vitro complete inhibition of aerobic and anaerobic glycolysis and respiration of suspensions of several types of tumor cells including leukemia types (Burk and Woods 1963). In vivo, NDGA combined with ascorbic acid is reported to reduce tumors in mice (Oliveto 1972). There is one unproven account that NDGA reduced a malignant melanoma of the cheek of one patient (Smart et al. 1969).

Other Properties of NDGA

Oliveto (1972) mentions that NDGA has analgesic and vasodepressant properties that inhibit dental caries formation in hamsters and increases the life span of rats fed with NDGA. It is also claimed to be effective in alcoholism treatment, liver ailments, and geriatrics (Oliveto 1972).

NDGA IN HUMAN DIET

Until 1967, when more effective antioxidants were introduced, creosote bush remained the best source of NDGA as an antioxidant for fats and oils.

The extraction, crystallization, and use of NDGA as a relatively nontoxic food antioxidant were patented several times (Gisvold 1945, 1946, 1947a, b; Adams 1947; Shipner 1945). Its addition to fats in concentrations up to 0.1 percent was approved by the Meat Inspection Division of the War Food Administration in December 1943.

NDGA has been fed to hamsters for long periods with no ill effect and was considered by most workers to be relatively nontoxic as a result of acute tests in rats and mice (Oliveto 1972). Two investigations were undertaken to study the effect of NDGA and its metabolites in rats in order to have more information on its safety for use as a food antioxidant (Grice et al. 1968; Goodman et al. 1970). NDGA was fed to rats in amounts up to 3 percent of their diet, and at this level the rats developed multiple dark cortical and medullary cysts in the kidneys. These later studies resulted in the U.S. Food and Drug Administration's removing NDGA from its GRAS (generally recognized as safe) list.

Further studies are now required in order to determine the level at which it is safe in foods.

LARREA AS A LIVESTOCK FEED

Larrea is unpalatable to livestock because of its high resin content. A few workers have treated the creosote bush chemically in order to remove the resin, thereby making this plant residue a good livestock feed.

Duisberg (1952b) and Abiusso (1962, 1971) extracted the resin with ether and ethanol, while Adams (1970) used NaOH solutions for the same purpose. Chemical analysis of the plant residue revealed important minerals, carotene, amino acids, and highly digestible proteins. The nutritive value of *L. tridentata* is nearly equal to that of alfalfa, as was shown in controlled experiments on animal digestion at the New Mexico Agriculture Experimental Station (Adams 1970) and by Duisberg (1952b).

Abiusso (1971) determined the content of cellulose, pentosans, and digestible proteins for the four species of *Larrea* in Argentina. All the species were shown to have good nutritive value (*L. divaricata, L. cuneifolia,* and *L. nitida* presented higher values than *L. ameghinoi*).

The utilization of this potentially valuable source for stock feed is a very promising possibility. Adams (1970) reported that most of the calves kept on a creosote bush diet were of good flavor and reasonably tender. Creosote bush is not utilized on a large scale because of the economic factors involved. However, one suggestion calls for the resin to be used for industrial applications after its extraction from the plant (Cruse 1949).

LARREA AS A MEDICINAL PLANT

Medicinal values were attributed to *L. divaricata* and *L. tridentata* by the Indian tribes from North and South America. They have long been using creosote bush in the treatment of many ailments. In Argentina, the medical properties of *L. divaricata* were mentioned by Hieronymus (1882) and Stuckert (1903). The various preparations made from the plant, especially extractions from the leaves and twigs, are still used in folk medicine in some of the areas where the plant grows. The Pima Indians boiled the leaves of creosote bush and used the decoction as an emetic and as a poultice for sores (Dodge 1968). The tea, "chaparral tea," is an old Indian remedy and is drunk for venereal disease, tuberculosis, bowel cramps and used as an antiseptic, expectorant, emetic, diuretic, and treatment for colds and rheumatism. It is also used as a hair tonic and to relieve pain in neuritis, sciatica and inflammation of the respiratory and intestinal tract (Waller and Gisvold 1945; Thaker 1971). The dried and powdered leaves are used to treat sores and wounds of humans and domestic animals. A bath for chickenpox and rheumatism is made by soaking the leaves in water.

Larrea nitida is used in Chile and Argentina as an excitant, vulneric, emmenagogue and to aid digestion (Hutchinson 1967). The crushed or cooked leaves of *L. nitida* are used for cataplasm and tumors (Garcia-Alcover 1950).

The medicinal potentials have not yet been fully explored. Evaluation studies of the "chaparral tea" have been initiated by scientists and medical centers to investigate the therapeutic possibilities of these desert plants (Jiu 1966; Hartwell 1971).

SUMMARY

The economic and practical uses of *Larrea* have only begun to be investigated. The properties of nordihydroguaiaretic acid (NDGA), the major phenolic component of *Larrea,* are as antioxidants in food and pharmaceuticals, lubricant, rubber, as fungicides, and as tumor inhibitors. NDGA was removed from the U.S. Food and Drug Administration's "generally recognized as safe list" (GRAS) list in 1970.

After removing the resin from *Larrea,* it can be used as a livestock feed. *Larrea* has been used by North and South American Indians for many medicinal purposes, mainly in the form of a tea prepared from its leaves.

RESUMEN

Los usos prácticos y económicos de *Larrea* día recien comienzan a investigarse. El ácido nordihidroguayarético (NDGA), principal componente fenólico de *Larrea,* tiene aplicación como antioxidante en alimentos y productos farmacéuticos, lubricantes y hule, además de propiedades fungicidas e inhibidoras de tumores. El NDGA fue eliminado en 1970 de la "lista generalmente reconocida como segura" (Gras) de la Administración de Alimentos y Drogas de los Estados Unidos.

Larrea puede usarse como forraje si se elimina la resina y ha sido usada por los indígenas norte y sudamericanos para muchos propósitos medicinales, principalmente preparando una infusión de las hojas.

References

Aasen, A. J., H. H. Hofstetter, B. T. R. Iyengar, and R. T. Holman. 1971. Identification and analysis of wax esters by mass spectrometry. Lipids *6*:502-07.

Abiusso, N. 1962. Composicion quimica y valor alimenticio de algunas plantas indigenas y cultivadas en la Republica Argentina. Rev. Inv. Agric. *16*: 93-247.

——. 1971. Digestibilidad de las "jarillas" (*Larrea* spp.) y su posible aprovechamiento en la alimentacion del ganado. Rev. Fac. Agr. La Plata *47*:37-44.

Abrahamson, W. G., and M. Gadgil. 1973. Growth form and reproductive effort in golden rods (*Solidago,* Compositae). Am. Natur. *107*:651-61.

Ackerman, T. L., and S. A. Bamberg. 1974. Phenology studies in the Mojave Desert at Rock Valley Nevada Test Site, Nevada. Presented at Phenology and Seasonality Symposium, AIBS, Minneapolis. 21 pp. mimeo.

Adams, D. W. 1970. A study of the possibilities of treating creosote bush with NaOH to make a good livestock feed. Master's Thesis. Sul Ross State Univ., Alpine, Tex. 51 pp.

Adams, J. 1947. Extraction and crystallization of nordihydroguaiaretic acid. U.S. Patent #2421109. May 27, 1947.

Adams, S., B. R. Strain, and M. S. Adams. 1970. Water-repellent soils, fire, and annual plant cover in a desert scrub community of southeastern California. Ecology *51*:696-700.

Allison, R. M. Factors influencing the availability of lysine in leaf protein, pp. 78-85. In N. W. Pirie (ed.) Leaf protein. Its agronomy, preparation, quality and use. IBP. Handbook #20. 192 pp.

Anderson, D. J. 1971. Pattern in desert perennials. J. Ecol. *59*:555-60.

Ashby, E. 1932. Transpiratory organs of *Larrea tridentata,* and their ecological significance. Ecology *13*:182-88.

Axelrod, D. I. 1950. Studies in late Tertiary paleobotany. VI. Evolution of desert vegetation in western North America, pp. 215-306. Carnegie Inst. Wash. Pub. 590. 323 pp.

——. 1970 Mesozoic paleogeography and early angiosperm history. Bot. Rev. *36*:277-319.

Bailey, H. 1977. Current climates. In G. H. Orians and O. T. Solbrig (eds.) Convergent evolution in warm deserts. Dowden, Hutchinson & Ross, Stroudsburg, Pa. (*in press*).

Ball, E. D., E. K. Tinkham, R. Flock, and C. T. Vorhies. 1942. The grasshoppers and other Orthoptera of Arizona, pp. 257-373. Tech. Bull. 93, Agric. Exp. Sta., Univ. of Arizona, Tucson.

Bamberg, S., A. Wallace, G. Kleinkopf, and A. Vollmer. 1973. Plant productivity and nutrient interrelationships of perennials in the Mojave Desert, pp. 1-52. In IBP Desert Biome report, RM 73-10.

Barbour, M. G. 1967. Ecoclinal patterns in the physiological ecology of a desert shrub, *Larrea divaricata.* Ph.D. Thesis. Duke Univ., Durham, N.C. 242 pp.

——. 1968. Germination requirements of the desert shrub *Larrea divaricata.* Ecology *49*:915-23.

——. 1969a. Patterns of genetic similarity between *Larrea divaricata* of North and South America. Am. Midl. Natur. *81*:54-67.

——. 1969b. Age and space distribution of the desert shrub *Larrea divaricata.* Ecology *50*:679-85.

——. 1973. Desert dogma reexamined: Root/shoot productivity and plant spacing. Am. Midl. Natur. *89*:41-57.

——. 1976. Plant-plant interactions, Chap. 6.1, Vol. 4. In R. Perry and D. Goodall (eds.) Structure, function and management of arid land ecosystems. Academic Press, New York (*in press*).

——, and D. V. Diaz. 1973. *Larrea* plant communities on bajada and moisture gradients in the United States and Argentina. Vegetatio *28*:335-52.

——, D. V. Diaz, and R. W. Breidenbach. 1974. Contributions to the biology of *Larrea* species. Ecology *55*:1199-215.

Bateman, G. C. 1967. Home range studies of a desert nocturnal rodent fauna. Ph.D. Thesis. Univ. of Arizona, Tucson. 115 pp.

Bate-Smith, E. C., and C. R. Metcalf. 1957. Leuco-anthocyanins 3. The nature and distribution of tannins in dicotyledonous plants. J. Linn. Soc. (London) *55*:669-705.

Beatley, J. C. 1965. Effects of radioactive and non-radioactive dust upon *Larrea divaricata* Cav., Nevada Test Site. Health Phys. *11*:1621-25.

——. 1969. Vascular plants of the Nevada Test Site, Nellis Air Force Range, and Ash Meadows, UCLA 12-705. Lab. Nucl. Med. Radiat. Biol. Univ. California, Los Angeles. 122 pp.

——. 1974. Effects of rainfall and temperature on the distribution and behavior of *Larrea tridentata* (creosote bush) in the Mojave Desert of Nevada. Ecology *55*:245-61.

Bedard, W. D., P. E. Tilden, D. L. Wood, R. M. Silverstein, R. G. Brownless, and J. O. Rodin. 1969. Western pine bettle: Field response to its sex pheromone and a synergistic host terpene. Myrcene Science *164*:1284-85.

Benson, L. B., and R. A. Darrow. 1954. The trees and shrubs of the southwestern deserts. Univ. of Arizona Press, Tucson. 437 pp.

Blair, W. F. 1941. Annotated list of mammals of the Tularosa Basin, New Mexico. Am. Midl. Natur. *26*:218-29.

——. 1943a. Ecological distribution of mammals in the Tularosa Basin, New Mexico. Univ. Michigan Contrib. Lab. Vert. Biol. *20*:1-24.

——. 1943b. Populations of the deer-mouse and associated small mammals in the mesquite association of southern New Mexico. Univ. Michigan Contrib. Lab. Vert. Biol. *21*:1–40.

Botkin, C. W., and P. C. Duisberg. 1949. The NDGA content of the creosote bush. New Mexico Agr. Exp. Sta. Bull. 349. 18 pp.

Bradley, W. G., and R. A. Mauer. 1973. Rodents of a creosote bush community in southern Nevada. Southwestern Natur. *17*:333–44.

Bragg, A. N. 1950. Observations on Scaphiopus, 1949. (Salientia:Scaphiopodidae). Wassmann J. Biol. *8*:221-28.

Branscomb, B. L. 1958. Shrub invasion of a southern New Mexico desert grassland range. J. Range Manage. *11*:129–32.

Braun, C. V., and J. A. MacMahon. 1975. Sampling characteristics of a desert scrub community with comments on dispersion. Ecology (*submitted*).

Bray, W. L. 1901. The ecological relations of the vegetation of western Texas. Bot. Gaz. *32*:99-123, 195-217, 262-91.

Bryson, R. 1957. The annual march of precipitation in Arizona. Univ. Arizona Inst. Atmosph. Physics. Tech. Rep. 6.

Burk, J. H., and W. A. Dick-Peddie. 1973. Comparative production of *Larrea divaricata* Cav. on three geomorphic surfaces in southern New Mexico. Ecology *54*:1094–102.

Burk, D., and M. Woods. 1963. Hydrogen peroxide, catalase, glutathione peroxidase, quinones, nordihydroguaiaretic acid, and phosphopyridine nucleotides in relation to X-ray action on cancer cells. Rad. Res. Suppl. *3*:212–46.

Cabrera, A. L. 1961. Anatomy of some xerophyllous plants of Patagonia, pp. 235-39. In Arid zone research, v. XVI, Plant-water relations in arid and semi-arid conditions. Proc. Madrid Symp., UNESCO, Paris.

Cain, S. 1950. Life forms and phytoclimate. Bot. Rev. *16*:1-32.

Cannon, W. A. 1905. On the water-conducting systems of some desert plants. Carnegie Inst. Wash. Pub. 98. 42 pp.

——. 1908. The topography of the chlorophyll apparatus in desert plants. Carnegie Inst. Wash. Pub. 98. 423 pp.

——. 1911. The root habits of desert plants. Carnegie Inst. Wash. Pub. 131. 96 pp.

Caplan, E. B. 1966. Differential feeding and niche relationships among orthoptera. Ecology *47*:1074–76.

Cates, R. G., G. H. Orians, D. F. Rhoades, J. C. Schultz, and C. S. Tomoff. 1977. Producer-consumer-predator interactions in hot deserts. In G. H. Orians and Otto Solbrig (eds.) Convergent evolution in warm deserts. Dowden, Hutchinson & Ross, Stroudsburg, Pa. (*in press*).

Chew, R. M., and B. B. Butterworth. 1964. Ecology of rodents in Indian Cove (Mojave Desert). Joshua Tree National Monument, California. J. Mammal. *45*:203-225.

——, and A. E. Chew. 1965. The primary productivity of a desert shrub (*Larrea tridentata*) community. Ecol. Monogr. *35*:355–75.

——, and A. E. Chew. 1970. Energy relationships of the mammals of a desert scrub (*Larrea tridentata*) community. Ecol. Monogr. *40*:1-21.

——, A. E. Chew, F. B. Turner, P. August, B. Maza, and J. Nelson. 1973. Effect of density on the population dynamics of *Perognathus formosus* and its relationships within a desert ecosystem, pp. 1-32. In IBP Desert Biome report, RM 73-18.

Childs, S., and D. W. Goodall. 1973. Seed reserves of desert soils, pp. 1-23. In IBP Desert Biome report, RM 73-5.

Chirikdjian, J. J. 1973a. Flavonoide von *Larrea tridentata.* Z. Naturforsch. Teil 3. *28c*:32-35.

——. 1973b. Isolierung von Quercetin-3-methyläther und Nicotiflorin aus *Larrea tridentata.* Sci. Pharm. *41*:206-09.

Clark, P. J., and F. C. Evans. 1954. Distance to nearest neighbor as a measure of spatial relationships in populations. Ecology *54*:445-52.

Cody, M. L. 1974. Optimization in ecology. Science *183*:1156-64.

Colless, D. H. 1967. An examination of certain concepts in phenetic taxonomy. Syst. Zool. *16*:6-27.

Cox, D. H., S. T. Coulter, and W. O. Lundberg. 1957. Effect of NDGA and other factors and stability of added vitamin A in dry and fluid milks. J. Dairy Sci. *40*:564-70.

Cozzo, D. 1948. Anatomía del leño secundario de las especies argentinas de la tribu "Zygophylleae" (Zigofiláceas). Rev. Inst. Nac. Investig. Cienc. Natur. Cienc. Bot. *1*:57-85.

Cruse, R. R. 1949. Chemurgic survey of desert flora in the American Southwest. Econ. Bot. *3*:111-31.

Cunningham, G. L. 1968. The ecological significance of seasonal leaf variability in a desert shrub. Ph.D. Thesis. Univ. California, Los Angeles. 59 pp.

——, and J. H. Burk. 1973. The effect of carbonate deposition layers ("caliche") in the water status of *Larrea divaricata.* Am. Midl. Natur. *90*: 474-80.

——, J. P. Syvertsen, J. M. Willson, T. Donahue, and F. R. Balding. 1974. The energy costs of reproduction in the creosote bush (*Larrea divaricata* Cav.). IBP Desert Biome progress report. 38 pp.

Cruden, R. W. 1966. Birds as agents of long-distance dispersal for disjunct plant groups of the temperate western hemisphere. Evolution *20*:517-32.

Dalton, P. D., Jr. 1962. Ecology of the creosote bush *Larrea tridentata.* Ph.D. Thesis. Univ. of Arizona, Tucson. 170 pp.

Dassow, J. A., and M. E. Stansby. 1949. Stabilization of vitamin A in halibut liver oil with NDGA. J. Am. Oil Chem. Soc. *26*:475-79.

Dement, W. A., and H. A. Mooney. 1974. Seasonal changes in the production of tannins and cyanogenic glycosides in the chaparral shrub, *Heteromeles arbutifolia.* Oecologia *13*:62-76.

Descole, H. R. 1943. Genera et species plantarum Argentinarum, vol. 1. Aedibus Guillermo Kraft, Buenos Aires.

——, C. A. O'Donell, and A. Lourteig. 1940. Revisión de las Zigofiláceas argentinas. Lilloa *5*:257-352.

——, C. A. O'Donell, and A. Lourteig. 1943. Zygophyllaceae *In* H. R. Descole. Genera et Species Plant. Argent. *1*:1-46.

Dodge, N. N. 1968. The desert wildflowers. S. W. Monuments Assoc. Phoenix, Arizona. 67 pp.

Dodson, C. H., R. L. Dressler, H. G. Hills, R. M. Adams, and N. H. Williams. 1969. Biologically active compounds in orchid fragrances. Science *164*: 1243-49.

Duisberg, P. C. 1952a. Some relationships between xerophytism and the content of resin, nordihydroguaiaretic acid, and protein of *Larrea divaricata* Cav. Plant Physiol. *27*:769-77.

——. 1952b. Development of a feed from the creosote bush and the determination of its nutritive value. J. Animal Sci. *11*:174-80.

——, L. B. Shires, and C. W. Botkin. 1949. Determination of NDGA in the leaf of *Larrea divaricata.* Anal. Chem. *21*:1393-96.

DuRietz, G. E. 1931. Life forms of terrestrial flowering plants. Acta Phytogeogr. Suecica *3*:1-95.

Dye, A. J. 1968. Correlation of age and size in creosote bush (*Larrea divaricata* DC.). Unpublished research report, New Mexico State Univ. 9 pp., mimeo.

Engler, A. 1896. Über die geographische Verbreitung der Zygophyllaceae im Verhältniss zu ihrer systematischen Gliederung. Phys. Abh. Königl. Akad. Wiss. Berlin *1896*:1-36.

Epstein, S., I. Saporoschetz, and S. Hunter. 1967. Toxicity of antioxidants to *Tetrahymena pyriformis.* J. Protozool. *14*:238-44.

Evenari, M. 1960. Plant physiology and arid zone research, pp. 175-95. In Arid zone research, v. 18, UNESCO, Paris.

Feeny, P. P. 1968. Seasonal changes in the tannin content of oak leaves. Phytochemistry 7:871-80.

——. 1969. Inhibitory effect of oakleaf tannin production on the hydrolysis of proteins by trypsin. Phytochemistry *8*:2119-26.

——. 1970. Seasonal changes in oakleaf tannins and nutrients as a cause of spring feeding by winter moth caterpillars. Ecology *51*:656-81.

Findley, J. S. 1969. Biogeography of southwestern boreal and desert mammals. Univ. Kansas Mus. Nat. Hist. Misc. Publ. *51*:113-28.

Fleming, T. H. 1973. Numbers of mammal species in North and Central American forest communities. Ecology *54*:555-63.

Gadgil, M., and O. T. Solbrig. 1972. The concept of *r* and *K* selection: Evidence from wild flowers and some theoretical considerations. Am. Natur. *106*:461-71.

Garcia, E., C. Soto, and F. Miranda. 1960. *Larrea* y clima. Anal. Inst. Biol. *31*:133-90.

Garcia-Alcover, B. 1950. Medicina Herbaria Chilena. Mexico. La vida naturista. 315 pp.

Garcia-Moya, E., and C. M. McKell. 1970. Contribution of shrubs to the nitrogen economy of a desert-wash plant community. Ecology *51*:81-88.

Gardner, J. L. 1951. Vegetation of the creosote bush area of the Rio Grande Valley in New Mexico. Ecol. Monogr. *21*:379-403.

Gates, D. M. 1968. Transpiration and leaf temperature. Ann. Rev. Pl. Physiology *19*:211-38.

Gentry, H. S. 1942. Río Mayo plants. Carnegie Inst. Wash. Pub. *527*. 328 pp.

Giannasi, D. E., and C. M. Rogers. 1970. Taxonomic significance of floral pigments in *Linum* (Linaceae). Brittonia *22*:163-74.

Gisvold, O. 1945. Plant extracts. U.S.Patent #2382475. Aug. 14, 1945.

——. 1946. Recovery of NDGA (a food antioxidant). U.S.Patent #2444346. June 5, 1946.

——. 1947a. Production of plant extracts. U.S.Patent #2421117. May 27, 1947.

——. 1947b. Extraction and crystallization of NDGA. U.S.Pattent #2421118. May 27, 1947.

——. 1948. Preliminary survey of the occurrence of NDGA in *Larrea divaricata.* J. Am. Pharm Assoc. *37*:194-96.

——, and E. Thaker. 1974. Lignans from *Larrea.* J. Pharm. Sci. *63*:1905-07.

Goldstein, J. L., and T. Swain. 1965. The inhibition of enzymes by tannins. Phytochemistry *4*:185-192.

Good, R. 1964. The geography of flowering plants. 3rd ed. Wiley, New York. 518 pp.

Goodman, T., H. Grice, G. Becking, and F. Salem. 1970. A cystic nephropathy induced by nordihydroguaiaretic acid in the rat. Light and electron microscopic investigations. Lab. Invest. *23*:93-107.

Grant, V. 1958. The regulation of recombination in plants. Cold Spring Harbor Symp. Quant. Biol. *23*:337-63.

——. 1963. The origin of adaptations. Columbia Univ. Press, New York. 606 pp.

——. 1971. Plant speciation. Columbia Univ. Press, New York. 435 pp.

Grice, H., G. Becking, and T. Goodman. 1968. Toxic properties of nordihydroguaiaretic acid. Food Cosmet. Toxicol. *6*:155-61.

Guenther, E. 1952. Essential oils of the plant family Zygophyllaceae. In The essential oils, Vol. 5, pp. 197-200. Van Nostrand Reinhold, New York. 507 pp.

Gustavson, K. H. 1956. The chemistry of tanning processes. Academic Press, New York. 403 pp.

Habermehl, G., and H. Möller. 1974. Isolierung und Struktur von Larreagenin A. Liebigs Ann. Chem. *1974*:169-75.

Halvorson, W. T., and D. T. Patten. 1974. Seasonal water potential changes in Sonoran Desert shrubs in relation to topography. Ecology *55*:173-77.

Harborne, J. B. (ed). 1972. Phytochemical ecology. Academic Press, New York. 272 pp.

Harper, J. L., and J. Ogden. 1970. The reproductive strategy of higher plants. I. The concept of strategy with special reference to *Senecio vulgaris* L. J. Ecol. *58*:681-98.

Hartwell, J. 1971. Plants used against cancer. A survey. Lloydia *34*:386–425.

Hastings, J. R., and R. M. Turner. 1965. The changing mile: An ecological study of vegetation change with time in the lower mile of an arid and semiarid region. Univ. of Arizona Press, Tucson. 317 pp.

——, R. M. Turner, and D. K. Warren. 1972. An atlas of some plant distributions in the Sonoran Desert. Univ. Arizona. Inst. Atmospheric Physics. Tech. Rep. 21.

Haworth, R. D., C. R. Mavin, and G. Sheldrick. 1934. The constituents of guaiacum resin. Part II. Synthesis of diguaiaretic acid dimethyl ether. J. Chem. Soc. *1934*:1423-29.

Hayden, P. 1966. Food habits of black-tailed jack rabbits in southern Nevada. J. Mammal. *47*:42–46.

Helfer, J. R. 1963. How to know the grasshoppers, cockroaches and their allies. W. C. Brown, Dubuque, Ia. 353 pp.

Hieronymus, J. 1882. Plantae diaphoricae florae argentinae. *45.*

Higgins, J. W., and H. C. Black. 1944. A preliminary comparison of the stabilizing effect of several recently proposed antioxidants for edible fats and oils. Oil and Soap *21*:277-79.

Holdridge, L. R. 1947. Determination of world plant formations from simple climatic data. Science *105*:367-68.

Hollander, M., and D. A. Wolfe. 1973. Nonparametric statistical methods. Wiley, New York. 68 pp.

Hopkins, B. 1954. A new method for determining the type of distribution of plant individuals. Ann. Bot. *18*:213-27.

Horigome, T., and M. Kandatsu. 1968. Biological value of proteins allowed to react with phenolic compounds in the presence of *o*-diphenol oxidase. Agr. Biol. Chem. *32*:1093-102.

Horn, G. M., and O. Gisvold. 1945. A phytochemical study of *Larrea divaricata* Cav. with special emphasis on its yellow pigments. J. Am. Pharm. Assoc. *34*:82-86.

House, H. L. 1974a. Nutrition. Chap. 1, Vol. 5 In M. Rockstein (ed.) The physiology of insecta. Academic Press, New York. 648 pp.

——. 1974b. Digestion. Chap. 2, Vol. 5. In M. Rockstein (ed.) The physiology of insecta. Academic Press, New York. 648 pp.

Hughes, M. N. 1973. The inorganic chemistry of biological processes. Wiley, New York. 304 pp.

Hull, H. M., S. J. Shellhorn, and R. E. Saunier. 1971. Variations in creosote bush (*Larrea divaricata*) epidermis. J. Ariz. Acad. Sci. *6*:195-205.

Hunziker, J. H. 1952. Las comunidades vegetales de la Cordillera de La Rioja. Rev. Investig. Agric. *6*:167-96.

——. 1971. El uso simultáneo de datos citogenéticos y moleculares en taxonomía experimental, pp. 129-137. In R. H. Majía and A. Moguilevsky (ed.) Recientes adelantos en Biología, Buenos Aires.

——. 1975. On the geographical origin of *Larrea divaricata* (Zygophyllaceae). Ann. Missouri Bot. Gard. *62*:497-500.

——, R. A. Palacios, and A. Soriano. 1969. Hibridación natural en especies sudamericanas de *Larrea* (Zygophyllaceae). Kurtziana *5*:55-66.

——, R. A. Palacios, A. G. de Valesi, and L. Poggio. 1972a. Evolución en el género *Larrea,* pp. 265-78. Memorias de Simposia, I Congreso Latinoamericano de Botánica, México.

——, R. A. Palacios, A. G. de Valesi, and L. Poggio. 1972b. Species disjunctions in *Larrea:* Evidence from morphology, cytogenetics, phenolic compounds and seed albumins. Ann. Missouri Bot. Gard. *59*:224-33.

——, R. A. Palacios, A. G. de Valesi, and L. Poggio. 1976. Hybridization in *Larrea* (Zygophyllaceae): A morphological, cytogenetic and chemosystematic study. Bol. Acad. Nac. Ciencias Córdoba (*in press*).

Hurd, P. 1957. Notes on the autumnal emergence of the vernal desert bee, *Hesperapis fulvipes* Crawford (Hymenoptera:Apoidea). J. Kansas Entomol. Soc. *30*:8.

——, and E. G. Linsley. 1975. *Larrea* bees of the southwestern United States. Smithsonian Contr. Entomol. (*in press*).

Hutchinson, J. 1967. The genera of flowering plants. Vol. *2*:612.

Janzen, D. H. 1973. Host plants as islands. II. Competition in evolutionary and contemporary time. Am. Natur. *107*:786-90.

Jiu, J. 1966. A survey of some medicinal plants of Mexico for selected biological activities. Lloydia *29*:250-59.

Johnston, I. M. 1940. The floristic significance of shrubs common to North and South American deserts. J. Arnold. Arboretum *21*:356-63.

Kearny, T. H., and R. H. Peebles. 1951. Arizona flora. Univ. California Press, Berkeley. 1032 pp.

Kennedy, J. S., and I. H. M. Fosbrooke. 1973. The plant in the life of an aphid, pp. 129-40. In H. F. Van Emden (ed.) Insect/plant relationships. Halsted Press, New York. 215 pp.

Kettlewell, H. B. D. 1961. The phenomenon of industrial melanism in Lepidoptera. Ann. Rev. Entom. *6*:245-62.

King, T. J., and S. R. J. Woodell. 1973. The causes of regular pattern in desert perennials. J. Ecol. *61*:761-65.

Knecht, G. N., and J. W. O'Leary. 1972. The effect of light intensity on stomate number and density of *Phaseolus vulgaris* L. leaves. Bot. Gaz. *133*:132-34.

Knipe, D., and C. H. Herbel. 1966. Germination and growth of some semidesert grassland species treated with aqueous extract from creosote bush. Ecology *47*:775-81.

Koller, D. 1955. The regulation of germination in seeds. Bull. Res. Council of Israel, section D *5*:85-108.

Köppen, W., and R. Geiger. 1936. Handbuch der Klimatolgie. Verlag von Gebrüder Borntraeger, Berlin. 5 vols.

Krukovsky, V. N., D. A. Theokas, F. Whiting, and E. S. Guthrie. 1949. The effects of NDGA, salt, and temperature of storage on the stability of fat and fat soluble vitamins in cream and butter. J. Dairy Sci. *32*:679–87.

Kurtz, E. B. 1958. Chemical basis for adaptation in plants. Science *128*: 1115–17.

Laban, E. 1950. Extraction and assay of NDGA in *Larrea nitida*. Tesis Quimica Univ., Chile (Sgo Chile) *2*:17–32.

Lawton, J. H. 1976. The structure of the arthropod community on bracken (*Pteridium aquilinim* (L.) (Kuhn)). In F. H. Perring (ed.) The biology of bracken. Academic Press, London (*in press*).

le Claire, J., and G. Brown. 1974a. Summary of qualitative phenology data. Origin and structure of ecosystems. IBP technical report 74-9 (unpaged).

——, and G. Brown. 1974b. Summary of qualitative phenology data. Origin and structure of ecosystems. IBP technical report 74–16 (unpaged).

——, P. Reppan, and P. Cantino. 1973a. Summary of qualitative phenology data. Origin and structure of ecosystems. IBP technical report 73–19 (unpaged).

——, P. Reppan, and P. Cantino. 1973b. Summary of qualitative phenology data, Origin and structure of ecosystems. IBP technical report 73–19 (unpaged).

Lee, A. K. 1963. The adaptations to arid environments in wood rats of the genus *Neotoma*. Univ. Calif. Publ. Zool. *64*:57–96.

Lesueur, H. 1945. The ecology of the vegetation of Chihuahua, Mexico, north of parallel twenty-eight. Univ. of Texas, Austin Pub. 4521. 92pp.

Levin, D. A. 1971. Plant phenolics: An ecological perspective. Am. Natur. *105*:157–81.

Levins, R. 1967. Evolution in changing environments. Princeton Univ. Press, Princeton, N.J. 120 pp.

Levy, E. C., I. Ishaaya, E. Gurevitz, R. Cooper, and D. Lavie. 1974. Isolation and identification of host compounds eliciting attraction and bite stimuli in the fruit tree bark beetle, *Scolytus mediterraneus*. J. Agric. Food Chem. *22*:376–78.

Linsley, E. G. 1958. The ecology of solitary bees. Hilgardia *27*:543–99.

Loomen, P. W., C. R. Schwintzer, C. S. Yocum, and D. M. Gates. 1970. A model describing photosynthesis in terms of gas diffusion and enzyme kinetics. Planta *98*:195–220.

Loomis, W. D., and J. Battaile. 1966. Plant phenolic compounds and the isolation of plant enzymes. Phytochemistry *5*:423–38.

Lowe, C. H. 1955. The eastern limit of the Sonoran Desert in the United States with additions to the known herpetofauna of New Mexico. Ecology *36*:343–45.

——. 1964. The vertebrates of Arizona. Univ. of Arizona Press, Tucson. 259 pp.

——, J. Morello, G. Goldstein, J. Cross, and R. Neuman. 1973. Analisís comparativo de la vegetación de los desiertos subtropicales de Norte y Sud ture of ecosystems. IBP technical report 72-6. 251 pp.

——, J. Morello, G. Goldstein, J. Cross, and R. Neuman. 1973. Analisís comparativo de la vegetación de los desiertos subtropicales de Norte y Sud America (Monte-Sonora). Ecologiá *1*:35–43.

Ludwig, J. A. 1975. Distributional adaptations of root systems in desert environments. In J. K. Marshall (ed.) The below ground ecosystem: A synthesis of plant-associated processes. Proceedings of U.S. IBP Interbiome Symposium, Fort Collins, Colo. Dowden, Hutchinson & Ross, Stroudsburg, Pa. (*in press*).

——, and W. G. Whitford. 1975. Short-term water and energy flow in arid ecosystems. In I. Noy-Meir (ed.) Arid ecosystem dynamics. IBP Synthesis, Vol. 2, Cambridge Univ. Press, London (*in press*).

Lundberg, W. O., H. O. Halvorson, and G. O Burr. 1944. Antioxidant properties of nordihydroguaiaretic acid. Oil and Soap *21*:33–35.

Lunt, O. R., J. Letey, and S. B. Clark. 1973. Oxygen requirements for root growth in three species of desert shrubs. Ecology *54*:1356–62.

Mabry, T. J., and B. L. Turner. 1972. The role of secondary compounds in the evolution of the desert scrub vegetation with emphasis upon taxa exhibiting disjunct distributions, pp. 73–98. In Origin and structure of ecosystems. IBP technical report 72-6. 251 pp.

MacArthur, R. H., and E. O. Wilson. 1967. The theory of island biogeography. Princeton Univ. Press, Princeton, N.J. 203 pp.

MacGillivray, A. D. 1921. The Coccidae. Scarab Company, Urbana, Ill. 502 pp.

MacSwain, J. W. 1946. The nesting habits of *Heteranthidium larreae* (Ckll.) (Hymenoptera, Megachilidae). Pan-Pacific Entomologist *22*:159–60.

Mares, M. A. 1973. Climates, mammalian communities and desert rodent adaptations: An investigation into evolutionary convergence. Ph.D. Thesis. Univ. of Texas, Austin. 345 pp.

——. 1975. South American mammal zoogeography: Evidence from convergent evolution in desert rodents. Proc. Nat. Acad. Sci. *72*:1702–06.

Marks, J. B. 1950. Vegetation and soil relations in the lower Colorado desert. Ecology *31*:176–93.

Matill, K. F., L. J. Filer, and H. E. Longnecker. 1944. A study of the antioxidant effectiveness of several compounds of vegetable fats and oil. Oil and Soap *21*:160–61.

Maximov. N. A. 1929. The plant in relation to water. MacMillan, New York. 451 pp.

Mayer, A. M., E. Harel, and R. Ben-Shaul. 1966. Assay of catechol oxidase. A critical comparison of methods. Phytochemistry *5*:783–89.

Mayr, E. 1942. Systematics and the origin of species. Columbua Univ. Press, New York. 334 pp.

——. 1963. Animal species and evolution. The Belknap Press of Harvard Univ. Press, Cambridge, Mass. 797 pp.

——. 1970. Populations, species and evolution. The Belknap Press of Harvard Univ. Press, Cambridge, Mass. 453 pp.

McCleary, J. A. 1968. The biology of desert plants, pp. 141-94. In G. W. Brown, Jr. (ed.) Desert biology, Vol. 1. Academic Press, New York. 635 pp.

McIntosh, R. P. 1967. The continuum concept of vegetation. Bot. Rev. *33*: 130-73.

McClure, J. W. 1975. Physiology and function of flavonoids, pp. 970-1055. In J. B. Harborne, T. J. Mabry, and H. Mabry (eds.) The flavonoids. Chapman and Hall, London. 1204 pp.

McKey, D. 1974. Adaptive patterns in alkaloid physiology. Am. Natur. *108*: 305-20.

Metcalfe, C. R., and L. Chalk. 1950. Anatomy of the dicotyledons, Vol. 1. Oxford Univ. Press, England. 724 pp.

Michener, C. D. 1965. A classification of the bees of the Australian and South Pacific regions. Bull. Amer. Mus. Nat. Hist. *130*:1-362.

Miles, P. W. 1969. Interaction of plant phenols and salivary phenolases in the relationship between plants and hemiptera. Entomol. Exp. Appl. *12*: 736-44.

Miller, N. C. E. 1956. The biology of the heteroptera. Leonard Hill, London. 162 pp.

Mizrahi, I. 1967. Aprovechamiento integral de las especies del género *Larrea* de la República Argentina. Estudio químico y físico. Rev. Inv. Agropec. INTA. Rep. Arg. Serie 2. Biol. y Prod. Veg. *4*:117-58.

Moldenke, A. R., and J. L. Neff. 1974. The bees of California: A catalogue with special reference to pollination and ecological research. Origin and structure of ecosystems. IBP technical reports 74-1, 74-2, 74-3, 74-4, 74-5, and 74-6.

Monsi, M., and Y. Murata. 1970. Development of photosynthetic systems as influenced by distribution of pattern, pp. 78-89. In Prediction and measurement of photosynthetic productivity. Wageningen: Cent. Agr. Publ. Doc.

Monticelli, J. V. 1939. El genero *Larrea* Cav.: Su historia y revision. Physis. *15*:331-56.

Mooney, H. A. 1972a. The carbon balance of plants. Ann. Rev. Ecol. and System. *3*:315-46.

——. 1972b. Carbon dioxide exchange of plants in natural environments. Bot. Rev. *38*:455-69.

——. 1977. Mediterranean climate ecosystems. U.S./IBP Synthesis Series, Vol. 5. Dowden, Hutchinson & Ross, Stroudsburg, Pa. (*in press*).

——, O. T. Solbrig, and B. B. Simpson. 1977. Phenology, morphology, physiology. In B. B. Simpson (ed.) Mesquite: Its biology in two desert scrub ecosystems. U.S./IBP Synthesis Series, Vol. 4. Dowden, Hutchinson & Ross, Stroudsburg, Pa. (*in press*).

Morello, J. 1955. Estudios botánicos en las regiones áridas de la Argentina. I. Ambiente, morfoligía y anatomía de cuatro arbustos resinosos de follaje permanente del Monte. Rev. Agron. Noroeste Arg. *1*:301-70.

——. 1956. Estudios botánicos en las regiones aridas de la Argentina, III. Rev. Agron. Noroeste Arg. *2*:79-152.

——. 1958. La provincia fitogeográfica del monte. Opera Lilloana II, Tucuman, Repub. Argentina. 153 pp.

——. 1972. Variables estructurales de la vegetación del Monte (Argentina) y desierto (E.U.A.), pp. 359-364. Memorias de Symposia, I Congreso Latinoamericano de Botánica, Mexico.

Muller, C. H. 1953. The association of desert annuals with shrubs. Am. J. Bot. *40*:53-60.

——. 1965. Inhibitory terpenes volatilized from *Salvia* shrubs. Bull. Torrey Botan. Club. *92*:38-45.

——, and R. del Moral. 1966. Soil toxicity induced by terpenes from *Salvia leucophylla*. Bull. Torrey Botan. Club. *93*:130-37.

Nagy, K. A. 1973. Behavior, diet and reproduction in a desert lizard, *Sauromalus obesus*. Copeia *1973*:93-102.

Norris, K. S. 1953. The ecology of the desert iguana *Dipsosaurus dorsalis*. Ecology *34*:265-87.

Odening, W. R. 1970. The effect of decreasing water potential on net CO_2 exchange of intact woody desert shrubs. Ph.D. Thesis. Duke Univ., Durham, N.C. 64 pp.

——, B. R. Strain, and W. C. Oechel. 1974. The effects of decreasing water potentials on net CO_2 exchange of intact desert shrubs. Ecology *55*: 1086-95.

Oechel, W. C., B. R. Strain, and W. R. Odening. 1972a. Tissue water potential, photosynthesis, ^{14}C-labeled photosynthate utilization, and growth in the desert shrub *Larrea divaricata* Cav. Ecol. Monogr. *42*:127-41.

——, B. R. Strain, and W. R. Odening. 1972b. Photosynthetic rates of a desert shrub, *Larrea divaricata* Cav., under field conditions. Photosynthetica *6*:183-88.

Oliveto, E. P. 1972. Nordihydroguaiaretic acid, a naturally occurring antioxidant. Chem. Indust. *1972*:677-79.

Oppenheimer, H. R. 1960. Adaptation to drought: Xerophytism, pp. 105-38. In Plant-water relationships in arid and semi-arid conditions, reviews of research. UNESCO, Paris. 225 pp.

Orians, G. H., and D. H. Janzen. 1974. Why are embryos so tasty? Am. Natur. *108*:581-92.

——, and O. T. Solbrig. 1976. A cost-income model of leaves and roots with special reference to arid and semi-arid areas. Am Natur. (*submitted*).

——, and O. T. Solbrig. 1977. Convergent evolution in warm deserts. U.S./IBP Synthesis Series, Vol. 3. Dowden, Hutchinson & Ross, Stroudsburg, Pa. (*in press*).

Otte, D. 1975. Plant preference and plant succession: A consideration of evolution of plant preference in *Schistocerca.* Oecologia *18*:129–44.

——, and A. Joern. 1975. Insect territoriality and its evolution: Population studies of desert grasshoppers on creosote bushes. J. Anim. Ecol. *44*: 29–54.

Page, J. O. 1951. Extraction and purification of NDGA. Anal. Chem. *23*: 296–98.

——. 1955. Determination of NDGA in creosote bush. Anal. Chem. *27*: 1266–68, correction p. 1399.

Painter, R. 1953. The role of nutritional factors in host plant selection. Trans. IX Intern. Cong. Entom., Vol. II, Symposia, Amsterdam.

Palacios, R. A., and J. H. Hunziker. 1972. Observaciones sobre la taxonomía del género *Larrea* (Zygophyllaceae). Darwiniana *17*:473–76.

Patterson, B., and R. Pascual. 1972. The fossil mammal fauna of South America, pp. 247–309. In A. Keast, F. C. Erk, and B. Glass (eds.) Evolution, mammals and southern continents. State Univ. of New York Press, Albany. 543 pp.

Penfound, W. T. 1931. Plant anatomy as conditioned by light intensity and soil moisture. Am. J. Bot. *18*:558–72.

Perry, C. W., M. V. Kalnins, and K. H. Deitcher. 1972. Synthesis of lignans. I. Nordihydroguaiaretic acid. J. Org. Chem. *37*:4371–76.

Philips, P. A., and M. M. Barnes. 1975. Host race formation among sympatric apple, walnut, and plum populations of the codling moth, *Laspeyresia pomonella.* Ann. Ent. Soc. Amer. *68*:1053–60.

Pianka, E. R. 1971. Comparative ecology of two lizards. Copeia *1971*: 527–36.

Pielou, E. C. 1959. The use of point-to-plant distances in the study of the patterns of plant populations. J. Ecol. *47*:607–13.

——. 1969. An introduction to mathematical ecology. Wiley, New York. 286 pp.

Pierpoint, W. S. 1969. *o*-Quinones formed in plant extracts. Their reaction with amino acids and peptides. Biochem. J. *112*:609–16.

Porter, D. M. 1963. The taxonomy and distribution of the Zygophyllaceae of Baja California, Mexico. Contrib. Gray Herb. *192*:99–135.

——. 1974. Disjunct distributions in the New World Zygophyllaceae. Taxon *23*:339–46.

Proctor, V. W. 1968. Long-distance dispersal of seeds by retention in digestive tract of birds. Science *160*:321–22.

Ragonese, A. M. 1951. La vegetación de la República Argentina. II. Estudio fitosociológico de las Salinas Grandes. Rev. Invest. Agr. *5*:1–234.

——. 1960. Estudio anatómico de las especies argentinas de *Larrea.* Rev. Invest. Agr. *14*:355–70.

Rand, A. S. 1967. Predator-prey interactions and the evolution of aspect diversity. Ata do Simpósio sobre a Biota Amazonica *5*:73–83.

Raunkier, C. 1934. The life-forms of plants and statistical plant geography. Clarendon Press, Oxford. 632 pp.

Raven, P. H. 1963. Amphitropical relationships in the floras of North and South America. Quart. Rev. Biol. *38*:151–77.

Rhoades, D. F., and R. G. Cates. 1976. Toward a general theory of plant anti-herbivore chemistry, Chap. 4. In J. W. Wallace, and R. L. Mansell (eds.) Biochemical interaction between plants and insects. Rec. Adv. in Phytochem. Vol. 10. Plenum, New York. 425 pp.

Richardson, G. A., and L. M. Long. 1947. The use of carotene for coloring butter. J. Dairy Sci. *30*:533.

Ricklefs, R. E., and K. O'Rourke. 1975. Aspect diversity in moths: A temperate-tropical comparison. Evolution *29*:313–24.

Rodriguez, E., and D. A. Levin. 1976. Biochemical parallelisms of repellents and attractants in higher plants and arthropods, Chap. 5. In J. W. Wallace, and R. L. Mansell (eds.) Biochemical interaction between plants and insects. Rec. Adv. in Phytochem. Vol. 10. Plenum, New York. 425 pp.

Rosen, H. 1957. A modified ninhydrin colorimetric analysis for amino acids. Arch. Biochem. Biophys. *67*:10–15.

Rozen, J. G., Jr. 1958. Monographic study of the genus *Nomadopsis* Ashmead (Hymenoptera, Andrenidae). Univ. Calif. Publ. Entomol. *15*:1–202.

Rudinsky, J. A. 1966. Scolytid beetles associated with douglas fir: Response to terpenes. Science *152*:218–19.

Runyon, E. H. 1934. The organization of the creosote bush with respect to drought. Ecology *15*:128–38.

Ruth, E. 1946. Acido nordihidroguayaretico en "Larreas" argentinas: *L. divaricata* y *L. cuneifolia.* Tesis 468 Facultad Ciencias Exactas y Naturales. Univ. Nacional de Buenos Aires.

——. 1947a. Aislamiento del acido nordihydroguayaretico de especies de *Larrea* argentinas. Anales Asoc. Quim. Arg. *34*:163–67.

——. 1947b. Acido nordihidroguayaretico en especies de *Larrea* argentinas. Ciencia e Invest. *3*:129.

Ryan, R. M. 1968. Mammals of Deep Canyon. The Desert Museum, Palm Springs, Calif. 137 pp.

Sage, R. D. 1973. Convergence of the lizard faunas of the chaparral habitats in central Chile and California, pp. 339–48. In F. di Castri and H. A. Mooney (eds.) Mediterranean type ecosystems: Origin and structure, ecological studies, Vol. 7. Springer-Verlag, New York. 405 pp.

Sakakibara, M., and T. J. Mabry. 1975. A new 8-hydroxyflavonol from *Larrea tridentata.* Phytochemistry *14*:2097–98.

——, B. N. Timmermann, N. Nakatani, H. Waldrum, and T. J. Mabry. 1975. New 8-hydroxyflavonols from *Larrea tridentata.* Phytochemistry *14*: 849–51.

——, D. DiFeo, Jr., N. Nakatani, B. Timmermann, and T. J. Mabry. 1976. Flavonoid methyl ethers on the external leaf surface of *Larrea tridentata* and *L. divaricata* (Zygophyllaceae). Phytochemistry *15*:727-31.

Sarmiento, G. 1976. Evolution of arid vegetation in tropical America, pp. 65-100. In D. W. Goodall (ed.) Evolution of desert biota. Univ. of Texas Press, Austin, 250 pp.

Saunier, R. E., H. M. Hull, and J. H. Ehrenreich. 1968. Aspects of the drought tolerance in creosote bush (*Larrea divaricata*). Plant Physiol. *43*:401-404.

Schimper, A. F. W. 1903. Plant geography upon a physiological basis. Clarendon Press, Oxford. 839 pp.

Schoonhoven, L. M. 1972. Secondary plant substances and insects, pp. 197-224. In V. C. Runeckles and T. C. Tso (eds.) Rec. Adv. in Phytochem. Vol. 5. Academic Press, New York. 350 pp.

Schratz, E. 1931. Vergleichende untersuchungen über den wasserhaushalt von pflanzen im trockengebiete des südlichen Arizona. Jahb. Wiss. Bot. *74*:153-288.

Schroeter, G., L. Lichtenstadt, and D. Irineu. 1918. Über die Konstituten der Guajacharz-Substanzen (I). Chem. Ber. *51*:1587-13.

Seigler, D. S., J. Jakupcak, and T. J. Mabry. 1974. Wax esters from *Larrea divaricata* Cav. Phytochemistry *13*:983-86.

Shelford, V. E. 1963. The ecology of North America. Univ. of Illinois Press, Urbana. 610 pp.

Sheps, L. O. 1973. Survival of *Larrea tridentata* S. E. M. seedlings in Death Valley National Monument, California. Israel J. Bot. *22*:8-17.

Shinn, A. F. 1967. A revision of the bee genus *Calliopsis* and the biology and ecology of *C. andreniformis* (Hymenoptera, Andrenidae). Univ. Kansas Sci. Bull. *41*:753-936.

Shipner, J. R. 1945. Treatment of fat with leaves or stems of *Larrea* or with extracts of these parts confer antioxidant properties to the fats. U.S. Patent #2457741. Oct. 15, 1945.

Shreve, F. 1940. The edge of the desert. Yearbook Assoc. Pacific Coast Geographers *6*:6-11.

——. 1942. The desert vegetation of North America. Bot. Rev. *8*:195-246.

——. 1951. Vegetation of the Sonoran Desert. Carnegie Inst. Wash. Pub. 591. 192 pp.

——, and A. L. Hinkley. 1937. Thirty years of change in desert vegetation. Ecology *18*:463-78.

——, and I. Wiggins. 1964. Vegetation and flora of the Sonoran Desert. Stanford Univ. Press, Calif., 2 vols.

Siddiqi, A. M., and A. L. Tappel. 1957. Comparison of some lipoxidases and their mechanism of action. Am. Oil Chem. Soc. *34*:529-33.

Simmons, N. M. 1966. Flora of the Cabeza Prieta Game Range. J. Arizona Acad. Sci. *4*:93-104.

Singh, S. P. 1964. Cover, biomass and root/shoot habit of *Larrea divaricata* on a selected site in southern New Mexico. Master's Thesis. New Mexico State Univ., Las Cruces. 36 pp.

Smart, C. R., H. H. Hogle, R. K. Robins, A. D. Broom, and D. Bartholomew. 1969. An interesting observation on NDGA (NSC-4291; NDGA) and a patient with malignant melanoma—A preliminary report. Cancer Chemot. Rep., part 1 *53*:147-51.

Smith, R. H. 1961. The fumigant toxicity of three pine resins to *Dendroctonus brevicomis* and *D. jeffreyi.* J. Econ. Entom. *54*:359-65.

Solbrig, O. T. 1972. The floristic disjunctions between the "Monte" in Argentina and the "Sonoran Desert" in Mexico and the United States. Ann. Missouri Bot. Garden *59*:218-223.

Soto-Ramirez, J., and H. L. Mitchell. 1960. The trypsin inhibitor of alfalfa. J. Agric. Food Chem. *8*:393-95.

Southwood, T. R. E. 1961. The number of species of insect associated with various trees. J. Anim. Ecol. *30*:1-8.

——. 1973. The insect/plant relationship—an evolutionary perspective, pp. 3-20. In H. F. Van Emden (ed.) Insect/plant relationships. Halsted Press, New York. 215 pp.

Spalding, V. M. 1904. The creosote bush (*Covillea tridentata*) in its relation to water supply. Bot. Gaz. *38*:122-38.

——. 1909. Distribution and movements of desert plants. Carnegie Inst. Wash. Pub. 113. 114 pp.

Stark, N., and L. D. Love. 1969. Water relations of three warm desert species. Israel J. Bot. *18*:175-90.

Stebbins, G. L. 1950. Variation and evolution in plants. Columbia Univ. Press, New York. 643 pp.

——. 1966. Processes of organic evolution. Prentice-Hall, Englewood Cliffs, N.J. 191 pp.

Stebbins, R. C. 1954. Amphibians and reptiles of western North America. McGraw-Hill, New York. 539 pp.

Stirton, A. J., J. Turer, and R. W. Riemenschneider. 1945. Oxygen absorption of methyl esters of fatty acids and the effect of antioxidants. Oil and Soap *22*:81.

Strain, B. R. 1969. Seasonal adaptations in photosynthesis and respiration in four desert shrubs growing *in situ.* Ecology *50*:511-13.

——. 1970. Field measurements of tissue water potential and carbon dioxide exchange in the desert shrubs *Prosopis juliflora* and *Larrea divaricata.* Photosynthetica *4*:118-22.

——, and V. C. Chase. 1966. Effect of past and prevailing temperatures on the carbon dixoide exchange capacities of some woody desert perennials. Ecology *47*:1043-45.

Strong, D. R. 1974a. Rapid asymptotic species accumulation in phytophagous insect communities: The pests of cacao. Science *185*:1064-66.

——. 1974b. Nonasymptotic species richness models and the insects of British trees. Proc. Nat. Acad. Sci. *71*:2766-69.

Stuckert, T. 1903. Las Zigofilaceas argentinas y sus aplicaciones. Am. Soc. Farm. Nac. Rosario. *1903*:36.

Stull, J. W., E. O. Herreid, and P. H. Tracy. 1948a. A study of the use of the antioxidant NDGA in dairy products. I. Its antioxygenic properties in milk. J. Dairy Sci. *31*:449-54.

——, E. O. Herreid, and P. H. Tracy. 1948b. A study of the use of the antioxidant NDGA in dairy products. II. Its antioxygenic properties in unsweetened frozen cream. J. Dairy Sci. *31*:1024-28.

Sugimoto, N., and K. Okumura. 1956. Synthesis of nordihydroguaiaretic acid. Annual Report G. Tamebe Co. Ltd., Japan. *1*:14-17.

Syvertsen. J. P., G. L. Cunningham, and T. V. Feather. 1975. Anomalous diurnal patterns of stem xylem water potentials in *Larrea tridentata.* Ecology *56*:1423-28.

Tappel, A. L., and A. G. Marr 1954. Effect of alpha-tocopherol, propyl gallate and NDGA on enzymatic reactions. J. Agr. Food Chem. *2*:554-58.

——, P. D. Boyer, and W. O. Lundberg. 1952. The reaction mechanism of soybean lipoxidase. J. Biol. Chem. *199*:267-81.

——, W. O. Lundberg, and P. D. Boyer. 1953. Effect of temperature and antioxidants upon the lipoxidase-catalized oxidation of sodium linoleate. Arch. Biochem. Biophys. *42*:293-304.

Thaker, A. K. 1971. A review of phenolic resins of *Larrea divaricata.* Ph.D. Thesis. Univ. of Minnesota, Minneapolis. 55 pp.

Timberlake, P. H. 1954. A revisional study of the bees of the genus *Perdita* F. Smith, with special reference to the fauna of the Pacific Coast (Hymenoptera, Apoidea). Univ. Calif. Publ. Entomol. *9*:345-432.

——. 1973. Revision of the genus *Pseudopanurgus* of North America (Hymenoptera, Apoidea). Univ. Calif. Publ. Entomol. *72*:1-58.

Tinbergen, N., M. Impekoven, and D. Franck. 1966. An experiment on spacing-out as a defence against predation. Behaviour *28*:307-21.

Tossi, J. A. 1960. Zonas de vida natural en el Peru. Turialba, Costa Rica. IICA, OEA. 271 pp.

Tukey, H. G. 1970. The leaching of substances from plants. Ann. Rev. Plant Physiol. *21*:305-24.

Turner, B. F., in collaboration with others. 1973. Rock Valley validation site report. IBP Desert Biome report, RM 73-2. 211 pp.

Turner, B. L. 1972. Chemosystematic data: Their use in the study of disjunctions. Ann. Missouri Bot. Gard. *59*:152-64.

Turner, R. M. 1963. Growth in four species of Sonoran Desert trees. Ecology *44*:760-65.

Twisselmann, E. C. 1956. A flora of the Temblor range and the neighboring part of the San Joaquin Valley. Wasmann J. Biol. *14*:161-300.

Valentine, D. A., and J. B. Gerard. 1968. Life-history characteristics of the creosote bush, *Larrea tridentata.* New Mexico Agri. Sta. Bull. *526*: 3-32.

Valentine, K. A., and J. J. Norris. 1964. A comparative study of soils of selected creosote bush sites in southern New Mexico. J. Range Manage. *17*:23-32.

Valesi, A. G., E. Rodriguez, G. Vander Velde, and T. J. Mabry. 1972. Methylated flavonols in *Larrea cuneifolia.* Phytochemistry *11*:2821-26.

Van Devender, T. R. 1973. Late Pleistocene plants and animals of the Sonoran Desert: A survey of ancient packrat middens in southwestern Arizona. Ph.D. Thesis. Univ. of Arizona, Tuscon, 199 pp.

Van Emden, H. F. 1973. Insect/plant relationships. Halsted Press, New York. 213 pp.

Van Sumere, C. F., J. Albrecht, A. Dedonder, H. De Pooter, and I. Pé. 1975. Plant proteins and phenolics, Chap. 8. In J. B. Harborne and C. F. Van Sumere (eds.). The chemistry and biochemistry of plant proteins. Plenum, New York. 425 pp.

Vasek, F. C., H. B. Johnson, and D. H. Eslinger. 1975. Effects of pipeline construction on creosote scrub vegetation of the Mojave Desert. Madroño *23*:1-12.

Vogel, R., I. Trautschold, and E. Werle. 1968. Natural proteinase inhibitors. Academic Press, New York. 159 pp.

von Ardenne, M., R. Chaplain, and P. Reitnauer. 1969. *In vitro* measurements of damage to cancer with a good substrate supply, following combined attack by nordihydroguaiaretic acid and 40 deg C hypothermia, with and without irradiation at a dose of 1000 r. Arch. Geswulstforsch. *34*:1-12.

Wallace, A., and E. M. Rommey, in collaboration with others. 1972. Radioecology and ecophysiology of desert plants at the Nevada test site. USAEC Report TID-25954. 439 pp.

——, E. M. Romney, and R. T. Aschcroft. 1970. Soil temperature effects on growth of seedlings of some shrub species which grow in the transitional area between the Mojave and Great Basin deserts. Bioscience *20*: 1158-59.

——, V. Q. Hale, G. E. Kleinkopf, and R. C. Huffaker. 1971. Carboxydismutase and phosphoenolpyruvate carboxylase activities from leaves of some plant species from the northern Mojave and southern Great Basin deserts. Ecology *52*:1093-95.

Wallace, J. W., and R. L. Mansell. 1976. Biochemical interaction between plants and insects. Rec. Adv. in Phytochem. Vol. 10. Plenum, New York. 425 pp.

Waller, C. W. 1942. A phytochemical study of *Larrea divaricata.* Ph.D. Thesis. Univ. of Minnesota, Minneapolis.

——, and O. Gisvold. 1945. A phytochemical investigation of *Larrea divaricata* Cav. J. Am. Pharm Assoc. *34*:78-81.

Walter, H. 1931. Die Hydratur der Pflanze und ihre physiologisch-ökologische bedeutung. G. Fisher, Jena. 174 pp.

Waterfall, U. T. 1946. Observations on the desert gypsum flora of southwestern Texas and adjacent New Mexico. Am. Midl. Natur. *36*:456-66.

Waterhouse, D. F. 1949. The hydrogen ion concentration in the alimentary canal of larval and adult Lepidoptera. Aust. J. Sci. Res. *B2*:428-37.

Webber, I. E. 1936. The woods of schlerophyllous and desert shrubs of California. Am. J. Bot. *23*:181-88.

Weberbauer, A. 1945. El mundo vegetal de los Andes Peruanos. Estudio fitogeográfico. Estación Experimental Agrícola de la Molina. Dirección de Agricultura. Ministerio de Agricultura, Lima. 776 pp.

Wellendorf, M. 1963. Nordihydroguajaretsyre (NDGA). 1. Stemplantens botanik. Dansk. Tidssker. Farm. *37*:257-69.

Wells, P. V. 1969. Preuves paléontologiques d'une végétation tardi-Pleistocène (datée per le ^{14}C) dans les anjourd'hui désertiques d'Amerique du Nord. Rev. Géog. Phys. Géol. Dynam. *11*:335-40.

——. 1977. Postglacial origin of the Chihuahuan Desert less than 11,500 years ago. In R. H. Wauer and D. H. Riskind (eds.) Symposium on the biological resources of the Chihuahuan Desert region. Science Associates, Washington, D.C. (*in press*).

——, and R. Berger. 1967. Late Pleistocene history of coniferous woodland in Mojave Desert. Science *155*:1640-47.

——, and J. H. Hunziker. 1977. Origin of the creosote bush (*Larrea*) deserts of southwestern North America. Ann. Missouri Bot. Gard. (*in press*).

Went, F. W. 1955. The ecology of desert plants. Sci. Am. *192*:68-75.

——, and M. Westergaard. 1949. Ecology of desert plants. III. Development of plants in the Death Valley National Monument, California. Ecology *30*:26-38.

Werner, F. G., W. R. Inns, and F. M. Parker. 1966. The Meloidae of Arizona. Tech. Bull. 175, Agri. Exp. Stat., Univ. of Arizona, Tucson. 96 pp.

Weinstein, B. R., and G. M. Trout. 1951. The solar activated flavor of homogenized milk. II. The role of oxidation and the effectiveness of certain treatments. J. Dairy Sci. *34*:559-64.

Whittaker, R. H., and W. A. Niering. 1964. Vegetation of the Santa Catalina Mountains, Arizona. 1. Ecological classification and distribution of species. J. Ariz. Acad. Sci. *3*:9-34.

Wigglesworth, V. B. 1972. The principles of insect physiology. 7th ed. Chapman and Hall, London. 827 pp.

Woodell, S. R. J., H. A. Mooney, and A. J. Hill. 1969. The behavior of *Larrea divaricata* (creosote bush) in response to rainfall in California. J. Ecol. *57*:37-44.

Wright, R. A. 1970. The distribution of *Larrea tridentata* (DC) Coville in the Avra Valley, Arizona. J. Ariz. Acad. Sci. *6*:58-63.

Yang, T. W. 1967a. Chromosome numbers in populations of creosote bush (*Larrea divaricata*) in the Chihuahuan and Sonoran subdivisions of the North American Desert. J. Ariz. Acad. Sci. *4*:183-84.

——. 1967b. Ecotypic variation in *Larrea divaricata.* Am. J. Bot. *54*:1041-44.

——. 1968. A new chromosome race of *Larrea divaricata* in Arizona, Western Reserve Acad. Nat. Hist. Museum. Spec. Publ. *2*:1-4.

——. 1970. Major chromosome races of *Larrea divaricata* in North America. J. Ariz. Acad. Sci. *6*:41-45.

——, and Y. Abe. 1973a. Summary of qualitative phenology data. Origin and structure of ecosystems. IBP technical report 73-1 (unpaged).

——, and Y. Abe. 1973b. Summary of qualitative phenology data. Origin and structure of ecosystems. IBP technical report 73-18 (unpaged).

——, and C. H. Lowe. 1956. Correlation of major vegetation climaxes with soil characteristics in the Sonoran Desert. Science *123*:542.

——, and C. H. Lowe. 1968. Chromosome variation in ecotypes of *Larrea divaricata* in the North American desert. Madroño *19*:161-64.

——, J. H. Hunziker, L. Poggio, and C. A. Naranjo. 1976. Hybridization between South American jarilla and North American diploid creosote bush (*Larrea* Cav., Zygophyllaceae). Plant System. and Evol. (*in press*).

York, J. C., and W. A. Dick-Peddie. 1969. Vegetation changes in southern New Mexico during the past 100 years, pp. 157-66. In W. G. McGinnies and B. J. Goldman (eds.) Arid lands in perspective. Univ. Arizona Press, Tucson. 421 pp.

Zavortink, T. J. 1974. A revision of the genus *Ancylandrena* (Hymenoptera: Andrenidae). Occ. Papers Calif. Acad. Sci. *109*:1-36.

Taxonomic Index*

**Larrea* and its species are not categorized in this index for obvious reasons.

Subject Index